PASSIONATE DEIFICATION

Passionate Deification

*The Integral Role of the Emotions
in Christ's Life and in Christian Life*

HENRY L. NOVELLO

◆PICKWICK *Publications* • Eugene, Oregon

PASSIONATE DEIFICATION
The Integral Role of the Emotions in Christ's Life and in Christian Life

Copyright © 2019 Henry L. Novello. All rights reserved. Except for brief quotations in critical publications or reviews, no part of this book may be reproduced in any manner without prior written permission from the publisher. Write: Permissions, Wipf and Stock Publishers, 199 W. 8th Ave., Suite 3, Eugene, OR 97401.

Pickwick Publications
An Imprint of Wipf and Stock Publishers
199 W. 8th Ave., Suite 3
Eugene, OR 97401

www.wipfandstock.com

PAPERBACK ISBN: 978-1-5326-6257-7
HARDCOVER ISBN: 978-1-5326-6258-4
EBOOK ISBN: 978-1-5326-6259-1

Cataloguing-in-Publication data:

Names: Novello, Henry L.

Title: Passionate deification : the integral role of the emotions in Christ's life and in Christian life / Henry L. Novello.

Description: Eugene, OR : Pickwick Publications, 2019. | Includes bibliographical references and index.

Identifiers: ISBN 978-1-5326-6257-7 (paperback) | ISBN 978-1-5326-6258-4 (hardcover) | ISBN 978-1-5326-6259-1 (ebook)

Subjects: LCSH: Emotions—Religious aspects—Christianity—History of doctrines. | Emotions (Philosophy) | Deification (Christianity)—History of doctrines.

Classification: BV4597.3 .N74 2019 (print) | BV4597.3 .N74 (ebook)

Manufactured in the U.S.A.   OCTOBER 28, 2019

PERMISSIONS

Emotion and Peace of Mind: From Stoic Agitation to Christian Temptation, by Richard Sorabji. Copyright © 2000 by Richard Sorabji. Oxford University Press, New York, NY. Selections reprinted by permission of Oxford University Press.

Jesus' Emotions in the Fourth Gospel: Human or Divine? by Stephen Voorwinde. Copyright © 2005 by T & T Clark, London. Selections reproduced with permission of Bloomsbury Publishing Plc.

Jesus' Emotions in the Gospels, by Stephen Voorwinde. Copyright © 2011 by T & T Clark, London. Selections reproduced with permission of Bloomsbury Publishing Plc.

[Scripture quotations are from] *Revised Standard Version* of the Bible, copyright © 1946, 1952, and 1971 National Council of the Churches of Christ in the United States of America. Used by permission. All rights reserved worldwide.

Upheavals of Thought: The Intelligence of the Emotions, by Martha C. Nussbaum. Copyright © 2001 by Martha C. Nussbaum. Cambridge University Press, New York, NY. Selections reproduced with permission of Cambridge University Press.

The Works of Jonathan Edwards, Vol. 2. *Religious Affections*. Edited by John E. Smith. Copyright © 1959 by Yale University Press. Selections reproduced with permission of the Licensor through PLSclear.

Dedicated to the memory of Frans Jozef van Beeck, SJ

Table of Contents

Introduction: Emotion Language as the Primary Language | 1

1. Emotion in Contemporary Thought: A Cognitive Theory of Emotion | 25
   A Critique of Stoicism on Emotion | 31
   Contemporary Cognitive Theories of Emotion | 45
      Robert Solomon: Emotions as Voluntary | 47
      Cheshire Calhoun: Emotions and Personal Biography | 50
      Richard Wollheim: Emotions as Attitudes to Reality | 52
      Aaron Ben-Ze'ev: The Logic of the Emotions | 54
      Martha Nussbaum: A Neo-Stoic Theory of Emotion | 55
   Components of Emotion, Basic Emotions, and Desire | 61
      The Emotion of Wonder: *Mysterium Fascinans et Tremendum* | 64
      Basic Emotions and Fundamental Desire | 68

2. Emotions and the Ascent to God in the Christian Tradition | 73
   Augustine of Hippo: The Restless Longing of the Heart | 75
   Gregory of Nyssa: The Progressive Education of Desire | 92
   Jonathan Edwards: True Religion Consists in Gracious Affections | 104
   Conclusion: Christian Emotions and the Problem of Sin | 114

3. Christ's Emotions in the Theological Tradition:
The Need to Go Beyond Stoicism | 122
   Patristic and Medieval Thought: Christ the Stoic Sage | 125
   Reformed and Contemporary Thought: Christ Assumed
      Our Adamic Flesh | 137
   A Progressive Incarnation: The Becoming of the Divine-Humanity | 149
   Jesus' Emotions as the Springboard of His Messianic Mission | 159

4. Jesus' Personal Biography in the Land:
The Full Course of His Emotional Life | 166
    The Formation of Jesus' Emotional Life | 168
        The Covenant Framework of Jesus' Life | 168
        Jesus' Mother as "Daughter Zion" | 183
        Jesus' *Modus Essendi*: Obedience to His Father | 192
    The Emotions of Jesus in the Gospels | 203
        Jesus' Love, Compassion, and Joy—The Congenial Emotions | 204
        Jesus' Amazement and Stern Warning | 210
        Jesus' Anger and Indignation | 213
        Jesus' Zeal for His Father's House | 216
        Jesus' Sighing and Weeping | 218
        Jesus' Grief, Distress, and Lament—The Suffering Emotions | 223
    Jesus' Involved Holiness and the Process
        of Passionate Deification in His Person | 228

5. Christian Life as the Transformation of the Emotions | 233
    Augustine of Hippo, Gregory of Nyssa,
        and Jonathan Edwards Revisited | 252

Bibliography | 263

Index | 271

Preface

IN JUNE OF 2013, I visited the old city of Jerusalem for the first time. One of the enduring memories of that visit is the image of Jewish men praying at the Wailing Wall. I was struck by the manner in which prayers raised to God at this holy site involve the physical movement of swaying back and forth—known as "davening"— which engages not only the mind but also the heart and body in conversation with God. The act of worship was conducted with palpable feeling which conveyed not only Jewish hope in God's coming reign, but also Jewish mourning and sorrow down the ages of covenant history. When will God finally reign from the hidden Zion? When will the Messiah come to fulfill the covenant promises of old? Since 1948 the Jewish people have regained statehood and have enjoyed the blessings of living in the land, but these blessings have not wiped away the horrors and sufferings of the Jewish Holocaust or the mourning over the ruins of the shattered Jerusalem Temple. The people in the land invariably exhibit an array of emotions in living their Jewish faith, from congenial emotions to suffering emotions, all of which are intelligible within the framework of the history of the covenant.

While observing Jewish prayer at the Wailing Wall, I began to wonder about Jesus praying in his local synagogue, and in the temple on the occasions of the religious festivals, or in quiet places alone during his ministry of proclaiming the kingdom of grace to his own. Did Jesus pray with all his heart, mind, and soul to God? Did he truly praise God with all his bones? Did he exhibit the full array of heartfelt emotions that have long defined Jewish life as the people of God? Was there a process of formation of Jesus' emotions as he grew up in the land and became aware of what it means to be the people of the covenant? Has Christian theology, because of a certain metaphysical notion of divinity, downplayed Jesus' emotional life in order to ensure that his divinity as the Son is exalted? To what extent did Jesus actually share in our Adamic flesh? What role did Jesus' emotions play in the development of his individuality and in carrying out his messianic mission? These questions arose in my mind as I observed the ritual of Jewish men praying wholeheartedly at the Wailing Wall. The questions all pertain to Jesus' true humanity and the idea of the kenosis of the divine Word. Has Christian theology sufficiently acknowledged the *real* participation of the divine in the human (kenosis), which aims at the participation of the human in the divine (theosis)? I began to suspect that the notion of kenosis had not been adequately developed in the past, due to the strong emphasis placed upon Christ's divinity and the strong influence of Stoic teaching on the passions and the life of virtue.

I did not seek to provide answers to these thought-provoking questions upon my return to Australia. It was not until a few years later that I took up these questions in earnest. Upon reading Martha Nussbaum's work *Upheavals of Thought*, which is a neo-Stoic cognitive theory of emotion, it occurred to me that an appraisal of the emotions as intelligent—because they involve judgments about things considered to be salient for human flourishing in the world—could provide a promising framework for a study of the Incarnation, the idea of kenosis, and Jesus' emotional life. The more I read on contemporary cognitive theories of emotion, the more I became convinced of their capacity to rethink the historical life of the incarnate Word, in terms of Jesus' subjective engagement with his world in a process of growth and development, through which he becomes conscious of his divinity as the Son of the Father. The words of Kierkegaard capture succinctly the line of thought that I became more and more focused upon: "God has come into being, has been born, has grown up, and so forth, precisely like any other individual human being."

The principal reason a cognitive approach to emotion is able to inform the process of a progressive Incarnation is that central to such a theory is the view that the emotions of adult life have a history of formation and are indicative of basic orientations to life, which motivate the person to act in particular ways in pursuing important goals in life. Once the emotions are recognized as action potentials in a person's subjective engagement in the world, then it is not possible to think of Jesus' identity or ministry to Israel without examining his emotional life. The picture is rendered more complex, though, by the fact that Jesus is no ordinary human person, for he is the Son who is in the bosom of the Father, so his identity has its origins in eternity and cannot be fathomed purely from the standpoint of the history of his birth and Jewish upbringing in the land. The God whom Jesus calls "Father" is the God of the covenant. Jewish Scripture speaks at length about the divine pathos, about how God is affected by his people. Here again, I realized that a cognitive theory of emotion is able to show that God's pathos is entirely reasonable and intelligible within the framework of the covenant relationship. For the emotions of God—such as love, joy, delight, wrath, jealousy, zeal, mercy, forgiveness, compassion, and lament—are actually communicable qualities of the divinity in relation to God's abiding fidelity to and personal engagement with his people. I therefore came to formulate the view that a cognitive theory of emotion is invaluable for reflection on both the human *and* divine emotions of Jesus, and for showing the richness and strength of Jesus' emotional life as the manifestation of the progressive and mutual interaction of the two natures in his person, which culminates in the suffering of Gethsemane and Calvary.

The title of this book is meant to convey the main thesis of the study; namely, that the emotional life of Christ is a special window through which to observe the process of deification in his person, which accomplishes our salvation. There are a few things, however, that must be made clear about the use of the adjective "passionate" in the title. (i) First, in contemporary language the term passionate conveys a person's depth of feeling and strength of conviction in relation to something deemed important in their lives. As used in the title, then, the term is intended to repudiate the view that Christ accomplishes our deification by displaying the detached attitudes and cool demeanor of a Stoic sage, who is unperturbed and unaffected by common passions such as love, joy, fear, anger, grief, and sorrow. (ii) Second, it will be noted that the modern term "emotions" is used in the subtitle, not the traditional term "passions." In this study I generally refer to the modern term emotions, not passions, although the two terms are used interchangeably. This is justified by the contention that both are forms of judgment concerning some present or prospective good or evil. (iii) Third, I am aware that the ancient term passions (*pathē*) refers to bad or false judgments, and not every experience we call an emotion today falls under this category; there are emotional experiences that are good judgments. When I say that I have used the terms passions and emotions interchangeably, it is the rightness or wrongness of the objects of the passions or emotions that makes them good or bad judgments. A passion is not a bad judgment in virtue of falling into the category of the passions; grief, for instance, is not a false judgment, but an ineluctable emotion that underscores human vulnerability due to dependency upon external objects over which we have little or no control. Jesus' anger, dread, grief, and sorrow are not passions in the pejorative sense of being bad judgments that he quickly overrides by the use of his superior reason as the divine Word, but very real emotions that are justified by the rightness of their objects, and concretely reveal what it cost the Son to win our glorious salvation.

Of course once I had reappraised the role of the emotions in Christ's life in a way that gives them greater integrity and importance than had been the case in past theological thinking, it became necessary to reconsider the role the emotions play in Christian life as a putting on Christ. As I examined writings on the Christian ascent to God in the theological tradition, I was especially drawn to the writings of Augustine of Hippo, Gregory of Nyssa, and Jonathan Edwards, inasmuch as all three thinkers in their respective ways repudiate a severe asceticism that follows the Stoic ideal of *apatheia* (i.e., extirpation of the passions). Yet notwithstanding the considerable merits of these thinkers, I also came to realize that all three envisage a restricted scope for the emotions of Christian life, since everything is reduced to the problem of sin and its consequences. In light of the formulation of my argument on the integral role of the emotions in Christ's life and mission, I turned my attention to considering a more expansive and integral role of the emotions in Christian life.

I came to see that putting on Christ means that his followers become the ongoing embodiment of God in the world, through a process of transformation of the emotions, wherein the crucified Christ becomes more and more the object of both the congenial *and* suffering emotions. In short, Christ's emotions are to become the emotions of his followers, who receive a "new heart" through the indwelling Spirit of the Lord. By virtue of this new sense of the heart, Christians see as God sees, and feel as God feels, and therefore become the living embodiment of Christ's "new commandment" to love one another as he has loved us (John 13:34). This perspective is certainly an attractive proposition that emphasizes the joy, peace, and hope that should reign in the lives of Christ's disciples, but it is also daunting and challenging insofar as it accentuates Christian life as the way of the cross, which takes the form of "love of enemies." I also came to see that such a perspective implies that the Christian churches of the future will have to be counter-cultural to a significant extent. For Christian emotions, as transformed emotions that have the ineffable God and the crucified Christ as their objects, motivate Christians to turn away from the corrupting influences of the technologies of desire in Western societies to pursue the loftier goods that pertain to the transcendent realm of the New Jerusalem. In pursuing these loftier goods as the embodiment of Christ in the world, Christian praise of God is not unlike the Jewish praise of God offered at the holy site of the shattered Jerusalem Temple. The similarity consists in the fact that Christian worship takes place at the foot of the cross of Christ; that is, before the shattered and broken body of the "Holy and Righteous One" (Acts 3:14), in whom the hidden Zion now dwells, until the time when the glory of Christ will be manifested to all in the coming age of the "New Jerusalem" (Rev 21:2).

I would like to extend my special thanks to Stephen Downs (Australian Catholic University), Robert Fitzsimons (Flinders University), and Fr. John Behr (St Vladimir's Orthodox Theological Seminary), for their encouragement and support in pursuing this particular study and seeing it through to its completion.

Introduction

Emotion Language as the Primary Language

EMOTION IS ONE OF the most integral and pervasive aspects of human experience. As people go about their business of living their daily lives in the world, they experience a wide range of emotions. Typical emotions include love for those who are close and important to us; the joy or delight of beholding some present good; jealousy when another person shows interest in one's partner; pity for someone who is beset by misfortune and suffers undeservedly; distress caused by a threatening situation, such as learning that one is likely to lose one's job or has cancer; anger when one suffers personal insult or injury, or confronts injustice in the world; anxiety about specific objects or the future state of things; fear of falling victim to harm; and grief at the death of a loved one. When we examine the concrete experiences of ordinary people, they are invariably expressed in the language of emotion. Emotion or affection language is the idiom of common discourse; it is what we may call the basic or primary or first-order language.

The emotions we experience are both positive and negative. They not only color and enrich and enliven human experience, they can also give rise to bad judgment and drastic action that results in a tragic end. This fact is recognized by the writers of literature, which thrives on the imagined emotions of its characters. The basic recipe is that the writer first paints a picture of a character with certain goals, standards, or attitudes, then goes on to construe a situation that readers will recognize as important given its implications for these known goals, standards, or attitudes. The character is then portrayed as correctly or incorrectly judging the situation as good or bad relative to these goals, standards, or attitudes, which leads to a description of the character's reaction to the situation. In the main plot of William Shakespeare's tragedy *Othello*, for example, the reader assumes that Desdemona's faithful love is something of great value to Othello, hence its preservation is an important goal for him. Hence when he (incorrectly) construes Cassio's (presumed) actions as a direct threat to this goal—because of the evil plan hatched by Iago—he becomes consumed with jealousy and anger. The dramatic deterioration in judgment that ensues is accompanied by tragic actions in which Othello first kills Desdemona and then subsequently takes his own life. "As readers, a certain suspension of disbelief is required, but only up to a point. The essential ingredients have to be believable. If literature is a microcosm of the real world, it has to be recognizable as such."[1] Emotions have enormous power to heal (benefit) or to wound (harm), and the range of emotions experienced by normal people in the course of their daily lives would undoubtedly support this perspective.

Notwithstanding the fact that emotion language is the idiom of common discourse, a number of common clichés have emerged in modern Western thinking on emotion that are at odds with the way people in general actually speak about specific emotions as they are experienced in concrete life. The usual clichés are as follows: emotions are irrational because they are simply bodily reactions, hence they must be sharply distinguished from reasoning which involves complex intentionality (mind-body dualism); emotions are innate or natural, whereas beliefs are formed and learned in a culture or society; and emotions are impervious to teaching, while beliefs can be modified by argument and teaching.[2] A divide between emotion and thought has become a feature of the modern Western cultural landscape and this split goes under many other rubrics, including the more academic and psychological "affect" and "cognition," the more romantic and philosophical "passion" and "reason," and the more prosaic "feeling" and "thinking."[3] To be emotional is to fail to process information rationally, to form erroneous judgments, and to forfeit the possibilities for sensible or intelligent action and the capacity for problem solving. A clear example of this view in popular Western culture is the character Mr. Spock of *Star Trek* fame, whose complete lack of emotions is depicted as integral to his superior Vulcan intelligence.

In conjunction with this notion of emotion as irrational—which is conveyed by everyday metaphors such as "insane with jealousy," "blind

---

1. Ortony et al., *Cognitive Structure*, 3.
2. Nussbaum, *Therapy of Desire*, 79.
3. Lutz, *Unnatural Emotions*, 56.

rage," and "love is blind"—is the related conceptualization of emotion as uncontrollable and involuntary. Everyday discourse is replete with metaphors that reflect this conceptualization: we speak of being "swept away" by our emotions; of allowing our emotions "to get the better of us;" of being "helplessly" in love or "hopelessly" confused; and daily we hear about "crimes of passion." An emotional person is one who is not in control of their actions because they allow themselves to be overpowered or buffeted by their emotions. It is the weak who are emotional, while rational persons are considered to be strong, reliable, and problem solvers. Yet while emotions are generally devalued as irrational, biological, and involuntary or unintended, they are also often regarded more positively as an expression of personal values relative to a particular situation. "The double-edged character of the Western cultural conceptualization of emotion is nowhere more evident than in the way the emotions are related to value, morality, and ethics."[4] It would therefore appear to be the case that the thinking on emotion in the modern Western world is somewhat ambivalent: there are a number of common clichés that tend to devalue the emotions yet there is also the recognition of emotion as an expression of personal values in a given context. In my personal world, emotions are attached to the things that I value, irrespective of how well or badly those valued things might fit together. If I value a particular person or my country of birth, I will inevitably experience certain emotions towards these cherished objects of value, which dispose me to action in upholding their value.

When we turn to examine the field of Western philosophical thought on the emotions, there is certainly a rich source of writings on the subject in the classic Hellenistic period. The non-cognitive approach to emotions—which has dominated Western thought on the topic until recently—can be traced back to Plato, who depicted the emotions (passions) as compulsive forces in opposition to the powers of reason. Aristotle, in contrast, proposed a "functionalist" model of mind, where something is analyzed in terms of "form" or how it functions. Emotions are distinguished on the basis of appraisal. The emotion of fear, for example, is based upon an appraisal of impending danger, while anger is associated with an appraisal of personal insult or injury. Aristotle's writings on emotion flowed on to the Stoic philosophers who maintained a lively debate over centuries on the emotions (*pathē*) and their place in ethics

---

4. Lutz, *Unnatural Emotions*, 76.

and the pursuit of the good life.[5] For the Stoics, emotions have a cognitive structure in that they are *forms of judgment*, but they are regarded as bad guides to good human behavior. What is wrong with the emotions is that they are based on false beliefs, thus the Stoic goal is the extirpation of the emotions (*apatheia*), which is integral to the pursuit of wisdom.

Those involved in the development of a contemporary cognitive theory of emotion, while accepting the Stoic notion that an emotion is a judgment concerning some present or prospective state of affairs, are united in rejecting the notion of *apatheia*. The general view today is that Stoic therapy can be effective in dealing with unwelcome and counter-productive emotions—such as anxiety and anger—but it is quite something else to maintain that none of the common emotions should be wanted. We can acknowledge the import of Stoic thinking on the cognitive nature of emotion without having to embrace the Stoic ideal of *apatheia*. This cognitive revival has been on the way for more than fifty years now, and its beginnings can be traced to Magda Arnold's book *Emotion and Personality* (1960), and Anthony Kenny's *Action, Emotion and Will* (1963). Cognitive theory now poses a serious challenge to non-cognitive theories that have dominated Western philosophical thinking since the time of René Descartes, who thinks of the emotions as just "epiphenomenal feelings without a function."[6]

The existentialist style of philosophizing was the first type of modern philosophy to seriously challenge the Cartesian view by attributing ontological significance to the affective aspect of human existence. The most obvious characteristic of existentialist thought is that "it is a philosophy of the subject rather than of the object."[7] One could rightly say that idealism takes its starting point in the subject as well, but what is distinctive about the existentialists is that the subject is "the existent in

---

5. Chryssipus and Seneca are two Stoic philosophers who deserve to be highlighted for their contribution to the philosophy of emotion. In this study the modern term "emotions" and the traditional term "passions" (*pathē*) are used interchangeably. This is justified by the assertion that both are forms of judgment concerning some present or prospective good or evil. However, it is acknowledged that the modern term "emotion" is a broader concept than the ancient term "passion," for not every experience we call an emotion today falls under the Stoic category of *pathē* (bad judgments); there are emotional experiences that fall under the Stoic category of *eupatheia* (good judgments). This will become clearer from the critique of Stoicism offered in chapter 1 of this study.

6. Power and Dalgleish, *Cognition and Emotion*, 26.

7. Macquarrie, *Existentialism*, 14.

the whole range of his existing. He is not only a thinking subject but an initiator of action and a centre of feeling. It is the whole spectrum of existing, known directly and concretely in the very act of existing, that existentialism tries to express."[8] For Descartes the individual is purely a thinking subject (*Cogito ergo sum*), whereas for the existentialists the existent is not only thinking subject but feeling subject and acting subject as well. Existentialism does not view emotion or feeling as antithetical to reason, but acknowledges that feelings too are a way of arriving at philosophical truth. As inward experiences of the existent, feelings are "perhaps our most direct openings on to the world."[9] In sense perception one is detached from the object, but in feeling the existent is united to that which is felt and is included in a whole.[10] Feelings are, in the language of phenomenologists, "intentional," which is to say that they are directed upon actual states of affairs.[11] Heidegger, for instance, uses the expression *Befindlichkeit*, which literally means "the-way-one-finds-oneself,"[12] to convey the intentionality of feelings. A feeling or emotion is understood as specifically disclosive of being inasmuch as it is the way the existent becomes aware of a given situation. For Heidegger, the fundamental affective state is "Angst" (anxiety).[13] The "facticity" of existence is the

8. Macquarrie, *Existentialism*, 15.

9. Macquarrie, *Existentialism*, 157.

10. Macquarrie points out that the kind of sense perception that comes nearest to inward experiences of feeling is touch. To touch something is to feel oneself in a peculiarly intimate relation to it.

11. A close link exists between existentialists and phenomenologists. Most existentialists are phenomenologists, for phenomenology offers the existentialist the sort of methodology that is required to pursue an investigation of human existence. There are many phenomenologists, though, who are not existentialists. Heidegger, for example, was a pupil of Edmund Husserl and dedicated his major work—*Being and Time*—to his old teacher, but Husserl was in fact quite critical of the use Heidegger had made of his ideas. See Macquarrie, *Existentialism*, 22–23.

12. Macquarrie, *Existentialism*, 161–62.

13. In addition to anxiety, Heidegger admits two other affects or moods as having ontological significance: joy and boredom (Macquarrie, *Existentialism*, 171–72). While existentialists claim that there are some fundamental feelings that are disclosive of being, they differ with regard to whether these fundamental feelings are of a negative or positive kind. For some, anxiety, boredom, and nausea are the primary ontological feelings, which reveal that the existent is not at home in the world (Heidegger, Sartre). For others, joy, hope, and the feeling of "belonging" are primary, with anxiety its derivative (Ricoeur). Here we appear to have a clash which undermines the very idea of ontological feeling, but as Ricoeur points out: "Perhaps this clash has no further import than the distinction between the *via negativa* and the *via analogiae* in the

primary disclosure of anxiety; it discloses the existent as "being-there" (*Dasein*), as possibility thrown into the world. Anxiety discloses the fact that the existent is responsible for an existence of which he can never be the master, thus the existent is not at home in the world.

The existentialists are focused not on the abstract problems of logic and epistemology, but on the problems of concrete "existence" in the world. Heidegger regards the fundamental category of the being of man as "being-in-the-world." This category is not understood spatially but existentially; that is, it does not mean that the existent is located in the world but that he is bound up with the world, he is engaged with it, he has to do with it, and endeavors to make something of himself by shaping his future. As Jean-Paul Sartre succinctly states the matter, "Man's existence precedes his essence." This is to say that we cannot posit a nature or essence of the existent, for he will be what he makes of himself through freedom, decision, and responsibility. Either the existent is himself, he is existing as this unique existent, standing out from the world of objects and emerging from any given state of himself; or he is not himself, he is being absorbed into the world of objects as just another object, he decides nothing for himself but everything is decided for him by external factors. These two possibilities are to exist authentically or inauthentically.[14] In the existentialist view, it is through our feelings that we learn some things about our world that are inaccessible to a merely objective beholding. Existentialism is not a philosophy of feelings, but it does acknowledge the legitimate place that feelings have in the totality of human existence. Against the ingrained tendency to conceive of the intellect, the emotions, and the will as separate faculties or activities of the soul, the existentialist style of philosophizing regards the *intellectual, emotional, and volitional elements as merely distinctions that belong within a living whole*, hence these elements "cannot be sharply marked off from each other."[15]

---

speculation on being." Ricoeur, *Fallible Man*, 161; cited in Macquarrie, *Existentialism*, 173. Macquarrie reminds us how religious language has traditionally spoken of God both negatively and positively—it has recognized both God's wrath and otherness, as well as God's love and closeness.

14. In addition to the themes of freedom, decision, and responsibility arises another prominent group of themes—finitude, guilt, alienation, despair, and death—that gives ample expression to the tragic dimensions of existence. These tragic elements are rooted in the fact that the human quest for authentic existence meets with inevitable resistance and existence ultimately ends in death.

15. Macquarrie, *Existentialism*, 156.

Kierkegaard's writings are worth noting for what they have to say about human existence in relation to God. It is impossible, says Kierkegaard, to objectively pursue knowledge of God because "God is a subject and therefore exists only for subjectivity in inwardness."[16] The human being's relationship to God is characterized by passion, which is the highest expression of subjectivity. The objective accent falls on "what" is said and does not recognize that it is "the decision" that is urgent and pressing, whereas the subjective accent falls on "how" it is said.[17] Only in subjectivity is there decisiveness, is there passion of the infinite. Here we see the central importance of decision and the affective aspect of human existence in Kierkegaard's thought. For Kierkegaard, without risk there is no faith and what is absurd is "that the eternal truth has come into being in time, that God has come into being, has been born, has grown up, and so forth, precisely like any other individual human being."[18] In the person of Jesus Christ, God himself enters the realm of existential being: Jesus Christ is *the* historical, *the* existential individual. In the event of the incarnation, the immutable becomes a changing being, the eternal takes on the temporal process, the suprahistorical enters into history. The object of faith is the "fact that God has existed," which cannot be grasped in any objective way. Without the "irruption of inwardness" the individual cannot appropriate the paradoxical nature of Christian faith, which leads to the attainment of truth and self-determination; that is, a true relationship to God, which constitutes authentic existence.[19]

The existentialists claim that feelings have a cognitive status insofar as they are disclosive of being and therefore render the existent aware of his total situation in the world. But the truth contained in the existentialist's ontological vision is not provable, for the ontological language "is not a language that describes but rather a language that evokes."[20] A language that is evocative and seeks to bring the other to the same disclosure of being has affinities with such religious experiences as revelation and mystical vision, as well as with aesthetic experiences of perceiving things in the depth of their inter-relatedness. The reflections of

16. Kierkegaard, *Concluding Unscientific Postscript*, 178. Kierkegaard wrote in opposition to the metaphysics of Hegel.

17. Kierkegaard, *Concluding Unscientific Postscript*, 181.

18. Kierkegaard, *Concluding Unscientific Postscript*, 188.

19. More recent theological thinkers who have sought to express the Christian faith in existentialist terms include Rudolf Bultmann and Paul Tillich.

20. Macquarrie, *Existentialism*, 244.

Friedrich Schleiermacher on the "feeling of absolute dependence" and of Rudolf Otto on the *mysterium tremendum et fascinans*, are further illustrations of affective language that is used evocatively to bring the other to a fundamental awareness of being. Schleiermacher wrote in response to the Enlightenment, which had reduced religion to knowledge of God (rationalistic deism) and to morality (Kantian emphasis on free will). He sought to correct the subject-object disjunction by appealing to the "principle of identity" which transcends the subject-object disjunction by positing God as the creative ground and unity of all that is. Paul Tillich explains that for Schleiermacher, "in order to derive a concept from reality one must be able to participate in the life of this reality."[21] Romanticism's principle of the infinite within the finite is apparent here. The word "feeling" is intended to describe the fundamental experience of the principle of identity; it expresses the immediate awareness of the divine within us, which transcends subject and object, and constitutes the essence of religious self-consciousness according to Schleiermacher.[22]

Rudolf Otto in his celebrated book *The Idea of the Holy* speaks of a "numinous" category of value and of a "numinous" state of mind, which is irreducible to any other.[23] The numinous experience transcends the sphere of the ordinary, the usual, the familiar, and awaits our discovery by being "felt" as objective and outside the self.[24] The idea of the holy comes to awareness in the human subject through the numinous experience of awe and wonder, and it contains a surplus of meaning above and beyond the meaning of moral goodness. The object of numinous experience is named by Otto as the *mysterium tremendum et fascinans*. The affective state referred to as *tremendum* conveys the sense of absolute majesty and awe, which produces in us the feeling of being but dust and ashes.[25] This element of daunting majesty is expressed biblically as the "wrath" of God. But there is another affective state, the *fascinans*, in which the mystery shows itself as something uniquely attractive and fascinating, so that we feel an impulse to turn our gaze towards it and allow ourselves to be captivated and entranced by it.[26] These philosophical reflections on

21. Tillich, *Perspectives*, 106.
22. Schleiermacher, *Christian Faith*, 12–22. Schleiermacher talks of the "feeling of absolute dependence."
23. Otto, *Idea of the Holy*, 6–7.
24. Otto, *Idea of the Holy*, 11.
25. Otto, *Idea of the Holy*, 19.
26. Otto, *Idea of the Holy*, 31.

religion offered by Schleiermacher and Otto serve to underscore further the existentialist view that there are certain affective elements to human existence that are disclosive of being, and thus have ontological import.

When we turn to consider the field of theological writings on the emotions, few thinkers in the Christian tradition have addressed themselves directly to the logical relations between emotion and theological thinking. The church fathers in general were very wary of the emotions or passions (*pathē*) and taught that Christian ascent to God requires either the elimination of the passions—in line with the Stoic notion of *apatheia*—or their transformation by directing them to God as their right object. Augustine's *Confessions* would have to stand out as a classic treatment of the emotions in the patristic period. As Augustine gave up on the idea of a vertical ascent to God in this life, he laid bare his innermost feelings to God, thereby exposing the inner world of his heart that yearned for the bliss of eternal rest in God—"Our hearts are restless, O Lord, until they rest in You." What we most ardently desire, according to Augustine, can never be more than a hope which points far beyond this life to the anticipated age to come. He speaks of moments of "delight," of clear vision of truth, but such moments are few and portrayed as consolations of a traveler on the long road of the spiritual life. When Augustine analyzed the psychology of delight, he came to the conclusion that nothing else but delight could motivate the human will. This implies that the source of action in human beings is the mobilization of our feelings; only if we are "affected" by an object of delight are we motivated to act. The language used by Augustine in the *Confessions* is the language of erotic longing, not the language the Stoic wise man would use in urging the extirpation of the passions. For Augustine, it is not a question of controlling the emotions or extirpating them altogether, but of directing them towards God as their right object. To seek to eliminate the emotions would amount to a denial of our human condition before God and of the means by which salvation in Christ comes to us sinners.

Gregory of Nyssa is another church father who deserves special mention on the topic of the emotions. In the past it was thought that Gregory was an extreme ascetic who advocated the purging of the emotions from the soul, but recent scholarship has challenged this view and shown that Gregory conceived of the emotions as playing a constructive role in the Christian ascent to God.[27] The emotions do pose a problem if

---

27. This will be discussed in chapter 2 of this study.

they are not properly ordered by the rational soul, however the remedy for this condition is not their elimination but the *proper training or educating of desire*. Gregory sees the rational soul as not merely controlling the appetitive faculties, but as transforming the bestial passions so that they are directed towards the lofty goods of God's kingdom. In such a scenario, the desires of the soul's lower faculties are not to be purged but harnessed and put to the service of the mind. In this fashion the soul rises above the drives of the spirited and appetitive faculties and the temptations of this world (vice) and ascends towards God (virtue). It is the educating or transforming of desire in an ascending order of creation—from vegetative or nutritive soul, to sensible or sentient soul, to rational soul— that is the guiding principle in Gregory's writings on Christian ascent to God. For Gregory, God is an object of *erōs* and even in the eschaton the perfected saints will still experience *erōs* as an ever-expanding, but not restless love.

During the medieval period, Thomas Aquinas, writing during a period in which Aristotelian philosophy had been recovered and put to theological use, reflected at length on the passions (*passiones*). Aquinas's *Treatise on the Passions* "probably constituted the longest sustained discussion of the passions ever written."[28] Aquinas's account of emotion is based on his concept of appetite, which plays a central role in his anthropology and metaphysics.[29] Aquinas offers us a positive evaluation of

28. Lombardo, *Logic of Desire*, 1. Questions 22–48 of the *Prima secundae* of the *Summa theologiae* have come to be known as the *Treatise on the Passions*. The fact that Aquinas was attentive to innumerable authorities—Jewish, Christian, Islamic, and pagan—and his reflections on the passions were set within the context of his entire corpus of philosophy and theology, means that his account of the passions poses "interpretative difficulties" that can be "difficult to penetrate." Lombardo, *Logic of Desire*, 272. Given these interpretative difficulties, Aquinas's account of the passions, while providing a rich source of material for contemporary study of the emotions, will not be reviewed in chapter 2 of the present study, both for the sake of brevity and for the purpose of adhering to a strictly cognitive theory of emotion. Aquinas does not limit his reflections to the cognitive character of emotions, but also attends to the appetitive dimension: emotions are thought of as movements or manifestations of sense appetite, caused by imagining good or evil.

29. It should be noted that Aquinas never used the term "emotion." The latter is a modern concept that is considerably broader than the ancient and medieval concept of passion. Aquinas wrote about appetites, passions, affections, habitus, virtues, vices, grace, and other subjects that relate to the contemporary category of emotion. The fact that in the contemporary climate there is no clearly defined category of emotion means that it is even more difficult to arrive at an etymological parallel to emotion in Latin. Perhaps the closest parallel would be *affectus* or *affectio* (affection). See

appetite, for appetite is what inclines or directs something toward its *telos*; that is, its perfection and completion.[30] Every existing thing tends by its own natural principles toward its proper end or good and Aquinas uses the term "love" to refer to the tendency an entity has to be itself. Even a stone, in tending to what is suitable to it, is said to love its own being.[31] Goodness is what evokes appetite in all existing things, but Aquinas goes further and proposes that appetite or desirability is the defining characteristic of goodness.[32] The goodness of appetite is thus bound up with the goodness of being, and since the world was created imperfect it is the appetite inherent in created reality that provides the dynamic movement toward perfection and completion.[33] At the heart of the *exitus-reditus* structure that Aquinas adopts in his *Summa theologiae* is the concept of appetite. His thought begins with God's act of creation, which flows from God's desire or appetite, and then proceeds to consider how created reality returns to God through the dynamic movement of appetite. "Appetite is the engine driving the *exitus-reditus*."[34]

As a passive power, appetite is triggered when certain objects come into view. Aquinas is most interested in the appetites that involve some kind of apprehension, that is, cognitive dimension.[35] Appetite is passive inasmuch as it is acted upon by objects via apprehension, and it is a power in that it acts in response to the apprehended object so as to move the subject toward its *telos*. Following Aristotle, Aquinas holds that humans

---

Lombardo, *Logic of Desire*, 15–19.

30. Lombardo, *Logic of Desire*, 26. This leads Aquinas to conceive of evil in terms of appetite. Evil is a privation of goodness; that is, a frustration or blocking of appetite's natural *telos*.

31. See Cates, *Aquinas on the Emotions*, 106–8.

32. Lombardo, *Logic of Desire*, 27.

33. Aquinas speaks of appetite in God as well; however, in God appetite is present only as an inclination toward a good already possessed. Appetite involves passivity, but God cannot become something other than what God already is. Aquinas identifies appetite in God with the divine will, which is a kind of intellectual appetite that is inclined toward unlimited goodness. We can attribute appetite to God but not passion, because the latter implies potential not yet actualized. See Lombardo, *Logic of Desire*, 28.

34. Lombardo, *Logic of Desire*, 30.

35. The power of sensory apprehension takes the form of "exterior" and "interior" senses. The former are the powers of sight, hearing, smell, taste, and touch; the latter include the "common sense," the "imagination," the "estimative" and "cogitative" powers, and the "memorative" power. See Cates, *Aquinas on the Emotions*, 112–16; Lombardo, *Logic of Desire*, 23–24.

have three kinds of appetite—natural, sensory, and intellectual—and he characterizes passion specifically as a motion of the sensory appetite.[36] A passion is "elicited by sensory images, impressions, associations, and judgments regarding the suitability or unsuitability of a particular object for one's life or well-being."[37] Aquinas lists eleven basic passions—love, desire, joy, hate, aversion, sadness, hope, daring, despair, fear, and anger—and structures these according to two appetitive powers; namely, the "concupiscible" power that is inclined to pursue sensible goods and avoid whatever is harmful to this end, and the "irascible" power that resists whatever might attack and get in the way of what the soul finds agreeable.[38] While Aquinas says that the passions do require the guidance of reason—given our fallen condition—nonetheless in their essential structure they continue to serve the perfection of our nature.[39] On Aquinas' account, it is apparent that the emotions involve a complex set of relationships, involving powers of apprehension and appetitive powers, by which we receive and process information about ourselves and our world.

---

36. Plants and inanimate objects are inclined toward a good by natural disposition, thus they have no cognition (natural appetite); sentient beings are inclined toward some particular good with some amount of cognition but they do not apprehend the good as good (sensory appetite); while still other things are inclined toward a good with the cognition proper to the intellect which is able to know the good as good (intellectual appetite or will). Aquinas distinguishes the species of appetite by the kind of object desired, that is, by *telos*. It is our intellectual appetite that shares an essential similarity with God's appetite; it has the capacity to love God and enjoy God. There are two kinds of cognition, sense cognition and intellectual cognition, which are mutually interpenetrating and pertain to different aspects of the world. Passion involves both kinds of cognition, for sense perception of an object is accompanied by evaluation of the object's relevance to the subject's interests—Aquinas refers to this as an "intention."

37. Cates, *Aquinas on the Emotions*, 121.

38. See Lombardo, *Logic of Desire*, ch. 2. The first of the positive concupiscible passions is love, which leads to desire (an affective movement toward an object that is not possessed) and pleasure (a kind of repose in an object that is possessed). The first of the negative concupiscible passions is hatred, which leads to aversion of an evil object and, if the evil becomes present, to sorrow or pain. The irascible passions have to do with the interests of the concupiscible passions in the face of some difficulty: hope arises when an arduous future good seems possible to attain; despair when an arduous future good seems impossible to obtain; daring when an arduous future evil seems possible to overcome; fear when an arduous future evil seems impossible to overcome; and anger when a present evil is challenged with the hope of overcoming it.

39. Lombardo, *Logic of Desire*, 41.

In Protestant theology, Jonathan Edwards in the eighteenth century should be singled out as having made a concerted effort to reflect deeply on the significance of the emotions for Christian life. Edwards acknowledges a primary role that the "affections" have to play in human life. The affections are seen as the spring of the busy and active world of humankind: "take away all love and hatred, all hope and fear, all anger, zeal and affectionate desire, and the world would be, in a great measure, motionless and dead; there would be no such thing as activity amongst mankind, or any earnest pursuit whatsoever."[40] Edwards wrote during a period dominated by revivalism in the region of New England, and he sought to repudiate two extreme poles of Christian religion of his time: on the one hand, he addressed the problem of religion being reduced to a lifeless morality; and on the other, he dissociated himself from hysteria, excessive enthusiasm, and the spectacular commotions of revivalism. He struggled with the central question of Puritan Protestantism—"What is the nature of true religion?"[41] In a climate where counterfeit religions abounded, Edwards recognized the necessity of articulating positive "signs" of true piety.[42] The true saints are those who have the "sense of the heart," by which is meant that they display gracious or holy affections as the fruits of the Spirit dwelling in their souls in its own proper nature. Edwards's thesis is stated thus: "True religion, in great part, consists in holy affections."[43] The phrase "in great part" has particular importance, for it indicates that Edwards did not want to swallow religion in the affections. The latter are necessary for true religion, but in the self they form a unity with the powers of understanding and will.

John Wesley, writing also in the eighteenth century, acknowledges, as does Edwards, that the emotions are a crucial part of human life. It was the desire "to stay close to concrete reality that made Wesley think long and hard about the importance of the emotions for the Christian life."[44] Wesley did not use affection-laden language merely for rhetorical purposes, but for communicating his theological grasp of the Christian faith: being a Christian consists, in larger measure, of having certain

---

40. Edwards, *Religious Affections*, 101.

41. Edwards, *Religious Affections*, 84. The express aim of Edwards's study is set forth in the Preface.

42. Edwards elaborated twelve distinguishing signs of "gracious" affections, which is the subject matter of part 3 of *Religious Affections*.

43. Edwards, *Religious Affections*, 95.

44. Clapper, *John Wesley*, 8.

religious affections. Affection language is the primary or first-order language for Wesley and while the notion of "religious experience" readily lends itself to confusion and misunderstanding—Wesley acknowledges the problems of fideism, quietism, and fanatical enthusiasm—this should not blind us to the fact that "certain affections do have a normative role to play in the Christian life, and to deny this is just as wrong as over-emphasizing it."[45] Wesley has recourse to the great range of scriptural language concerning the "heart" to support his claim that certain patterns of affectivity belong to the Christian life. Far from being mere ornamentation or clouding the real message of the Gospel, affection language actually conveys and constitutes, in large measure, the real message.[46] For Wesley, the religious affections must be considered on their own terms as evaluations of reality, which have God as their object and dispose the Christian to action in the world. The religious affections for Wesley were not, as is often thought, merely inner and subjective feelings, but "fundamentally rational, relational and, in some respects, even public, manifestations of the Christian character."[47]

This introduction started by pointing out the paradoxical or contradictory attitude to emotion in the modern Western world. On the one hand, emotion or affection language is the idiom of common discourse and reflects the crucial part played by the emotions in our lives; yet, on the other hand, there are a number of common clichés that have emerged in modern Western thinking on emotion, which are at odds with the way we commonly speak about emotion in our concrete life. The common clichés have their roots in the rationalist philosophies of the Enlightenment, epitomized by René Descartes whose non-cognitive conception of the emotions persisted for centuries and influenced the important psychological work of William James. James interpreted feelings as a physiological set of bodily sensations. So, if I feel afraid, it is because I tremble; if I feel sad, it is because I cry. The body sensation according to James *is* the emotion. We have seen that by the turn of the twentieth century some philosophical challenges to the Cartesian view of emotion began to emerge and these challenges came mainly from the existentialist style of philosophizing (Kierkegaard, Heidegger, Sartre), as well as the philosophy of religion (Schleiermacher, Otto). But it is in the latter half

---

45. Clapper, *John Wesley*, 5.
46. Clapper, *John Wesley*, 1.
47. Clapper, *John Wesley*, 14.

of the twentieth century, beginning with the works of Magda Arnold and Anthony Kenny, when we witness a genuine revival of interest in the cognitive nature of emotion, which continues to gain momentum amongst philosophers, psychologists, and social scientists.[48]

While philosophers, psychologists, and social scientists are earnestly engaging with a cognitive approach to emotion, theologians and scriptural scholars to date have not seen any particular need to consider the implications of cognitive theory for the Christian life, or, indeed, for reflection on the mystery of Christ. In our time, the only notable exceptions to Christian scholarly neglect of the role of the emotions in Christian life or in life of Christ are to be found in the writings of Benjamin Warfield, Matthew Elliott, and Stephen Voorwinde.[49] Warfield writes as a theologian who contends that as we examine the emotional life of Christ, we must not lose sight of the fact that "we are not only observing the proofs of the truth of his humanity, and not merely regarding the most perfect example of a human life which is afforded by history, but are contemplating the atoning work of the Savior in its fundamental elements."[50] Warfield rejects the idea that the emotional movements in Jesus never ran their full course as we experience them, claiming instead that in order to secure our salvation Jesus' emotional life did not differ at all from his fellow humans, sin only excepted. Every manifestation of the truth of our Lord's humanity is an exhibition of the reality of our redemption: "In his sorrows he was bearing our sorrows, and having passed through a human life like ours, he remains forever able to be touched with a feeling of our infirmities . . . we are observing his fitness to serve our needs."[51] Warfield's welcome approach to the emotional life of Christ has the considerable merit of avoiding "a dualizing sort of christology," where Christ is thought of as both a divine subject with regard to the active aspects of his mission and a human subject in respect of the passive and emotional aspects of his life.[52]

---

48. For evidence of the explosion of academic interest in the emotions, see Corrigan, *Religion and Emotion*, 1–31.

49. Warfield, "Emotional Life," 93–145; Elliott, *Faithful Feelings*; Voorwinde, *Jesus' Emotions in the Fourth Gospel*; Voorwinde, *Jesus' Emotions in the Gospels*.

50. Warfield, "Emotional Life," 145.

51. Warfield, "Emotional Life," 144.

52. Gregersen in his article, "Emotional Christ," 247–61, makes the claim that Leo's Tome introduced in the Western church "a dualizing sort of christology." That is to say, not enough emphasis was given to the activity of Christ as a single divine-human

Voorwinde writes as a scriptural scholar and his focus in his first monograph on John's Gospel is doctrinal; that is to say, he is interested in the significance of Jesus' emotions for the Christology of John's Gospel. The question that Voorwinde investigates is: "Do the emotions of Jesus as recorded in the Fourth Gospel demonstrate (a) his humanity, (b) his divinity, or (c) both his humanity and his divinity?"[53] His study upholds the third option. In Voorwinde's second book, he examines Jesus' emotions in each of the four Gospels with a view to showing how Jesus' emotions contribute to the overall picture that each Gospel paints of Jesus. Voorwinde seeks to illustrate how each Gospel writer uses the emotions of Jesus to move his Gospel forward. But that is not the only express purpose of Voorwinde's study, for he also raises the fundamental question of whether Christians should emulate the emotions of Jesus as presented in the Gospels?

The monograph by Elliott is more of a general work that lacks the exegetical depth of Voorwinde's work or the theological acumen of Warfield's writings, and, moreover, it is largely concerned not with the emotions of Jesus but the emotions of his disciples. Elliott's work is nonetheless of value in seeking to draw attention to the potential significance of interpreting emotion in the New Testament from an explicitly cognitive viewpoint. The acceptance of the gospel, says Elliott, leads to a renewing of our mind and thus to a renewing of our emotions: "To be like Christ is not only to behave like Christ but also to feel like Christ."[54] Stephen Barton in the conclusion to his article on the emotions in early Christianity makes this very same point when he asserts that "more attention needs to be given to the various ways in which conversion to Christ involved an ongoing *conversion of the emotions.*"[55] G. Walter Hansen is of the same mindset, although he expresses his thought in a more dramatic and compelling fashion in his article on the emotions of Jesus:

> I am spellbound by the intensity of Jesus's emotions: not a twinge of pity, but heartbroken compassion; not a passing irritation, but terrifying anger; not a silent tear, but groans of anguish.

---

subject. We must conceive of the divine and human aspects as working in tandem, rather than being parceled into two separate subjects—a divine subject with regard to the active aspects of Christ's mission, and a human subject with regard to the passive and emotional life of Christ.

53. Voorwinde, *Jesus' Emotions in the Fourth Gospel*, 13.
54. Elliott, *Faithful Feelings*, 261.
55. Barton, "Eschatology," 591.

> Not a weak smile, but ecstatic celebration. Jesus' emotions are like a mountain river, cascading with clear water. My emotions are more like a muddy foam or feeble trickle. Jesus invites us to come to him and drink. Whoever is thirsty and believes in him will have the river of his life flowing out from the innermost being (John 7:37–38). We are not to be merely spellbound by what we see in the emotional Jesus; we are to be unbound by his Spirit so that his life becomes our life, his emotions our emotions, to be "transformed into his likeness with ever increasing glory" (2 Cor 3:18).[56]

With regard to the structure of the present work, the first chapter of this study will seek to provide a contemporary cognitive framework for reflection on the emotions. Several eminent advocates of a cognitive theory will be surveyed—Martha Nussbaum, Robert Solomon, Richard Lazarus, Aaron Ben-Ze'ev, Cheshire Calhoun, and Richard Wollheim—with a view to elucidating what could reasonably be identified as the fundamental ingredients or components of a cognitive approach to emotion. It will emerge that emotions are judgments about important things, that they embody beliefs about their objects, that they have a personal biography of subjective engagement in the world, that they have action potentials, that they register our vulnerability before parts of the world that we do not fully control, and that they are no mere bodily sensations but are judgments of the body. The discussion will not be exhaustive since this is not a study of cognitive theory per se, but rather the application of a contemporary cognitive understanding of emotion to the emotional life of Jesus as depicted in the gospels, and the implications of the latter findings for Christian life and mission in the world. The first chapter is therefore a preparatory chapter that will provide the framework for the remainder of the work.

A necessary part of the first chapter will be a critique of the Stoic view of emotion, not only because of the revival today of cognitive theory in emotion studies, but because of the pervasive influence of Stoic teachings on the development of Christian thought on the emotions.[57] A number

---

56. Hansen, "Emotions of Jesus," 46.

57. For example, the Stoic idea of first movements, conveyed by the Stoic term *propatheia* (pre-passion), was taken over by church fathers such as Origen, Jerome, Didymus the Blind, Evagrius of Pontus, and Augustine. The first movements are thought of as temptations and sin comes in when assent is given to the pleasure of the thought, be it a thought of fornication, gluttony, avarice, distress, anger, depression, vainglory, or pride. By dealing with these first movements the Christian works towards the Stoic

of reasons will be given for a repudiation of the Stoic ideal of *apatheia*, after which it should be clear to the reader what elements of Stoic teaching can continue to be useful today, both for emotion studies and for Christian reflection on the person and work of Christ. Consideration will also be given in chapter 1 to the basic emotion of wonder—philosophy in the past regarded wonder as the hallmark of the human being—and how it is to the transcendent object of wonder, insofar as it is invested with a surplus of meaning and unsurpassable value, that all our goals in this life are referred for their ultimate fulfillment and transformation. The chapter will conclude with a discussion of whether or not desire should be considered as a basic emotion. Desire in the past has often been presented as a basic emotion, but the discussion will contend that desire is a different kind of mental disposition to emotion. It is best not to think of desire as a basic emotion, although the discussion will suggest that it is legitimate to think of the human subject as having a *fundamental desire*—i.e., created in the image and likeness of God—that accounts for the dynamic movement of its historical existence. It will be proposed that the notion of transcendental experience (see Karl Rahner) is helpful for illuminating human subjectivity as a dynamic movement beyond its own finitude toward an infinite horizon known as "holy mystery." This fundamental desire of the human subject will be portrayed as referred to the ineffable object of wonder, and it is within this framework that the life of the emotions will be examined so as to unveil their importance and significance for human life in general and for Jesus' life in particular. With regard to Jesus Christ, it is apparent from the gospels that the God whom he calls "Father" is the object of wonder—*mysterium tremendum et fascinans*—who is invested with unsurpassed value and a surplus of meaning, and Jesus' fundamental desire is to make known and present the Father's compassionate love in his saving mission to the covenant people. The emotions of Jesus unfold and assume importance within this framework, for they appear as manifestations of a profound struggle and agonizing tension that obtains between Jesus' fundamental desire to make known the Father's unfathomable love for his people on the one hand, and, on the other, the increasing resistance, isolation, and ultimate rejection of Jesus by his own people who pretend that the kingdom of

---

ideal of *apatheia*. When applied to the gospel story, the church fathers tended to assert that Christ only "began" to be troubled, that he experienced certain pre-passions, but he halted the disturbances by the exercise of his rational soul so that they did not develop into passions. See Sorabji, *Emotion*, chs. 22–24.

God is something they can exercise control over according to their own self-serving interests.

Chapter 2 will offer reviews of the writings of three major Christian thinkers in respect of the emotions: one is representative of Western Latin Christianity (Augustine of Hippo); the other is representative of Eastern Greek Christianity (Gregory of Nyssa); and the final one is representative of Protestant Christianity (Jonathan Edwards).[58] These particular thinkers have been selected because each in their own way attempts to show the constructive role that the emotions play in the ascent to God. Often in Christianity the ascent of the soul to God has featured quite a severe asceticism, where the ideal was defined as the extirpation of the passions.[59] We will see that neither Augustine, nor Gregory, nor Edwards subscribes to this view, and instead they propose that Christian life consists largely in the right ordering of the emotions, which are recognized as having a cognitive character. This latter aspect will be drawn out by comparing each thinker with the cognitive theory of emotion presented in chapter 1.

Augustine's thought is considered significant inasmuch as he situates Christian ascent within the context of the present human condition with all its inadequacies, sinfulness, weakness, longing, and incompleteness, so that ascent involves the redirecting of desire away from earthly objects toward the heavenly God as the new object of the emotions. Gregory's thought is especially significant in that he seeks to elaborate the erotic relation of humanity to God, and, moreover, he proposes the transformed nature of *erōs* in the eschaton, which he depicts as a "soaring *stasis*." Like Augustine, Gregory contends that human desire is something which can be rightly or wrongly ordered, which leads him to conceive of Christian ascent as the educating or transforming of desire. But unlike Augustine who depicts his erotic longing for God as finally satisfied in the blissful peace of eternal life, Gregory goes further and retains an essential role for *erōs* even in the age to come. This means that emotions such as love of God and joy in God are simultaneously fulfilled and yet not sated

---

58. Aquinas's writings on the emotions, which were introduced earlier, will not be treated in chapter 2 given the complexity and intricacies of his thought which lends itself to various interpretations, as well as the fact that his treatment of emotion is not a purely cognitive theory. Wesley's thought is not discussed either, given that it is similar to that of Edwards, and, moreover, Edwards's thought on the affections is more accessible in that it is concentrated in specific works on the topic, whereas Wesley's insights are more dispersed in his sermons, essays, and biblical commentaries.

59. The severe forms of asceticism are metaphysical or dualistic, whereas the type of asceticism in view in Augustine, Gregory, and Edwards is eschatological.

in the eschaton. There is a progressively fuller participation in God and the emotions are central to this perpetual progress in God, for increased knowledge of God's goodness and beauty cannot take place without an ever expanding emotional life that delights in the infinite God.

Edwards's thought is given considerable attention because he maintains that true religion consists, in great part, in gracious affections, which he depicts as the springboard of all the actions of Christ's faithful. Edwards insists that the holy affections of Christ must become the gracious affections of the saints. Just as the emotional life of Christ appears as a movement of "action," the affectionate life of the saints becomes the springboard for carrying out Christ's healing mission in the world. Edwards, like Gregory and Augustine, envisages Christian ascent as the redirecting or transforming of love and desire away from earthly objects toward God as the new object of ineffable delight and exalted joy. Human affections and Christian affections are not seen as two different stories, but two parts of one and the same story. The effects of God's grace in Christ do not involve new faculties of the soul, but a new inward perception that inclines the soul toward God as its ultimate end. Yet for all the positive things that are said about these three eminent thinkers of the great tradition, the chapter will conclude by pointing out how they are still beholden to the Stoic idea of the passions as sicknesses of the soul, inasmuch as they restrict the scope of the Christian emotions to the problem of sin.

Chapter 3 will offer a treatment of some notable shortcomings in the various understandings of Jesus' emotions in patristic theology as well as medieval theology. There is not an abundance of material that directly addresses the question of the role of Jesus' emotions in the mystery of the incarnation and in his redemptive-salvific work. The sorts of christological questions that should be asked today, but were perhaps not possible in the intellectual and historical contexts of earlier centuries of Christian thought, include the following: Do the emotions of Jesus undergo a process of formation from childhood to adulthood? Is the formation of Jesus' emotional life integral to the development of Jesus' own individuality? Is it acceptable to restrict the emotions of Jesus to his passive humanity or should they be conceived more broadly as the outworking of the interaction of the two natures in his person? This chapter is perhaps the most technical of all the chapters, but it provides the linchpin for the main argument and focus of this study. Augustine, Aquinas, Gregory of Nyssa, Cyril of Alexandria, Maximus the Confessor, and John of Damascus will all receive attention as they are brought into conversation with the writings of John Calvin, Jonathan Edwards, Martin Luther, Karl Barth, Eberhard Jüngel, and Sergius Bulgakov. The purpose of this conversation will be to highlight the inability of especially patristic thought to admit that the incarnate Word truly descended into the temporal-historical realm; that is, that Jesus clothed himself with our Adamic flesh (sin excepted). Patristic thought is characterized by a particularly strong emphasis on the divinity of Christ, which admitted no possibility of Christ being subject to human becoming or the temptation of evil. The human nature of Christ was not seen, it will be argued, as existing for the divinity itself, but as passive in relation to the divine nature which is the active element in Christ's mission of redemption. The human nature is thought of merely as a passive instrument of redemption. This perspective represents a failure to formulate an adequately developed notion of kenosis. Therefore, the emotional life of Christ is not presented in any strong or moving language that conveys the genuine struggle in bringing Christ's Adamic flesh under the guidance of the spirit. An adequately developed notion of kenosis is one that allows Christ to be subject to human becoming and development—which gives rise to the idea of a gradual or progressive incarnation—so that the deification of humanity in his person is not rendered possible without his *real* solidarity with our Adamic flesh. Integral to chapter 3 will be a discussion not only of the inadequacies of past thinking on kenosis, but also the concomitant inadequacies in respect of the interpenetration of the two natures in the person of the God-Man. The chapter will conclude with the following key proposition: *the emotional life of Jesus is the outworking of the mutual interaction of the two natures in his person and the springboard of his messianic ministry to Israel, and as such provides a privileged window through which to observe the process of salvation (deification) in his person.*

The first part of chapter 4 will be focused on the development of an adequate understanding of kenosis by giving considerable attention to the formation of Jesus' emotions according to his personal biography, which will include: an historical picture of his Jewish background in terms of the covenant framework; the influence of Jesus' family upbringing from the standpoint of his mother Mary understood as Daughter Zion; and the development of Jesus' individuality from the standpoint of his divinity conceived in relational and dynamic terms as his *modus essendi* of being related to the Father in ineffable love, which reaches a defining and climactic point in his sacrificial death. The result of the first part of chapter

4 will be to show that the traditional view of Jesus' emotions as belonging solely to his human nature, which is held to be passive in relation to his divine nature, is simply unsatisfactory and should be repudiated. It will be proposed that a more satisfactory viewpoint is one that acknowledges Jesus' emotional life as tending in both a human and divine direction. This is consistent with the view that Jesus' humanity mediates his divinity; that is to say, his divinity expresses itself in the sphere of his humanity and his humanity expresses itself in the presence of his divinity, so that his emotional life is the product of the mutual interaction of the two natures in his person. This line of thinking will lead to the conclusion that when we reflect on Jesus' emotions, we are gazing on the very process of our salvation—understood as the deification of our Adamic humanity.

The remainder of chapter 4 will then offer a discussion of the emotions of Jesus as recorded in the gospels. The purpose of the discussion in the second part of chapter 4 will be threefold. First, it aims to demonstrate how a cognitive theory of emotion is able to illuminate the intelligence of Jesus' emotions and provides insight into his emotional life as the springboard of his messianic ministry. A second intention will be to repudiate the Stoic notions of *apatheia* and *propatheia* as incompatible with the gospel figure of Immanuel. These Stoic teachings should not be applied to Jesus as a way of underscoring a particular metaphysical conception of his divinity, which bears no real relationship to his humanity. A third aim will be to better appreciate the subtle interplay of the human and the divine in the person of Jesus. This will assist us in the task of developing a more satisfactory understanding of the kenosis of the Son, as well as forming a better appreciation of the Pauline statement: "For in him the whole fullness of deity dwells bodily" (Col 2:9). The Son genuinely shares in the infirmities of our Adamic flesh in order to exalt the present human condition to the glory of eternal life—the humiliation of the Son of God (kenosis) aims at the divinization of the Son of Man (theosis).

The intention of this study is to provide the reader with a more profound sense of Jesus' holiness as an "involved holiness." Too often in Christian thought the God-Man's holiness is conceived as an ahistorical holiness cut-off from the harsh and testing realities of life in first-century Galilee. An involved holiness is one that does justice to the idea of the divine Son's condescension into the fray of the historical-existential realm. It means that the incarnate Son is not exempt from the human condition: he undergoes a process of formation in his pious Jewish family; he is confronted by human sin, failure, and misery; he subjectively engages with his surroundings and is subjected to the temptation of evil; he grows in wisdom and understanding; he experiences mounting opposition and rejection as he proclaims the advent of the kingdom of grace; and he suffers overwhelming dread and grief in the suffering of his passion. An appreciation of the richness and strength of Jesus' emotional life—both his congenial and suffering emotions—is crucial to shedding light on what is involved in the process of a progressive incarnation which reaches its zenith in the garden of Gethsemane and on the hill of Golgotha. The Son is involved in a veritable struggle to carry forward his proclamation of the Father's kingdom—driven by his emotions of love, compassion, and joy—as he faces the hardness of heart of his own people in general and the mounting opposition from Jewish religious authorities in particular, who seek to destroy him—hence his suffering emotions of anger, indignation, sighing, weeping, grief, distress, and sorrow.

When we examine the emotional life of Jesus, we are actually gazing on the mystery of salvation in his person and we come to realize afresh what it cost the Son to bring us the glad tidings of the Father's benevolent love for us: "For God so loved the world that he gave his only Son, that whoever believes in him should not perish but have eternal life" (John 3:16). In order to proffer us mortal sinners the gift of eternal life, the incarnate Son is subjected to the infirmity of this life—i.e., the pathos of the flesh, the reality of sin, and the weight of death—and is truly tested in his obedience to the Father, who sent him into the realm of existential being to proclaim the eschatological kingdom of grace. Since the emotions of Jesus are expressive of his whole person and give insight into the basic orientation of his life, they are invaluable in shedding light on the dynamics of the gospel story and the dramatic and costly manner in which the decisive victory over the powers of death was won by the Son.

Once we come to terms with the fundamental role played by the emotions of Jesus in the mystery of the incarnation, this will lead to the further acknowledgement that to be disciples of Jesus entails that his affections become our affections, by the grace of the indwelling Spirit. The Christian life understood as the ongoing transformation of the emotions is the focus of the concluding chapter of this study. To put on Christ means to possess a "new heart" from which springs the exercise of gracious affections, chief amongst which is love of God: "You shall love the Lord your God with all your heart, and with all your soul, and with all your might" (Deut 6:4). Love of God is the motivating force for the Christian life of virtue, which includes "love of enemies" (Matt 5:44).

Ascent to God is not a question of extirpating the emotions, but of redirecting love and desire away from earthly objects toward the merciful God—manifested in the crucified Christ—as the new object of ineffable delight, exalted joy, and abundant hope in the blessed life to come. The ascent can never be a facile matter, for the congenial emotions of love, compassion, and joy will always be accompanied by suffering emotions such as grief, sorrow, dread, and lament, as Christians proclaim the Gospel to the world by bearing in their bodies the dying of Jesus in order that the life of Jesus may be manifested to the world. The congenial emotions, together with the suffering emotions of the Christian life, will therefore be portrayed as integral to the process of deification that springs from the life, death, and resurrection of the Lord Jesus Christ. When the process of our deification is understood as the ongoing transformation of our emotions in imitating Christ's involved holiness, then the incarnation should be regarded not merely as a past event but as the "ongoing embodiment of God in those who follow Christ."[60]

---

60. Behr, *John the Theologian*, Preface.

1

Emotion in Contemporary Thought
A Cognitive Theory of Emotion

IN THE WESTERN TRADITION of philosophy, emotions have been typically dismissed as mere subjectivity, by which is meant that they are irrational and therefore can have no cognitive content at all. A sharp dichotomy between emotion and intellect has been a central theme of Western philosophy. The roots of such a non-cognitive approach to emotions can be found in the Platonic tradition where emotions (passions) are depicted as compulsive forces in opposition to the powers of reason.[1] The Platonic tradition, with its dualistic theory of mind, has exerted a strong influence on the development of Western thought on emotion. This is especially evident in the philosophy of Descartes, who thinks of the emotions as just "epiphenomenal feelings without a function."[2] This notion of epiphenomenal, non-functional feelings is central to the feeling theory of emotion. William James took the philosophical framework of Descartes and modified it for the field of psychology. James interpreted feelings as a physiological set of sensations—the bodily changes that follow the perception of the exciting fact *is* the emotion.[3] On this interpretation, we feel afraid

---

1. Plato taught that besides reason and its judgments, there are irrational forces at work in the soul. He compared reason and the two irrational parts of the soul with a charioteer and two horses: the emotional capacities are involuntary, although we can be trained to control the irrational parts of the soul. See Sorabji, *Emotion*, 95–96.

2. Power and Dalgleish, *Cognition and Emotion*, 26. Descartes was the first to suggest that some emotions might be more basic than others. He listed six basic emotions: wonder, joy, sadness, love, hatred, and desire.

3. James, "What is an Emotion?," 17–36. Prior to William James, John Locke and

because we tremble, we feel sorry or sad because we cry, and we feel angry because we strike. In the aftermath of James's work, the behaviorist theory of emotion gained rapid ascendency. The behaviorists reject the idea of emotions as inner states that can only be known through introspection. The psychological behaviorist James Watson, for instance, argues that introspection forms no essential part of the methods of psychology, which he views as a purely objective experimental branch of natural science, the goal of which is the prediction and control of behavior. To Watson's mind, an emotion is "an hereditary 'pattern-reaction' involving profound changes of the bodily mechanisms as a whole."[4] Emotions are nothing more than inherited physiological reactions. Watson's theory is identical to the physiological part of James's theory, although Watson does not regard the emotions as inner states known through introspection. While non-cognitive theory has experienced a number of changes and revisions in the twentieth century, many psychologists still regard emotions as being independent of cognition. When taken to its logical conclusion, as in the writings of Griffiths, non-cognitive theory leads to the view that "the general concept of emotion has no role in any future psychology."[5]

At the same time, however, the latter half of the twentieth century has witnessed a move towards a cognitive approach to emotion. There has recently been much renewed interest in the Aristotelian tradition with its non-dualistic conception of mind.[6] What is attractive about Aristotle nowadays is that he was the first to propose a "functionalist" model of mind, which is an approach that dominates contemporary cognitive science.[7] Functionalism is any approach that analyzes something in terms of how it functions; that is, in terms of "form." To Aristotle's mind, emotions are distinguished on the basis of what he calls "stimulus," which today is more commonly referred to as *appraisal*.[8] Fear is based upon an

---

David Hume also developed their own versions of feeling theory. The tendency in non-cognitive theories is to stress the animal-like nature of emotions.

4. Cited in Power and Dalgleish, *Cognition and Emotion*, 34. The authors also discuss Skinner's behaviorist theory of emotions and Gilbert Ryle's philosophical behaviorism, which need not concern us here.

5. Griffiths, *What Emotions Really Are*, 247.

6. The cognitive revival began with Magda Arnold's book *Emotion and Personality* (Penguin, 1968) and Anthony Kenny's book *Action, Emotion and Will* (Routledge & K. Paul, 1963).

7. Power and Dalgleish, *Cognition and Emotion*, 38–39.

8. Aristotle considers ten emotions: four are positive (calm, friendship, favor, and pity), and six are negative (anger, fear, shame, indignation, envy, and jealousy).

appraisal of impending danger; anger is associated with an appraisal of personal insult or injury; pity is characterized by an appraisal that something evil or unfortunate has occurred to one who does not deserve it; jealousy is based upon an appraisal that a person one loves has affections for someone else; and so forth. In such a perspective it is the *cognitive element*—belief, judgment, or evaluation in respect of an object—that allows one emotion to be distinguished from another, and the function of the emotions is related to the propensity for certain types of action or behavior. For instance, if when walking in the forest I suddenly notice a grizzly bear approaching me, I would appraise the situation as one of danger, which causes the emotion of fear followed by the physiological changes associated with fear, such as increased adrenalin secretion, which affords me the action potential to run faster than normal. Fear has the form or function of flight from the grizzly bear, although it might also have the unlikely function of fight—I could stand up to the bear.

Aristotle's considerable interest in the philosophy of emotion flowed on to the Stoic philosophers[9] who maintained a lively debate over centuries on the nature of emotion and its place in ethics and the pursuit of the good life. According to the ancient Stoic view, emotions are *forms of judgment*, hence they have a cognitive element. The problem with emotions, though, is that they are regarded as bad guides to good human behavior, hence the Stoic goal is *apatheia*; that is, the extirpation of the emotions, which is integral to the pursuit of wisdom. What is wrong with emotion is that it is not discerning or aimed at truth, for it "latches onto false beliefs"[10] and in this sense it is irrational. Insofar as emotion is cognitive we can say that it is rational in a descriptive sense and is not opposed to reason—against Platonism—yet it is irrational in the normative sense of discourse that claims to engage in persuasive reasoning. Hence philosophy's task is to "liberate the human being from bondage to emotion."[11] Contemporary philosophers engaged with the development of a cognitive account of emotions, while they all stand in a broadly functionalist framework and acknowledge the Stoic contribution to an analysis of emotions, are also united in rejecting the notion of *apatheia*.

Mick Power and Tim Dalgleish, for instance, are committed to the belief that what they have called "the strong cognitive theory of emotions"

9. Chryssipus and Seneca are two Stoic philosophers who deserve to be highlighted for their contribution to the philosophy of emotion.
10. Nussbaum, *Upheavals of Thought*, 370.
11. Nussbaum, *Upheavals of Thought*, 370.

is the only approach that has the makings of a truly comprehensive theory.[12] With regard to the constituent parts of an emotion, they contend that a concept of emotion must include the following: an instigating event; an interpretation of the event; an appraisal of the interpretation; physiological change; an action potential; and, most probably, conscious awareness.[13] The authors maintain that the emotions are distinguished on the basis of different types of *appraisals*, not different types of interpretation. The appraisal, then, is a "logically necessary ingredient of emotion."[14] So, in the instigating event of a grizzly bear approaching me in the forest, I interpret the event as the bear will eat me, hence I appraise the situation as one of danger, which is causal of physiological changes in my body and a state of potential for action; namely, flight from the bear. My experience of the emotion of fear is associated with my appraisal of danger. The function of the emotion is to provide me with the action potential to avoid a situation of danger. In the functionalist view of Power and Dalgleish, action potentials are a conceptually necessary constituent of the emotional experience. When we consider the question of why we have emotions, the answer must be related to the speed of response involved in emotion-provoking situations, to the physiological readiness required to execute that response, and to the need to effectively communicate our evaluations to others. Even with the emotion of grief, the authors argue that there are action potentials, but "the goals to which they are directed either cannot be realized or consist of elicitations of support and sympathy from others or the reassessment of psychological coping resources through internal reflection."[15]

Martha Nussbaum also operates within a broadly functionalist framework, although she is committed to the development of a "neo-Stoic theory" of the emotions, in which the basic Stoic idea of emotions as

---

12. The comprehensive nature of a strong cognitive theory of emotions is illustrated by its ability to address eight key questions: (1) What distinguishes an emotion from a non-emotion? (2) What are the constituent parts of an emotion? Or are emotions irreducible? (3) What distinguishes one emotion from another? (4) What is the process of having an emotional experience? (5) Why do we have emotions? (6) What is the relationship between emotional states, moods, and temperament? (7) How many emotions are there and what is the nature of their relationship to one another? (8) What is the difference between, and the relationship of, the so-called normal emotions and the emotional disorders? See Power and Dalgleish, *Cognition and Emotion*, 55–64.

13. Power and Dalgleish, *Cognition and Emotion*, 58.

14. Power and Dalgleish, *Cognition and Emotion*, 52.

15. Power and Dalgleish, *Cognition and Emotion*, 61.

evaluative judgments is retained while rejecting the ancient Stoic notion of *apatheia*. Nussbaum writes that emotions "involve judgments about important things, judgments in which, appraising an external object as salient for our own well-being, we acknowledge our own neediness and incompleteness before parts of the world that we do not fully control."[16] A notable part of this definition is the understanding that emotions involve appraisals of external objects that we consider to be important for our "human flourishing" (*eudaimonia*).[17] Because we invest objects with value, they are integral to our well-being; yet, at the same time, emotions register our vulnerability and passivity before a world that we do not fully control. As with Power and Dalgleish, appraisal is still at the center of Nussbaum's cognitive theory of emotion, but she relates emotions as evaluative judgments to the notion of human well-being, which is inseparable from an awareness of our incompleteness and vulnerability in the world. The Stoics insisted that virtue by itself suffices for a completely good life (*eudaimonia*), which is to say that virtue is something unaffected by external contingency.[18] But Nussbaum repudiates this particular aspect of Stoic teaching on the detachment of the sage, who is free from what happens externally in the world and therefore is free from the emotions—free from fear, distress, pity, hope, anger, jealousy, passionate love, and intense joy. Self-sufficiency of the virtuous person is not something that Nussbaum advocates, insisting instead, like Aristotle, that the good life consists in activity and the stage for this activity is the external world with all its contingencies. Freedom from all vulnerability and passivity toward the world is just not a feasible position to hold as far as Nussbaum is concerned, and this becomes especially apparent when she gives much consideration to the role of social norms, as well as the history of childhood development, in the shaping of emotions. A good cognitive theory of emotion will not ignore the developmental phase of childhood, nor the role of cultural-social norms, in disposing persons to the formation of certain emotions. By treating human beings as living creatures immersed in the vicissitudes of history, and not as minds only, Nussbaum is keen to underscore the view that the complexity of emotional dispositions evolves over time and has a history.

16. Nussbaum, *Upheavals of Thought*, 19.

17. Nussbaum cautions against a rendering of the term *eudaimonia* as "happiness." Such a rendering of the term misses the emphasis on activity and suggests that what is at issue is a state or feeling of satisfaction. See Nussbaum, *Therapy of Desire*, 15.

18. Nussbaum, *Therapy of Desire*, 359.

Richard Lazarus is another eminent thinker who has done much to dispel the myth that emotions are non-cognitive or irrational, claiming that "emotions and intelligence go hand in hand, which is why humans, highly intelligent beings, are such emotional animals."[19] Lazarus insists that emotions are "products of *personal meaning*, which depends on what is important to us and the things we believe about ourselves and the world."[20] When we feel angry, anxious, happy, loving, envious, proud, and so forth, it is the meaning we attach to the events and conditions of our lives that makes us feel these emotions. Emotions may appear to be irrational, but when we dig deeper we realize they are far from being irrational; emotions have a logic of their own which can be fathomed by analyzing the dramatic plot in which they arise. To understand why a person experiences a particular emotion, we must inquire about the plot and the personal meaning it contains. For example, if I were to find myself in a situation where I failed to live up to my own personal ideal, I would experience shame in such a plot. If I were to feel jealous every time my spouse showed interest in someone else, I might be reacting in this fashion because I think of myself as less lovable than others, and, therefore, I fear my spouse may lose interest in me.

The discussion hitherto has served as an introduction to this chapter on a cognitive theory of emotion. The remainder of the chapter will elaborate on the introductory material by providing, in part one, a critical discussion of Stoicism's teaching on the emotions, and, in section two, a select presentation of the views of some eminent thinkers in this area, namely; Robert Solomon, Cheshire Calhoun, Richard Wollheim, Aaron Ben-Ze'ev, and Martha Nussbaum. The final part of the chapter will then outline what could reasonably be considered to be fundamental components of a complex cognitive theory of emotion, and it will present the idea of basic emotions from which will ensue a discussion of the importance of the basic emotion of wonder, as well as the transcendental nature of desire, which is not considered to be a basic emotion. It will emerge that a cognitive view of emotions should not be regarded as a simple approach to the study of emotions; rather, emotions are "highly complex phenomena that rely upon both our conscious and unconscious mind,

---

19. Lazarus and Lazarus, *Passion and Reason*, 3. In this work, fifteen emotions are discussed: anger, anxiety, fright, shame, joy, love, sadness, guilt, envy, jealousy, pride, relief, hope, gratitude, and compassion.

20. Lazarus and Lazarus, *Passion and Reason*, 5.

memories, cultural factors, family upbringing, and our personalities."[21] These various factors interact with one another in a complex web of beliefs and values to produce particular emotions in our subjective engagement with the world. The aim of this chapter is to present a credible—not exhaustive—picture of emotions as cognitive, which will form the framework for the remainder of this study on the emotional life of Christ and the role of the emotions in the Christian ascent to God.

A Critique of Stoicism on Emotion

In today's English, "Stoicism" is generally taken to mean an absence or suppression of emotion. This interpretation is supported by the fact that the aim of Stoic ethics is to be completely free of emotion (*apatheia*). While many admire those who submit calmly to the assaults of fortune and display bravery in the face of adversity, at the same time it would be fair to say that most would not affirm the Stoic ideal of *apatheia* as something they could realistically give assent to, simply because it does not seem to fit with what they actually experience as human beings. The capacity to experience emotions—especially grief and loss—is generally held to be an important, inalienable, and integral dimension of our being in the world, so that the suppression of emotion would amount to a suppression of our genuine humanity. Be that as it may, modern cognitive therapy has many things in common with Stoic therapy, which is based on the Stoic notion that emotion itself consists of judgments. The defining of emotions by their *propositional content*—an emotion is a judgment concerning some present or prospective state of affairs—is the one aspect of Stoic teaching that has attracted much attention in recent years, as the foregoing discussion has sought to draw attention to. Judgments are not, like appearances, involuntary. If it appears to me that I am in a bad situation, Stoicism teaches that I can withhold giving my assent while I question the appearance. Judgments can be either true or false, and the chief Stoic claim about emotions (*pathē*) is that they imply false judgments; they involve erroneous ways of thinking that are in need of correction. Emotions such as anger and anxiety are generally unwelcome emotions that prevent us from living well and attaining peace of mind, and Stoic therapy can be effective in dealing with these counter-productive emotions. As Richard Sorabji says, "we can learn from the Stoics in treating

---

21. Elliott, *Faithful Feelings*, 42.

unwanted emotions, without agreeing that none should be wanted."[22] We can, in other words, acknowledge the import of Stoic thinking on the cognitive nature of emotion without having to embrace the Stoic ideal of freedom from disturbance and upheaval (*apatheia*).

It was the Stoic Chrysippus (c.280–c.206 BCE) who developed the standard Stoic view on emotion as value judgments. He argued that emotion involves two judgments: there is the judgment that there is good or bad (benefit or harm) at hand; and the judgment that it is appropriate to react in specific ways.[23] Four emotions are affirmed as the most generic ones, under which all other emotions could be arranged by species.[24] Emotions of the genus "delight" or "pleasure" (*hēdonē*) see their objects as good and present; those of the genus "distress" (*lupē*) see their objects as evil and present; emotions of the genus "desire" or "appetite" (*epithumia*) see their objects as prospective goods; and those of the genus "fear" (*phobos*) see their objects as prospective evils.[25] These four generic emotions, furthermore, are depicted as accompanied by contractions or expansions of the soul. The founder of Stoic philosophy, Zeno, had tended to identify the generic emotions of distress and pleasure with the contractions and expansions of the soul respectively, but what Chrysippus did "was to turn the cause (the judgment) into the emotion itself."[26] The emotions often involve physiological movements that are felt as either sinking or expansive sensations, and these are often judged to be appropriate responses to specific situations. On this view, distress is the judgment that there is evil at hand and that it is appropriate to feel a sinking sensation; pleasure or delight is the judgment that there is a good present and it is appropriate to feel an expansive sensation; fear is the judgment that there is a prospective evil and that it is appropriate to avoid or lean away from it; and appetite or desire is the judgment that there is a prospective good and that it is appropriate to reach for it. It therefore becomes quite

---

22. Sorabji, *Emotion*, 173. Also Nussbaum, *Therapy of Desire*, 41.

23. Sorabji, *Emotion*, 29–33.

24. The four basic passions are based upon two distinctions: the distinction between good and bad, and the distinction between present and future.

25. Graver, *Stoicism and Emotion*, 53–54; Sorabji, *Emotion*, 29. The ordinary emotions are further broken down into a number of species within each genus. The genus distress, for example, is broken down into the species-emotions of envy, rivalry, jealousy, pity, grief, anxiety, misery, worry, anguish, and agony.

26. Sorabji, *Emotion*, 35, also 36–41.

apparent what Chrysippus meant when he argued that emotion involves two judgments.[27]

The ancient Stoics sought to identify unwanted emotions with the aim "not to eliminate feelings as such from human life, but to understand what sorts of affective responses a person would have who was free of false belief."[28] Not every experience we call an "emotion" in our language falls under the Stoic *pathē*. There are varieties of affective response that are entirely rational and good, such as awe and reverence, certain forms of joy and gladness, particular kinds of love and friendship, and some types of longing and wishing—these fall into the category of *eupatheiai* which are the affective responses of the sage. A typical Stoic list of species of good affections is arranged under three generic kinds: joy (*khara*); will in the strict sense (*boulēsis*); and caution (*eulabeia*). These are presented as analogues of the generic emotions (*pathē*), although there is no eupathic analogue of the emotion of distress. The reason for this is that the sage does not judge contraction of the soul as appropriate, inasmuch as it detracts from his peace of mind.[29]

The judgment involved in the sage's affective response of joy is seen as having the same structure as the judgment involved in the emotion of pleasure, but the difference lies in that the expansive sensation in the former is regarded as reasonable. It is the element of reasonableness (*eulogon*) that characterizes all three generic kinds of *eupatheia*. Joy is a reasonable expansion or elevation directed at objects perceived as present

---

27. Sorabji offers four reasons why Chrysippus argued for a second "appropriate to react" judgment. First, it was the main thing to be attacked in consoling the distressed. Second, in the process of seeking to attain virtue in a bad situation, the appropriate reaction should not be a sinking sensation but a determination to improve. Third, because emotion involves a particular type of judgment, namely an impulse, the latter is stirred not by the first appearance that there is good or bad at hand, but by how it is appropriate to react. Fourth, in connection with emotions fading despite the retention of the first judgment that the present situation is bad, Chrysippus is able to maintain that it is the second judgment concerning the appropriateness of the contraction that fades. See Sorabji, *Emotion*, 32–33.

28. Graver, *Stoicism and Emotion*, 2.

29. Sorabji presents a list of good feelings as follows: (i) There are four species of will: good will (*eunoia*) is wishing good things to another for his sake; kindness is lasting *eunoia*; welcoming is uninterrupted *eunoia*; love (*agapēsis*). (ii) There are three species of joy: delight (*terpsis*) is a fitting joy at one's advantages; gladness (*euphrosunē*) is joy at the deeds of the temperate; cheerfulness (*euthumia*) is joy at the conduct of the universe. (iii) There are two species of caution: modesty (*aidōs*) is caution about due blame; piety (*hagneia*) is caution about sins towards the gods. See Sorabji, *Emotion*, 48.

goods; will is a reasonable desire directed at objects perceived as good and in prospect; and caution is a reasonable disinclination or withdrawing directed at objects perceived as prospective evils. In light of the teaching that eupathic responses are corrected versions of ordinary human emotions, the Stoic ethical system speaks in terms of "virtue" (condition of the sage) and "vice" (condition of ordinary people). The virtuous person is free of erroneous judgments associated with *pathē*, yet the wise person still remains subject to other categories of affective responses (*eupatheiai*). There is a real sense in which our ordinary emotions have us under their control,[30] and we are all familiar with this state of affairs, yet the Stoics maintain that the human task is to commit to the maturing process of attaining virtue (wisdom). What is also notable about the eupathic responses of the sage is that they are few, and, moreover, the range of affective responses of will in the strict sense is narrow because the four species listed have to do with willing things for others, not for oneself.[31] It should also be noted, as Nussbaum observes, that Stoic joy is an emotion-free joy: "There is joy here; joy without enervating uncertainty, joy without fear and grief, a joy that really does move and lift the heart."[32] But this type of joy "is like a child that is born inside of one and never leaves the womb to go out into the world. It has no commerce with laughter and elation."[33] Stoic joy appears too self-sufficient and lacking in recognition of our vulnerability, and is removed from any sense of hope forged in the conflicts, ambiguities, frailties, and sufferings of historical beings. No wonder Richard Sorabji says that "Stoic sages were rarer than the phoenix."[34]

In the Stoic system of thought the only thing that matters is that which can be brought under our control; namely, our character or virtuous behavior. Only virtue is worth choosing for its own sake and by itself it suffices for a completely good life. "For the Stoics virtue admits of no trade-offs in terms of any other good."[35] External goods—all goods other than virtue—are invested with no intrinsic value at all. In order

---

30. That emotions have us under their control is implied in the Greek word *pathos*, which is the noun form of *paschein*, to suffer or undergo. The very word pathos expresses a sense of passivity.

31. Sorabji, *Emotion*, 50.

32. Nussbaum, *Therapy of Desire*, 399.

33. Nussbaum, *Therapy of Desire*, 400.

34. Sorabji, *Emotion*, 169.

35. Nussbaum, *Therapy of Desire*, 361.

for something to be genuinely good it must benefit us all the time, not just on some occasions. What is genuinely good belongs to a logically coherent and ethical system in which beliefs can be brought into line with one another so as to achieve a full, consistent, and harmonious self-understanding, which makes the good life attainable. The things that ordinary people generally regard as desirable—e.g., life, wealth, health, comfort, beauty, pleasure, and reputation—are regarded by the Stoics as a matter of indifference. What is more, it is incorrect to regard the opposite of these naturally desirable objects as harmful. To have ill health, for example, may be beneficial if it prevents one from being conscripted into the death squad of a brutal dictator,[36] and if one is starving or incarcerated or in exile this need not prevent one from being virtuous. What matters is not external circumstance, but simply whether one is virtuous. The Stoics do teach that one should do everything in one's power to secure naturally desirable objects for oneself and others—this is the Stoic attitude of preferred indifferents—but whether one does secure them should matter no more than whether one wins at cricket: what matters is the way one has played the game. "The only question that matters is whether you aimed aright. The natural objectives are merely the subject matter (*hulē, materia*) of virtuous action."[37] The preferred indifferents, in other words, are invested with a certain value by classing them as instrumental goods (*poiētika*, not *telika*)—they are instrumental for approaching virtue, but have no intrinsic ethical value in themselves. It is not difficult to see how this Stoic theory of indifference ties in with the Stoic aim of taking freedom from emotion (*apatheia*) as an ideal of the life of virtue.[38] It is natural, for instance, to treat the welfare of one's family as rightly preferred, but this means incurring the risk of grief and desolation due to misfortune, which the Stoics regard as unwanted emotions that must be extirpated in order to advance in virtuous character and attain tranquility and dignity.[39] Tranquility is attainable only if the wise person is free from

---

36. Graver, *Stoicism and Emotion*, 49.

37. Sorabji, *Emotion*, 171.

38. Even before the Stoics, in Aristotle's time, a debate was on the way amongst the various philosophical schools concerning whether the emotions (*pathē*) should only be moderated (*metriopatheia*) or actually eradicated (*apatheia*). Aristotle was an advocate of *metriopatheia*, while the Stoics taught the extirpation of the emotions (*apatheia*). See Sorabji, *Emotion*, 194–210; Nussbaum, *Therapy of Desire*, 390.

39. One major objection to emotions is that they are disturbing and so preclude tranquility. Cicero underscores this by using the Latin term *perturbatio*. Cicero also stresses that emotions must be rejected because it is a fault of character not to be

all vulnerability and passivity toward the external world—free from fear, distress, pity, hope, anger, jealousy, passionate love, and intense joy.

In light of this aim of attaining peace of mind, much attention is paid in Stoic philosophy to the emotions of fear and grief, which are emotions due to human mortality. By changing our views regarding the badness of death, we can overcome fear and grief. The Stoic philosopher Seneca (1 BCE–65 CE) pays much attention to fear and grief, and he contributed much to the formulation of the philosophical genre of "consolation." In order to appreciate what Stoic thought on the emotions and the pursuit of wisdom entails, it will be instructive to briefly examine Seneca's writings on consolation, as well as Boethius's writing on consolation.

In his *De Consolatione ad Marciam* (To Marcia on Consolation), Seneca writes to console his sister Marcia who is grieving the death of her son aged fourteen. He writes that Nature does bid us to grieve for our dear ones, but grief must be tempered. Ultimately, no amount of grieving will bring back the dead, thus we must acknowledge "moderation even in grieving."[40] Seneca points out that the death of Marcia's son was already proclaimed at his birth; his fate "attended him straightway from the womb."[41] Death lurks beneath the very name of life. The ordinary person does not think about death, but to think about our mortality is to acknowledge the truth that all fortuitous things that "adorn life's stage have been lent, and must go back to their owners."[42] It is common to hear ordinary people exclaim that a dear one might have lived longer, might have been greater than they were, but "it is better for us to have blessings that will flee than none at all."[43] The wise person does not complain about what has been withdrawn from her, but gives thanks for what was given fortuitously for a while.

Marcia, like every other human person, is subject to the affronts of fortune. Her reward lies in having loved her son and her bitter fortune can be sweetened by "enduring it calmly."[44] She is reminded by Seneca that all things unfold according to a fixed plan, that there is an underlying order to Nature, thus no one dies too soon because "he lives only as long

---

dignified (*gravis*). See Sorabji, *Emotion*, 182.

40. Seneca, *De Consolatione ad Marciam*, III.2–4.
41. Seneca, *De Consolatione ad Marciam*, X.2–6.
42. Seneca, *De Consolatione ad Marciam*, IX.4–X.2.
43. Seneca, *De Consolatione ad Marciam*, XII.3–5.
44. Seneca, *De Consolatione ad Marciam*, XII.5–XIII.1.

as he was destined to live."⁴⁵ Marcia is urged to estimate her son not by his years, but by his virtues. What is more, the premature death of Marcia's son brought no ill; rather it has "released him from suffering ills of every sort."⁴⁶ There are no ills to be suffered after death. Marcia's son has been restored to that peaceful state in which he lay before he was born. Those who are treated most kindly by nature are "those whom she removes early to a place of safety."⁴⁷ To be removed early from this earthly life is advantageous, says Seneca, insofar as the person does not become too contaminated by the weight of material things and can therefore more easily journey towards the gods. The soul struggles against the weight of the flesh and ever strives to rise to that place whence it once descended. The virtuous life is easier to attain for those souls that are free before they become hardened, defiled, and stained. Marcia must therefore contemplate all these things and by doing so she will be able to endure her bitter fortune calmly, nobly, and with dignity. Her grieving must exhibit moderation and be short-lived because tempered by the consolation offered by mature and proper thinking on the matter.

This theme of enduring the affronts of fortune calmly and nobly in the pursuit of virtue is continued in Seneca's *De Consolatione ad Helviam*. His mother Helvia is grieving Seneca's exile in Corsica, and he writes to console her. He begins by saying that he is suffering no ill and he is "happy under circumstances that usually make others wretched."⁴⁸ Seneca underscores the typical Stoic teaching that external things are invested with no importance and that the only thing that matters is the character of the person and the life of virtue. The wise person relies entirely upon himself and is able to derive his own joy and make his own good life.⁴⁹ The wise man anticipates the affronts of fortune and regards misfortune as bringing a certain blessing; namely, it "fortifies" those whom it assails.⁵⁰ Exile is seen by most as a misfortune, but Seneca writes that it is nothing more than a "change of place."⁵¹ It is simply folly to think that the mind is troubled by changing its home, for wherever we go we take with

---

45. Seneca, *De Consolatione ad Marciam*, XXI.2–6.
46. Seneca, *De Consolatione ad Marciam*, XX.5–XXI.2.
47. Seneca, *De Consolatione ad Marciam*, XII.2–4.
48. Seneca, *De Consolatione ad Helviam*, IV.1–V.2.
49. Seneca, *De Consolatione ad Helviam*, IV.1–V.2.
50. Seneca, *De Consolatione ad Helviam*, II.2–5.
51. Seneca, *De Consolatione ad Helviam*, V.6–VI.2.

ourselves two things that are most admirable: universal nature and our own virtue.[52] The human mind should not be directed to earthly things but should turn from these to those above, where true goods are found. "It is the mind that makes us rich."[53] The mind goes with Seneca into exile, but the mind can never suffer exile since it is free and at home in every world and every age. The mind bursts through to heights above and there enjoys the noblest spectacle of things divine. Once the mind attains to the state of virtue it is invulnerable from every quarter, and the wise man is much admired for his bravery in adversity.[54] Seneca concludes by reminding Helvia of the consolations she still has, besides philosophic studies; namely, Helvia's sister, her grandchildren, and Seneca's brothers.

In his *De Consolatione ad Polybium*, Seneca writes to Polybius to console him for the loss of his brother. The arguments here are very similar to those in his writings to Marcia. Seneca writes that no one is exempt from the law of Nature that brings all things to their end; no one can be protected from the assaults of fortune. The life of humankind is but a journey towards death: "Every man who is brought into life is appointed to die. Let us rejoice, therefore, in whatever shall be given us, and let us return it when we are asked for it."[55] Polybius is urged to accept the law of mortality and to bear the assaults of fortune "bravely" just as great generals act in times of disaster.[56] Seneca concedes that to be human is to feel misfortunes and to be sorrowful, but maturity requires us to bear them and conquer them. "Nature requires from us some sorrow ... Let your tears flow, but let them also cease, let deepest sighs be drawn from your breast, but let them find an end; so rule your mind that you may win approval both from wise men and from brothers."[57] It is madness to never cease to grieve for one who will never grieve any more, who is "at rest," who is "free," who is at last "safe" and "immortal."[58] Polybius is urged by Seneca to bring his mind to a state of equanimity by accepting all that he has wisely said on the topic of consolation for death.

---

52. Seneca, *De Consolatione ad Helviam*, VIII.2–6.
53. Seneca, *De Consolatione ad Helviam*, XI.3–7.
54. Seneca, *De Consolatione ad Helviam*, XII.7–XIII.4.
55. Seneca, *De Consolatione ad Polybium*, XI.2–5.
56. Seneca, *De Consolatione ad Polybium*, V.4–VI.2.
57. Seneca, *De Consolatione ad Polybium*, XVIII.4–8.
58. Seneca, *De Consolatione ad Polybium*, IX.6–X.1.

Seneca's focus on logic and how reason shows the right path to the truth of reality is also exhibited in Boethius's *Consolation of Philosophy*. This work, written in 523 CE, is considered Boethius's masterpiece and was written while he experienced the turn of fortune's wheel—i.e., exiled and imprisoned at Pavia, awaiting imminent death by execution. Imprisoned and despairing, Boethius receives a theophany: his former teacher Lady Philosophy appears and chides him for his miserable state of mind. She brings him to recognize that it is purely his own distorted perception that has allowed temporal circumstances and mundane ill-fortune to affect him.[59] Boethius is reminded that chains and imprisonment are self-imposed. He must not neglect logic, for "unless reason shows the right path, the incorrupt truth of reality cannot be found."[60] Reason will show him the unreality of his physical situation and imprisonment.[61] Consolation proper begins in Book II, which is almost wholly Stoic in its inspiration, with many parallels in Seneca. A state of equanimity is achieved by reconciling oneself to a world of determined inevitability. We should not try to change things, but adapt ourselves to the way things are. The human task in life is to learn to bear oneself nobly before the blows of outrageous fortune.[62] For the Stoics, no real distinction exists between providence and fate and the inexorable chain of causation, so one must accept the assaults of fortune and comfort oneself by reconciling oneself to the way things are.

The foregoing summary presentations of the development of the philosophical genre of consolation show clearly the Stoic perspective on the proper way to deal with grief and how the proper use of reason makes us rich, how it makes us wise and virtuous, thereby freeing us from the strong hold that ordinary emotions have over us. Salvation is regarded as a matter of the mind, of utilizing the faculty of reason to fortify ourselves, to learn to bear oneself nobly before the affronts of fortune so as to attain peace of mind and the good life. The example of consolation for grieving persons serves as a powerful illustration of Stoic teaching on the need for *pathē* to come under the guidance and correction of proper reasoning, so as to be transformed into the class of affective responses known as *eupatheiai*.

---

59. Gibson, *Boethius*, 238.
60. Chadwick, *Boethius*, 173.
61. Gibson, *Boethius*, 242.
62. Chadwick, *Boethius*, 228.

There are a number of questions that the modern thinker would put to classical Stoic thought on the emotions. One of the obvious questions was already alluded to earlier; namely, if emotions have us under their control yet we are free to pursue the affective responses of the sage, does this not amount to a logical incongruity? One could legitimately question whether an apparent incongruence lies at the heart of the Stoic teaching on emotion, for how can our ordinary emotions be volitional, how can we assume responsibility for them, if they are seen as having us under their control? The key to overcoming this apparent impasse lies in keeping before us the Stoic understanding that human beings are not helpless. Ordinary emotions can be corrected precisely because they are also assents; that is, they are judgments with a certain belief or propositional content, and sets of beliefs can, through the power of reasoning, undergo change and correction in the ongoing process of maturation.[63]

The basic problem with this argument consists in the degree to which emotions have us under their control. An emotion is thought of as an excessive impulse turned away from reason, so that once the mind propels itself into emotions of anger, fear, love, and desire, there is extremely limited scope for the mind to check such powerful impulses. Seneca, for example, is very clear on this point:

> For once the mind is stirred into motion, it is a slave to that which is driving it. With some things, the beginnings are in our power, but after that they carry us on by their own force, not allowing a return. Bodies allowed to fall from a height have no control of themselves: they cannot resist or delay their downward course, for the irrevocable fall has cut off all deliberation, all repentance; they cannot help but arrive where they are going, though they could have avoided going there at all. Even so the mind, once it propels itself into anger, love, and other emotions, is not permitted to check its impulse. Its own weight must carry it to the bottom.[64]

Seneca has no doubt that once the mind is propelled into emotion, there is no way of stopping it. Yet because emotions are also regarded as assents or judgments with a certain content, the Stoics at the same time maintain that emotions can be corrected by the normative sense of the word rational. A mental conflict is therefore set up in which it is difficult to see how normative reason might be able to conquer the overriding impulses

---

63. Graver, *Stoicism and Emotion*, 65.
64. Seneca, *On Anger* 1.7. Cited in Graver, *Stoicism and Emotion*, 69–70.

that have us under their firm control. Who can realistically be counted amongst the wise when our emotions are more powerful than the wise counsel of normative reasoning? Is it really possible to reverse the process of entrenchment in an erroneous set of deeply held beliefs and habitual behaviors through the mere exercise of reason, which alone shows us the path to the truth of reality?

Augustine of Hippo in his *Confessions* came to the view that the ideal of perfect wisdom is not achievable in this life, insisting that the compulsive force of habit (*consuetudo*)—which is firmly etched in the memory—persists in the present life.[65] The life of the spirit is therefore never wholly removed from the common ways of life, and Augustine appealed to the writings of Paul to underpin his depiction of a basic, unresolved tension between "flesh" and "spirit."[66] There could be no complete renewal of the "inner" person that would represent a clear break from the burdens of compulsive habit. For Augustine, the unresolved tension between flesh and spirit means that we must acknowledge human life as having an enduring tragic dimension. Recourse could be made to Samuel Johnson's poem *The Vanity of Human Wishes*, published in 1748, as a powerful expression and recognition of the tragic dimension of human life, which poses a permanent obstacle to achieving perfection. Jackson Bate, one of Johnson's biographers, describes the argument of the poem as follows:

> In the first place [Johnson] dwells on the helpless vulnerability of the individual before the social context – the tangled, teeming jungle of plots, follies, vanities, and egoistic passions in which anyone – the innocent and the virtuous no less than the vicious – is likely to be ambushed . . . In the second place Johnson traces the inevitable doom of man to inward and psychological causes. The medley processes of hope and fear, desire and hate intercept each other and make it impossible for the heart to be satisfied if only because its own basic impulses are in conflict. More than this Johnson makes clear the inevitable self-deception by which human beings are led astray. Because the betrayal is from within, the human being seems peculiarly defenseless before it.[67]

Given the depth and complexity of the tragic dimension of human existence, both within and without, it would seem delusory to suppose that

---

65. Augustine is discussed in chapter 2 of this study.
66. See Brown, *Augustine of Hippo*, 151.
67. Bate, *Samuel Johnson*, 281–82. Cited in Greer, *Christian Hope*, 6.

the tragic could ever be eliminated from the present life so as to attain perfection, whether the individual's perfection in wisdom or the ushering in of a golden age of social justice. The Stoic thinker would maintain that human tragedies, since they are occasions for exercising right reason and acquiring wisdom, must be borne nobly and calmly, but this would not be a position that is tenable to most people today. The truth is that tragedies are not seen as occasions for exercising clear logic in the pursuit of the mature state of wisdom; rather, they defy logic and give rise to enduring suffering which weighs heavily on the human soul. This perspective leads us to raise further critical questions in respect of the classical Stoic teaching on *apatheia* and the inner life of virtuous perfection detached from the external world.

A second critical question that should be put to classical Stoic thought would be: Is not the humanist notion of salvation too cerebral and rational to the exclusion of ordinary human feelings? Augustine of Hippo, for instance, unlike Stoic thought, came to the conclusion that nothing else but delight can motivate the human will, which is to say that the source of action is the mobilization of our feelings. "Now, 'feeling' has taken its rightful place as the ally of the intellect."[68] In his *Confessions*, Augustine says there are moments in which he has an inward sense of delight, of glimpses of supreme good. This delight is beyond human control though; what we desire—"Our hearts are restless, O Lord, until they find their rest in You"—can never be more than a *hope* which points to a distant homeland. All we can do is yearn for blissful perfection: "It is yearning that makes the heart deep."[69] The *Confessions*, as a manifesto of Augustine's inner world of feelings (*affectus*), is a moving piece of writing offering consolation for our wanderings on the long and difficult road of the spiritual life as it strains forward to the final goal of eternal rest in God.

The view of Augustine on the yearnings of the human heart are bolstered by the writings of John Calvin. In his *Institutes of the Christian Religion*, Calvin criticizes the view of faith as an intellectual assent and elevates the heart above the mind in matters of faith and salvation. Calvin maintains that it is not enough for the mind to be illuminated by the Spirit of God "unless the heart is also strengthened and supported by his power. In this matter the Schoolmen go completely astray, who in considering

---

68. Brown, *Augustine of Hippo*, 155.
69. Brown, *Augustine of Hippo*, 156.

faith identify it with a bare and simple assent arising out of knowledge, and leave out confidence and assurance of heart."[70] Calvin is critical of Stoic philosophy, asserting: "Especially let that foolish and most miserable consolation of the pagans be far from the breast of the Christian man; to strengthen their minds against adversities, they charged these to fortune."[71] The Christian, unlike the Stoic, accepts his sorrow and suffering, just as Christ accepted his sorrow and sufferings in bringing salvation to the world. The Stoics condemn weeping and groaning, yet Christ "groaned and wept both over his own and others' misfortunes."[72] Calvin asserts that we are affected by adversity and we must not reject our emotions, for all our emotions — sadness, sorrow, desire, grief, dread, and mourning — are emotions shared by Christ. Calvin bolsters his argument by appealing to the agony in the garden of Gethsemane when Christ sweated drops of blood (Luke 22:44), as well Christ's teaching on the Mount, "Blessed are those who mourn, for they shall be comforted" (Matt 5:4). While Calvin owed much to the ancient Stoics, he frequently condemns features of their writings incompatible with Christian faith, especially the notion of *apatheia* and their doctrine of fate.

Related to the foregoing two critical questions arises a third that could legitimately be raised as a challenge to the classical Stoic view of emotion: Do not our emotions serve to register our neediness and vulnerability to external objects that are not fully in our control? Martha Nussbaum, for instance, in the formulation of her neo-Stoic theory of the emotions, claims: "Emotions involve judgments about important things, judgments in which, appraising an external object as salient for our well-being, we acknowledge our own neediness and incompleteness before parts of the world that we do not fully control."[73] To Nussbaum's mind, emotions are related to items that we regard as important for our human flourishing or well-being (*eudaimonia*); yet they also register our deep sense of vulnerability and passivity before the world.[74] The emotion of grief, for example, contains not only the judgment that something important in my life has been lost, but that *it is right* to be genuinely upset by the irrevocable loss. One of the limitations of Stoicism's eudai-

---

70. Calvin, *Institutes*, III, 2.33.
71. Calvin, *Institutes*, III, 7.10.
72. Calvin, *Institutes*, III, 8.9.
73. Nussbaum, *Upheavals of Thought*, 19.
74. Nussbaum, *Upheavals of Thought*, 43.

monistic picture, Nussbaum argues, is that it simply fails to recognize that emotions are "localized"—that my mother has died, for instance, is not simply a fact like any other fact about the world; it is the fact that *my* mother has died.[75]

A good Stoic strives to distance himself from emotions such as grief, which arise from attachment to things in the external world, and claims that virtue is sufficient for *eudaimonia*; but a neo-Stoic, such as Nussbaum, would argue otherwise. To struggle with grief is to acknowledge an irrevocable loss in my life and to accept the reality of my human existence in its passivity and vulnerability before the world. If I grieve for the death of my beloved mother, who was an important part of my life, I struggle to forge a view of the world in which my beloved mother's face appears no more; without her, my own life is *not* complete.[76] The spiritual writer Henri Nouwen captures beautifully the emotion he felt when his mother had died in hospital and he and his father were returning to the family home:

> When we turned into the road leading to our house, I suddenly felt a deep, inner sadness. Tears came to my eyes and I did not dare look at my father. We both understood. She would not be home. She would not open the door and embrace us. She would not ask how the day had been. She would not invite us to the table and pour tea in our cups. I felt an anxious tension when my father drove into the garage and we walked up to the door. Upon entering the house it was suddenly clear to us: it had become an empty house . . . I wandered from room to room, and felt a shiver throughout my entire body. Everything that for years had spoken of her presence now reminded me of her absence. Everything that had always told me that she was home now told me that I would never hear her warm voice again . . . Only now did I fully recognize that I had become a different man, a man without a mother, a man alone in a new way.[77]

There are other limitations of the ancient eudaimonistic picture which are worth mentioning. Of particular note is the idea that my own scheme of goals concerning what it is for me to live well, because they form a system of some sort, can be commended to others for their good living. "But real people are usually not this systematic. We value things,

---

75. Nussbaum, *Upheavals of Thought*, 52–53.
76. Nussbaum, *Upheavals of Thought*, 82, 86.
77. Nouwen, *In Memoriam*, 48–49.

often, without asking how all our goals fit together; sometimes they do not fit together well, and sometimes painful emotional conflicts ensue."[78] The fact is, contrary to the ancient theory, there is usually no well-structured system of value where one thing fits neatly together with all the others. In my personal world, emotions are attached to the things that I do value, however well or badly those valued things might fit together. I might be able to commend some very general goals as good for human beings—e.g., friendship, parental love, and civic responsibility—but what concrete specification each of these goals takes will vary from individual to individual.[79] What's more, people value things that they do not necessarily think good. At times people actively disapprove of someone or the country they love, but they still continue to love and cherish that person and their country. Nussbaum therefore points out that "thoughts about the good may prove less powerful, in shaping a conception of importance for me, than habit and time."[80] All in all, these critical observations serve to underline the complexity of our emotions, as well as how deeply embedded they are in our personal history of engagement with the external world. Changing our character to arrive at the norm of perfection—corrected versions of ordinary human feelings—as taught by the ancient Stoics, will not prove to be an attainable goal, and may, in fact, only succeed in wreaking emotional havoc rather than leading to good or proper feelings (i.e., *eupatheiai*).

Contemporary Cognitive Theories of Emotion

Since the 1970s there has been a resurgence of philosophical interest in emotions. Emotions, especially in the Anglo-American tradition, were typically dismissed as mere subjectivity, which is to say that they were regarded as having no cognitive content at all. A sharp divide was maintained between emotions and rationality. This view is still apparent today when we say that someone is being "emotional," meaning that they are not being reasonable and have lost control of themselves. It is also readily apparent in our language where metaphors for the supposed irrationality of the emotions abound, such as: "insane with jealousy," "blind rage," and "love is blind." Many today have begun, though, to seriously question

---

78. Nussbaum, *Upheavals of Thought*, 49.
79. Nussbaum, *Upheavals of Thought*, 50.
80. Nussbaum, *Upheavals of Thought*, 51.

this sharp divide between emotions and rationality. Robert Solomon, for instance, has strongly challenged this traditional divide, arguing for more than forty years now that emotions are not involuntary, but voluntary, inasmuch as they involve evaluative judgments. Solomon's voluntarist thesis, which can be traced back to the Stoics, has come under considerable fire, yet the cognitive approach to emotion has managed to gain broad appeal; it has become "the touchstone of all philosophical theorizing about emotion, for or against."[81] Solomon developed his voluntarist thesis in opposition to what he calls the "primitivist" conception of emotions, which is concisely captured by William James's well-known theory that, "Our feeling of [bodily changes] as they occur *IS* the emotion."[82] Solomon stresses that emotion is no mere feeling, if feeling is interpreted, together with James, as a bodily set of sensations.

With regard to cognitive theories of emotion, there exists a diversity of opinion concerning what the term "cognition" refers to: is it best conceived as a belief, a thought, a judgment, a perception, or something else? A lively debate is still taking place over this fundamental question. There are those, such as Jeffrey Murphy and Kendall Walton, who regard the cognitive element as beliefs. Jerome Neu, on the other hand, proposes that thoughts constitute the cognitive element. Many others, including Robert Solomon and Martha Nussbaum, defend the Stoic view that emotions are evaluative judgments. Then there are those, such as Cheshire Calhoun who thinks in terms of "seeing as" and Robert Roberts who speaks in terms of "construal," who argue for more perceptual ways of conceiving cognition in emotion. There are also psychologists involved in this debate, such as Richard Lazarus, who argue that "appraisals" are cognitions, while others, such as A. Ortony, G. Clore, A. Collins, and R. Gordon play it safe by preferring to talk of "cognitive elements" or "cognitive structures" of emotion.[83] It will simply not be possible, of course, to offer critical analyses of all the current thinking on this topic. The task here will be to identify major lines of thought and what could reasonably be taken as fundamental components of a complex cognitive theory of emotion. The complex picture will not be limited to the life of the mind, but will include the role of the body and "feelings," as well as the role played by a person's individual history and social-cultural context.

81. Solomon, "What is a 'Cognitive Theory'?," 1.
82. Solomon, "Emotions as Engagements," 76.
83. This overview is provided by Solomon, "Emotions as Engagements," 79.

Robert Solomon: Emotions as Voluntary

Solomon has always maintained that emotions are judgments and that they are *about the world*. The scholastic concept of "intentionality" was intended to express the understanding that emotions are always "about" something, that they have an intentional object. But Solomon began to think that the traditional concept of intentionality is unsatisfactory insofar as it merely affirms that emotions are "directed to" the world, whereas he now prefers stronger language that conveys the sense of emotions as *engagement* with the world:

> So I now want to improve my analysis by making this central point, that *emotions are subjective engagements in the world*. I still favor the use of "judgment" to make this point, but I now want to stress even more than I have before the idea that a judgment is not a detached intellectual act but a way of cognitively *grappling* with the world. It has at its very basis and as background a complex set of aspirations, expectations, evaluations ("appraisals"), needs, demands, and desires (which says something about why the reigning "belief-desire" analysis of emotions and intentions is so hopelessly impoverished).[84]

Solomon has certain reservations about the using the term "cognitive theory of emotions," because it suggests that desire or active engagement in the world has no essential part to play in emotion, and, instead, promotes an exclusive focus on the intellect or affectless "information."[85] But the reality is that we are stuck with the label, in which case the question he then proceeds to address is: What is a cognitive theory if one thinks of emotions as engagements in the world? In providing a reply to this question, Solomon admits that in the past bodily feelings had been "left out" of his cognitive account and he now wishes to acknowledge the role of feelings or "affect" in emotions. As part of this rethinking on feelings or affect, Solomon has had to revisit William James in determining what role the body plays in emotion. This is one of the more interesting aspects of his latest thinking on the topic. Before we turn to consider the role of the body in emotion, we must first discuss what sort of a phenomenon an emotion might be.

There is significant debate about whether the type of cognition involved in emotion is best thought of as a belief, a thought, a judgment,

---

84. Solomon, "Emotions as Engagements," 77.
85. Solomon, "Emotions as Engagements," 78.

or a perception. Solomon acknowledges that while beliefs and emotions are related in important ways, beliefs cannot constitute our emotions; beliefs are necessarily dispositions and/or propositional attitudes, but an emotion is, at least in part, an *experience*.[86] The view that a thought is the essential element of emotion is also problematic, to Solomon's mind, in that a thought is too specific, too intellectual, too demanding in terms of linguistic ability, articulation, and reflection, and too episodic to apply to all emotions. These doubts or shortcomings in respect of beliefs and thoughts explain the appeal of perception as the cognitive element in emotion. Solomon is supportive of the proposal concerning a close link between emotion and perception, seeing it as particularly helpful in repudiating the insidious distinction that perception is one thing, while appraisal, evaluation, interpretation, and emotional response are all something else.[87] The concept of judgment maintains close ties to perception, yet is conceivable apart from perception. He continues to think, though, that judgment is "the most versatile candidate in the cognitive analysis of emotion,"[88] while maintaining that "some emotions might be better analyzed in terms of perception, others in terms of thoughts or judgments, others in terms of construal."[89] The real work in this area of inquiry is directed to a particular instance of a particular sort of emotion. Solomon proposes the following complex view of the essential features of emotion and judgment:

> They are about the world (including oneself in the world). They are episodic but possibly long-term processes as well. They must span conscious and nonconscious awareness (in fact, I would argue, these are ill conceived as a simple polarity—there are many "levels" of consciousness). Emotions as judgments must accept as their "objects" both propositions and ordinary objects of perception (imagination, memory, etc.). They must be appropriate both in the presence of their objects and in their absence. They must involve appraisals and evaluations without necessarily involving (or excluding) reflective appraisals and evaluations. They must stimulate thoughts and encourage beliefs (as well as

---

86. Solomon, "Emotions as Engagements," 80.

87. Solomon, "Emotions as Engagements," 81.

88. A judgment need not be articulate or deliberate, as, for example, in the case of animals that make all sorts of judgments—whether something is worth chasing, or worth eating, or worth courting—or in the case of infant emotions, or in the case of kinaesthetic judgments. See Solomon, "What is a 'Cognitive Theory'?," 10.

89. Solomon, "What is a 'Cognitive Theory'?," 12.

being founded on beliefs) without being nothing more than thoughts or beliefs themselves. And, of particular importance to my larger view, they must artfully bridge the categories of the voluntary and the involuntary.[90]

As part of this "larger view" of emotions as judgments, Solomon revisits the issue of feelings or affect, in response largely to the accusation that the cognitive theory neglects feelings.[91] He continues to argue, against William James, that emotion is no mere feeling—interpreted as a bodily set of sensations—but now reconsiders what role the body plays in his larger perspective of cognitive theory. He wants to acknowledge the *role of the body*, and not just the brain, in emotional experience. The feeling, for instance, of our "making a face" in anger or disgust is integral to our experience of those emotions. Moreover, a certain "action readiness" is associated with the experience of anger, insofar as we take up a defensive posture which manifests itself in the tensing of various muscles in readiness for physical aggression. Solomon is now keen to acknowledge that there are feelings critical to emotion, yet at the same time he is clear on asserting that they are "not distinct from cognition or judgment and they are not mere 'read-outs' of processes going on in the body. They are judgments *of* the body, and this is the 'missing' element in the cognitive theory of emotions. They are profound manifestations of our many ways of emotionally engaging with the world."[92]

Solomon's revised understanding of feelings as judgments of the body, I would note, is consistent with, and supported by, an evolutionary view of the world, where cosmology and anthropology are to be taken in their "ontological interrelatedness."[93] The relationship between the cosmos and humanity is one of mutuality or interdependence: humanity continues to borrow from or need the cosmos as a physical and biophysical matrix, but it also affects the structures of the cosmos in turn by endeavoring to make something of them in a deliberate and purposeful fashion. This is the phenomenon of human self-transcendence, which manifests itself in the transforming of our environment into a world of culture. These processes of mutuality are mediated by our *bodiliness*. The

---

90. Solomon, "Emotions as Engagements," 82–83.

91. Michael Stocker and Peter Goldie, for instance, have accused the cognitive theory of neglecting feelings or "affect."

92. Solomon, "Emotions as Engagements" 88.

93. Beeck, *God Encountered*, vol. 2/3, 47.

latter implies that the body is not altogether discrete—against Cartesian philosophy—and is not radically individuated; rather, it is the common matrix in and through which individual human persons are related to humanity and the cosmos as a whole. Through the medium of our bodiliness "we are natively predisposed to *action*—to engagement with the world we live in."[94] This notion of bodiliness is useful for highlighting how the body, and not just the brain, is involved in emotional experience, which is rooted in humanity's engagement with, and grappling with, the world in which we live, move, and have our being.

Cheshire Calhoun: Emotions and Personal Biography

Cheshire Calhoun's thought is significant and helpful for clarifying and elaborating on Solomon's contention that "emotions are subjective engagements in the world." When we say emotions are subjective, what does this mean exactly?[95] Calhoun surveys several concise responses from eminent thinkers in the past—Plato, Hume, Freud, James, Brentano, Dewey, Kierkegaard, Buber, and Sartre—from which he is able to distill out two quite different conceptions of emotional subjectivity; namely, "epistemic subjectivity" and "biographical subjectivity." The former has a pejorative sense, implying that emotions distort perception, that they are prejudiced, untrustworthy, lack adequate justification, and imbue objects with unreal qualities. This type of understanding drives the wedge between reason and emotion, resulting in the philosophical devaluation of emotion. With the category "biographical subjectivity," by contrast, the attention falls on a person's individuality, personal history, and social-cultural context; in short, emotional beliefs have a strong connection to our personal biographies. Calhoun explores the idea of biographical subjectivity with the intention of showing that this type of subjectivity allows us to distinguish emotions from non-emotional beliefs, without invoking epistemic subjectivity.

Once we give assent to Calhoun's central argument that *the connection with personal biography is what makes emotions subjective*, then the line between emotion and reason will have to be drawn very thinly.[96]

---

94. Beeck, *God Encountered*, vol. 2/3, 113.

95. Calhoun, "Subjectivity and Emotion," 107–21.

96. The philosopher Richard Wollheim, it is worth noting, also thinks of emotional subjectivity in this way. He asserts that the "specific function" of an emotion and the

What Calhoun calls for is a revised notion of epistemic objectivity, in which truth is not divorced from an at least partially personal point of view. He urges us to think of emotions as both personal (biographically subjective) and sources of knowledge (epistemically objective). That way we will begin to trust our emotions "to deliver truth in the same way that we trust our perceptions or our chains of reasoning or the voice of experts."[97] Ever since the Enlightenment, knowledge has been promoted as theoretical, abstract, impersonal knowledge that all people can give intellectual assent to. What has also occurred is a polarization of the public and personal spheres, with true knowledge—the fields of science, mathematics, logic, and ethics—being situated squarely in the public realm. But significant challenges have been raised to this Enlightenment perspective on knowledge and progress, challenges that highlight the personal, historical, and cultural conditioning of all knowledge. The problem with knowledge that is abstracted from everyday concrete life is that it "cannot engage the biographical self."[98] It is a kind of knowledge that has no valence because it simply does not speak to our personal needs, aspirations, desires, fears, and hopes. From the standpoint of everyday life, knowledge that matters most is knowledge that is relevant to our way of life and is biographically loaded. This type of personal knowledge includes the recognition of emotional beliefs associated with our personal biographies (past and present). So, for Calhoun, biographical subjectivity is understood as follows:

> I hope "biographical" evokes the image of a subject about whom we tell stories. We are, after all, individuals with histories, growing up in Panama or New York, born into middle-class or lower-class families, suffering childhood traumas, becoming paranoid or generous, learning philosophy, learning to be careful, disadvantaged or advantaged, suffering loss, and sometimes getting lucky. This is the subject who has a past, a psychological profile, and allotted or elected social roles. Biographical subjectivity is the viewpoint of that subject.[99]

What makes emotions subjective on this view is the connection with personal biography. Once we begin to look for the biographical

---

"life-history" of the person are "closely bound up." See Wollheim, "Emotions and their Philosophy," 29.

    97. Calhoun, "Subjectivity and Emotion," 110.

    98. Calhoun, "Subjectivity and Emotion," 112.

    99. Calhoun, "Subjectivity and Emotion," 113.

meaningfulness of our emotions we will be able to conduct a deeper analysis of the nature of emotion. Calhoun explores, for instance, "appropriate emotions" as ones that are epistemically objective; that is, "there is some sense in which they fit the facts."[100] In order to fathom what this "fitting the facts" might entail, Calhoun has recourse to Ronald de Sousa's work on "paradigm scenarios."[101] We learn, identify, and judge the appropriateness of emotions by reference to paradigm scenarios embedded in our culture. The paradigm scenario for love in *Romeo and Juliet*, for example, is not a good fit for love relations in the twenty-first century, or for love between elderly people. Where a variety of emotional paradigm scenarios may fit a given situation, de Sousa suggests the most appropriate one should be chosen by considering the consequences of adopting one paradigm over another—for instance, fortitude may preserve relationships, while anger destroys them—and the cultural rankings of paradigms—for example, fortitude is a virtue, anger is not. Calhoun wants to add to this picture, however, our own emotional temperaments as playing a part in the choices we make regarding appropriate emotions.

Richard Wollheim: Emotions as Attitudes to Reality

Richard Wollheim's writings on the emotions further bolster the view that a wedge must not be driven between reason and emotion, and that emotions are inextricably related to personal biography. Wollheim is of the opinion that a theory of the emotions needs a theory of the mind to go with it, and he adopts a broad map of the mind according to which a divide exists between "mental states" and "mental dispositions": the emotions are placed amongst the mental dispositions.[102] Other salient examples of kinds of mental disposition are beliefs and desires. Wollheim maintains that the kinds of mental disposition can be distinguished on the basis of the role or function that they perform. The function of beliefs is to provide us with a picture of reality that claims to be true; the role

---

100. Calhoun, "Subjectivity and Emotion," 118–20.
101. De Sousa, *Rationality of Emotion*.
102. Wollheim, "Emotions and their Philosophy," 20–21. Examples of a mental state would be perceptions, sensations, pangs of hunger and lust, daydreams and hallucinations, and passing thoughts. These are transient events. Examples of a mental disposition would be desires, beliefs, skills, virtues and vices, and habits. These have a history and endure over a period of time. Wollheim underscores the need to appreciate that mental dispositions and mental states interact.

of desires is to provide us with goals or targets at which to aim in life; and the role of emotions is to provide us with orientations or attitudes to reality, or some part of reality.[103] Emotions are thought of according to the specific function of *formation of attitudes*, and this process of formation takes place within the particular life-history of the person. Like Calhoun, Wollheim acknowledges that emotions have a history and are connected with personal biography. The history of an emotion is thought of as follows:

> One, the person has a desire; two, the desire may be satisfied or frustrated; three, when either happens, the person . . . is led to trace the fact of satisfaction or frustration to a precipitating factor, which may be a person, or a thing, or an event; four, though this precipitating factor is often settled upon only after much thought . . . the whole process may be clouded by the imagination, and therefore the selection of the precipitating factor need not be on rational grounds; five, . . . the experience of satisfaction or frustration (as the case may be) is projected on to the precipitating factor, and this gives rise to an attitude on the part of the person; six, the attitude persists, an emotion forms; and, seven, the newly formed emotion will in the course of time give rise to a variety of mental dispositions, and will manifest itself in a number of mental states. Prominent amongst the mental states that arise will be feelings, and prominent amongst the dispositions that form will be desires. It is only when desires form that the emotion has motivational force.[104]

According to this citation, the formation of an orientation or attitude (emotion) towards reality or some part of reality has two major components to it: the personal experience of satisfaction or frustration of a pre-existing desire, and the projection of this experience on to what is taken as the precipitating factor. The satisfaction of a pre-existing desire gives rise to a positive emotion associated with pleasure—e.g., gratitude, joy, hope, or love—while the frustration of desire gives rise to a negative emotion associated with displeasure—e.g., grief, hatred, anger, or anxiety. Since in this perspective we cannot reduce or identify emotions with desires, it would be wrong to think of desire as a basic emotion. Desire and emotion pertain to different kinds of mental disposition: the role of desire is to provide targets or goals in life, whereas the role of emotion is

---

103. Wollheim, "Emotions and their Philosophy," 25–26.
104. Wollheim, "Emotions and their Philosophy," 30.

to provide attitudes to the world which color our future experience, leading us to attend to one aspect of things rather than another, and to view the things we attend to in one light rather than another. It is wrong to identify emotions with desires or beliefs, although there are similarities between emotions and beliefs on the one hand, and emotions and desires on the other.[105]

Aaron Ben-Ze'ev: The Logic of the Emotions

Wollhiem's contention that a theory of the emotions needs a theory of the mind to go with it is shared by Aaron Ben-Ze'ev, who has done much study on the unique logic of emotions. What is especially interesting about his work is the proposal that the emotional mode is a general mode of the mental system, which is to be distinguished from the perceptual and intellectual modes.[106] He explains that typical emotions have the characteristics of urgency and heat, great intensity, and brief duration, since they indicate a transition during which the preceding context has changed and no new context has yet stabilized. Emotions are functional in that they "help us to mobilize many resources in order to face the unstable situation."[107] This concurs with the view of Power and Dalgleish as to why we have emotions. Of particular importance in Ben-Ze'ev's analysis of the logic of emotions is the understanding that emotions are not rational in the "descriptive" sense of being the result of deliberate, intellectual calculations; rather, they are rational in the "normative" sense of generating appropriate (optimal) responses in the given circumstances, in a regular and consistent fashion.[108] By abandoning the exclusivity of the traditional descriptive sense of rationality, Ben-Ze'ev is able to conduct an insightful discussion about a type of logic that is different from the logic of intellectual deliberations.[109]

---

105. Wollhiem, "Emotions and their Philosophy," 28. Nussbaum also regards emotions as different from desires, although they are closely connected. See Nussbaum, *Upheavals of Thought*, 135–36.

106. Ben-Ze'ev, "Logic of Emotions," 147–62.

107. Ben-Ze'ev, "Logic of Emotions," 149.

108. Ben-Ze'ev, "Logic of Emotions, 150–51. Note that what Ben-Ze'ev calls the "descriptive" sense of rational is what Nussbaum refers to as the "normative" sense of rational, and vice versa.

109. Ben-Ze'ev asserts that neither intellectual reasoning nor emotional reasoning violate "analytic" rules of formal logic, which ensure valid argumentation. With regard

One salient aspect of intellectual deliberations worth highlighting is that they do not necessarily address personal and practical concerns of the thinker, who is "more of a detached, objective observer looking for regularities independent of her existence."[110] Emotions, on the other hand, are not detached theoretical states, for they "address a practical concern from a personal and interested perspective."[111] In the emotional mode the world is seen from our own personal perspective, and we apply our own sense of personal importance to unstable, changing events. Ben-Ze'ev therefore lends support to the functionalist views of both Lazarus and Nussbaum. But his distinctiveness lies in the way he develops an understanding of emotional reasoning as having a different logic to that typical of intellectual reasoning. As Blaire Pascal poignantly stated the matter: "The heart has its reasons which reason does not understand." When we acknowledge that both types of logic are useful in different circumstances, it will be to our benefit, Ben-Ze'ev concludes, "to integrate them"[112] as best we might.

Martha Nussbaum: A Neo-Stoic Theory of Emotion

Finally, it is fitting to complete this brief review of current thinking on the emotions by discussing Martha Nussbaum's comprehensive neo-Stoic cognitive theory of the emotions. Her analysis of emotions gives further expression and weight to the arguments of both Wollheim and Calhoun concerning the intimate connection of emotions with personal biography, as well as Solomon's contention that emotions as judgments are subjective engagements in the world. According to Nussbaum, emotions "involve judgments about important things, judgments in which, appraising an external object as salient for our own well-being, we acknowledge our own neediness and incompleteness before parts of the world that we do not fully control."[113] In order to illustrate the evaluations associated with emotions such as fear, hope, grief, anger, and love,

---

to "synthetic" rules of reasoning, which deal with content, the author seeks to describe some synthetic principles underlying emotional reasoning that are absent from intellectual reasoning. By doing so, the author intends to show that emotional reality differs from intellectual reality.

110. Ben-Ze'ev, "Logic of Emotions," 157.
111. Ben-Ze'ev, "Logic of Emotions," 156.
112. Ben-Ze'ev, "Logic of Emotions," 162.
113. Nussbaum, *Upheavals of Thought*, 19.

Nussbaum discusses the story of her beloved mother's death. In telling the story of her mother's death, Nussbaum identifies several features of the emotions that her neo-Stoic cognitive theory will have to elaborate upon:

> In this story we see several features of the emotions that it will be the business of my argument to try to explain: their urgency and heat; their tendency to take over the personality and to move it to action with overwhelming force; their connection with important attachments, in terms of which a person defines her life; the person's sense of passivity before them; their apparently adversarial relation to "rationality" in the sense of cool calculation or cost-benefit analysis; their close connections with one another, as hope alternates uneasily with fear, as a single event transforms hope into grief, as grief, looking about for a cause, expresses itself as anger, as all of these can be the vehicles of an underlying love.[114]

In light of highlighting these features of emotions, it might seem surprising that Nussbaum defends the thesis that emotions are forms of judgment, yet that is precisely the thesis she is committed to defending. She appeals to the ancient Greek Stoic view of the emotions as evaluative judgments that ascribe to things and persons great importance for the person's own flourishing. "Emotions always involve thought of an object combined with thought of the object's salience or importance; in that sense, they always involve appraisal or evaluation."[115] Emotions are therefore acknowledgements of neediness and lack of self-sufficiency. But Nussbaum rejects the Stoic ideal of *apatheia*, claiming that emotions are not bad guides to wise human behavior, and she undertakes an investigation of the role of social norms in emotions, as well as the development of the emotions in infancy and early childhood. She refers to her thesis as a "cognitive-evaluative" perspective, where the term cognitive means nothing more than "concerned with receiving and processing information."[116]

Nussbaum's cognitive-evaluative thesis has an adversary, namely, the view that emotions are non-reasoning, unthinking energies that push the person around like gusts of wind. The adversary's view is contained in the common misconception that emotions are "bodily" rather than "mental." As bodily, emotions are reduced to unthinking forces with no

---

114. Nussbaum, *Upheavals of Thought*, 22.
115. Nussbaum, *Upheavals of Thought*, 23.
116. Nussbaum, *Upheavals of Thought*, 23.

connection to our thoughts, evaluations, or plans.¹¹⁷ In such a perspective, it would be easy to explain the urgency of the emotions and why they are experienced as passive, as something we suffer. The Stoic view of emotions as evaluative judgments would therefore seem to be in trouble: if emotions are a kind of judgment or thought, how could one account for their urgency since thoughts are usually imagined as detached and calm? How can judgments be passive when they are usually regarded as things that we actively do, not suffer? What, then, according to Nussbaum, makes the emotions unlike unthinking energies?

First of all, they are *about* something, which is to say that they have an object.¹¹⁸ Second, the object is an *intentional* object; that is, it figures in the emotion as it is seen by the person whose emotion it is.¹¹⁹ Emotions are not about their objects merely in the sense of being pointed at them; rather, their aboutness is more internal, it embodies a way of seeing. "In fear, one sees oneself or what one loves as seriously threatened. In hope, one sees oneself or what one loves as in some uncertainty but with a good chance for a good outcome. In grief, one sees an important object or person as lost; in love, as invested with a special sort of radiance."¹²⁰ Third, emotions embody not just ways of seeing an object, but *beliefs* about the object, often a complex set of beliefs. In order to have fear, I must believe that something bad is about to happen and that I am not entirely in control of warding it off. In order to have anger, I must believe that some damage has occurred to me or to someone close to me, and that the damage is significant, not trivial, and that it was done deliberately, not accidentally. Emotions, then, involve thoughts, and it "seems necessary to put the thought into the definition of the emotion itself."¹²¹ Finally, emotions are concerned with *value*. They see their object as invested with value, as important for the person's own flourishing. The emotions, then, appear to be *eudaimonistic*; they are concerned with what it is for the person to live well. "Most of the time emotions link us to items that we regard as important for our well-being, but do not fully control. The

---

117. Nussbaum, *Upheavals of Thought*, 25.

118. Nussbaum, *Upheavals of Thought*, 27.

119. Nussbaum's thought here is the same as Solomon's when he proposes that emotions are subjective engagements with the world (i.e., emotions are not merely "about" something, but "engagements" with the world).

120. Nussbaum, *Upheavals of Thought*, 28.

121. Nussbaum, *Upheavals of Thought*, 30.

emotion records that sense of vulnerability and imperfect control . . . a certain passivity before the world."[122]

In light of the above characteristics of the emotions, Nussbaum returns to the adversary's view to show that her position responds well to the experiential points raised by the adversary.[123] (i) First, her argument can explain why the emotions have heat and urgency—because they concern our most important goals and projects. The urgency derives not from an unthinking force, but from the thought that my well-being is threatened by that force. In her synthesis, Nussbaum shows that it is the emotion itself, and not some further reaction to it, that has urgency and heat. (ii) Second, the experience of passivity in emotion is explained by the fact that the objects of emotion are people and things whose activities we do not ourselves control, and in whom we have invested a good measure of our own well-being. (iii) Third, the reason why in some emotional experiences we feel torn apart, or, at the opposite end of the spectrum, a marvelous sense of wholeness, is that these are transactions with a world about which we care deeply, a world that may complete us or may tear us apart. The *world enters into the self* in emotion, with enormous power to heal or to wound. It enters in a cognitive way, in our perceptions and beliefs about what matters in life.

When we consider the passage from one emotion to another, Nussbaum says that we arrive at a deeper understanding of why the emotions should be grouped together as a class.[124] It is not only that the emotions all share certain features, it is also that they have a dynamic relationship to one another. Given a deep attachment to an object outside our own control, combined with the very accidents of life, we will experience intense joy when the beloved object is at hand, fear when it is threatened, and grief when catastrophe befalls it.[125] When another fosters the beloved object's good, we feel gratitude; when another damages the object, we feel anger. When another has such a valuable object and we do not, we feel envy; when another becomes our rival in respect of such an object, we feel jealousy. In this scheme of thinking, we begin to have "some idea of

---

122. Nussbaum, *Upheavals of Thought*, 43.
123. Nussbaum, *Upheavals of Thought*, 77–78.
124. Nussbaum, *Upheavals of Thought*, 87.
125. Nussbaum, *Upheavals of Thought*, 87.

what it is to understand emotions as a certain sort of vision or as value-laden ways of understanding the world."[126]

Nussbaum then proceeds to give attention to the ways in which emotions are shaped by individual history and social norms. With regard to the latter, Nussbaum gives the examples of the Ifaluk who believe that it is necessary to "cry big" when someone dies otherwise sickness will set in afterwards, and the Balinese who believe that sad feelings associated with someone's death are dangerous to a person's health, thus one should distract oneself with happy thoughts.[127] With regard to the grieving of her mother's death, Nussbaum notes that there were elements of both the Ifaluk and Balinese cultures: her grief was shaped not only by her attachment to her mother, but also by social norms concerning appropriate ways to mourn the loss of a parent. She felt the need to "cry big" at times, yet at the same time American culture expects the mourner to help themselves and be distracted by getting on with their work and their commitments without making a big fuss.

Emotions such as fear, love, anger, and grief are universal human elements; they belong to our common humanity. Yet emotions are also shaped differently by different societies, so that emotional repertories differ between different societies. What is more, it is likely that the differences run deeper, "affecting the experience of the emotion itself."[128] In all three above cases of grieving, a loss is suffered, yet the responses take very different forms that affect the inner experience itself. If we accept the proposition that beliefs about what is important or valuable in life play a central role in emotions, we can readily see how those beliefs can be shaped by social norms. Emotions themselves are therefore ethical and social-political inasmuch as they are tied up with our responses to the questions, "What is worth caring about?" and "How should I live?"[129] As we study different societies it becomes apparent that they have different normative teachings regarding the importance of objects such as honor, money, bodily beauty, health, friendship, children, and political

---

126. Nussbaum, *Upheavals of Thought*, 88.
127. Nussbaum, *Upheavals of Thought*, 139.
128. Nussbaum, *Upheavals of Thought*, 141.
129. Nussbaum, *Upheavals of Thought*, 149. At times, Nussbaum notes, human emotions go beyond their eudaimonistic framework in a way that animal emotions more rarely do. Few, if any, nonhuman animals experience wonder and awe, emotions that depart from the focus on one's own scheme of goals and projects.

power. "They therefore have many differences in anger, envy, fear, love, and grief."[130]

In addition to recognizing the relevance of social-cultural factors in emotional life, Nussbaum accords due recognition to a person's individual history. The child's interactions with parents, siblings, and other caretakers are important factors in the development of emotional traits. The way in which parents and caretakers treat children is, to some extent, determined by culture, yet at the same time we must acknowledge that an infant has "a separate history in a separate body, intertwined with other specific individuals in a history of great depth and intensity."[131] Some recent attempts to defend a cognitive account of emotion in philosophy have severed emotions from their past in wanting to depict them as fully determined by present input relating to one's current situation. But Nussbaum repudiates such attempts, arguing that "in a deep sense all human emotions are in part about the past, and bear the traces of a history that is at once commonly human, socially constructed, and idiosyncratic."[132] The *emotions of adult life have a history*, and they originate in infancy.[133]

Nussbaum is critical of cognitive views that ignore infancy altogether, and, at the same time, she is critical of non-cognitive views that fail to recognize that differences in the emotions of one adult in contrast to another are at root a cognitive difference: "a difference in one's perceptions of value and salience, a difference in the narratives of need and dependency one has come to accept."[134] Nussbaum is also critical of any position, such as classical Stoic teaching, according to which every emotion must be brought into line with the dictates of reason in order to achieve the norm of perfection. Once we acknowledge that the emotions have grown out of human ambivalence and neediness, which is to say that "the roots of anger, hatred, and disgust lie very deep in the structure of human life,"[135] then the normative goal of perfection is not only unachievable, but is the very thing that can wreak emotional havoc. Nussbaum's argument is therefore a neo-Stoic theory of emotion which diverges from normative Stoic ethics by providing the emotions with a history that does justice to

130. Nussbaum, *Upheavals of Thought*, 157.

131. Nussbaum, *Upheavals of Thought*, 173.

132. Nussbaum, *Upheavals of Thought*, 177.

133. Both Cheshire Calhoun and Richard Wollheim, we saw above, also espouse the view that emotions have a history.

134. Nussbaum, *Upheavals of Thought*, 230.

135. Nussbaum, *Upheavals of Thought*, 234.

the complexity, neediness, and frailty of human life, and underscores the difficulty and upheaval involved in changing one's character.

Components of Emotion, Basic Emotions, and Desire

It has been argued in this chapter that emotions and intelligence go hand in hand, that emotions are not unthinking energies but have their own unique logic, particular history, and process of formation. Emotions make sense when they are considered from the standpoint of our important goals in life (desires) and the beliefs we hold about ourselves, other people, and the world in which we live. When a personal goal is at stake we experience the arousal of an appropriate emotion, and the more important the goal from a personal and interested perspective, the stronger the emotion will be. Integral to the experience of emotions is the action potential or motivational forces associated with them, so that when an emotion is aroused we are mobilized to gain something of benefit (e.g., love), or to prevent something harmful from occurring (e.g., fear), or to inflict harm on someone (e.g., hatred). It is apparent from the foregoing discussion of the various philosophical studies on emotion that there are many interrelated aspects of emotion that one should consider carefully in seeking to arrive at the truth regarding the significance of our emotional life. The picture is indeed a complex one. A key issue that a cognitive theory of emotion has to grapple with is what the term "cognition" actually refers to—a belief? a thought? a judgment? an appraisal? a perception? To my mind, since beliefs, interpretations, judgments, appraisals, and perceptions are all of a cognitive nature and related to one another, it would be preferable to talk of cognitive elements or cognitive structures of emotion, rather than confine or restrict cognition to a single term.[136] Therefore, on the basis of the various arguments and selected reviews presented hitherto, the following points could reasonably be taken as fundamental components of a complex cognitive theory of emotion:

1. Emotions are evaluative *judgments* about important things, judgments in which we appraise objects as valuable and essential to our goals (desires) of human flourishing.

---

136. This is the view espoused by Ortony et al, *Cognitive Structure*.

2. Emotions are directed to *intentional* objects and register our vulnerability and passivity before parts of the world that we do not fully control.
3. Emotions embody not just ways of perceiving an object, but *beliefs* about the object, although emotions cannot be identified with beliefs (or desires).
4. Emotions have a *personal biography* of subjective engagement in the world, thus they provide attitudes to reality or some part of reality.
5. Emotions have *action potentials* in the given circumstances of our life—they have power to heal or to wound, to gain some benefit or prevent some harm from happening to us.
6. Emotions are *no mere bodily feelings*, yet the body is involved by producing facial expressions and physiological changes appropriate to the emotion—we can think of emotions as judgments of the body.

On this complex cognitive view, not only do the emotions share certain common features but they also have *a dynamic relationship to one another*. When someone forges a deep and important attachment to an external object outside of their control, the ineluctable accidents and unpredictability of life "will bring the person who is so attached now into intense joy, when the beloved object is at hand, now into fear, when it is threatened, now into grief, when catastrophe befalls it."[137] Once we begin to see the way in which emotions are closely related to one another, we begin to appreciate them as subjective engagements with the world, as value-laden ways of seeing the world that enters into the self with power to heal (benefit) or to wound (harm). Without the emotions there simply would be no earnest pursuits whatsoever and human existence would be rendered motionless and dead. Of all the components outlined above, emotions as action potentials should be singled out for special recognition inasmuch as the other components collectively account for the motivating force of the emotions.

Connected to this understanding of emotions as being dynamically related to one another arises the idea that some emotions are more basic than others, and, therefore, more complex emotions are to be thought of as elaborations or combinations of the basic few. We saw earlier that the Stoics taught the notion of basic emotions when they proposed four

---

137. Nussbaum, *Upheavals of Thought*, 87.

emotions as the most generic ones, under which all other emotions could be arranged by species: emotions of the genus "delight" see their objects as good and present; those of the genus "distress" see their objects as evil and present; emotions of the genus "desire" see their objects as prospective goods; and those of the genus "fear" see their objects as prospective evils. We saw that Thomas Aquinas affirms eleven basic passions, which he divides into the two basic categories of concupiscible passions and irascible passions.[138] In modern philosophy, Descartes was the first to propose that some emotions may be more basic than others and he listed six primary emotions or passions: wonder, joy, sadness, love, hatred, and desire.[139] He saw other emotions as a compound mixture of these basic emotions. But what really generated interest in this question of basic emotions was the publication of Darwin's *On the Expression of the Emotions in Man and Animals* (1872). This particular work was a catalyst for drawing attention to the potential importance of basic emotions in biology and psychology.[140] Many different writers have pledged the cause of basic emotions from their own particular research perspective, and while much work remains to be done, what is noteworthy is that the list of basic emotions produced by different research approaches is very similar: the basic emotions are regarded as being anger, fear, disgust, sadness, and happiness.[141] In terms of the cognitive theory of emotions proposed in this chapter, these basic emotions would involve judgments about important things integral to our well-being, in which we appraise our goals in life as being compromised in some way (harm) or successfully maintained and furthered (benefit). The short list of basic emotions reflects, in other words, basic appraisal scenarios that are apparent in most, if not all, human cultures. Although it should be kept in mind, as Nussbaum has reminded us, that emotions are shaped differently by different societies

---

138. The eleven basic passions are love, desire, joy, hate, aversion, sadness, hope, daring, despair, fear, and anger.

139. Power and Dalgleish, *Cognition and Emotion*, 29, 62.

140. The notion of basic emotions is supported by scholars such as William James, Magda Arnold, Paul Ekman, Jeffrey Gray, and Keith Oatley, while those who reject the idea include Andrew Ortony, Terence Turner, and James Russell. See Power and Dalgleish, *Cognition and Emotion*, 100.

141. See Power and Dalgleish, *Cognition and Emotion*, 102–10. Part 2 of the latter work is devoted to an elaboration of the basic emotions and their disorders.

and it is likely that the differences could run at the deeper level of "affecting the experience of the emotion itself."[142]

The Emotion of Wonder: *Mysterium Fascinans et Tremendum*

Descartes included wonder in his list of six basic emotions, but he gave wonder a special place by regarding it as "the first of all the passions."[143] Wonder is assigned a primary place because it disposes human beings towards the acquisition of knowledge; that is, the sciences. The ancient Greek philosophers spoke of philosophy as beginning with wonder and continually sustained by wonder, hence they saw wonder as the hallmark of the human species. In more recent times, this philosophical recognition of wonder has been given renewed expression by Rudolf Otto in his celebrated book *The Idea of the Holy*, where he speaks of a "numinous" category of value and of a "numinous" state of mind which is irreducible to any other.[144] The numinous experience transcends the sphere of the ordinary, the usual, the familiar, and awaits our discovery by being "felt" as outside the self.[145] The idea of the holy comes to awareness in the human subject through the numinous experience of awe and wonder, and it contains a surplus of meaning above and beyond the meaning of moral goodness.[146] The rational and moral, on this view, is an essential part of the holy, but it is not the whole of it.

The object of numinous experience is named by Otto as the *mysterium tremendum et fascinans*. The affective state referred to as *tremendum* conveys the sense of absolute majesty and awe, which produces in us the feeling of being but dust and ashes.[147] This element of daunting majesty is expressed biblically as the "fear" or "wrath" of God. But there is another affective state, the *fascinans*, in which the mystery shows itself as something uniquely attractive and fascinating, so that

142. Nussbaum, *Upheavals of Thought*, 141.

143. Descartes, *Passions of the Soul*, Article 53.

144. Otto, *Idea of the Holy*, 6–7.

145. Otto, *Idea of the Holy*, 11.

146. Otto's assertion regarding a surplus of meaning is not dissimilar to Jean-Luc Marion's concept of the "saturated phenomenon." When speaking of the logic of the gift that precedes being, Marion holds that what is given is obscure, not because it is defective or deficient, but because it is excessive. What is given, in other words, "dazzles the beholder." See Horner, *Jean-Luc Marion*, 69.

147. Otto, *Idea of the Holy*, 19.

we feel an impulse to turn our gaze towards it and allow ourselves to be captivated and entranced by it.[148] On the rational side of the element of fascination are concepts such as love, mercy, pity, and comfort, all of which belong to our natural psychical life, but here they are thought of as absolute and complete, hence there is always a surplus of meaning which is non-rational (i.e., ineffable). The *mysterium* is experienced in its positive character as something that bestows on us "a beatitude beyond compare."[149] St. Paul has this positive character of fascination in view when he writes: "What no eye has seen, nor ear heard, nor the heart of man conceived, what God has prepared for those who love him" (1 Cor 2:9). It is in the religious feeling of longing for union with God that the moment of wonder is recognized as a living factor.

The writings of Thomas Merton on contemplation are helpful for shedding further light on this discussion. Merton's interest lies not in contemplation as something that is the fruit of our own intellectual efforts, but in the "religious apprehension of God" as a transcendent gift.[150] What is experienced in contemplation is the awakening of our "deep transcendent self," which is opposed to the superficial external self that we usually associate with the first person singular "I." The latter is not our real self, it is not the true "I" that subsists before the eyes of God. For Merton, nothing could be more alien to contemplation than the *Cogito ergo sum* of Cartesian philosophy; this is the declaration of an alienated being who reduces himself to a concept, who thinks of himself as a "thing" and then goes on to convince himself that God is also a "thing" like other limited objects of thought.[151] But God is neither a "what" nor a "thing," but a pure "Who" or "Thou" or "I AM" before whom our inmost "I" springs into awareness.[152] This means that contemplation is "the experiential grasp of reality as *subjective*" and we arrive at reality "by an intuitive awakening in which our free and personal reality becomes *fully alive* to its own

148. Otto, *Idea of the Holy*, 31.
149. Otto, *Idea of the Holy*, 33.
150. Merton, *Seeds of Contemplation*, 3.
151. Merton, *Seeds of Contemplation*, 6.
152. Merton, *Seeds of Contemplation*, 11. The idea of our inner "I" awakened by a "Thou" or "I AM" receives a comprehensive treatment by Martin Buber in his celebrated work *I and Thou*. Buber makes a distinction between the "I" of the basic word "I-It" (the world of experience) and the "I" of the basic word "I-Thou" (the world of relation). The realm of "It" is characterized by activities of controlling and predicting the future, but whoever says "Thou" stands in relation and has no control over the other and the future.

existential depths, which open out into the mystery of God."[153] What is in view here is a special dimension of inner experience and discipline, a certain integrity of personal development, which is not compatible with a purely external, busy existence. This does not mean that contemplation is incompatible with action; rather, action is thought of as the creative work of dedicated love. "A certain depth of disciplined experience is a necessary ground for fruitful action."[154] Without a profound awareness of our inmost "I" before the "I AM," our personal life will not be deepened and enriched, love will tend to remain superficial and deceptive, and our capacity to serve others will be limited and defective.

Nussbaum in her study of emotion contends that the emotion of wonder is exceptional in that it makes no reference to our important goals and projects, which is to say that wonder is not eudaimonistic. She holds that when we experience the emotion of wonder we are maximally aware of the value of the object, and only minimally aware of the object's relationship to our own plans.[155] Wonder is therefore likely to issue in contemplation, rather than action toward the object. This statement, to my mind, is only partly true. Wonder does issue in contemplation, to be sure, but this type of contemplation involves much intellectual activity, such as: acknowledging a transcendent source of life outside of the human subject; reflecting on the meaning and purpose of our subjective engagements in the world; weighing up and judging our current set of values to determine whether they are in need of undergoing some reform; deciding on the ultimate ground or basis of our hope; and identifying the type of social relationships that we would do well to pursue if we wish to live better and good lives. If we then proceed to further consider contemplation as an intuitive awakening in which we become "fully alive" to our own existential depths which open out into God, then

---

153. Merton, *Seeds of Contemplation*, 7. Merton's argument here bears a family resemblance to Karl Rahner's notion of a "supernatural existential." If God created creatures with whom he could share his own divine life in knowledge and freedom, then the offer and possibility of grace—God's self-communication—is given with human existence. We are intrinsically ordered to the life of grace as our deepest dynamism and final goal. The offer of this grace is an existential; that is, an intrinsic component of human existence, a possible way of being. See Rahner, *Foundations of Christian Faith*, 126–33.

154. Merton, *Contemplation*, 172.

155. Nussbaum, *Upheavals of Thought*, 54. The author sees reverence or awe as a related emotion. In a religious context, awe is the acknowledgement of the surpassing value of the object.

the understanding that action potentials are associated with contemplation is significantly bolstered. The awakening of our inmost "I" gives rise to "fruitful action" in dedicated service to others, and we come to the awareness that union with God, which is our final goal in life, expresses and manifests itself in the creative work of a profound and dedicated love. This type of contemplation, moreover, is assisted by the communal activities of public worship, as well as individual activities of private devotion and study of religious traditions, all of which give symbolic expression to the *mysterium tremendum et fascinans*. Our own personal goals and projects, incomplete and corrupted as they might be, find their transformation and fulfillment and completion in the object of wonder, which defies rational explanation and human manipulation because it always retains a surplus of meaning.

This last point should be elaborated a little further. Nussbaum asserts that the emotion of wonder does not make reference to our important goals and projects. In her definition of emotion she states that emotions invest their objects with value, and they register our neediness, vulnerability, and incompleteness before a world that is not fully in our control. When we consider the emotion of wonder as I have presented it above, the object of wonder is invested with surpassing value (surplus of meaning), the emotional experience of wonder underlines our passivity before the world (we are captivated by the object of wonder), and it registers our neediness and incompleteness (the object of wonder bestows on us "a beatitude beyond compare"). The rational side of wonder (fascination) contains concepts such as love, mercy, pity, and comfort, all of which belong to our natural psychical life, but here in the emotional state of wonder they are thought of as absolute and complete. In such a framework, all our goals and projects, which always remain incomplete and subject to the accidents of life, are ultimately referred to, and find their completion, in an ineffable object acknowledged in the emotional experience of wonder. Even if only obscurely and somewhat dimly, wonder does make reference to our important goals and projects (i.e., our desires), although it will require us to modify and transform them in striving to make our relationships, both in the service of others and of creation, right and true and good.

Basic Emotions and Fundamental Desire

In the lists of basic emotions enumerated by Aquinas and Descartes, desire is included as a basic emotion. The Stoics, as well as Augustine and Gregory of Nyssa who will be discussed in chapter 2 of this study, also regard desire as a basic emotion. But is it right to consider desire as a basic emotion? We saw earlier that Wollheim conceives of emotions, desires, and beliefs as three different kinds of mental disposition, from which it follows that desire cannot be affirmed as a basic emotion. Nussbaum is also of the view that emotions are different from desires, although they are closely related to them. Desires provide targets or goals in life that are considered integral to our human flourishing, while the emotions arise in connection with judgments we make about intentional objects that bear on the attainment of those important goals. This is a reasonable position to hold, to my mind, but more needs to be said about desire. The foregoing discussion on wonder and contemplation suggests the human being has a fundamental desire that accounts for its movement toward perfection and completion (*telos*).[156] When the human subject becomes fully alive to its own existential depths which open out into the mystery we call God, such transcendental experience points to human subjectivity as a dynamic movement beyond its own finitude toward an infinite horizon known as "holy mystery."

Karl Rahner's transcendental thought, which was alluded to earlier in relation to the concept of the supernatural existential, is particularly effective in demonstrating how this fundamental desire operates in the human subject, and underlies all categorical desires. For Rahner, self-transcendence is characterized by the two dimensions of knowledge and freedom. In knowing some object in the world, the drive or desire of the intellect is never satisfied because each act of knowing in turn raises a new question. Since this questioning never ceases, it becomes apparent that human knowing is situated between the finite and the infinite. It is precisely in the finite that the human subject becomes aware of the infinite as the horizon of its transcendence. Rahner says the same about freedom. In every act of choice, the human subject decides upon something finite in the world. But each act of freedom reveals the gap between what is chosen and the dynamism of human subjectivity, thus freedom

---

156. This point is underlined by Aquinas' conception of desire or appetite as playing a central role in the *exitus-reditus* structure of his *Summa theologiae*. This was discussed in the introduction to this study.

also refers to an infinite horizon. It is only within this horizon that the subject's freedom is recognized as finite. It is precisely in the recognition of the limits of knowledge and freedom that the human subject is driven beyond finitude to the infinite as the condition of possibility of its transcendence, the term of which is "holy mystery."[157] This is a philosophical analysis of what in theological terms is meant by the doctrine of humanity's natural desire for the beatific vision of God. The human subject, since it is intrinsically ordered to holy mystery as the basis of its action in the world, has a fundamental desire that expresses itself in the categorical goals (aspirations) of its life. The *emotional life of the human subject emerges within this framework of desire*. When the longing for objects deemed important and valuable to the human subject is threatened or undermined in some way, it experiences the negative emotions of fear, anger, sadness, or contempt. On the other hand, when the yearning for important things is successfully maintained and nurtured, the human subject experiences the positive emotions of love, joy, and hope. It is human desire that keeps the human subject indelibly rooted in holy mystery.

Augustine acknowledges this fundamental desire at the heart of human existence in more psychological language when he famously wrote in his *Confessions*, "Our hearts are restless, O Lord, until they rest in you." To Augustine's way of thinking, the human subject is characterized by a fundamental desire for union with God as its final goal or end. The restless heart is invested with a transcendent dimension and yearns for blissful perfection in the age to come, and in this yearning the heart grows deep. The whole thought of Augustine in his *Confessions* is developed in terms of Christ the Savior as the fulfillment of the true desire of the human heart. Gregory of Nyssa, whose thought will also be examined in chapter 2 of this work, adds weight to this position when he regards the Christian life as the progressive education of desire, the right object of which is love of God. Daniel Bell, somewhat reminiscent of both Augustine's and Gregory's thought on the true desire of the heart or soul, has recently written about Christianity as the transformation of our corrupted desire in a capitalist system. Bell appeals to Bernard of Clairvaux's sermons on the Song of Songs to develop his portrayal of Christianity as a "therapy of desire" that resists capitalism's ensemble of "technologies of

---

157. For Rahner, the two words "holy mystery" constitute a unity: they express equally the transcendentality of knowledge (mystery) and freedom/love (holy). In the human subject is rooted an innate natural desire for the beatific vision of God.

desire" which shapes and corrupts desire.[158] Diarmuid O'Murchu echoes Bell's call for the transformation of our desire. He asserts that desire is not within our control, it defies any rational attempt at manipulation, yet it manifests itself through our "aspirations for advancement, growth, achievement, and fulfilment."[159]

In the New Testament we find some key texts that talk of desire. For example, Jesus says, "I have earnestly desired to eat this Passover with you before I suffer" (Luke 22:15). This text can be set in relation to the text in the Letter to the Hebrews, where Christ says that God does not desire sacrifices according to the law; rather, it is through the offering of the body of Christ, once for all, that we humans come to perfection (Heb 10:5–10). Jesus earnestly desires to eat the Passover with his disciples in order to inaugurate the new covenant in his blood, with a view to finally consummating God's work of bringing to perfection (*telos*) all created things. Paul is clear in his writings that desire has a transcendent dimension: he exhorts us "to eagerly desire the greater gifts" (1 Cor 12:31), and his greatest desire is to "depart and be with Christ" (Phil 1:23). As in the Jewish Scriptures where the final object of desire is God himself (see Prov 3:3–6; Isa 43:1), in the New Testament the ultimate object of desire is union with God through Christ (see 2 Pet 1:4). Both in the Jewish and Christian Scriptures, when the Lord God is our greatest desire, all other desires find their true and proper expression.

To conclude, it is best to think of desire not as a basic emotion, but in terms of the final end or inalienable goal of the human subject, which is acknowledged in transcendental experience. Desire is integral to every act of human knowing and willing, and seeks to weave patterns of meaning and growth in the drama of personal life. While desire finds expression in the categorical plans and goals of the human subject, it defies all human categories inasmuch as it relates to the object of wonder—i.e., holy mystery—which simply cannot be contained or manipulated, thus there is always unsurpassable value and a surplus of meaning in respect of desire.[160] The deepest and truest expression of humanity is desire drawing

---

158. Bell, *Liberation Theology*, 85–96.

159. O'Murchu, *Transformation of Desire*, 139.

160. This perspective is applicable to the portrait of Christ in the gospels. The God whom Jesus calls "Father" is the object of wonder—*mysterium tremendum et fascinans*—who is invested with unsurpassed value and a surplus of meaning. Jesus' fundamental desire is to make known and manifest the Father's benevolent love for the people of God through his saving mission as the Son. The emotions of Jesus arise

the soul to God, and when this longing or yearning for communion with God is recognized as our final end (goal), the emotions of the human subject are progressively transformed by being directed to their right and proper object—love of God, joy in God, and hope in God. All the basic emotions experienced by ordinary people undergo transformation when God becomes the new object of desire. Augustine, for example, expresses this idea of the transformation of the basic emotions when he says that the citizens of the city of God fear to sin and fear eternal punishment, they desire eternal life and thus desire to persevere to the end, they grieve for sin and because they groan for the redemption of their body, and they rejoice in good works and in the hope that death will be swallowed up in victory. Augustine does not see Christian life as a matter of eradicating the affections, but of redirecting them to the ultimate goal of union with God, to the firm hope of eternal peace with God in eternity. When emotions are regarded as having a cognitive structure, this implies that a modification or change in our thoughts, beliefs, and values—which occurs with the acceptance of the gospel of Christ—will give rise to transformed affections that are expressive of Christian discipleship, the life of virtue, and hope in the resurrection life to come.

In this chapter the focus has been on showing how the contrast that Western philosophical thought habitually draws between reason and emotion, has recently been subjected to serious challenges by advocates of a cognitive theory of emotion. In the next chapter the intention will be to illustrate how the Christian theologians Augustine of Hippo, Gregory of Nyssa, and Jonathan Edwards, in their respective ways, all think along lines that are congruous with a basically cognitive view of emotion as portrayed in the discussion hitherto. Emotions, we have seen, are always about something, they have intentional objects, are intimately related to our beliefs and values, reveal our passivity and vulnerability before the world as we pursue our goals, and are springs of action in our personal lives. In such a framework where emotions are defined by their propositional content, any change in our thoughts, beliefs, and values in relation to personal existence in the world will be accompanied by

---

and assume importance within this framework, for they appear as manifestations of a profound struggle between Jesus' fundamental desire to make known the unsurpassable worth of the Father's love for his people on the one hand, and, on the other, the increasing resistance, isolation, and ultimate rejection of Jesus by his own people who pretend that the kingdom of God is something that is containable and acceptable on their own terms.

a transformation of our emotions in the pursuit of the good life. Can theology, as the church's ongoing reflection on the gospel of Christ, afford to neglect the role of the emotions in Christian life, worship, and teaching? Is the affective language of "heart" that features both in Jewish and Christian Scriptures to be ignored as clouding the gospel message, or does it poignantly express the real message about the work of redemption-salvation in the person of the incarnate Word? And, more importantly, if emotion and cognition are inseparable, what role does Jesus' emotional life play in the mystery of the incarnation, understood as the interpenetration of divinity and humanity in his person? It is the task of the remainder of this study to address these questions.

2

Emotions and the Ascent to God in the Christian Tradition

THE STOIC ACCOUNTS OF the emotions had considerable influence on the development of Christian thought on the emotions, especially in the patristic period. We saw in the previous chapter that the Stoic philosopher Seneca, for example, paid much attention to overcoming the emotions of fear and grief, which are emotions attributed to human mortality. Early Christian thinkers, armed with the doctrine of Adam's sin as responsible for the mortality that all must suffer and wrestle against, were also focused on death and the associated emotions of fear and grief. Sin is a negative reality that wreaks havoc and leads to death, and the fear and grief associated with death are, of course, negative emotions. Consolation for the Christian, however, unlike Stoic thinkers such as Seneca, comes not from the right judgments of the mind leading to the wise state of *apatheia*, but from the crucified Christ who has conquered sin and death, and graciously offers sinners the joyous prospect of sharing in his resurrection life. The focus for the Christian is not on the elimination of the passions, but on directing them toward their right objects. Fear, for example, is retained because the Christian is aware of the tenacious reality of sin and dreads eternal condemnation for sin; grief is likewise retained, but now one grieves for one's sins and groans for the redemption of the body; joy is also retained, but one rejoices and delights in one's good works and in the hope of death being swallowed up by Christ's victory; desire continues to feature in Christian life, but longing is fundamentally desire to be in ecstatic union with God, through the grace of Christ who is the mediator between God and humanity.

In this chapter the task is to examine the writings of three prominent Christian thinkers, namely, Augustine of Hippo, Gregory of Nyssa, and Jonathan Edwards, all of whom have been selected on the basis of their understanding of the emotions as playing an integral role in the Christian ascent to God. At times in Christianity the ascent to God has featured a strong type of asceticism where the ideal of *apatheia* was upheld, but it will be shown in what manner each of these Christian thinkers of the Great Tradition repudiate the Stoic ideal of the extirpation of the emotions. Augustine's thought is considered to be significant in that he situates Christian ascent within the present human predicament with all its attendant weaknesses, longings, and incompleteness; Gregory's writings are notable for attempting to elaborate the ascent to God in terms of the educating of desire and the erotic relation of humanity to God; and Edwards's work is highlighted for his thesis that true religion consists, in great part, in gracious affections. All three of these thinkers, in their own particular way, portray the Christian life of ascent as the redirecting—i.e., transforming—of emotions away from earthly objects toward God as the new object of ineffable delight. This means that the emotions are envisaged as playing a vital role in the process of the soul's ascent to God, and, moreover, human affections and Christian affections are not seen as two different stories, but two parts of one and the same story. The effects of God's grace in Christ, through the indwelling Spirit, do not involve new faculties of the soul, but a new inward perception and mode of willing that inclines the soul toward God as its ultimate end.[1]

A further task of this chapter will be to compare each of the three thinkers with the cognitive theory of emotion presented in the previous chapter 1. It will become apparent that all three, in their respective ways, acknowledge the cognitive nature of emotions as judgments and share many of the aspects of the cognitive theory outlined in chapter 1. After these comparisons have been made, the final section of the chapter will discuss the similarities that can be discerned between the three thinkers, as well as some notable differences that highlight different accents and emphases in their thinking. Gregory, for example, talks of the educating of desire within an ascending order of creation, and of the virtuous life as "participation" in God in the here and now. Augustine's emphasis, on

---

1. The type of asceticism in view here is eschatological, not metaphysical or dualistic.

the other hand, is more on a descending order of creation, where the Christian emotions serve to underpin the "anticipation" of blissful peace in the age to come. While it is important to note the different accents in the three thinkers, the focus toward the end of the chapter will be on the overlapping ideas amongst the three, including: desire as having a malleable quality; emotions as playing a constructive role in the Christian ascent to God; emotions as the spring of action in the world; grace in the soul as not involving new faculties of the soul; and the heavenly life as consisting largely in holy affections. These are all positive overlapping ideas, however the chapter will conclude with what is considered to be an overlapping idea with a negative note; namely, the influence of the Stoic idea of the passions as sicknesses of the soul. The result of the adoption of this Stoic idea into Christian theology has been the reduction of the negative emotions—i.e., fear, grief, sadness, and anger—to the problem of sin. Reasons will be given as to why this traditional position should be challenged as an inadequate portrayal of the ascent to God.

Augustine of Hippo: The Restless Longing of the Heart

By the time Augustine came to write the *Confessions*, he had undergone quite a radical change of thought in respect of attaining the ideal of perfect wisdom as understood by the Platonic tradition. The earlier Augustine, from the time of his conversion in 386 CE to the time of being ordained a priest in 391 CE, had aspired to becoming a Christian wise man, to growing godlike in his twilight years. He believed that the Apostles had become perfect men of wisdom, hence he believed that the ideal of the contemplative life could be reached in the present life. His great hope had vanished, though, by the time he sat down to write the *Confessions* (circa 397 CE), when he had been a bishop for only a few years. As a bishop, Augustine tells his readers how he still had to struggle with his own temptations. He was a man who was terrified by the weight of his sins, who was burdened by his many infirmities, and his hope is fixed on God, who, through Christ, offers a medicine to heal all his diseases. In writing his *Confessions*, Augustine was forced to come to terms with his true human condition, hence his piece of writing is at heart "an act of therapy."[2]

---

2. Brown, *Augustine of Hippo*, 165.

Augustine had begun his Christian life with optimism concerning the attainment of perfection through a Christian Platonism. But by the time he sat down to write his *Confessions*, he had given up on optimism: "he would never impose a victory of mind over body in himself, he would never achieve the wrapt contemplation of the ideal philosopher."[3] The problem that Augustine saw with the Greek philosophical tradition is that it was guilty of the sin of pride, insofar as it teaches that through our own efforts we can make ourselves godlike. What Augustine had come to understand was that because bodily and carnal desires tenaciously persist in the present life, the life of the spirit can never be thought of as wholly removed from the common ways of life. This awareness forced him to reassess human potentialities and to propose that the human will does not enjoy complete freedom, all of which gave rise to a new humility in Augustine.

In his reassessment of the human predicament, Augustine came to affirm the permanence of evil in our will and he did so in purely psychological terms; namely, in terms of the compulsive force of habit (*consuetudo*), which derives its strength from the workings of the human memory. Because the pleasure of past actions—especially sexual pleasure—is recorded in the memory, the force of habit rooted in the past persists in the present. Augustine writes, "Yet in my memory, of which I have spoken at length, sexual images survive, because they were imprinted there by former habit."[4] The writings of Paul, in which is depicted a basic unresolved tension between "flesh" and "spirit," resonated with Augustine's experience of the lingering weight and burden of his sins.[5] There could be no clear break for the baptized Christian from his past life, no complete renewal of the inner self that would leave behind the burdens of compulsive habit firmly etched in the memory. "In the last resort, the individual Christian, like the Church, remains always deeply infected with sin."[6] Baptism launches the Christian on a life-long process of convalescence, rather than curing him all at once and enabling him

---

3. Brown, *Augustine of Hippo*, 147.

4. Augustine, *Confessions*, X, 30. Augustine talks about various temptations, such as: concupiscence, gluttony, excess drink, wealth, self-complacency, and love of praise.

5. Brown, *Augustine of Hippo*, 151. Augustine's view of flesh and spirit is discussed below.

6. Markus, *End of Ancient Christianity*, 54. Since Augustine had learnt to appreciate the insidious force of habit, Markus, in chapter 4 of his work, portrays Augustine as the defender of Christian mediocrity.

to make a clean break from his past life. In the course of this life-long process, the hearts of the faithful are stirred by the love of God's mercy and the sweetness of God's grace, by which every weak person is given power. While Augustine was not in the least anti-intellectual, he nonetheless "did not think that intellect had the last word and he pioneered a highly positive evaluation of human feelings. We owe to him our sense of the word 'heart' in this sense."[7]

With regard to Christian life as not representing a clear break from the past, Augustine also makes the point that if the Christian were, in Platonic fashion, to dissociate himself from his past life, this would amount to forfeiting the sense of self. Memory, while it keeps the sinner embroiled in the force of habit, is nonetheless required to give a sense of self and continuity. Without memory, "the soul cannot progress at all."[8] Progress of the soul is, however, characterized as a long unbroken period of trials, which means that Augustine is resigned to knowing no more than occasional glimpses of the supreme good:

> Nowhere amid all these things which I survey under your guidance do I find a safe haven for my soul except in you; only there are the scattered elements of my being collected, so that no part of me may escape from you. From time to time you lead me into an inward experience quite unlike any other, a sweetness beyond understanding. If ever it is brought to fullness in me my life will not be what it is now, though what it will be I cannot tell. But I am dragged down again by my weight of woe, sucked back into everyday things and held fast in them; grievously I lament, but just as grievously am I held. How high a price we pay for the burden of habit![9]

In the *Confessions* gone is the talk of a vertical ascent in this life and in its place Augustine affirms the image of a traveller on a long journey.[10] There are moments of delight, of clear vision of truth, but these moments of great value are now seen as consolations of a traveller on the long, winding road of the spiritual life. Augustine analyzed the psychology of delight and concluded that *nothing else but delight can motivate the human will.* The source of action in human beings is the mobilization of our feelings; only if we are affected by an object of delight can we act.

7. Chadwick, *Augustine*, 2.
8. Nussbaum, *Upheavals of Thought*, 538.
9. Augustine, *Confessions*, X, 40.
10. Brown, *Augustine of Hippo*, 152.

"Now, 'feeling' has taken its rightful place as the ally of the intellect."[11] Augustine lays bare his feelings (*affectus*), he exposes the inner world of his heart, yet at the same time he regards the experience of delight as beyond human control.[12] We cannot attain it by our own resources or power; what we most ardently desire can never be more than a hope which points far beyond this life to the life to come. All we can do is to yearn for the state of blissful perfection, to feel its loss intensely, to pine for it: "It is yearning that makes the heart deep."[13] The language used by Augustine in the *Confessions* is the language of erotic longing, which is "not language that the Stoic or Spinozistic wise man would use, extirpating the passions."[14] The following citation illustrates the erotic longing of Augustine's soul that seeks God and thirsts after his delight:

> Late have I loved you, Beauty so ancient and so new, late have I loved you! Lo, you were within, but I outside, seeking there for you, and upon the shapely things you have made I rushed headlong... You were with me, but I was not with you... You called, shouted, broke through my deafness; you flared, blazed, banished my blindness; you lavished your fragrance, I gasped, and now I pant for you; I tasted you, and I hunger and thirst; you touched me, and I burned for your peace.[15]

In light of the initiative that God takes in the divine-human encounter, Augustine is critical of any view that depicts the human being as sufficient for its own salvation. It is sinful to think and live as though we humans were sufficient, and Augustine uses the language of erotic longing to highlight *the emotions as acknowledgments of the truth of our profound neediness*.[16] To be without the basic emotions of desire, joy, fear, and grief would be simply inhuman; "they are an inescapable feature of our psychological condition."[17] In the prelapsarian state of paradise, Adam and Eve were not troubled by emotions such as fear, grief, or

---

11. Brown, *Augustine of Hippo*, 155. An intellectual work was valued by Augustine not simply because it changed his views, but because it changed his way of feeling.

12. For Augustine, when God is known at all, he is known as the self-evident. Augustine espouses a doctrine of divine illumination as the *dynamic source* of all our knowledge of divine reality.

13. Brown, *Augustine of Hippo*, 156.

14. Nussbaum, *Upheavals of Thought*, 530.

15. Augustine, *Confessions*, X, 27.

16. Nussbaum, *Upheavals of Thought*, 542.

17. O'Daly, *Augustine's Philosophy*, 50.

sadness, but they did experience emotions of love for each other and for God and the joy ensuing from this good state of affairs. Similarly, in the blissful condition of heavenly life the blessed will also feel certain positive emotions: they will experience splendid love and joy, though not fear or grief for all suffering and weeping will be wiped away. This pilgrim life of ours, though, as distinct from prelapsarian or heavenly life, is characterized by emotions other than love and joy: we also experience emotions that have a disturbing and distressing nature, such as fear, grief, anger, and sadness, all of which Augustine attributes to the universal condition of human sinfulness and mortality. Yet notwithstanding this present state of affairs with regard to our historical condition and the wrecking potential of misused emotions, Augustine cannot give his approval to the Stoic notion of impassibility (*apatheia*).[18]

The crucial point for Augustine is *the rightness of the object of the emotions*, which are regarded as forms of volition: the emotions are good if accompanied by a morally right will, and evil if accompanied by a wrong will. Emotions such as desire, fear, and joy are common to both the good and the evil, "but the good have these emotions in a good way and the evil in a bad way, just as the human will is either rightly or wrongly directed."[19] The Christian who feels appropriate emotions will, for example: desire eternal life, fear eternal punishment, feel sorrow for sins committed, feel gladness at performing good works, feel compassion for fellow sinners, grieve for the redemption of their body, and rejoice in the hope that death will be swallowed up in victory.[20] Augustine is critical of philosophers who do not admit the passions or "perturbations" of desire, joy, fear, and sorrow in the soul of the wise person, and argues instead that the perturbations of the soul appear as right affections in the life of the righteous when leading to repentance in Jesus Christ, about which Paul writes (2 Cor 7:8–11).[21] The upshot of all this is that *Augustine situates Christian ascent squarely within the context of the present human condition* with its concomitant emotions or passions that must

---

18. The Stoics argue that the wise man, who has learnt to extirpate the passions, experiences corresponding "stable states" (*eupatheiai*): the wise man "wills" rather than desires; feels "gladness" rather than joy; and "caution" rather than fear. No stable state is identified that corresponds to distress or pain. This was discussed in chapter 1.

19. Augustine, *City of God*, XIV, 8. Emotions as modes of willing is discussed further below.

20. Augustine, *City of God*, XIV, 9.

21. See O'Daly, *Augustine's City of God*, 155–56.

be rightly directed to appropriate objects. It is not a question of controlling the emotions or extirpating them altogether, but of directing them towards the right objects. Augustine portrays the present realities of human inadequacy, sinfulness, weakness, longing, and incompleteness not as impediments to attaining the goal of delightful union with God, but as the very condition of God's definitive address to humankind in the person of Jesus Christ, through whom comes the blessedness of eternal life and final peace. It is not difficult to understand why Nussbaum describes Augustine's account of Christian ascent as "a major philosophical achievement and a decisive progress beyond the Platonic accounts."[22]

The major problem Augustine encountered with the Greek philosophical tradition was that it promotes the sin of pride, inasmuch as it teaches that we sinners can make ourselves godlike. The human being simply cannot ascend towards God by some neat intellectual progression, and to convey this basic point Augustine makes much use of images of "descent" which are more prevalent than images of "ascent." The prolific use of images of descent indicates that Augustine feels himself to be in constant danger of falling away from the object of his delight. For instance, instead of talking of exaltation, Augustine tends to speak of poverty and lowness, dust and ashes; instead of the fullness of the Platonic soul, we find emptiness and barrenness; instead of the ease with which the soul, once purified, turns to contemplation, we read about toil and labor; instead of safety, danger; instead of light, darkness and obscurity, fog and mist; instead of purity and health, we find sickness, hunger, and thirst—God is invoked as "my intimate doctor."[23] The following words of Augustine convey his view of the ordeal of earthly life that simply shows no refrain:

> When at last I cling to you with my whole being there will be no more anguish or labor for me, and my life will be alive indeed, because filled with you. But now it is very different. Anyone whom you fill you also uplift, but I am not full of you, and so I am a burden to myself. Joys over which I ought to weep do battle with sorrows that should be matter for joy, and I know not which will be victorious. But I also see griefs that are evil at war in me with joys that are good, and I know not which will win the day. This is agony, Lord, have pity on me! It is agony! See, I do not hide my wounds; you are the physician and I am sick;

---

22. Nussbaum, *Upheavals of Thought*, 547.
23. Nussbaum, *Upheavals of Thought*, 544.

> you are merciful, I in need of mercy. Is not human life on earth a time of testing? Who would choose troubles and hardships? You command us to endure them, but not to love them... In adverse circumstances I long for prosperity, and in times of prosperity I dread adversity. What middle ground is there between the two, where human life might be free from trial? Woe and woe again betide worldly prosperity, from fear of disaster and evanescent joy! But woe, woe, and woe again upon worldly adversity, from envy of better fortune, the hardship of adversity itself, and the fear that endurance may falter. Is not human life on earth a time of testing without respite?[24]

God, the exceedingly merciful one, is the object of Augustine's delight; God is beloved and desired. The happy life, which is the thing that all desire, is to rejoice in God and for God and because of God, and there is no other happy life.[25] Yet the earthly life is not experienced as filled by God, thus Augustine feels he is a burden to himself and life is an ongoing ordeal to be endured in the hope of being wholly filled by God in the life to come. Augustine is sick and God is the physician who heals his flaws and frailty, but complete healing does not belong to this life, thus life on earth is a long unbroken period of trial and toil. It is not within Augustine's power to save himself, thus he exhorts God, "Give what you command, and then command whatever you will."[26] Eternal life is the supreme good that Augustine's heart is set upon and to attain this final good, "The just person lives by faith" (Rom 1:17). Since we sinners do not yet see our good, although we may have occasional glimpses of the supreme good, we must seek it by believing. "Nor is it in our power to live by our own efforts unless we are helped in believing and praying by the one who gave us the very faith by which we believe that we must have his help."[27]

In his *City of God*, Augustine presents his understanding of life according to the "flesh" and life according to the "spirit." The flesh is not simply equated with the pursuit of bodily or sensual pleasure; rather, it is thought of as a misdirection of the human being that does not live according to God. As a result of Adam's sin the human being was given over to himself, not in a way that he became his own master, but rather in such a way that he was set at odds with himself: "in the punishment of that sin

---

24. Augustine, *Confessions*, X, 28.
25. Augustine, *Confessions*, X, 20, 22.
26. Augustine, *Confessions*, X, 29.
27. Augustine, *City of God*, XIX, 4.

the retribution for disobedience was simply disobedience itself. For what is man's misery if not his own disobedience to himself, with the result that, because he would not do what he could, he now cannot do what he would?"[28] It is not because of having flesh that the human being has become like the devil; it is rather by living according to self and not living according to God.[29] The punishment for disobedience to God was the human being's disobedience to himself. The body, then, is not the source of the misdirection of the self, for the body is good. It is true that in the present life the corruptible body weighs upon the soul, but Augustine argues that the sinful soul inherited from Adam is what made the body corruptible. The goodness of the body, and the proper functioning of the passions prior to the sin of Adam, comes to the fore in the following text:

> In paradise, then, man lived as he wanted for as long as what he wanted was at one with God's command. He lived in the enjoyment of God, from whose goodness he himself was good. He lived without any lack, and he had it in his power to live this way forever. There was food to keep away hunger, drink to keep away thirst, and the tree of life to keep away the decay of old age. There was no corruption in the body, or arising from the body, to inflict distress on any of his senses. There was no fear of disease from within or of injury from without. He had supreme health in his flesh and complete tranquillity in his soul . . . There was no grief at all, nor was there any empty joy. Rather, true gladness flowed continually from God, for whom there burned *love from a pure heart, and a good conscience, and genuine faith* (1 Tm 1:5).[30]

The influence of the body cannot be blamed for the basic emotions—i.e., desire, joy, fear, and sorrow—that beset the personal self in this life. Prior to Adam's sin all the human passions were properly directed to God, who is the true enjoyment and happiness of the human being. There was no lack of any sort, no fear, no grief, no empty joy; rather, there was a state of supreme health in the body, complete tranquility of the soul, true

---

28. Augustine, *City of God*, XIV, 15. The deep flaw in human nature as a result of Adam's sin is expressed by distinguishing between true freedom (*libertas*), which consists of the human's whole-hearted directedness to its true goal of love of God, and freedom of choice (*liberum arbitrium*), which refers to the voluntary character of this directedness. As a consequence of the fall, true freedom has been lost, hence we are no longer free to love God, but we retain freedom of choice in our self-love or pride.

29. Augustine, *City of God*, XIV, 3.

30. Augustine, *City of God*, XIV, 26.

gladness, and love for God that burned from a pure heart. In created beings that possess merely an irrational soul, Augustine sees peace as attained through the satisfaction of the appetites. But in the human being who has a rational soul, the appetites which it shares with the animals must be subordinated to the peace of the rational soul which is referred to God: the desire in human nature must be directed into the paths willed for it by God.[31] Peace in a rational being is attained through the harmonizing of knowledge and action, rather than by the satisfaction of the appetites. This state of peace has been lost as a result of Adam's sin and remains ever elusive in this pilgrim life. The present human condition before God is one in which the corruptible body labors under the burden of concupiscence and mortality, yet this corruptible body is referred to the merciful God and longs for total redemption in the risen Christ.

From the foregoing discussion it becomes apparent that Augustine regards the will as involved in the emotions. In fact, he states that the emotions are nothing more than *modes of willing*.[32] Desire and joy are simply the will consenting to the seeking of things that we want or wish to happen, while fear and sorrow are the will dissenting from things that we do not want or wish to happen. In respect of the appropriateness of the emotions, it is the character of the will that makes the emotions of the soul right or wrong. Hence the emotions are regarded as good when a person's will is directed toward the right objects, and evil when a person's will is directed toward the wrong objects. One who lives according to God and not according to the flesh is a "lover of the good." Thus at times Augustine defines the emotions in terms of love: the emotions are bad if the love is bad, and good if the love is good.[33] Love, just like the will, is defined by its direction or goal. Good emotions are a foretaste of the blessed life, and bad emotions will be punished in the life hereafter.

To Augustine's way of thinking, to be truly human is to lay bare our affections, to be stirred into action by our affections, for nothing else but

---

31. See Daly, *Creation and Redemption*, 140. Note that this implies that desire has a malleable quality; that is, desire can refer to the blind impulse to satisfy physical appetites—i.e., eating, drinking, and sexual drive—or it can be focused on God as the right object of desire.

32. Augustine, *City of God*, XIV, 6. Because good and bad emotions are alike modes of willing, the behavioral sequence is emotion (e.g., anger) > will (consent to emotion) > action (angry words and/or hitting somebody). See O'Daly, *Augustine's Philosophy*, 52–53. The one exception to this rule is sexual desire, which activates the sexual organs directly; that is, with or without consent.

33. See O'Daly, *Augustine's City*, 155.

delight can motivate the human will. Any teaching that seeks to restrain or extirpate the emotions—as the Stoics do with their ideal of *apatheia*—is rejected by Augustine who argues in terms of the rightness of the object of the emotions. The philosophic view that the emotions are irrational and thus have no integral part to play in the soul of a wise person runs the risk of forfeiting our humanity, rather than gaining true peace of mind, as the following citation makes clear:

> And, if this city [of the ungodly] has any citizens who appear to control and in some way to temper these emotions, they are so proud and puffed up in their impiety that, for this very reason, the tumors of their pride expand as the pangs of their pain shrink. And, if some of these, with a vanity as monstrous as it is rare, are so enamored of their own self-restraint that they are not stirred or excited or swayed or influenced by any emotion at all [cf. the Stoics], the truth is that they are losing all humanity rather than gaining real tranquility. For the fact that something is difficult does not make it right, nor does the fact that something has no feeling mean that it is in good health.[34]

In sum, Augustine more than anything else was a seeker. He embraced the idea that humankind was created with a natural longing for God, yet this longing for union with God, who is sheer delight, becomes a kind of home sickness for fallen beings. Despite the fact that we bear our mortality as evidence of our own sin, we still nonetheless cannot be content unless we praise God, "because you have made us and drawn us to yourself, and our heart is unquiet until it rests in you."[35] The longing for God is not portrayed, though, as having a positive character; rather, it is seen primarily in negative terms. The restless heart finds no peace in the pilgrim life and our tragic restlessness will cease only in the life of the age to come. Rowan Greer, in his analysis of Augustine's view of hope, concludes that because Augustine makes so sharp a distinction between the pilgrim life on earth and the life in the age to come, it makes more sense "to think of his understanding of the Christian hope as an *anticipation* of what will be."[36] The Christian life is conceived as a bridge of hope that

---

34. Augustine, *City of God*, XIV, 9.
35. Augustine, *Confessions*, I, 1.
36. Greer, *Christian Hope*, 155. I have added the emphasis. Greer compares Gregory of Nyssa to Augustine, and contends that Gregory's vision is one of *participation* in the new age even now in the earthly life, whereas Augustine's vision is more of an *anticipation* of the new age to come (see Greer, *Christian Hope*, 113). Augustine, in

joins the two ages. Augustine recognizes many blessings—i.e., God's operative grace—in this life, but the desires of the heart remain unfulfilled so that the Christian life becomes a stretching forth toward the blissful new age to come, when our hearts will find eternal rest in God. Augustine regards salvation in the here and now as very incomplete and as straining forward to fullness in the there and then. Given the pervasiveness of tragedy both within us and outside us, Augustine does not entertain the hope that the tragic can ever be eliminated within the present state of affairs in the world.[37] Nussbaum, while applauding Augustine's work for restoring compassion to a place of centrality in this life—since human beings are to relate to one another as vulnerable, incomplete, and needy—at the same time questions whether the type of compassion Augustine has in view adequately promotes the task of earthly politics, such as feeding the hungry and caring for the persecuted.[38] But so strong was Augustine's personal sense of the inner sickness of the divided self, and so grim was the specter of worldly affairs of his day, that he felt compelled to seriously question the effectiveness of human agency in transforming either the tragedy within or the tragedy without. Jackson Bate, one of Samuel Johnson's biographers, reverberates this pessimistic Augustinian perspective rather poignantly when describing the argument of Johnson's celebrated poem titled *The Vanity of Human Wishes*:

> In the first place [Johnson] dwells on the helpless vulnerability of the individual before the social context–the tangled, teeming jungle of plots, follies, vanities, and egoistic passions in which anyone—the innocent and the virtuous no less than the vicious—is likely to be ambushed.... In the second place Johnson traces the inevitable doom of man to inward and psychological

---

other words, stresses discontinuity, whereas Gregory is more focused on continuity between the two ages.

37. Given the horrific events of the twentieth century, Augustine's position on the limits of progress seems especially warranted. In light of the Holocaust can we really entertain the hope that evil can be removed from our world by political action? Is not earthly peace at best the accommodation of conflicting wills in a fragile social-political order? Is the advancement of science and technology a panacea for the world's problems or a contributor to instability, injustice, and inequality in our world? How can we resist capitalism's ensemble of technologies of desire that shapes and corrupts the desire of the human being created in the image and likeness of God?

38. Nussbaum, *Upheavals of Thought*, 555. What is without doubt problematic in Augustine's thought, as Nussbaum rightly points out, is his highlighting of revenge and anger against God's enemies—heretics, pagans, unbelievers, and Jews—which undermines social cohesion and religious tolerance.

causes. The medley processes of hope and fear, desire and hate intercept each other and make it impossible for the heart to be satisfied if only because its own basic impulses are in conflict. More than this Johnson makes clear the inevitable self-deception by which human beings are led astray. Because the betrayal is from within, the human being seems peculiarly defenseless before it.[39]

In light of the foregoing review of Augustine's moving portrayal of the restless human heart on pilgrimage toward an anticipated blissful union with God, we can now turn to critique his understanding of human emotions by comparing it with the cognitive theory of emotion elaborated in chapter 1 of this study. To begin with, it is abundantly clear that Augustine's use of the language of erotic yearning for God is worlds apart from the language of the Stoic sage whose ideal is *apatheia*, or from the language of contemplative ascent toward God. If by *apatheia* is meant that no emotion (*pathē*) at all can affect the soul, so that no fear frightens and no grief or sorrow pains the virtuous person who lives right and well, such a state is denounced by Augustine on the grounds that the emotions serve to highlight the true human condition in the aftermath of Adam's sin. In the absence of God's redemptive grace in Christ, the emotions are not good because they are not directed toward the right choice of object. Only when the will, under the influence of grace, is directed toward God and eternal life, can the emotions be affirmed as good: Christians fear eternal punishment, they desire eternal life, they grieve because they are groaning for the redemption of their bodies, and they rejoice in the hope that death shall be swallowed up in victory.[40] The difference between the present Christian life and the pre-Christian life lies not in the elimination of strong emotions, but in *directing them to the right choice of objects*. This shows that human love and Christian love, human emotion and Christian emotion, are for Augustine but two parts of the same story: "there is only one faculty of love and desire in the human being."[41] Christian ascent is thought of as the redirecting of human love and desire away from earthly objects towards the heavenly God as the new object of ineffable delight. The emotions do involve judgments, but Augustine regards them as erroneous unless illuminated by the grace of Christ, who has conquered sin and death for our sake.

39. Bate, *Samuel Johnson*, 281–82. Cited in Greer, *Christian Hope*, 6.
40. Augustine, *City of God*, XIV, 9.
41. Nussbaum, *Upheavals of Thought*, 547.

As a second area of convergence with our cognitive theory of emotion, there can be no doubt that for Augustine the emotions register the human subject's deep vulnerability, incompleteness, neediness, and longing before parts of the world that will always remain beyond our control. Gone is any talk of the sublime contemplation of the ideal wise person who attains perfection through their own intellectual efforts, and in its place Augustine highlights the impossibility of extricating ourselves from the habitual sin of the past etched in the memory, so much so that he envisages no possibility of achieving happiness and fulfillment in this life. There are moments of an inward sense of delight, which are regarded as pure receptivity (grace) and chance happenings, but the intermittent nature of delight means that the final end of permanent delight and blissful peace remains an anticipated hope in this conflicted life of toil. The goal of human flourishing in this world, which is a feature of the ancient ethical project, is denounced by Augustine as infected by the sin of pride. The mind should not be focused on its own self-sufficient activity, as if we sinners were sufficient for our own salvation. Christian ascent is a matter of receptivity and love, although Augustine depicts the ascent as precarious and beyond our firm grasp since we are always in danger of falling away from the object of delight. Those who live in that inscrutable mystery of the call of God and through faith are able to maintain that openness of receptivity and hopeful expectation of blissful union with God in the life to come, live the good life according to Augustine. By distancing himself from the Platonist and Stoic accounts of the wise person, Augustine has created a *new Christian norm* inasmuch as the ascent now takes place within the context of our concrete human condition with all its tangled web of conflicting emotions, not by attempting to depart from it. Christian emotions therefore register our ongoing vulnerability, incompleteness, and neediness before parts of the world that are beyond our control.

As a third point, I would observe that there is considerable overlap between our cognitive theory and Augustine's writings when it comes to acknowledging emotions as subjective engagements in the world. It is very clear that Augustine holds that it is not possible to disassociate ourselves from the temporal past, which would not only amount to a loss of personal identity but would also diminish responsibility for our past sins. The emotions of adult life have a history, they have a personal biography, and this is most evident in Augustine's conception of memory and the compulsive force of habit, which places limits upon the renewal of the conflicted and divided inner self. So terribly burdensome is the memory of Augustine's past history that he feels himself to be a sick man in need of God the merciful physician, who alone can heal his chronic sickness. The Stoic sage would seek to remove himself from the common ways of his past, but Augustine's thought remains firmly connected with the memory of the past, which is set in relation to the much anticipated age to come that the yearning heart is set upon.

A potential criticism of Augustine here would be that while he acknowledges that what makes emotions subjective is the connection with personal biography, he tends to reduce subjective engagements in the world to the problem of sin. This means that the individuality of each person, which is forged by their unique personal biography in their encounter with the world, is not genuinely recognized in the Augustinian perspective, for all individuals are the same in that they are sinners in need of God's redeeming grace. The Christian loves his neighbor not for what the neighbor is as a unique person with a personal biography, but because of what God through his boundless mercy has done for the sinner. The Christian, in other words, loves his neighbor because of what the neighbor might be through God's redeeming grace. This represents, to my mind, a diminishment of the richness of individuality and a restricted way of interpreting the proposition concerning emotions as subjective engagements in the world.

A fourth area of congruity between Augustine's thought and our cognitive theory of emotion has to do with emotions as motivating forces or action potentials in the given circumstances of a person's life. This aspect of emotions is apparent in Augustine's thinking when he claims that nothing else but delight can motivate the human will, and it is more generally in play when Augustine discusses the emotions as modes of willing. The human will according to Augustine does not enjoy complete freedom, though, as is evident when he talks of a perverse will that persists in the compulsive force of habit. A right will, which is correctly set in motion by the gift of faith, always finds itself locked in battle with a perverse will, hence there are limits to the possible extent of our inner-self renewal. Be that as it may, the point here is that emotions, whether they are directed toward right or wrong objects, are seen by Augustine as providing us with motivation to act in the circumstances of our daily lives.

Given the argument that the emotions are properly directed when God becomes their new object, so much so that the sole focus of the emotions becomes the other-worldly life beyond death, Augustine could legitimately be criticized for failing to promote the dignity of this-worldly moral agency. The task of involvement in earthly politics with a desire to promote social justice in our world was not something that Augustine embraced passionately. This is quite fathomable in the light of his doctrine of original sin and his conception of the compulsive force of habit indelibly etched in the memory. What the latter teachings certainly do positively achieve with a high degree of effectiveness, however, is the restoration of *compassion*, as well as other emotions such as *lament*, to a place of centrality in this pilgrim life.[42] Once the universality of sin and the concomitant universal need for God's redeeming grace in Christ is established by Augustine's doctrine of original sin, what the Christian sees in his neighbor is a profound sinfulness and neediness that only God's grace can remedy and put right. This recognition of the genuine need in the other, who is the object of God's love, gives rise to compassion on the part of the Christian, although, once again, it could and should be asked whether this Augustinian compassion is able to give any motivating force to issues of social justice, inasmuch as it is too confined to the hope of sharing in the beatitude of the heavenly life beyond death.[43]

In addition to the emotion of compassion, it is not difficult to see how Augustine's treatment of the basic emotions readily gives rise to the acknowledgment of the emotion of lament. Christian lament is appropriate to a state of affairs in which evil is so pervasive that it persists in the human subject until the time of death and continually wreaks havoc in the socio-political world. Augustine is certainly not too starry-eyed when it comes to the possibilities of transformation, either of the inner self or the external social-political world. The inner self is portrayed as such a dark and tangled mess of perverse vanities and egoistic passions, and the world as so terribly unjust and out of kilter, that the redirecting of human desire away from earthly objects and events towards the heavenly God can only be met with very partial success at best. Little wonder that Augustine is a burden to himself and feels himself to be in constant danger of falling away from God, who is such sweet delight. The images of descent—rather than ascent of the soul—which were referred to above, convey the strong sense of burden and darkness and barrenness that Augustine attributes to the human condition. While he desires eternal life,

---

42. Compassion and lament will be discussed at greater length in chapter 4 and the conclusion to this study.

43. See Nussbaum, *Upheavals of Thought*, 552.

he can never be assured of being counted amongst those who will enjoy blissful union with God, hence he simultaneously fears the danger of eternal punishment as a real possibility. What is more, Augustine grieves in the sense that he groans for the redemption of the body, yet at the same time he rejoices in the hope that death shall be swallowed up in victory. The intrinsic and innate human desire for union with God, as Augustine understands it, always remains unfulfilled and frustrated and threatened by the darkness of sin in this life, hence it is accompanied by fear and grief and groaning.

It would be reasonable to maintain at this point that what we are looking at is indeed a very lamentable situation. Augustine movingly describes his profound wrestling with God and he does not shy away from vigorous dialogue with God. Lament as a speech form in the Bible is precisely the recovery of the human voice before God. In his *Confessions*, Augustine lays bare his restless soul in a dramatic and beautiful prayer that honestly defines the reality of the human condition before God. Patrick Miller captures the significance of the lament speech form thus:

> If the lament is the voice of pain, it is also the voice of prayer. To recover the voice of lament is to recover the voice of prayer as it has defined the human reality before God. The lament is utterly human and profoundly theological. It arises out of the reality of human existence; it assumes there is something beyond that reality that can transform human existence without destroying it. The laments of Scripture make clear what is present in every human cry for help, the assumption that God is there, God can be present, and God can help. As such, the voice of lament, the cry for help we call lament, is always our prayer. It is our humanness, the sign of our being here as man and woman, as sentient beings, who feel and hurt, who remember and despair, who cry and try to speak. We cannot avoid these prayers. They are who we are.[44]

This citation, to my mind, succinctly encapsulates the distinctive tenor of the *Confessions* as Augustine's prayer to God arising out of the depths of his heart. The older Augustine was compelled to re-evaluative Christian ascent and he came to a new understanding of the lamentable reality of the human condition, and he does not hold back his feelings and hurts as he cries out to God the physician to help him overcome his crippling and painful sickness. Augustine acknowledges that God, as delight, has

---

44. Miller, "Heaven's Prisoners," 17.

been present to him in the past, and on that basis he prayerfully petitions God to help him in the present so as to make a way forward into a better future. Patrick Miller in the citation above says that in the lament prayer the lamenter assumes that God "can transform human existence without destroying it," and this Augustine certainly does assume. It is apparent when Augustine understands transformation of human existence in terms of redirecting human desire and love to a new object, namely, God. There is only one faculty of love and desire in the human existent as far as Augustine is concerned, thus salvation in Christ is not about destroying our present human condition; rather, it has to do with the illumination of the mind to know the true object of our innate longing, and the strengthening of the will to pursue the right object of our desire. There can be no doubt that the lament speech form is very palpable in the *Confessions*, for Augustine patterned his *Confessions* after the book of Psalms and so addresses God directly from the depths of his heart.[45]

A fifth and final point in this critique concerns the involvement of the body in emotions. What does Augustine have to say about this? Well, the first thing to say is that Augustine regards the body as good, not bad; he does not attribute the misdirection of the self to the body. What is bad is termed "flesh," which denotes a state of affairs consequent upon Adam's sin, whereby one lives according to self and not according to God. Prior to the advent of sin, Adam's appetites and passions are seen as properly directed to God, but in the aftermath of the fall they become disorderly or misdirected (concupiscence). Furthermore, fallen humanity now experiences emotions such as fear, grief, and longing, since there is no longer freedom from death.[46] It is the sinful soul that is seen as responsible for the problems associated with the corruptible body. When fallen humanity becomes the recipient of God's grace in Christ, Augustine describes these intermittent moments of delight in very physical terms that denote a close relationship between emotions and bodily sensations. In moments of delight, Augustine says that God fills him with a feeling quite unlike his normal state of being, and this feeling is communicated by language pertaining to all the senses of the body: "You called, shouted, broke through my deafness; you flared, blazed, banished my blindness; you lavished your fragrance, I gasped, and now I pant for you; I tasted

---

45. See Studer, *Grace of Christ*, 78.

46. What was lost by Adam's sin was the set of qualities referred to as *original justice*: namely, freedom from disorderliness of desire or freedom from concupiscence, and freedom from death.

you, and I hunger and thirst; you touched me, and I burned for your peace."[47] The effects of Christ's grace dwelling in the soul can never be divorced from the reality of the corruptible body, for body and soul form an integral unity in the thought of Augustine. Further evidence of the involvement of the body in emotions can be gleaned from the fact that what Augustine yearns and groans for is the final redemption of the body. The blissful state of eternal union with God in the age to come cannot be envisaged without the body. Perfect ascent to God perforce involves the body, which was created by God as essentially good and destined to partake of the glorious life of God.

By way of concluding this section on Augustine, it has been shown that there is considerable overlap between the cognitive theory of emotion presented in chapter 1 of this study and the perspective on the basic emotions provided by Augustine. At times certain criticisms were leveled against Augustine, especially in respect of his restricted view of emotions as subjective engagements in the world and his somewhat limited capacity to inspire Christians to take up the struggle for social justice as a requirement of a loving God who hears the cries of a suffering world. But these criticisms certainly did not occupy center stage. Instead, the spotlight was very much on the manner in which Augustine situates Christian ascent within the concrete human condition with all its deep-seated vulnerability and neediness, and repudiates any philosophy—Platonic or Stoic—that wishes to depart from or eliminate the emotions. This represents, it was argued, a major philosophical achievement.

Gregory of Nyssa: The Progressive Education of Desire

There has been much recent interest in Gregory of Nyssa's theory of asceticism, which has led to a reassessment of his thought on Christian asceticism and the relationship of desire to the rational soul. In the past it was thought that Gregory endorsed a disjunction between reason and passion, but recent scholarship has challenged this view and argued that Gregory envisages the animal instincts and appetites as included in the rational soul. The studies of Mark Hart, John Behr, Rowan Williams, Morwenna Ludlow, and Martin Laird, since they have featured largely in this reappraisal of Gregory's anthropological foundations in his theory of asceticism, will be briefly discussed below to illustrate the main lines of

47. Augustine, *Confessions*, X, 27.

thinking in the reassessment of Gregory's thought. This will be followed by a review of the study by J. Warren Smith, which is significant in that it elaborates on Gregory's understanding of the erotic relation of humanity with God in this life, as well as the transformed nature of human *erōs* in the eschaton. It will become apparent by the end of the reviews that Gregory is not an extreme ascetic who sought to purge the soul of all its emotions; rather, Gregory sees the emotions as playing a constructive role in the Christian ascent to God.

Let us begin with Mark Hart's study. Hart undertakes a re-evaluation of Gregory's *De virginitate* with the aim of showing that Gregory does not—as thought by many—clearly exalt celibacy over marriage. In this work Gregory holds that "the chief thing which interests one in marriage is the attaining of gratifying companionship."[48] The true object of Gregory's criticism of marriage is not marriage per se, but the desire for pleasure and misguided expectations of happiness that are the basis of most marriages. The pleasure Gregory has in view is not sexual pleasure, though; instead, the greatest danger for the soul lies with the pleasure of companionship (*symbiōsis*).[49] The problem with this kind of pleasure is its tendency to produce the delusion of believing that one can "live" in the mind and body of another, and find therein a certain permanency, security, and even immortality. This mistaken judgment forms, in turn, the basis for the preoccupation with vainglory, reputation, greed, fame, and survival of one's *own* children. What Gregory seeks to warn against is the danger of attachment and the desire for symbiosis in marriage.

One who does not live a symbiotic life but lives "according to himself," by contrast, is one who is not passionately attached to others out of fear of his frailty and mortality, and thus has a better understanding of what can be legitimately expected of human relationships. The celibate who lives according to himself is not disinterested in and withdrawn from others; rather, to live a celibate life means that one is not attached to others as a solution to overcoming the fear of one's frailty and mortality, and is therefore available for the service of others (*philanthrōpia, leitourgia*). For Gregory, explains Hart, the term "marriage" becomes a metaphor for passionate attachment in general, just as the term "virginity" comes to be a metaphor for a general attitude of non-attachment, which is also

---

48. *De virg.* 3.2.6–9. Cited by Hart, "Reconciliation," 451.
49. Hart, "Reconciliation," 455.

possible in marriage.⁵⁰ Marriage is viable for the Christian to the extent that it is founded on the very quality that makes Christian celibacy viable; namely, non-attachment. Gregory envisages a viable Christian marriage as being one that exercises "moderation" and "duty" inasmuch as it is based upon public service (*leitourgia*), which includes the service of bringing children into the world.⁵¹ With respect to the ultimate Christian goal of union with God, the problem of desire is located not in the body per se, but in the soul when it allies itself with the body and seeks ultimacy in what is not God.⁵² What is evil is "the attempt by what is most divine and highest in the soul to satisfy itself in the animal side of our nature."⁵³ The remedy for this condition, according to Gregory, is the proper training of desire, whether one is celibate or married. The goal is not disembodiment, but dispassion (*apatheia*), which seeks the fulfillment of erotic longing not in another mortal human being but in God.

John Behr in his study supports Hart's conclusion that for Gregory the remedy to the problem of desire is not its extirpation but its proper training, although the focus of Behr's study is Gregory's anthropology contained in *De hominis opificio*. Behr is keen to challenge two things: (i) the generally accepted "synthetic" presentation of a dual creation, according to which God first created the human being in the divine image, then God added the distinction of male and female in foresight of the fall; (ii) and a prelapsarian angelic mode of reproduction, which holds that humans prior to the fall would have multiplied as the angels and sexual reproduction became operative with the postlapsarian addition of the "garments of skin." Behr is critical of those who interpret Gregory's thought in *De hominis opificio* through the idea of garments of skin, which is not even alluded to in *De hominis opificio*.⁵⁴ The task that Behr sets himself is to expound Gregory's anthropology in *De hominis opificio* within its own terms and framework.

At the heart of Behr's study is a presentation of Gregory's notion of an ascending order of creation. The human being appears as the culmination of creation's "ascent by steps from the smaller things to that which

---

50. Hart, "Reconciliation," 458.

51. Hart, "Reconciliation," 470–71.

52. Gregory's thought is very similar to that of Augustine who regards the sinful soul as responsible for the corruptibility of the body.

53. Hart, "Reconciliation," 463.

54. Behr, "Rational Animal," 223.

is perfect."⁵⁵ In the Genesis account of creation we are presented with the successive appearance of plants, animals, and finally human beings, and Gregory sees in this account three distinctions of the power of life and soul: there is the power of increase and nutrition (nutritive soul); there is the activity of sense and perception that is found in sentient beings (sensitive soul); and, finally, there is the perfect bodily life of the rational human being created in the image of God (rational soul).⁵⁶ The rational soul encompasses and fulfills the lower levels of the nutritive and sensitive souls, and Gregory expresses its novelty within an ascending perspective of creation by saying that the human being is "a word-bearing animal."⁵⁷ If the human mind ascends towards God it will "adorn our body as a mirror of the mirror;" but if, conversely, human beings turn towards the lower levels in their lust, "they are transformed by the shapelessness of that which should be adorned by them"⁵⁸ and are no longer able to manifest the divine image.

The passions in this perspective are not caused by the mere presence of irrational or bestial aspects in the human being, but by the "evil husbandry of the mind" that perverts the irrational motions of the body into passions.⁵⁹ Gregory conceives of human beings as the "midpoint" of the divine-incorporeal nature and the irrational-bestial life, which enables him to see a potential in creation for ascent as well as the possibility of descent.⁶⁰ We humans were never meant to be solely intellectual beings, like the angels; we were not created male and female in foresight of the fall. Rather, the creation of male and female, which establishes humanity's "community and kinship" with the irrational animals, is seen by Gregory as something essential to our God-given role as the midpoint of creation. This means that we should not seek to eliminate desire, for it is not a question of ridding oneself of desire but training or educating desire in order to attain union with God.

Behr's focus on Gregory's view of an ascending order of creation is reinforced by Rowan Williams's study. Williams writes in response to a

55. Behr, "Rational Animal," 231.
56. Behr, "Rational Animal," 226.
57. Behr, "Rational Animal," 231.
58. Behr, "Rational Animal," 232.
59. Behr, "Rational Animal," 238. Again, this is very similar to how Augustine sees the body as essentially good and attributes the corruptibility of the body to the sinful soul.
60. Behr, "Rational Animal," 235.

claim made by the scholar Christopher Stead that Gregory proposes the separation of reason from the passions.[61] Stead contends that Gregory repeats "Aristotle's mistake of regarding man simply as an animal with reason added on as an extra capacity."[62] The picture of the human subject as a hybrid of rationality and impulse implies that there is no single or integrated good—the goods sought by one element are inimical to the goods of the other, thereby creating a disjunction of reason and passion. The rational soul's goal of attaining union with God would therefore involve the separating of impulse out of the equation of human realization. For Williams, such an understanding of Gregory will not do, and he undertakes a closer reading of Gregory's *De anima et resurrectione* in order to show that it "reveals a good deal more nuance than Stead's summary might suggest."[63]

Williams carefully builds his argument to show that Gregory views the animal as included in the rational, which is to say that the animal "is part of how mind realizes itself."[64] Gregory envisages a concrete unity of body and soul, which is evident in the idea of the rational soul as including the lower forms of soul; namely, the vegetative or nutritive soul, and the sensible or sentient soul. The "power of animation" is seen as advancing through the different levels of material life, from vegetative to animal to rational, so that "active intelligence has no reality apart from the materiality which it animates and with which it interacts."[65] The mind is thought of as governing impulses that are in some sense included in its life, and is unable to realize its own goals without deploying impulse or affect—"passion" is impulse or affect divorced from the proper ends of a reasoning being.

Williams believes that one of the most notable contributions that Gregory makes to anthropology is his account of a "progressive integration" of the power of animation with the material world: in the human being the power of animation "at last comes to full awareness, to the capacity for freely shaping its animality and its environment."[66] Desire is problematic, to be sure, yet how could the human being long for God or

---

61. Williams, "Macrina's Deathbed," 227–46.
62. Stead, "Concept of Mind," 48.
63. Williams, "Macrina's Deathbed," 230.
64. Williams, "Macrina's Deathbed," 235.
65. Williams, "Macrina's Deathbed," 233.
66. Williams, "Macrina's Deathbed," 239.

battle against evil if desire and aggression were taken away? To underscore this point Gregory talks of God as an object of *erōs*, and, moreover, he advances the novel idea that *erōs* persists even in the eschaton. The wholly inexhaustible otherness of God implies that even the perfected saint in heaven undergoes an endless or perpetual progress in the good, so that a kind of *erōs*—i.e., an ever-expanding but not restless love—can be said to persist in the life to come. Gregory paints a picture of desire in the eschaton as simultaneously fulfilled and yet not sated.

The study by Morwenna Ludlow, which is focused on eschatology, sheds further light on the nature of desire in the writings of Gregory.[67] She first highlights the point that Gregory in his *De mortuis* talks about different types of desire: there is the desire for physical things such as food, drink, procreation, and protection; there is desire directed toward materialistic impulses such as pleasure, wealth, and vainglory; and there is the purified desire of the good belonging to the kingdom of God. Ludlow explains that Gregory does not so much envisage many different types of desire, but rather regards human desire as "something which can be rightly or wrongly directed."[68] Desire can be mistakenly aligned with materialistic impulses and passions, or it can be aligned with the true good if it is purified of its impurities. This gives desire a malleable quality, thereby allowing Gregory to think along the lines of the training of desire. This means that *apatheia* is "not absence of desire but freedom from any materialistic impulse or passion."[69]

In *De anima*, Gregory elaborates on appetite and how it cannot be the driving force of the soul's advance toward God. It is the godlike qualities of the human soul that allow our advance toward God. Not only the intellectual qualities of the soul are in view here, for it is also a case of "beauty attracting beauty and of the soul's love of God."[70] This language of love is especially prominent in Gregory's *In canticum canticorum*. In the Song of Songs, Gregory interprets the bride's desire for the bridegroom as the soul's desire or love for God. Gregory uses the word *erōs* to stress the intensity of the soul's desire for God, as well as to convey the dynamic sense of the soul's advance toward God. Desire drawing the

---

67. Ludlow, *Universal Salvation*, 56–64.
68. Ludlow, *Universal Salvation*, 57.
69. Ludlow, *Universal Salvation*, 58. Ludlow also says that Gregory's use of the Greek words *orexis* and *epithymia* comes close to meaning "will." The thinking here is very similar to that of Augustine who regards the passions as modes of willing.
70. Ludlow, *Universal Salvation*, 61.

soul to God "is the deepest and most true expression of humanity."[71] The dynamic sense of desire or love of God is reinforced by Gregory's idea of perpetual progress in God, according to which a progressively fuller participation in God takes place not only in this life but also in the life to come.

Martin Laird commences his study with a brief survey of the four authors considered above, which he regards as the *status quaestionis* on the topic of desire in Gregory of Nyssa.[72] All four studies summarized above challenge the former view of a bifurcated anthropology—reason over here, desire over there, thus desire must be rooted out in order to attain union with God. In place of this older scenario we now have to consider an intrinsically unified and dynamic anthropology in which desire is "part of how mind realizes itself" (Williams). Taking Hart, Behr, Williams, and Ludlow as a new point of departure in the question of educating rather than extirpating desire, Laird examines what sort of education Gregory paints for us in his *Homilies on the Song of Songs*.

Laird examines the Solomonic books Proverbs, Ecclesiastes, and the Song of Songs, and finds that each in its own way serves to train desire so as to attain communion with God. Wisdom in Proverbs exhorts us to desire virtue, to fall in love with divine beauty, thus desire should be trained to yearn not for corporeal things but the incorporeal. The philosophy contained in Ecclesiastes also exercises what Gregory calls "the passionate faculty," "the movement of soul's desire."[73] The goal is not to eradicate desire but to educate it by inflaming it, so that it might long for virtue and fall in love with the beauty of all things divine. This "noetic-erotic" capacity for God is also to be found in the Song of Songs, but what is most distinctive about this Solomonic book is the deeply apophatic character of the training of the soul. "Unlike the pedagogy found in either Proverbs or Ecclesiates, the Song of Songs wants to lead the soul into the apophatic space of the inner sanctuary, the hidden chamber of the heart, where the Beloved is encountered in the embracing darkness."[74] The faculty of desire is placed in the soul to create longing for God, and the Song of Songs uses erotic images to inflame this desire and train it to long for communion with God. Yet ultimately the noetic-erotic capacity for God

---

71. Ludlow, *Universal Salvation*, 63.
72. Laird, "Under Solomon's Tutelage," 507–25.
73. Laird, "Under Solomon's Tutelage," 512.
74. Laird, "Under Solomon's Tutelage," 515.

must be abandoned in order to enter the hidden sanctuary where all images and concepts are left behind. When desire arrives at its final end of union with God, it enters a state of "dispassionate passion."

Finally, J. Warren Smith in his study examines Gregory's understanding of the erotic relation of humanity with God, as well as the transformed nature of human *erōs* in the eschaton, to make the case for the constructive role played by the emotions in Gregory's thought. Smith argues that Gregory is not an extreme ascetic who sought to purge the soul of all its emotions. Instead, Gregory retains the language of desire (*epithymia*), although he thinks in terms of a purified or transformed desire—what he refers to as "impassible desire."[75] By the latter term is meant desire that ceases to be a passion in the pejorative sense, because it shifts its focus from the fleshy to the goodness of God himself. The passions do pose an anthropological problem, yet Gregory sees the problem as located not in human flesh per se, but with the judgments of the mind. Hence the need to purify the soul, to transform desire so as to attain the ultimate end of eternal participation in God.

With regard to Gregory's eclectic psychology where he appeals to both Plato and Aristotle's theory of the soul, Smith makes the point that when Gregory discusses the vegetative soul, the sentient soul, and the rational soul, he does not think in terms of the soul as being divided into three parts; rather, Gregory has in mind three "activities and powers" all of which are united in the human being.[76] The nutritive and sentient powers of the soul, because they are conjoined to the rational faculties, should be ordered by the mind that operates through the senses. We humans have a sensual awareness of our surroundings, but we also possess an intellectual awareness of the intelligible realm and its goods, which transcend our immediate sense experience. Hence a basic tension is experienced in our appetitive faculty between our desire for sensual goods and our desire for intellectual goods. At the same time, however, it is precisely because the embodied rational soul is a blending of the rational and non-rational faculties "that it produces a metamorphosis within the appetitive faculties of the soul's lower elements."[77] This means that the rational and non-rational need not be treated as opposing impulses; rather, they should be seen as forming an "alliance" (*oikeiōsis*) that not

---

75. Smith, *Passion and Paradise*, 3, 184, 193, 205.

76. Smith, *Passion and Paradise*, 65–67. Gregory has in mind a trichotomous, not tripartite, soul.

77. Smith, *Passion and Paradise*, 69.

only transforms our sensual nature, "but also aids the rational nature in achieving its natural end."[78]

In *De anima et resurrectione*, Gregory's sister Macrina argues that desire (*epithymia*) and our spirited faculty (*thymos*), because they pertain to the appetitive impulses, must be purged in order to realize our godlikeness. Gregory, though, challenges this understanding, arguing that emotions are not inherently evil; rather, they can be directed toward a good end or an evil end.[79] Human reason serves to exert control over the appetitive impulses by discerning the proper end for which material goods were created, and by directing appetitive faculties to "lofty goods"—the soul, excited by the mind's glimpse of divine beauty, is filled with desire for God. When emotions are rightly ordered by human reason they not only cease to be an impediment to the soul's ascent to God "but actually enable it to attain this end."[80] The soul's advance toward God is aided by the spirited faculty (*thymos*), which spurs the soul on in the face of obstacles such as the temptations of Satan. Christian love, viewed as sublimated *epithymia*, is the principal cause of the soul's ascent to God, and *thymos* is regarded by Gregory as a secondary necessary emotion "associated with the ascetic discipline necessary for the ascent."[81] The drives of the soul's lower faculties are not to be eradicated or purged; rather, their power should be harnessed and put to the service of the intellect if the soul is to move toward God. What Gregory offers us is a picture of "the ascent to God through the interplay of reason, spirit, and desire."[82] Gregory does not teach that emotions must be eradicated, but that they must be directed toward lofty goods and therefore transformed. He envisages the transformation of the bestial passions into holy desires and in this *process of transformation* is to be found the solution to the problem of the passions.

---

78. Smith, *Passion and Paradise*, 70. This important point, note, was highlighted by Rowan Williams above when he asserted that the animal in humankind is part of how mind realizes itself.

79. Smith, *Passion and Paradise*, 81.

80. Smith, *Passion and Paradise*, 85.

81. Smith, *Passion and Paradise*, 87.

82. Smith, *Passion and Paradise*, 149. This is not unlike Augustine, who talks of the Gospel of Christ as illuminating the human mind in respect of the divine beauty and goodness, and, through the Spirit, as strengthening the human will to desire union with God as our final end.

The foregoing picture is reinforced by Gregory's view of desire in the eschaton. The end of the soul's journey is eschatological union with God, but this blissful end does not represent the end of desire. Gregory proposes that there will be no end to the soul's love of God—this is his theory of *epectasy*—and this eschatological love is referred to as "impassible desire" so as to convey the sense that desire is wholly focused on God rather than carnal pleasures.[83] There are, however, Smith explains, two different accounts of *epectasy* contained in Gregory's writings. In *On the Soul and Resurrection*, when God becomes "all in all," the soul's erotic longing is eliminated because the eschatological state admits no lack or deficiency of any good. The result is the transformation of erotic desire (*epithymia*) into a holy enjoyment (*apolausis*) of God's beauty that Gregory identifies with *agape* (holy love).[84] A decade later when Gregory wrote *Commentary on the Song of Songs*, as well as *Life of Moses*, a shift in his thinking about the role of desire in the eschaton is apparent. The language of enjoyment (*apolausis*) is retained to affirm the soul's blissful communion with God, but now intellectual enjoyment of God's beauty is viewed as the beginning of desire, not its end.[85] The renewed desire of God is still *erōs*, inasmuch as it is the most intense and pleasurable of all passion, but it is passion for the incorporeal and thus is regarded by Gregory as a dispassionate form of *erōs*. "The reorientation of desire is not so much the elimination of *pathos* as it is the purging of *orexis*, the drive for pleasure, glory, and wealth."[86] Since desire in the eschaton is focused on God's goodness and beauty, it is a sanctified desire and every enjoyment of God kindles a still more intense desire of God, who is without limit. God, then, is the object of endless desire.

Smith seeks to offer a constructive synthesis of the two different accounts of *epectasy* to be found in Gregory's writings. He proposes that the early and late works be seen as giving expression to different dimensions of the soul's love of God. The earlier work stresses that God as the "all in all" is the perfect fulfillment of the soul, in the sense that the soul experiences perfect joy. Insofar as the soul need look nowhere else for its complete satisfaction, Gregory speaks of the end of desire in the eschaton.[87] In

83. Smith, *Passion and Paradise*, 183–84.
84. Smith, *Passion and Paradise*, 197.
85. Smith, *Passion and Paradise*, 202.
86. Smith, *Passion and Paradise*, 205.
87. Smith, *Passion and Paradise*, 218.

his later works Gregory no longer regards eschatological union with God as independent of desire and holds that "there is not intellectual movement that is not accompanied or driven by desire."[88] What is emphasized in the later writings is that desire is an essential component of our participation in God, whether in this life or in the life to come. The difference between the two ages is that while *erōs* is retained, it is transformed, and this is where, suggests Smith, it is possible to formulate a synthesis of Gregory's various writings. The *erōs* of this life is not tragic,[89] for it is a passionate longing and hopeful striving *toward* the blissful enjoyment of eschatological union with God. In the life to come, *erōs* will no longer be a striving toward God but a blissful enjoyment of being *fully within* the eschatological embrace of God.[90] Since the soul is eternally excited by God's infinite goodness and beauty, the eschatological *erōs* is thought of as a "soaring *stasis*."[91] It is soaring because ever ascending, ever more deeply participating in God, so that it is eternally satisfied, yet not satiated; it is *stasis* because the soul is perfectly satisfied or situated in God's presence. The synthesis that Smith proposes, then, consists in viewing *epectasy* as the transformation of the erotic.

In conclusion, the various reviews of recent studies undertaken on Gregory's theory of asceticism have argued that he is not an extreme ascetic who advocated the extirpation or purging of the emotions from the soul: rather, Gregory conceives of the emotions as playing a constructive role in the Christian ascent to God. The emotions do pose a problem if they are not properly ordered by the rational soul, however the remedy for this condition is not their elimination but the proper training and educating of desire. Desire for Gregory is an essential component of participation in God, whether in this life or in the age to come: how could we long for God and battle against evil in our lives if desire were taken away? Gregory proposes a scenario in which the rational soul not merely controls or governs the appetitive faculties but *transforms the bestial passions* so that they are directed towards the lofty goods of God's kingdom. The understanding of desire as a malleable quality implies that it can be

---

88. Smith, *Passion and Paradise*, 219.

89. Smith explains that Gregory's *erōs* is not the same as *erōs* in Plato's *Symposium*, where it is symptomatic of a state of lack, impermanence, imperfection, and nonsatisfaction. *Erōs* is tragic because it bespeaks futility and disappointment in this life. See Smith, *Passion and Paradise*, 219.

90. Smith, *Passion and Paradise*, 222.

91. Smith, *Passion and Paradise*, 222.

trained to desire virtue—imitation of Christ's virtues—and to fall in love with divine beauty. In this perspective, the bestial passions are part of the reality of how mind realizes itself, which is to say that the desires of the soul's lower faculties are not to be purged but harnessed and put to the service of the mind—this is referred to as "dispassionate passion." In this fashion the soul rises above the drives of the spirited and appetitive faculties and the temptations of this world (vice) and ascends towards God (virtue). It is the *educating or transforming of desire in an ascending order of creation* that is the guiding principle in Gregory's writings on asceticism. The problem of the passions is resolved by proposing the sublimation of the soul's impulses or affects, which involves the elimination of errant judgment by adhering to Christian orthodoxy and nurturing the theological virtue of hope in the resurrection life to come.

When Gregory's understanding of the passions is considered from the standpoint of the cognitive theory of emotion presented in chapter 1 of this study, there are obvious areas of overlap in thought. One of the fundamental elements of cognitive theory is that emotions are judgments about important things in relation to human flourishing. Gregory certainly does maintain a close connection between emotions and judgments, which is most evident when he asserts that emotions per se are morally neutral and thus not inherently evil: they can be directed toward a good end (virtue) or an evil end (vice). Evil passions ensue when what is highest in the soul seeks to satisfy itself in the animal side of our nature (bad judgment). Conversely, when the emotions are rightly ordered by the rational soul, they actually enable the soul to ascend toward God and pursue the lofty intellectual goods of God (good judgment). The view of the animal as included in the rational implies the recognition of the cognitive nature of the emotions as good or bad judgments. Rightly ordered the passions are love (sublimated love of God) and courage (required for the ascetic discipline), and these two passions are most essential to the soul's ascent toward God. Wrongly ordered the passions are lust (leads to adultery) and anger (leads to murder), and these two passions result in a movement away from the lofty goods of God's kingdom.

It is quite apparent that the passions for Gregory, whether rightly or wrongly ordered, are seen as motivating forces or springs of action for good or evil respectively. Here we can recognize another aspect of Gregory's thought that is shared with our cognitive theory of emotion. Since the passions serve as motivating forces for both good and evil, the task is not to eliminate them from the Christian life but to direct them in pathways that attain to God as the supreme good.[92] The Christian has a history of subjective engagement in the world, and what this personal biography reveals in light of the gospel of Christ is the problematic nature of the passions and how they tend toward an evil end. The good news is that the transformation or right ordering of the passions comes by way of God's redemptive grace in Christ. Through the indwelling of grace in the soul the Christian is able to flourish through the sublimation of the soul's impulses, the elimination of errant judgments, steady growth in the virtues, and the firm hope of participating in the resurrection life to come.

Finally, our cognitive theory asserts that emotions are no mere feelings or bodily sensations, although the body is involved in emotional life by manifesting physiological changes appropriate to the particular emotion. Gregory's portrayal of the conjoining of the nutritive and sentient powers of the soul to the rational faculties serves to underscore the involvement of the body in emotional life. In such a perspective, the soul at each stage adds a new set of faculties to those of the stage immediately below it, from which it follows that the judgments of the reasoning mind are inseparable from the lower powers and activities of the soul. The unity of the trichotomous structure of the soul in Gregory's writings implies not only that the body is involved in emotional life, but ensures that the emotions are not reduced to mere bodily sensations or feelings.

Jonathan Edwards: True Religion Consists in Gracious Affections

No serious discussion of the emotions in the Christian tradition can avoid the writings of Jonathan Edwards on religious affections. Edwards wrote during a period dominated by revivalism in the region of New England, and especially that segment of it called The Great Awakening in the 1740s. There were two extreme poles of Christian religion that Edwards was concerned to address and repudiate: on the one hand, he addressed the problem of religion being reduced to a lifeless morality; and on the

---

92. For Gregory, reactions of fear and anger (*thymos*) to painful sense data, and reactions of desire and longing (*epithymia*) to pleasing sense data, are the principal emotions (*pathē*) by which all other actions are derived. This is quite similar to Augustine who speaks of four basic emotions, based on the two distinctions of good and bad, present and prospective: desire (object seen as good and prospective); joy (object seen as good and present); fear (object seen as evil and prospective); and grief (object seen as evil and present).

other, he dissociated himself from hysteria, excessive enthusiasm, and the spectacular commotions of revivalism. He therefore struggled with the central question of Puritan Protestantism: What are the distinguishing qualifications of those in whom the divine Spirit dwells? Or, which comes to the same thing, "What is the nature of true religion?"[93]

In his treatment of this fundamental question, Edwards made a concerted effort to articulate the "sense of the heart" required for individuals to be persuaded of the truth of the gospel. By being equipped with this new sense received by the "gracious" operation of the Spirit, people could directly apprehend or "see" the truth of the gospel.[94] In a climate where counterfeit religions abounded, Edwards recognized the necessity of articulating positive "signs" of true piety.[95] The true saints are those who have the sense of the heart, by which is meant that they display gracious or holy affections as the fruits of the Spirit dwelling in their souls in its own proper nature. Edwards's thesis is stated thus: "*True religion, in great part, consists in holy affections.*"[96] The phrase "in great part" has particular importance, for it indicates that Edwards did not want to swallow religion in the affections. The latter are necessary for true religion, but in the self they form a unity with the powers of understanding and will. The following text sets forth Edwards's view of true religion as consisting largely in holy affections:

> For although to true religion, there must indeed be something else besides affection; yet true religion consists so much in the affections, that there can be no true religion without them. He who has no religious affection, is in a state of spiritual death, and is wholly destitute of the powerful, quickening, saving influences of the Spirit of God upon his heart. As there is no true religion, where there is nothing else but affection; so there is no true religion where there is no religious affection. As on the one hand, there must be light in the understanding, as well as an

---

93. Edwards, *Religious Affections*, 84. The express aim of Edwards's study is set forth in the Preface to *Religious Affections*.

94. Calvinists distinguished between "common" and "saving" operations of the Spirit, and the term "gracious" applies to the latter alone. In the common work of the Spirit, the Spirit is thought of as operating on the self, as externally related to it; whereas in the gracious work of the Spirit, the Spirit is regarded as dwelling in the self in its own proper nature. See Edwards, *Religious Affections*, 6, 24, 202.

95. Edwards elaborated twelve distinguishing signs of gracious affections, which is the subject matter of part 3 of his *Religious Affections*.

96. Edwards, *Religious Affections*, 95.

affected fervent heart, where there is heat without light, there can be nothing divine or heavenly in that heart; so on the other hand, where there is a kind of light without heat, a head stored with notions and speculations, with a cold and unaffected heart, there can be nothing divine in that light . . . If the great things of religion are rightly understood, they will affect the heart.[97]

In this citation we clearly see that Edwards acknowledges the role played by the faculty of understanding in true religion, which he relates to the affections. For the sake of clarity, Edwards often makes rather sharp distinctions between the human powers of understanding, affections, and will, but the editor of *Religious Affections* makes the important point that "we must not overlook the extent to which these initial distinctions are overridden in the course of the argument."[98] The integrity of the self requires that its faculties be related to one another so as to preserve unity of the self. What is meant by the affections is clarified by how they stand in connection with the understanding and the will, which to Edwards's mind are the two faculties of the soul. The faculty of understanding is the capacity for perception and speculation, as well as discernment and judgment of things; while the faculty of will is that by which the soul not only perceives and views things, but in some way is inclined (attraction) or disinclined (aversion) to the things it views or considers.[99] When the inclination of the soul is expressed in action it is called "will," and when it is expressed through the mind alone it is called "heart." The affections form a class of more "vigorous" and "sensible" exercises of the will—they are vigorous enough to carry the self well beyond indifference.[100] The judgment involved in attraction or aversion to things in view is intimately related to what Edwards means by "heart." Inclination is not a blind affair since it is based on judgment of the objects of perception.

Edwards explains that the exercises of the inclination and will in the common actions of life are not ordinarily called affections; yet the latter are not essentially different from the will and inclination, differing

97. Edwards, *Religious Affections*, 120.
98. Edwards, *Religious Affections*, 11.
99. Edwards, *Religious Affections*, 96.

100. Edwards, *Religious Affections*, 97. Edwards makes a distinction between the "affections" and the "passions." He says that affection is something more extensive than passion, inasmuch as it refers to vigorous exercises of the will; whereas passion refers to "more sudden" and "violent" effects on the "animal spirits," so that the mind is "less in its own command." Edwards, *Religious Affections*, 98.

only in the degree and manner of exercise. What is more, just as all the exercises of the inclination and will are either in approving (liking) or disapproving (rejecting) of what is in view, so the affections are of two kinds: those by which the soul is "carried out" and cleaves to what is in view; and those by which the soul is "averse" from what is in view and opposes it. Of the former kind are the affections of "love, desire, hope, joy, gratitude, complacence," and of the latter sort are "hatred, fear, anger, grief, and such like."[101] The affections, though, are not merely regarded as a class of more vigorous exercises of the will, but are thought of as expressing the whole person, as giving insight into the basic orientation of the person's life; that is, his or her heart. The affections, says Edwards, are the *spring of human actions*, they carry us forward in life, they give vigor to human affairs: "take away all love and hatred, all hope and fear, all anger, zeal and affectionate desire, and the world would be, in a great measure, motionless and dead; there would be no such thing as activity amongst mankind, or any earnest pursuit whatsoever."[102] The true saints are those who have the sense of the heart, the essence of which is "holy love" as the springboard of all their actions.

As Edwards studied the Scriptures he discovered that true religion is based upon the chief affection of love of God. The essence of true religion lies in holy love. Edwards searched for a model of true religion in the Scriptures and he chose the text 1 Peter 1:8: "Without having seen him you love him; though you do not now see him you believe in him and rejoice with unutterable and exalted joy." What Edwards found especially convincing about this text is that it is a word addressed to the early Christian community during a time of persecution. He reasoned that in a time of suffering and affliction, when faith is tested in the fire of persecution and disbelief, religion will appear in its true form. True religion, according to the biblical text 1 Peter 1:8, consists in the affections of *love* and *joy*

---

101. Edwards, *Religious Affections*, 98. Note that Edwards's scheme is very similar to the Stoics who taught four generic types of emotions, according to whether what is in view is good (like) or bad (dislike), present or future. That which is present and good = joy or delight; prospective good = desire; present evil = grief or sorrow; prospective evil = fear. Edwards also talks of the soul being "carried out" to what is in view, which corresponds with the Stoic notion of the expanding soul in respect of present or prospective good, and he speaks of the soul being "averse" to what is in view, which corresponds to the Stoic idea of the contracting soul in respect of present or prospective evil.

102. Edwards, *Religious Affections*, 101.

in Christ. Love is treated not merely as one of the affections, but is held to be the first and chief of the affections, as the following text explains:

> For love is not only one of the affections, but it is the first and chief of the affections, and the fountain of all the affections. From love arises hatred of those things which are contrary to what we love, or which oppose and thwart us in those things that we delight in: and from the various exercises of love and hatred, according to the circumstances of the objects of these affections, as present or absent, certain or uncertain, probable or improbable, arise all those other affections of desire, hope, fear, joy, grief, gratitude, anger, etc. From a vigorous, affectionate, and fervent love to God, will necessarily arise other religious affections: hence will arise an intense hatred and abhorrence of sin, fear of sin, and a dread of God's displeasure, gratitude to God for his goodness, complacence and joy in God when God is graciously and sensibly present, and grief when he is absent, and a joyful hope when a future enjoyment of God is expected, and a fervent zeal for the glory of God. And in like manner, from a fervent love to men, will arise all other virtuous affections towards men.[103]

On the basis of Edwards's understanding that in every act of the will the soul is either inclined or disinclined to what is in view, when the liking or disliking of the perceived object is experienced to a high degree the person experiences the affections of love and hatred respectively. Once the soul is affected by the indwelling Spirit and is inclined toward God and experiences love of God, that primary and fundamental religious affection becomes the cornerstone of all other religious affections such as: joy and delight in Christ the Redeemer, hatred and fear of sin, gratitude to God for what he has done for us in Christ, hope of sharing in Christ's resurrection life, zeal for the glory of God, and grief when God is experienced as absent. A lively and vigorous love of God in turn gives rise to a fervent love of one's fellow human beings, from which ensues virtuous affections towards them. Here we have before us the two great commandments as taught by Christ: "You shall love the Lord your God with all your heart, and with all your soul, and with all your mind. This is the great and first commandment. And a second is like it, You shall love your neighbour as yourself. On these two commandments depend all the law and the prophets" (Matt 22:37–40).

---

103. Edwards, *Religious Affections*, 107–8.

With regard to the holy affections that arise through the Spirit as dwelling in the soul in its own proper nature, Edwards makes the point that no new faculties of the soul are involved in order to experience this new spiritual sense of the heart. The new dispositions that attend the heart of the true saints are regarded as new "principles of nature." The latter term refers to that foundation which is laid in nature and forms the basis for any particular kind of exercise of the faculties of the soul. Edwards explains this point thus:

> So this new spiritual sense is not a new faculty of understanding, but it is a new foundation laid in the nature of the soul, for a new kind of exercises of the same faculty of understanding. So that new holy disposition of heart that attends this new sense, is not a new faculty of will, but a foundation laid in the nature of the soul, for a new kind of exercises of the same faculty of will.[104]

When Edwards talks of a new spiritual sense, he means that which is born of the Spirit, a relation to the Spirit of Christ dwelling in the soul, influencing the heart as a principle of "new nature." The gracious affections are supernatural inasmuch as the effects of the indwelling Spirit are "above nature;" that is, they cannot be produced as a compounding of things natural. Grace involves a new inward perception or sensation, which is regarded as a principle of new nature. The new foundation laid in the nature of the soul is expressed through the powers of the self—i.e., understanding, will, and affections—without destroying their essential natures.[105] This perspective of a new nature through the Spirit dwelling in the soul is no different from the picture painted by Augustine or Gregory of Nyssa, who both, we saw earlier, contend that Christian ascent involves the *redirecting* of human love and desire away from earthly objects towards God as the new object of ineffable delight and exalted joy. Human affections and Christian affections are therefore to be seen not as two different stories, but two parts of one and the same story, for the effects of grace do not involve new faculties of the soul but the introduction of a new principle of nature—a new inward perception that inclines the soul towards God through the exercises of gracious affections. One of the signs of gracious affections is that they are attended by a "change of

---

104. Edwards, *Religious Affections*, 206.

105. The editor of *Religious Affections* points out that Edwards thus sides with the theological tradition which regards the finite as having a capacity for the infinite: the Spirit expresses itself through the created world. See Edwards, *Religious Affections*, 26.

nature," which is to say they are "transforming."[106] To use more biblical language, gracious affections "turn a heart of stone more and more into a heart of flesh."[107]

Another distinguishing sign that Edwards advances, which is worth drawing attention to, concerns the spiritual appetite or longing of gracious affections. This is presented as the eleventh distinguishing sign of gracious affections. Edwards argues that the higher the gracious affections are raised, the greater the spiritual longing of the soul, which is quite distinct from the false affections that rest satisfied in themselves. His thinking on this particular sign is set forth as follows:

> The more a true saint loves God with a gracious love, the more he desires to love him, and the more uneasy is he at his want of love to him: the more he hates sin, the more he desires to hate it, and laments that he has so much remaining love to it: the more he mourns for sin, the more he longs to mourn for sin: the more his heart is broke, the more he desires it should be broke: the more he thirsts and longs after God and holiness, the more he longs to long, and breathe out his very soul in longings after God: the kindling and raising of gracious affections is like kindling a flame; the higher it is raised, the more ardent it is; and the more it burns, the more vehemently does it tend and seek to burn.[108]

The thought of Edwards here is akin both to Augustine's portrayal of the restlessness of the heart that yearns for blissful union with God, and to Gregory of Nyssa's dynamic view of desire (*erōs*) as never exhausted either in this life or in the age to come. In the true saints, says Edwards, there is no abating of desire for more spiritual maturity and perfection; there is "no tendency to satiety."[109] The true saints on earth know what divine love and joy in the soul are, and Edwards envisions the religion of heaven as consisting in a much higher degree of the same holy affections of love and joy. The affections of the saints in heaven are "exceedingly great and vigorous; impressing the heart with the strongest and most lively sensation, of inexpressible sweetness, mightily moving, animating,

---

106. Edwards, *Religious Affections*, 340. That gracious affections are attended by a change of nature is discussed as Edwards's seventh sign of gracious affections.
107. Edwards, *Religious Affections*, 360.
108. Edwards, *Religious Affections*, 377.
109. Edwards, *Religious Affections*, 377.

and engaging them, making them like a flame of fire."[110] The language here certainly is dynamic and tends to convey the idea of an ever-deeper participation in the ineffable sweetness, beauty, and glory of God. This would suggest that Edwards's position is not all that far removed from Gregory of Nyssa's doctrine of *epectasy*.

The primary focus of Edwards's writing is the gracious affections of the true saints, but in elaborating his understanding of the nature of true religion Edwards perforce has to consider the holy affections of Jesus Christ, whose spirit lives in the heart of the saints as an "internal vital principle," exerting its own proper nature, in the exercise of the faculties of the soul.[111] On the view that the saints are those who bear the image of Christ who lives in their hearts "as in his temple and as one that is alive from the dead," it follows that the *holy affections of Christ must become the gracious affections of the saints*.[112] The gracious affections of the saints are attended with a change of nature; that is, "with the lamblike, dovelike spirit and temper of Jesus Christ . . . they naturally beget and promote such a spirit of love, meekness, quietness, forgiveness and mercy, as appeared in Christ."[113] Edwards asserts that he whom God sent into the world to be the Light of the world and the perfect example of true religion, was a person of affectionate heart: "his virtue was expressed very much in the exercise of holy affections."[114] The holy affections of Christ are seen as expressing the whole man, as giving insight into the basic orientation of his life, and as providing the springboard of his redemptive activity. This is especially evident in Edwards's depiction of Christ's passion. He writes that it was the vigor and strength of Christ's holy love, to both God and fallen humanity, that won the victory on Calvary. This holy love did not overcome the heightened sense of fear or dread on the part of Christ in a facile manner, but was involved in a veritable and mighty struggle, which the following text makes plain:

> It was these affections that got the victory, in that mighty struggle and conflict of his affections, in his agonies, when he prayed more earnestly, and offered strong crying and tears, and wrestled

110. Edwards, *Religious Affections*, 114.
111. Edwards, *Religious Affections*, 392.
112. Edwards, *Religious Affections*, 392. This point emerges from Edwards's discussion of the twelfth distinguishing sign; namely, that gracious affections have their exercise and fruit in Christian practice.
113. Edwards, *Religious Affections*, 344–45.
114. Edwards, *Religious Affections*, 111.

in tears and in blood. Such was the power of the exercises of his holy love, that they were stronger than death, and in that great struggle, overcame those strong exercises of the natural affections of fear and grief, when he was sore amazed, and his soul was exceedingly sorrowful, even unto death.[115]

The virtues of Christ—such as humility, meekness, love, forgiveness, and mercy—were most dramatically on display in his passion, and the strong language used by Edwards leaves us in no doubt about the reality of the immensity of Christ's wrestling with his natural affections of utter dread and fear, which he was able to endure and overcome by the exercises of his holy love, thereby winning for us the victory over the powers of death. All the virtues of the Lamb of God are exhibited in those unutterable sufferings that he endured as the dreadful effects of our sins. Edwards then goes on to discuss how Christ was full of affection not only in his passion, but also in the entire course of his life. Edwards gives examples from the Scriptures of Christ's great zeal, his being grieved for the hardness of people's hearts, his bitter weeping over Jerusalem, the tenderness of his heart full of pity and compassion, his being moved by the mourning of Mary and Martha over the death of Lazarus, and his earnest desire to eat the Passover with his disciples. A special place is given to Jesus' dying discourse in John 17, about which Edwards writes: "Of all the discourses ever penned, or uttered by the mouth of any man, this seems to be the most affectionate, and affecting."[116]

Finally, how does Edwards's portrayal of the religious affections compare with the cognitive theory of emotion presented in chapter 1 of this study? To begin with, Edwards certainly does affirm a broadly cognitive view of the affections insofar as he relates the faculty of the will to the faculty of understanding. An attraction (love) or aversion (hatred) to something in view is based on *judgment* of the object of perception, thus affection is not thought of as a blind affair. The judgment involved in attraction or aversion to things is very closely related to what Edwards means by the term "heart." Sin is referred to as hardness of heart, by which is meant an unaffected or stony heart, whereas the saints, who display gracious affections, have a heart of flesh. Conversion becomes possible when the soul is affected and the will inclined to God, and at this point Edwards's writings share another major feature of the cognitive model presented in chapter 1; namely, the affections are motivational

---

115. Edwards, *Religious Affections*, 111–12.
116. Edwards, *Religious Affections*, 112.

forces or the *spring of human actions* in the circumstances of our lives. If we were to take away the affections, there would no longer be any potential for action, no power to heal (benefit) or to wound (harm), or for any earnest pursuit whatsoever in the world. And it would also be difficult to account for the steadfast actions of God in relation to his created reality, as recounted in the Jewish and Christian scriptures.

A third component of Edwards's work that overlaps with our presentation of a cognitive theory of emotion is his understanding of the *interrelatedness of the affections*. He takes love as the first and chief of the affections, from which arises hatred of those things that are contrary to what we love and delight in. From the various exercises of love and hatred, according to the circumstances of the objects of these affections as present or absent, certain or uncertain, arise all those other affections such as desire, hope, fear, joy, grief, gratitude, and anger. Edwards gives the example of how fervent love to God, manifested by the true saints, will inevitably give rise to intense hatred of sin, fear of sinning, gratitude to God for his merciful goodness, joy when God is graciously present, grief when God is absent, hope in expected enjoyment of God beyond death, and zeal for the glory of God. In like manner, from a fervent love to our fellow human beings will arise all other virtuous affections towards them. The affections, then, do not merely share common features, but are closely intertwined and logically related to one another in the argument proffered by Edwards.

A fourth and final point that Edwards's thought shares with our cognitive theory of emotion is that the affections of adult life have a history. While Edwards does not expressly talk of the affections as arising from a history of personal engagement in the world, he does nonetheless implicitly acknowledge the affections as having *a personal biography* when he asserts that they give insight into the basic orientation of a person's life. The basic attitudes of a person are formed over a period of time and emerge from the historical circumstances of a person's upbringing and social-cultural conditioning. A person's basic orientation to life can change, though, and Edwards conceives of such a change as involving a transformation of the affections inasmuch as they are directed toward a new intentional object. The religious affections of the saints represent a transformation of their basic orientation to life, for love of God becomes the first and chief of their affections, from which flow all the other affections integral to the life of putting on Christ and bearing his image in the world. In sum, there can be no doubt that Edwards's view of the religious affections is basically a cognitive view that shares most of the major points highlighted and elaborated in chapter 1 of this study.

Conclusion: Christian Emotions and the Problem of Sin

It is clear from the foregoing discussion that Augustine, Gregory, and Edwards all conceive of the human being as a union of body and soul, and do not attribute the problems posed by the emotions to the body per se, but to the judgments of the rational soul. It is the mind that is the proper seat of the emotions, and their cognitive character as judgments is what underpins the contention that emotions can undergo change and transformation. All three thinkers conceive of desire as having a malleable quality and hence as something that needs to be *rightly directed* by being carried out to God as the true object of its seeking. Gregory refers to the purified state of the soul as "impassible desire" or "dispassionate passion," by which is meant desire that ceases to be a passion in the pejorative sense because it is directed toward God as its right object. This is not the same as the Stoic position on *apatheia*, which is evident when Gregory talks of rightly ordered desire in terms of *erōs*. Augustine is certainly explicit about the notion of *apatheia*, which he regards as a denial of our true human condition before God. Augustine repudiates *apatheia* if by this term is meant that no negative emotions can affect the soul, that no fear frightens and no grief pains the virtuous man. He says that Christians fear eternal punishment for their sinfulness, they desire eternal life by God's grace, they grieve in that they are groaning for the redemption of their bodies, and they rejoice in the hope that death will be swallowed up in Christ's victory. Edwards is certainly closer to Augustine's thought in respect of *apatheia*, for he gives much emphasis to the true saints as having a fear of sin and a dread of God's displeasure, as experiencing grief when God is absent, and sorrow that arises from a contrite heart. If by *apatheia* is meant the extirpation of disturbing emotions such as fear, dread, and grief, as well as the acceptance of only those affective responses that fall under the Stoic category of *eupatheiai*, then Edwards is certainly not an advocate of the Stoic position. For he argues that true religion consists, in large measure, in the fervent exercises of the heart, in vigorous and sensible exercises of the will, which he calls gracious affections. All three thinkers share the view that the Christian task is not to eliminate the emotions but to redirect them toward God as their proper object.

In this process of redirecting the emotions of love and desire away from earthly objects towards God as their new object, all three thinkers share the understanding that the dwelling of Christ's grace in the soul does not involve new faculties of the soul but the introduction of a new principle of nature; that is, a new inward perception that inclines the soul towards God and gives rise to a new kind of exercises of the same faculties of the soul. The participation of nature in grace is expressed through all the created powers of the soul without destroying the essential nature of the soul. The emotions are thought of as modes of willing—i.e., motivational forces—and we have seen how all three theologians attribute a foundational role to the emotion of love—love of God is the first and chief of the emotions. Differences do arise, nonetheless, in relation to the degree to which one can ascend towards God in this life. Gregory, informed by his distinctive idea of perpetual progress (*epectasy*) in the knowledge and love of God's goodness and beauty, is more optimistic than Augustine about the training or educating of desire in this life. "There is a sense for Gregory in which we can even now *participate* in the new age, but for Augustine the best we can hope for is an *anticipation* of the rest in eternal peace."[117] Augustine's emphasis is on the gap between the here and now and the there and then; and yet he is unwilling to make the gap between the two ages an absolute, bridging it not with knowledge and fulfillment, but with the theological virtues of faith, hope, and charity.[118] Gregory is more confident that already in the here and now we can participate in God and grow in virtue, and this present participation in the supreme good bolsters Christian hope in the resurrection life to come.

Gregory has much to say concerning the moral qualities or virtues of the Christian, which enable the soul to attain to God. To follow God means to pursue the life of virtue, to become involved in an ever-greater imitation of Christ in action, word, and thought. What we are taught by Gregory is to have but one purpose in life: "to be called servants of God by virtue of the lives we live."[119] To become a servant of God is to become a friend of God, which is the only thing worthy of honor and

---

117. Greer, *Christian Hope*, 113.
118. Greer, *Christian Hope*, 117.
119. Gregory of Nyssa, *Life of Moses*, 135.

desire. Christianity is "an imitation of the divine nature,"[120] and whoever lives a virtuous life free from evil lives a transformed life; that is, they live already in heaven. By participating in Christ, the Christian shares in the "lofty ideas" which such participation implies. The names of the virtues, each referring to the divine nature of Christ, convey these lofty ideas.[121] Christ is given to us as a great gift from God, and Gregory sees it necessary to conduct our lives as a testimony to the great name of Christ. Gregory writes as if Christian perfection is an attainable ideal, and this is consistent with his view of rightly ordered emotions as being love (erotic desire for God) and courage (for the ascetic discipline).

This perspective is very different to what Augustine has to say in his later writings, where we are presented with a mediocre Christianity still caught in an ongoing and bitter struggle between the desired good and the persistence of evil temptation. Unlike Gregory, Augustine magnifies the Lord's name as a sinful and wretched man, not as someone whose virtuous life gives testimony to the great name of Christ. Augustine considers himself among the weak members of Christ's body; he casts all his cares upon the Lord who is exceedingly merciful and his only happiness is to take joy in praising God's abundant grace in Christ. Worship and prayer is primarily the way to God for Augustine, not the moral life of virtue. What the emotions serve to register is the true human condition before God, thus it is the language of lament and anticipation that shines through Augustine's portrayal of the Christian life. His *Confessions* is a moving portrayal of the lament genre and its ability to bring consolation to the faithful who are suffering and grieving over the loss of goods. The lament speech form is aptly suited to conveying the complex and baffling profundities of the human condition in the world, and effectively warning us not to expect a smooth and linear development of moral character or a golden age of justice in the world. The battle both within and without is a veritable struggle, punctuated by moments of success and joy and justice, to be sure, but our sighing and yearning for the New Jerusalem remains an integral part of our existential landscape. As stated earlier, "To recover the voice of lament is to recover the voice of prayer as it has

---

120. Gregory of Nyssa, "On What it Means," 85.

121. The virtues are those things associated with the great name of Christ; namely, justice, wisdom, power, truth, goodness, life, salvation, permanence, incorruptibility, and lack of change. See Gregory of Nyssa, "On What it Means," 84. We cannot imitate all the traits implied by the name of Christ; we imitate some in pursuing the life of moral perfection, while we revere and worship others.

defined the human reality before God." The voice of lament is the voice of our humanity; it is the expression of our being here as sentient and existential beings, who feel and hurt, who suffer and despair, who cry and try to speak in order to renew faith in God and firm up our hope in the life to come.

Edwards is certainly closer to Augustine's thought when it comes to rejecting the notion of *apatheia* and acknowledging the ongoing role played by negative emotions in the life of the saints—the true saints have a fear of sin and a dread of God's displeasure, and experience grief when God is absent and sorrow that arises from a contrite heart. But when the discussion turns to the issue of the virtuous life of Christians, Edwards is definitely closer to the more optimistic position held by Gregory. The life of the saints must reflect evermore the holy affections of Christ—Christ's holy affections must become the gracious affections of the true saints. The language used by Edwards is very much intended to convey the idea of the present participation of nature in grace. The Spirit of Christ indwelling the soul influences the hearts of the saints as a principle of new nature, as a divine spring of life and action, hence gracious affections are attended with "the lamblike, dovelike spirit and temper of Jesus Christ." The Christian life for Edwards, similar to Gregory, is understood as a bearing of the image of Christ, as a putting on Christ.

This chapter has sought to elaborate the views of three eminent thinkers in the theological tradition who do not espouse a severe asceticism, but recognize the constructive role that the emotions play in the Christian ascent to God. The conversion to Christ involves not the extirpation of the emotions but the right ordering of the emotions away from earthly objects toward the heavenly object of God, who alone can satisfy the deep yearning and longing of the human heart. Yet despite the generally positive appraisals given of these three thinkers, there is, to my mind, a basic problem that is discernible in their writings: namely, the influence of the Stoic idea of the passions as sicknesses of the soul. It is clear that Augustine regards the present perturbations of his soul as signs of the enduring consequences of Adam's sin. Adam prior to committing sin was in a state of *apatheia*—i.e., freedom from the passions of fear, grief, sadness, and anger—and Augustine laments the tragic results of Adam's transgression as his soul is burdened with the sickness of sin.[122] The *negative emotions of fear, grief, sadness, and anger serve merely to bring to*

---

122. For Augustine's view on *apatheia* as a desirable quality, see Augustine, *City of God*, XIV, 9.

light the profound sickness of sin in his soul, which can only be healed by God, who is the all-merciful physician. A basic problem with Augustine's thinking is that since everything is geared to the sickness of human sin, we are presented with a perspective of the Christian's emotional life that is too pessimistic and limited. Augustine's fundamental desire is to enjoy the blissful peace of eternal life, but since his soul is plagued by the tragedy and sickness of sin, the congenial emotions of love of God and joy in God are not depicted as the atmosphere of the Christian life. Instead, Augustine is more focused on images of descent than ascent to God. He talks a lot about how he fears eternal condemnation for sin, feels sorrow for sins committed, struggles with the life of virtue, has a restless heart, and grieves for the redemption of his mortal body. Moments of delight in God are few and irregular, and joy is more of a prospective joy in the hope that death will be swallowed up in victory. Augustine paints a picture of his soul as so terribly burdened by sin that sighing and lament appear as the atmosphere of the Christian life.

Gregory's thought on the Christian ascent to God also restricts the passions to the problem of sin. This is apparent in his notion of the erotic desire for God as an "impassible desire." By the latter Gregory means desire that shifts its focus from the flesh—i.e., errant judgment due to sin—to the divine goodness and beauty—i.e., good judgment due to the workings of grace—and is therefore free from the common passions. Gregory highlights the common passions of lust and anger in particular, given that they lead to adultery and murder, and thus wreak much havoc in people's lives and in the social order. But fear and grief, since they are associated with mortality, are also recognized as common passions experienced by fallen humanity. As in Augustine, the negative emotions serve no other purpose than to bring to light the sickness of the soul burdened by the realities of sin and mortality. The good news is that by virtue of the redeeming grace of Christ, the rational soul of the Christian is able to turn its attention to the divine goodness and beauty, and so desires to progress in the life of virtue. The conception of the Christian life as a progressive participation in the divine nature does not allow Gregory to assign any significance to the role of the negative and suffering emotions beyond illuminating the problem of sin, and the mortality that is the result of sin. There can be no real cause for lament in this life, for the Christian is called a servant and friend of God by virtue of the life they lead, which is thought of as an imitation of the divine nature. The focus in Gregory is very much on the ascent to God through the positive emotions of love of God and courage for the ascetic discipline, which engender Christian hope in the resurrection life to come.

Edwards's thought on the new sense of the heart displayed by the saints is no different from that of Augustine or Gregory in that his focus too is on the problem of sin, and the common passions are closely tied to this fundamental sickness of the soul. In a manner similar to Augustine, Edwards repudiates *apatheia* as the ideal of the Christian life and maintains that from the chief emotion of love of God arise other emotions, such as: hatred of sin; fear of sin; dread of God's displeasure; gratitude to God for his goodness; joy when God is present and grief when God is absent; hope when enjoyment of God is expected; and zeal for the glory of God. Yet in all this it is apparent how Edwards's thought limits Christian emotions to the problem of sin. Fear is limited to the prospect of eternal condemnation for individual sins; grief is restricted to moments when God is felt to be absent; sorrow arises only from a contrite heart; anger is not acknowledged as a legitimate emotion that expresses indignation in the face of injustice and evil; and compassion is confined to a spirit of forgiveness towards other sinners. Despite the notable optimism regarding the transforming power of the gracious affections of the saints, Edwards's reflections are nonetheless confined to the problem of individual sin. No reflections are offered on the distinctive character of the Christian life as the way of the cross, on the dread associated with Jesus' radical command to love our enemies, on grieving for people's hardness of heart, on suffering as the vocation of the faithful who bear in their bodies the dying of Jesus so that the life of Jesus is manifested to the world, or on the role of Christian lament as ontologically joined to Christ's cry of lament on the cross. The same can be said of Augustine and Gregory, both of whom also restrict the role played by the suffering emotions in the Christian life. It is true that Augustine's soul endures much suffering, but his suffering is due to the enduring problem of sin in his life and his deep yearning for the peace of eternal life. It is not a suffering that springs from having before us the crucified Christ as the object of the suffering emotions. Gregory too acknowledges that there is suffering in the Christian life, but the suffering in view stems from the difficulty of pursuing the life of virtue, which is why courage is required to continue with the soul's ascent to God. As in the case of Augustine, suffering is limited to the individual's ongoing struggle with the reality of sin, although Gregory is considerably more optimistic about the educating of desire in this life than Augustine is.

All three thinkers display the tendency not to attribute any significance to the negative emotions of the Christian life, other than their ability to expose the defects of soul and individual sufferings consequent upon Adam's sin. This fundamental point will be returned to in the concluding chapter to this study, where reflections will be offered on the important roles played by the negative and suffering emotions over and above their function in revealing the problem of individual sin. The reflections on the Christian emotions offered at the end of this study will seek to draw attention to integral dimensions of Christian life that give voice to the corporate and social elements of the Gospel of Christ, such as the following: the distinctive character of Christian life as the way of the cross; suffering as the vocation of the faithful who bear in their bodies the dying of Jesus so that the life of Jesus may be manifested to the world; the notion of righteous anger as reflective of the Christian's strong moral sense in the face of evil in the world; a broader conception of compassion that goes beyond recognizing the other person's need for God's forgiveness in Christ; and the indispensable role played by lament which should not be restricted to the grief caused by the individual's awareness of abiding sinfulness in oneself, but opens out onto a broader horizon when Christian lament is regarded as ontologically joined to Christ's cry of lament on the cross.

When the mystery of the incarnation of the eternal Word is reflected upon in dynamic and truly historical terms as the fullness of divinity that dwells bodily in the developing humanity of the man Jesus—which accomplishes the deification of humanity in his person—then the incarnation should be regarded not merely as a past event but as the "ongoing embodiment of God in those who follow Christ."[123] To follow Christ means that his congenial *and* suffering emotions are to be reflected in his followers who bear his image as a beacon of light, salvation, and hope to the world. Christian life as an imitation of the richness, depth, and transforming power of Christ's emotional life is nowhere better summed up than in Jesus' radical teaching in the Beatitudes concerning love of enemies: "But I say to you, love your enemies and pray for those who persecute you, so that you may be sons of your Father who is in heaven; for he makes his sun rise on the evil and on the good, and sends rain on the just and on the unjust" (Matt 5:44–45). Dietrich Bonhoeffer reflected at length on this distinctive teaching of Jesus in the Beatitudes, in order

---

123. Behr, *John the Theologian*, Preface.

to underscore the hallmark of Christian life as the "extraordinary," the "unusual," that which is not "a matter of course."[124] When we merely love those who love us, says Bonhoeffer, we behave in a manner that is no better than the heathen or publican, whose love is ordinary and natural. What Jesus the Savior intends by the quality of love is something very different, for it takes his followers along the way of the cross, which is the victory of divine love over the enemy's hatred and hardness of heart. The disciples of Christ are required not only to passively and patiently endure evil, but *to actively engage in heartfelt love towards their enemies.*[125]

In the next chapter the focus will shift to offering a critique of the theological tradition's treatment of the emotions of Christ. If the process of putting on Christ involves an ongoing conversion of the emotions as the Christian faithful increasingly imitate the emotions of Christ, then it follows that Christ's emotional life becomes a foundational consideration for theology. How did the affirmation of Christ's full divinity influence the treatment of his emotional life? What influence did Stoic teaching on the passions as sicknesses of the soul, as well as the Stoic teaching on first movements of the soul (*propatheia*), have in respect of christological reflection on Christ's emotional life? Did the emotions run their full course in Christ as they do in us? Were the emotions of Christ real? Can we credibly affirm the humanity of the incarnate Word and the process of kenosis in his person if his emotions did not run their full course? Does the theological tradition portray Christ as a Stoic sage? What significance, if any, does the theological tradition accord to Christ's emotions in respect of the deification of humanity in his person? These probing questions will be addressed in the following two chapters, before returning to discuss a contemporary understanding of the emotions of Christian life—a "new heart"—in the concluding chapter.

---

124. Bonhoeffer, *Cost of Discipleship*, 152.
125. Bonhoeffer, *Cost of Discipleship*, 148.

3

Christ's Emotions in the Theological Tradition

The Need to Go Beyond Stoicism

THE DISCUSSION IN THE previous chapter was focused not on the emotions of Christ, but on the role that the emotions play in the Christian ascent to God. It was shown in what manner Augustine of Hippo, Gregory of Nyssa, and Jonathan Edwards all maintain the basic position that the emotions are not to be eradicated but corrected by redirecting them to the love of God and the goal of beatific union with God in eternity. All the discussion hitherto has been about the emotions of baptized Christians, but it is now time to turn our attention to how the emotions of Christ have been depicted and conceived in the theological tradition, and what role they might play in the mystery of the incarnation and the work of redemption and salvation wrought by the God-Man. In the field of patristic theology, "scholars have noted a certain patristic reserve toward Christ's emotions."[1] While patristic thinkers affirmed the reality of Christ's humanity, they tended to hesitate when confronted with the implications of affirming a human nature in Christ. The Dominican scholar Jean-Paul Torrell makes the point that "the general influence of Stoic philosophy, with its estimation of the passions as sicknesses of the soul, offered little encouragement to Christian thinkers to pause and reflect on Christ's human feelings."[2] The discernible patristic reserve

---

1. Coolman, "Hugh of St. Victor," 529.
2. Gondreau, *Passions of Christ's Soul*, 8.

toward Christ's emotions, which will become apparent during the course of the discussion in this chapter, is not, by contrast, something that can be said of the medieval theologians, many of whom pursued the topic with considerable vigor. Aquinas, for example, reflected at length on the topic of Christ's passions and he has bequeathed to us a profound treatment of Christ's human affectivity "in a way that few theologians have had the determination to do in the history of Christian thought."[3]

Yet notwithstanding Thomas's positive account of human passions, which was briefly reviewed in the introduction to this study, his treatment of Christ's passions is restricted to the "defects of soul" that belong to the condition of human nature in the aftermath of Adam's sin.[4] This narrow approach focuses exclusively on those passions of Christ that involve suffering and a reaction to evil, while ignoring the congenial side of Christ's passions that relate to the good, such as love (see Mark 10:21), joy (see Luke 10:21), and desire (see Luke 22:15).[5] Paul Gondreau in his comprehensive study of Aquinas notes that the scholastics tended to follow the standard set by John Damascene who "restricts the scope of inquiry to only those passions in Christ that ensue upon the sense perception of some evil, such as fear, agony, sorrow, and the like, and hence, to those passions that bring about suffering, or those passions that emerge as consequences of sin."[6] In addition to this restricted inquiry of Christ's passions, a further potential problem, as will become apparent in this chapter, is that Aquinas regards each passion of Christ as a "propassion" (*propatheia*), which denotes a passion that is under the control of reason and therefore never amounts to a perturbation of Christ's soul. In effect, Christ is depicted as being in the same situation as Adam before the fall, whereby the sensitive appetite, under the influence of original grace, submitted perfectly to reason and will, thereby enabling Adam to live in full harmony both with himself and with God. Aquinas also holds, on the other hand, that Christ shares in the condition of Adam after the

---

3. Gondreau, *Passions of Christ's Soul*, 457.

4. *Summa theologiae* III 15. Cited in Lombardo, *Logic of Desire*, 203. The most significant of Aquinas's predecessors on the topic of Christ's passions were Hilary of Poitiers, Augustine, John Damascene, Peter Lombard, Alexander of Hales, Albert the Great, and Bonaventure. See Gondreau, *Passions of Christ's Soul*, 48–100.

5. Aquinas discusses five passions in Christ: sensible pain, sorrow, fear, wonder, and anger. Christ is depicted as taking on these passions voluntarily, and so gives them soteriological value.

6. Gondreau, *Passions of Christ's Soul*, 66.

fall, which is to say that he assumed our humanity with its passibility and mortality, for soteriological reasons. Yet Christ's experience of assuming humanity is conceived as much more harmonious than our own, for he was free of original sin and its associated effects, which is why the notion of "propassion" is applied to Christ. The "spirit-flesh" conflict that characterizes all other human beings is not something that can be applied to Christ, for the hypostatic union guarantees the perfection of grace and harmony in Christ's soul. The humanity of Christ is affirmed as real and genuine, yet at the same time it is clearly different from the rest of humanity in significant ways, which does raise difficulties for a contemporary theology of the incarnation where the concern is to conceive of Christ's humanity as being the same as ours, sin only excepted—i.e., a true kenosis of the eternal word of God.

This chapter will often refer to Augustine and Aquinas, but several other notable theologians will be brought into the discussion, including Gregory of Nyssa, Hilary of Poitiers, Cyril of Alexandria, Maximus the Confessor, John Damascene, John Calvin, Jonathan Edwards, Martin Luther, Karl Barth, Eberhard Jüngel, and Sergius Bulgakov. The purpose of the discussion will be to highlight the inability of patristic thought in particular to admit that the divine Word truly descended into the temporal realm of human being. The strong emphasis on the divinity of Christ—which is a feature of medieval Christology as well as patristic theology—admits no possibility of Christ being clothed with our Adamic flesh and subject to human becoming or the temptation of evil. It will be argued that this traditional perspective represents not only a failure to formulate an adequately developed notion of kenosis, but is also an obstacle to appreciating the depth and richness of Christ's emotional life as the manifestation of the process whereby each of the two natures advances through the other in his historical life and mission of proclaiming the kingdom of grace to Israel. The main problem with Christian thinking in the past is that the strong emphasis on Christ's divinity as the Word gave rise to the conception of his humanity as merely a passive instrument of his redemptive mission. Once the passivity of Christ's humanity in the work of redemption is affirmed, the result is that his emotional life is not described in strong affective language that conveys the veritable struggle in bringing his Adamic flesh under the guidance of his spirit, so as to live a life of perfect obedience to the Father. Also integral to this chapter will be a critical discussion of the related inadequacies in the theological

CHRIST'S EMOTIONS IN THE THEOLOGICAL TRADITION   125

tradition with regard to the issue of the interpenetration of the two natures in the person of the God-Man.

The critical reviews will prepare the way for the final section of the chapter that features the formulation of a proposition that is the main thesis of this study. It will be proposed that Jesus' emotional life should be viewed as the outworking of the mutual interaction of humanity and divinity in his person and the springboard of his messianic mission to Israel, and thereby provides a privileged window through which to observe the process of salvation—understood as deification—in his person. The kind of deification in view here is a truly "passionate deification" that acknowledges a number of crucial elements that should feature in a contemporary Christology, including: a properly developed idea of kenosis; the real participation of divinity in the human realm; the notion of a progressive incarnation where each of the natures advances through the other; and Jesus' veritable struggle in bringing his Adamic flesh into perfect communion with the Father through the agony, anguish, and sorrow of his passion. In all this dramatic story of God's visitation of his people is revealed the truth of Immanuel's humanity as an exhibition of the reality of our redemption and salvation, as well as the truth of what God is really like. What will also emerge is the view that the crucified Lord, since he has borne our sorrows in his sorrows and has passed through a truly human life like ours, remains forever able to be touched by our infirmities, and we are forever able to be touched by his holy affections towards us.

I. Patristic and Medieval Thought: Christ the Stoic Sage

Let us begin the discussion with Augustine, whose thought was discussed at some length in the previous chapter 2 of this study. After having discussed the manner in which the perturbations of the soul appear as right affections in the righteous or baptized, Augustine then goes on to relate these emotions of the Christian to the emotions of Christ. He writes:

> For this reason, even the Lord himself, when he condescended to live a human life in the form of a servant (although wholly without sin), showed these emotions where he judged that they ought to be shown. For there was nothing fake about the human emotion of one who had a true human body and a true human mind. It is certainly not false, therefore, when the Gospel reports that he was grieved and angered at the Jews' hardness of heart (Mk 3:5), or that he said, *For your sake I am glad so*

> *that you may believe* (Jn 11:15), or that he even shed tears when he was about to raise Lazarus (Jn 11:35), or that he desired to eat the Passover with his disciples (Lk 22:15), or that his soul was grieved when his passion drew near (Mt 26:38). Rather, for the sake of his fixed purpose, he took on these emotions in his human mind when he willed, just as he became man when he willed.[7]

In this key text Augustine clearly states—as a rejoinder to Stoic and docetic views that were common in his day—that because Christ possessed a true human body and a true human soul, there was nothing fake about the human emotions he showed. This passage also reveals that any discussion of Christ's passions must include an unequivocal acknowledgement that he is wholly without sin, given the view that the affective side of human existence shares in the consequences of sin. The Lord had no sin whatever and yet he showed emotions when he willed to show them. A problematic tension arises here between a sinless passible Christ on the one hand, and a Christ who shares in the defects of human affectivity on the other. This tension "will pervade the entire Medieval discussion on Christ's passions, Thomas Aquinas included."[8] In order to resolve this tension, Augustine proposes that all affective movements in Christ's soul are strictly controlled by the commands of reason: the Lord "showed these emotions where he judged that they ought to be shown," and "he took on these emotions in his human mind when he willed." In the same chapter of his *City of God* Augustine explains that our emotions are peculiar to this life and they arise from human infirmity or weakness, but it was not so with the Lord Jesus, "for even his weakness was an expression of his power."[9] Christ was not liable to infirmity, yet by his power he chose to lay down his life for the sake of our redemption—forgiveness of sins and the swallowing up of our mortality—and when it pleased him he exercised certain emotions to show that he shared in the consequences of Adam's sin.[10] Augustine is keen to uphold Christ's genuine humanity and

---

7. Augustine, *City of God*, XIV, 9.
8. Gondreau, *Passions of Christ's Soul*, 54.
9. Augustine, *City of God*, XIV, 9.
10. Elsewhere Augustine writes: "taking for our example Christ who, although He was not liable to death by any sin, and was the Lord, whose life no one could take away, Himself laid down His life, so that even for Him there was *an issue of death*" (*Enar, in Ps*. 67. XX.29). Cited by Bonner, "Augustine's Conception," 383.

possession of a human soul that accounts for the emotions of Christ,[11] but his line of thinking does raise some critical questions about the true solidarity of Christ with the human condition. This becomes clearer when attention is drawn to Augustine's teaching that Christ's human nature was preserved from original sin by his taking flesh from the Virgin Mary,[12] and his refusal to admit, despite the gospel statements that would seem to indicate the contrary, any human ignorance in Christ.[13]

This means that to Augustine's mind there is a basic difference between Christ's humanity and our Adamic fleshliness, and this difference is further in evidence in his understanding of *apatheia*. If by the latter is meant a state of freedom from those emotions which perturb the mind—such as fear, grief, anger, and sadness—then Augustine says that it is "clearly a good and is much to be desired, but it does not belong to this life."[14] This is because the present human condition is marked by deep-seated perturbations of the soul—guilt, concupiscence, mortality, and fear of eternal damnation—which are signs of the enduring consequences of Adam's sin. The soul in this life suffers many perturbations and has an ongoing need for the healing power of God's redeeming grace in Christ. To claim that the state of *apatheia* is attainable in this life would amount to the refusal to acknowledge the tenacious reality of sin and the tragic restlessness of the human heart in its deep longing for God, who is sheer delight. The medley of emotions introduced by Adam's sin simply makes it impossible in this life for the human soul to attain blissful peace and enduring joy, for its own basic impulses are in conflict. Only

---

11. In his *De diversis Quaestionibus* 83, Augustine writes: "Just as the reality of Jesus' body was attested by his being scourged, crucified and buried, so too was his soul revealed through his emotions, since only the soul can give rise to the emotions." Cited in Gondreau, *Passions of Christ's Soul*, 56. The emotions of Christ reveal that he has a human soul, which is an anti-docetic stance.

12. Augustine, *Enchiridion*, 34, 41. According to Augustine, what was lost by the sin of Adam was that complex of qualities referred to as original justice; namely, freedom from concupiscence and freedom from mortality. If Christ was preserved from original sin, then the assumption of flesh in his person is not the same as our Adamic flesh. To Augustine's mind, although Christ was not liable to death because he was preserved from original sin, Christ nevertheless laid down his life on the cross for the sake of proffering us the medicine of redemption (see *Enar. in Ps.* 67. XX.29). By Christ partaking of our mortality, we become partakers of his immortality by exaltation (see *Serm* 166. iv.4).

13. See, for instance, Augustine, *On the Trinity*, I, 23.

14. Augustine, *City of God*, XIV, 9.

in the blessedness of the age to come, when sin will be no more, will the righteous possess the quality of *apatheia*.

What does such a perspective imply about Christ's human nature and emotions? Well, if Christ's human nature was preserved from original sin and there was no human ignorance or development in his individuality, then this would imply that Christ had the mind of a Stoic sage. At this point it is worth drawing attention to a particular section of Augustine's *City of God* where he gives us some valuable insight into his understanding of Stoic philosophy when he uses Aulus Gellius, rather than Seneca, as his teacher.[15] What is significant about Gellius's report on Stoicism is that he mistakenly interprets Stoic first movements (*propatheia*) or pre-passions as actual passions, and Augustine does likewise.[16] Stoic thinkers such as Seneca did not teach that pre-passions are passions; rather, they become passions only when assent is given by the mind to the first movements. Augustine concedes that assent plays a role after the appearances or first movements, but he views the latter as already passions, so that the difference between the mind of the wise man and of the fool is that the mind of the fool yields to these passions by giving assent of the mind. The mind of the wise man, on the other hand, does not yield to the first movements of passion, but retains a true opinion about the things that rationally ought to be chosen or avoided.

It would therefore seem reasonable to hold that Augustine conceives of Christ according to his mistaken understanding of Stoic first movements. Christ must have had the mind of a Stoic sage, given that he was born free of original sin and had full knowledge of all things, but this does not preclude him from experiencing pre-passions, which Augustine regards as actual passions. As a Stoic sage Christ was still liable to experiencing perturbations of the soul, which is why Augustine says in the passage above that Christ experienced certain emotions "when he willed," for the sake of his fixed purpose. The way the emotions are described in the above citation—Christ was "grieved," "angered," and "shed tears"—does not convey a high degree of perturbation of the soul, and

---

15. Augustine, *City of God* IX, 4.

16. For a comprehensive discussion of Augustine's misunderstanding of Stoic first movements, see Sorabji, *Emotion*, ch. 24. Augustine says that the supposed differences between the Platonists and the Stoics are purely verbal and not based in reality: "the controversy is one of words rather than of things" (Augustine, *City of God* IX, 4). The Stoic sage, on this view, does experience perturbation (*perturbatio*) of the soul to a limited degree.

this would be consistent with Augustine conceding a limited degree of perturbation of soul in the Stoic sage. It is significant that Augustine does not employ dramatic language when speaking of Christ's emotions, and this would be in keeping with his understanding that the passions do befall the Stoic wise man, albeit the mind of the wise man does not yield to those passions. Augustine in the citation above makes no reference to more disturbing and truly deep emotions experienced by Christ, such as his terrible dread of "the cup," his fervent anger in the episode of the cleansing of the temple, his bitter weeping over Jerusalem, or his suffering of God-forsakenness expressed in his loud cry of lament on Calvary.

Notwithstanding Augustine's explicit assertion that Christ possessed a true human body and a true human soul, and thus true human emotion, the problem with his thought is that he does not think in dynamic terms of there being a genuine reciprocity and mutual participation of one nature in the other in the person of the God-Man. This is further illustrated by the manner in which Augustine attributes a mediatory role to the human soul of the God-Man. The emphasis on the real humanity of Christ is apparent when, for instance, Augustine writes: "The whole man was taken by the Word, that is, a rational soul and body, that the one Christ, the one God, the Son of God, should not only be Word, but Word and man."[17] In attempting to account for the personal unity of the Word who "takes up" the whole man, Augustine employs the famous analogy of the unity of body and soul in the human being. Just as the soul (immaterial substance) is united to the body (material substance) in order to constitute a human person, God is united to man in one person so as to constitute Christ. The former is a more difficult case of union inasmuch as it involves the unity of the spiritual and the corporeal, whereas the latter is an easier case since we are dealing with the unity of two spiritual substances in the person of Christ—the Godhead and the rational soul are directly united in him.[18] It is the rational soul of Christ that provides the point of union between the Word and the flesh; the body is joined to the Godhead by means of the rational soul—the key phrase is *anima mediante*. Up to this point the argument is quite reasonable insofar as it attempts to establish the connecting link between the divine and the human in the person of Christ. Problems arise, however, when Augustine lays great stress on the mediatory role of Christ's rational soul in order

---

17. *Serm.* 214, 6. Cited by Grillmeier, *Christ*, 407.
18. See Grillmeier, *Christ*, 410; also Kelly, *Early Christian Doctrines*, 336.

to demonstrate that the Godhead is not polluted through its conjunction with the material body—the soul is not only portrayed as a connecting link between the two natures in the person of Christ, but becomes *a protective screen* between the immaterial and the material.[19]

The upshot of all this is that Augustine does not conceive of Christ's humanity as being the same as our Adamic flesh, and he does not entertain the notion of Christ being subject to human becoming and development. The two natures are thought of statically as being in mere juxtaposition, so that the human nature "taken up" into the person of the divine Word does not exist for the divinity itself. The notion of a dynamic reciprocity of divinity and humanity, where there is a real mutual interaction of the two natures in Christ's person, does not guide Augustine's reflections on the christological mystery. The inevitable result is that *the human nature is regarded as passive in relation to the divine nature*; there is no real participation of the divine in the human nature, for the divinity is regarded as the active element in Christ's mission of redemption. It is this passivity which transforms the human nature into a mere instrument for redemption, which is thought of as the deification of human beings: participation in the divine nature, which is appropriated through the sacraments of baptism and Eucharist, is for Augustine the heart of redemption.[20]

But if the human essence of the incarnate Word is regarded as playing no active part in our redemption, if there is no real participation of the Son of God in human essence, then the notion of kenosis is rendered unsatisfactory because it remains undeveloped. In the text cited earlier, Augustine does speak of the word of God condescending to live a human life in the "form of a servant," but from the discussion hitherto it is apparent that the humiliation of the Word is attributed not to his divinity but to his human nature that has a passive and servile relation to his divinity,

---

19. Grillmeier, *Christ*, 412.

20. While Augustine does not often use the term deification, nonetheless his writings echo the guiding idea of Irenaeus and Athanasius that Christ became man that we might become gods. Some examples are: "And so the only Son of God was made the mediator of God and man, when being the Word of God with God, He both brought down His majesty to human affairs and raised human lowliness to the realms of the divine, that He might be a mediator between God and men, being made a man by God above men" (*Ep. Ad Galatas Exp.* 24.5); "He descended that we might ascend" (*Ep.* 140); "He became a partaker in our weakness, bestowing on us a participation in his divinity" (*Enar. In Ps.* 58). See Russell, *Doctrine of Deification*, 331–32; and Bonner, "Augustine's Conception," 369–86.

which is the active element in the work of redemption. This explains Augustine's rather limited and restrained portrayal of the emotional life of Christ, for no mighty and dramatic struggle is entertained between his Adamic flesh and the grace communicated to it through the Spirit by virtue of his divine origin as the eternal Son of the Father.

This particular problem of not according the notion of kenosis its full ontological realism is the basic problem with patristic thought in general. Gregory of Nyssa, for all his rich theological anthropology concerning how the emotions play a constructive role in the Christian ascent toward God, also does not think of the event of the incarnate Word in terms of a real participation of the divine in the human essence. This is evident, for instance, in his famous image of *the divine swallowing up the human like a drop of vinegar absorbed by a boundless ocean.*[21] The human is not annihilated on this view, for the drop of vinegar in the ocean still exists, but it is no longer perceptible as it is "taken up" into divinity so as to be endowed with the divine attributes of eternity and incorruptibility. At the moment of Christ's conception in the virgin's womb, the flesh of the Word already begins its deification, which reaches its completion and utter transformation with Christ's resurrection and glorification when the humanity is changed into divinity.

While the characteristics of the two natures are no longer distinguishable in the risen and glorified Christ, with respect to the earthly Jesus Gregory does regard the characteristics of the two natures as remaining distinguishable—when Christ endured suffering or other human experiences, it was not his divinity which experienced them, but his humanity. Since Gregory in his day was in dispute with Apollinaris, he tended to hold the two natures apart, hence his language is more diphysite in tone and owes much to the Antiochene school. Flesh and Logos are each considered as a separate physis to combat the Apollinarian "one physis" doctrine (see below). The unity of Christ is explained in categories of "mingling" of the two natures, where the flesh is passive and the Logos is the active element. As with Augustine's thought, the creaturely nature has a servile relation to the divine nature—the two natures are thought of statically as being in mere juxtaposition, so that the human nature taken up into the person of Christ does not exist for the divinity itself but is portrayed as a passive instrument of redemption.

---

21. Gregory of Nyssa, *Antirrheticus adversus Apollinarium* 42; and *Contra Eunomium* 3.4. See also Russell, *Doctrine of Deification*, 229; Grillmeier, *Christ*, 371; and Kelly, *Early Christian Doctrines*, 300.

Special mention should be made of Hilary of Poitiers (c. 315–367) whose problematic writings on Christ's passibility were immensely influential and had an enduring influence on medieval theology. Hilary's polemic with the Arians sets the historical context for his statements on Christ's human affectivity. In order to prove the reality of Christ's body, Hilary says that Christ experienced suffering at the time of his crucifixion, but without feeling his body's pain in his soul. The Arians regarded Christ's suffering as a rejoinder to the tenet of his full divinity, and Hilary counters this view by denying that Christ's suffering penetrated his divine person.[22] In order to safeguard the divine nature of Christ, Hilary writes:

> But when, in his humanity, He was struck with blows, or smitten with wounds, or bound with ropes, or lifted on high, He felt the force of suffering, but without its pain . . . He had a body to suffer, and He suffered: but He had not a nature which could feel pain. For His body possessed a unique nature of its own; it was transformed into heavenly glory on the Mount, it put fevers to flight by its touch, it gave new eyesight by its spittle. It may perhaps be said, 'We find Him giving way to weeping, to hunger and thirst: must we not suppose Him liable to all the other affections of human nature?' . . . His weeping was not for Himself; His thirst needed no water to quench it; His hunger no food to stay it. It is never said that the Lord ate or drank or wept when He was hungry, or thirsty, or sorrowful. He conformed to the habits of the body to prove the reality of His own body, to satisfy the custom of human bodies by doing as our nature does. When he ate and drank, it was a concession, not to His own necessities, but to our habits.[23]

Hilary adopts this position in part to uphold the divinity of Christ against Arian beliefs, but also because he advocates the commonly held view regarding the impassibility of the divine nature. The result is a less than realistic account of Christ's passions, which medieval theologians, such as Aquinas, had to address in a respectful and accommodating manner while attempting to formulate a more credible account of Christ's passions, that takes more seriously the gospel narratives concerning the emotional life of the Savior.

---

22. For a discussion of Hilary's historical context and his enduring influence on medieval theology, see Gondreau, *Passions of Christ's Soul*, 48–51, 388–402.

23. Hilary of Poitiers, *On Trinity*, 10.23.

In addition to Hilary of Poitiers, special mention should also be made of John Damascene's *De fide orthodoxa*, which was a highly influential eighth-century work on the topic of Christ's passions. Book III, chapters 20–28 of the *De fide orthodoxa* offer a comprehensive defense of the reality of Christ's suffering and death. The historical context of Damascene's writings was his polemic with the docetic-Monophysitic group, the Aphthartodocetae, who, similar to Hilary of Poitiers, proposed a glorified Christology that excluded passibility from Christ's human nature.[24] Damascene unequivocally affirms that Christ assumed not flesh without a soul, but flesh together with a soul, which allows him to admit passion in the human experience of Christ. He writes:

> We confess, then, that He assumed all the natural and innocent passions of man. For he assumed the whole man and all man's attributes save sin. For that is not natural, nor is it implanted in us by the Creator ... the natural and innocent passions are those which are not in our power, but which have entered into the life of man owing to the condemnation by reason of the transgression; such as hunger, thirst, weariness, labour, the tears, the fear, the agony with the bloody sweat, the succour at the hands of angels because of the weakness of the nature, and other such like passions which belong by nature to every man[25]

The assertion that sin is not natural is fundamental to Damascene's conception of Christ's human affectivity. For it means that the absence of sin in Christ in no way detracts from his full consubstantiality with us, and in no way does it exclude the passions from the life of Christ. Equipped with this understanding it is possible to resolve the quandary of a Christ who is sinless yet possesses a passible nature that suffers the consequences of sin. The "natural and innocent passions" that Christ assumed are the result of Adam's sin, but they need not imply any moral defect in his person.

In order to safeguard, though, against the possibility that Christ might have experienced disordered passion, Damascene asserts—in a manner reminiscent of Augustine—that Christ exercised supreme willful command over his passions. All his passions are depicted as voluntary. "For no compulsion is contemplated in Him but all is voluntary. For it was with His will that He hungered and thirsted and feared and died."[26]

24. Gondreau, *Passions of Christ's Soul*, 60–61.
25. Damascene, *Exposition*, 20.
26. Damascene, *Exposition*, 20.

This volitional self-mastery of Christ means that a perfect harmony pervades his psyche, which stands in sharp contrast to the spirit-flesh conflict that characterizes the rest of humanity. Damascene does not permit any rebellious conflict arising from the lower appetitive powers to assail Christ's interior life, and he goes on to compare Christ to Adam in the state of original integrity. Just as the wicked one made his assault on Adam not by interior thoughts but by the serpent, so too with Christ he "made his assault from without, not by thoughts prompted inwardly."[27] Damascene, and Aquinas later follows his line of thinking here, does not allow any interior temptations in the life of Christ. Gondreau observes that Damascene does at times display "hesitation in his endeavor to drive the theological regard for Christ's full human affectivity forward."[28] This is especially the case with Damascene's interpretation of Christ's prayers, "Father, not as I will, but as you will" (Matt 26:39), and, "My God, my God, why have you forsaken me?" (Matt 27:46). Rather than treating these prayers as windows to shedding light on the true state of Christ's soul in the mystery of the incarnate Word, Damascene proposes the interpretation that Christ offered these prayers "as appropriating our personality."[29] The prayers of Christ are regarded as nothing more than lessons to his followers to ask help in our trials only to God, and to always prefer God's will to our own. Despite the originality of Damascene's christological thought, it remains the case that he (i) offers a less than realistic account of Christ's passions, and (ii) restricts the scope of inquiry to the disagreeable or suffering passions in Christ, which are regarded as a consequence of Adam's transgression.

This position became standard for the scholastic discussion, as evidenced in the writings of Aquinas, whose treatment of Christ's passions is restricted to the "defects of soul" consequent upon Adam's sin. Aquinas has much to say about disagreeable passions such as sensible pain, sorrow, fear, and anger, but offers no reflections on congenial emotions such as Christ's compassion, love, joy, or desire, which also feature in the gospel narratives. Moreover, while Aquinas has bequeathed to posterity a comprehensive treatment of Christ's human affectivity, it remains the case that the emphasis falls very much on Christ's divinity. This is apparent in the way Aquinas conceives of Christ as born free of original sin, as

---

27. Damascene, *Exposition*, 20.
28. Gondreau, *Passions of Christ's Soul*, 65.
29. Damascene, *Exposition*, 24.

imbued with sanctifying grace, as possessing all the virtues, and all the gifts of the Holy Spirit. Even if we were graced and sinless like Christ, there would still be dissimilarities between Christ and us, especially in respect of Christ's knowledge as a divine person. Aquinas speaks of three kinds of knowledge in relation to Christ; namely, acquired empirical knowledge, infused supernatural knowledge, and immediate beatific knowledge of God. It is the third type in particular that presents a serious challenge for Aquinas when it comes to upholding Christ's genuine humanity and fully human affectivity. He writes that, "from the first instance of his conception, Christ had the full vision of God in his essence."[30]

The immediate beatific knowledge of God means that Christ constantly experiences supernatural joy, which sets him apart from the rest of humanity. Since this beatific joy is immense and the soul's joy normally flows to the body, this would mean that it was not possible for Christ to suffer, to experience sorrow, to know fear the same way we do, or to experience finite human joys.[31] Aquinas seeks to overcome this serious problem by proposing that Christ prevented the normal process of overflow by a special exercise of divine power. He writes: "By a dispensation of divine power, the pleasure of divine contemplation remained in the mind of Christ, and did not flow into the sense powers, which would have prevented the experience of any sensible pain."[32] It is only by virtue of this divine dispensation that Christ is able to keep his beatific joy shut up in his intellectual appetite, thereby preventing it from flowing into his sense powers. Throughout his *Treatise on the Passions*, Aquinas describes a kind of interpenetration of sense appetite and intellectual appetite in the human being. Yet when it comes to the affectivity of Christ, the affections of the will (intellectual appetite) are no longer presented as fully engaging the passions of the sense appetite; Aquinas isolates the operation of the different appetites for the sake of resolving the difficulties introduced by his doctrine of Christ's beatific vision of God. The result is that Christ, despite Aquinas's attempts to uphold the contrary, is not fully in solidar-

---

30. Aquinas, *Summa theologica* III 7.3.

31. In us sorrow is often in the intellectual appetite, but Aquinas holds that in Christ sorrow was only in the sense appetite; in us fear involves the element of uncertainty, but Aquinas maintains that since Christ had full knowledge of the future this prevented him from experiencing fear in the same way we do; since human joy is a movement of the intellectual appetite, Aquinas's thought does not allow Christ to experience ordinary human joy because it would be swallowed up by his beatific joy.

32. *Summa theologica* III 15.6. Cited by Lombardo, *Logic of Desire*, 216.

ity with the human condition; there is no genuine participation of the divine Son in the infirmities of human existence lived in the constraints and limitations of the temporal realm.

This is further illustrated by the fact that there is no struggle or conflict at all between the flesh and spirit in the person of Christ. Despite the fact that Aquinas's anthropology and metaphysics—where appetite plays a central role—provides the foundation for a positive evaluation of Christ's passions, he gives considerable attention to ways in which the passions of Christ differ from ours. The differences are centered on the relationship between reason and passion. Aquinas sees Christ's passions as instinctively following the guidance of reason, which leads him to sometimes refer to them as "propassions."[33] In us the passions are commonly drawn toward illicit objects, but in Christ the movements of the sense appetite are directed toward their proper objects according as they arise from the dictates of perfect reason. Aquinas also highlights these differences between Christ and us by referring to the theme of the *fomes peccati* (the tinder of sin). He writes: "Since Christ's virtue was utterly perfect, it follows that there was no *fomes peccati* in him."[34] Aquinas does not permit any inclinations toward sin in Christ, for his passions were perfectly virtuous because always under the spontaneous guidance of reason.

This leads Aquinas to say that Christ never experienced "interior" temptation, but only "exterior" temptation.[35] When the devil tempts Christ to turn stones into bread, or when Christ prays in the garden of Gethsemane, these are examples of the latter kind of temptation. In these episodes the penetration of Christ's passions by reason does not prevent him from desiring something inappropriate for him to seek, although reason does prevail in remaining obedient to the will of God. So, while the gospels narrate some episodes in the life of Christ where a tension exists between Christ's natural will (sensory appetite) on the one hand, and his intellectual appetite (will) and the divine will on the other, to Aqui-

---

33. Lombardo, *Logic of Desire*, 210. The term *propassio* was coined by Jerome in the fourth century. The Latin term is equivalent to the Stoic term *propatheia* (pre-passion). Origen, in Rufinus's Latin, speaks of first movement (*primus motus*), as well as of pre-passion (*propatheia*). According to Jerome, Christ was subject to first movements, which did not linger in his mind. Christ was truly saddened, for instance, but Jerome insists that Christ's beginning to be sad was only a pre-passion. Emotion thus did not dominate in Christ's mind. See Sorabji, *Emotion*, ch. 22.

34. *Summa theologica* III, 15.2. Cited by Lombardo, *Logic of Desire*, 211.

35. *Summa theologica* III, 15.2 ad 3. Cited by Lombardo, *Logic of Desire*, 211.

CHRIST'S EMOTIONS IN THE THEOLOGICAL TRADITION 137

nas's mind there was never any conflict between Christ's appetites. In his perspective, Christ assumed a human nature in which he experienced suffering so he could make satisfaction for sin, yet "it was not necessary that he take upon himself all of our defects."[36] By asserting that Christ was not able to experience the *fomes peccati* or any interior temptation, Aquinas intends to ensure that his work of redemption is not obstructed in any way. There are only some weaknesses that are integral to the work of redemption, while others are excluded as a threat to achieving the objective of final redemption for humanity. The upshot of all this is that Christ in effect can be seen as possessing the virtuous qualities of a Stoic sage. The emotional life of Christ is therefore not conceptualized in sufficiently strong and comprehensive terms that do full justice to the mystery of the divine condescension into the human temporal realm.

Reformed and Contemporary Thought: Christ Assumed Our Adamic Flesh

The fundamental problem with patristic and medieval thinking is that the essence of the Word become flesh is not the same as our Adamic flesh. There is no acknowledgement of a *real* participation of the Son of God in a human life lived in the constraints and limitations of the temporal realm. This poses a basic problem, for if the man Jesus does not truly share in the limitations and weakness of our flesh, which means that he does not experience the full course of emotions in relation to this pilgrim life of ours, how can Jesus be affirmed as the Redeemer who is in solidarity with the human condition and has raised it to the exalted level of glorious immortality? Benjamin Warfield, commenting on John Calvin's portrayal of Jesus' emotional life, says that Calvin turned away from "the tendency from which even an Augustine is not free, to reduce the affectional life of our Lord to a mere show."[37] Calvin stresses that the Son of God having clothed himself with our flesh means that Christ did not differ at all from us, sin only excepted. The Stoic principle of *apatheia* is condemned by Calvin as incompatible with the Gospel of Christ and the essence of Christian life. The repudiation of Stoic philosophy is clear from the following text:

---

36. *Summa theologica* III, 14.4 ad 2. Cited by Lombardo, *Logic of Desire*, 221n.72.
37. Warfield, "Emotional Life," 142–43.

> Yet we have nothing to do with this iron philosophy which our Lord and Master has condemned not only by his word, but also by his example. For he groaned and wept both over his own and others' misfortunes. And he taught his disciples in the same way: "The world," he says, "will rejoice; but you will be sorrowful and will weep" [John 16:20]. And that no one might turn it into a vice, he openly proclaimed, "Blessed are those who mourn" [Matt. 5:4]. No wonder! For if all weeping is condemned, what shall we judge concerning the Lord himself, from whose body tears of blood trickled down [Luke 22:44]? If all fear is branded as unbelief, how shall we account for that dread with which, we read, he was heavily stricken [Matt. 26:37; Mark 14:33]? If all sadness displeases us, how will it please us that he confesses his soul "sorrowful even to death" [Matt. 26:38]?[38]

This citation indicates the realism with which Calvin depicts the emotional life of the Word become flesh. He conveys the intensity of Christ's weeping by referring to the tears of blood that trickled down the body of Christ during his passion, he underscores the depth of fear experienced by Christ when he speaks of the dread with which Christ was heavily stricken, and he highlights the degree of sadness experienced by Christ whose soul was sorrowful even unto death. The descriptions of Christ's emotional life offered by Calvin are much stronger and more palpable than those of Augustine, who talks of Christ in more sanguine terms: Christ merely being "sorrowful" when his hour drew near, or "desiring" to eat the Passover with his disciples, or "shedding tears" when he was about to raise Lazarus. The tenor of Augustine's writing is such that he prefers to depict Christ as not being too perturbed by the affections, which he displayed when it pleased him. Calvin, on the other hand, does not reduce Christ's emotional life to a mere show, but acknowledges the *strong emotions of Christ as evidence of his being subjected to the infirmity of this life*, and of the manner in which redemption and salvation comes to the world. The Christian, unlike the Stoic, gives concrete expression to their pain, suffering, and sorrow, and in so doing is united with the person of the Word who clothed himself with our flesh in order that we might be "more fully clothed [II Cor. 5:2–3]" with the blessed inheritance of his life and glory.[39] Just as Christ the Redeemer experienced the whole gamut of emotions related to life in this world, the disciples of

---

38. Calvin, *Institutes*, III, 8.9.
39. Calvin, *Institutes*, III, 9.5.

Christ likewise must patiently bear even the greatest tribulations of mind on the way to receiving the blessed inheritance of Christ's life and glory. Amid the many adversities of this life, says Calvin, there must be but one thought that dominates the minds of Christians: "to incline our heart to bear cheerfully those things which have so moved it."[40]

So as to make very clear the true and full humanity of Christ as integral to the proclamation of redemption and salvation in his person, Calvin contends that Christ is our righteousness according to his human nature, in contradistinction from the traditional approach of attributing righteousness to the divine nature alone. We have been justified by Christ's obedience to the Father, says Calvin, and this obedience was performed in the "form of a servant" (Phil 2:7). This biblical text is interpreted as meaning that Christ justifies us "not according to his divine nature but in accordance with the dispensation enjoined upon him."[41] Calvin does of course adhere to the orthodox teaching that Christ is both God and man—he is the person of the mediator—but he is at pains to underscore the view that "the matter of both righteousness and salvation resides in his flesh."[42] This perspective certainly does compel us to reconsider the traditional patristic and scholastic notion of kenosis and affirm a renewed appreciation of the depth of Christ's emotions. Yet despite the considerable merit of Calvin's perspective, which is an advance on patristic and scholastic thought on Christ's emotional life, what remains underdeveloped in his thought is the role played by the divinity of the mediator in the generation of his emotional life. If Christ's soul in Gethsemane was heavily stricken by dread and sorrowful even unto death, are these strong emotions purely accounted for by the fact that he assumed the "form of a servant," or do they also have something to say about the divinity of Christ as the Son and the interpretation of his impending death by crucifixion? To state the matter more formally, *can the strong emotions of Christ be attributed purely to his humanity or do they point to the mutually reciprocal interaction of humanity and divinity in his person?*

Jonathan Edwards's writings on the affections of Christ, which were reviewed in the previous chapter 2 of this work, largely reflect the mindset of Calvin on the topic. Like Calvin, Edwards thinks in terms of the Word condescending to the sphere of Adamic flesh. He makes a persuasive case

---

40. Calvin, *Institutes*, III, 8.10.
41. Calvin, *Institutes*, III, 11.8.
42. Calvin, *Institutes*, III, 11.9.

for the view that Christ's virtue and victory over the powers of death in the world was expressed very much in the exercise of holy affections. The term "holy" affections is significant, for it suggests that when we observe Christ's emotional life we should not think of his emotions simply as proofs of his humanity, but in more complex terms as manifesting divine affections that interact with "natural" affections experienced by Christ. This line of thinking, to my mind, represents an advance on Calvin's understanding of Christ's emotional life. In the following citation, where we see Christ's affectionate heart on display in his passion, Edwards makes an explicit distinction between holy and natural affections:

> He was the greatest instance of ardency, vigor and strength of love, to both God and man, that ever was. It was these affections which got the victory, in that mighty struggle and conflict of his affections, in his agonies, when he prayed more earnestly, and offered strong crying and tears, and wrestled in tears and in blood. Such was the power of the exercises of his holy love, that they were stronger than death, and in that great struggle, overcame those strong exercises of the natural affections of fear and grief, when he was sore amazed, and his soul was exceedingly sorrowful, even unto death.[43]

Edwards is certainly not of the view that Christ's affections are a mere show. The strong emotive language used to express Christ's affections serves to convey the mighty struggle involved in securing the victory of holy love over the powers of sin and death in the world. Holy love was involved with a great struggle with the natural affections of fear and grief: it manifested itself in Christ's wrestling in tears and blood, his loud and bitter cries, and his bleeding heart which was exceedingly sorrowful, even unto death. Here Edwards is asserting not merely that Christ truly knows fear and grief the same way we do, but his suffering emotions are greater than ours in virtue of his identity as the Son who endures the agony of being forsaken by God on Calvary. This veritable struggle of Christ's affections was played out for the sake of the redemption of God's enemies, so as to bring them "to unspeakable and everlasting joy and glory."[44] There is no room in Edwards's dramatic portrayal of the passion of Christ for allowing Stoic teaching on the affections to corrupt the gospel picture of Christ the Redeemer. What is more, Edwards displays ample recognition

---

43. Edwards, *Religious Affections*, 111–12.
44. Edwards, *Religious Affections*, 123.

of the congenial emotions of Christ; not only his holy love, but also the tenderness of his heart full of mercy and compassion, the great zeal with which he carries forward his mission, and his earnest desire to eat the Passover with his disciples. The suffering emotions of Christ are depicted as the concrete manifestation of his holy affections, which provide the basic orientation to his life and mission.

For all the richness of Edwards's portrayal of Christ's emotional life, there are areas of his thought that are still not sufficiently developed. The main weakness, to my mind, revolves around the distinction Edwards makes between natural and holy affections. The problem is the lack of any recognition of the considerable overlap between human and divine emotions. The congenial emotions—such as love, mercy, compassion, zeal, and desire—are depicted as holy affections in Christ, but how plausible is it to think of them as purely divine emotions? Are not the emotions of love, joy, mercy, compassion, and zeal experienced as common human emotions or natural affections? What is lacking in Edwards's comprehensive work, in other words, is reflection on the mutual interaction of natural and holy affections in Christ. As fully human, Christ has natural emotions, and as fully divine he expresses divine emotions. But the latter should be thought of as divine properties communicated to and mediated by his humanity in a process of mutual interaction of the two natures, which accounts for the strength and depth of Christ's emotional life as he makes known the Father's benevolent love towards his people. What is basically lacking in Edwards's work, in other words, is the recognition of the *process of development of Jesus' divine-humanity in the temporal-historical realm.*

In contemporary Reformed theology, Benjamin Warfield adds his voice to this chorus of protest against the corruptive influence of Stoic teaching on the biblical figure of Christ. Warfield treats the emotional life of Jesus as proof of his true humanity and rejects the traditional idea that the emotional movements of Jesus never ran their full course as we experience them.[45] In a similar vein to Calvin and Edwards, Warfield asserts that to observe the movements of Jesus' emotions as recorded in the gospels is to gaze upon the very process of our salvation. Also like Calvin and Edwards, Warfield says that it is not sufficient to merely gaze upon the Redeemer and admire him, for Christians are to be metamorphosed into the image of Christ, which is not to eradicate the emotions but "to

---

45. Warfield, "Emotional Life," 137–38.

correct and subdue that obstinacy which pervades them, on account of the sin of Adam."[46] Warfield talks about how Jesus in his sorrows was bearing our sorrows, so that he is forever able to be touched with a feeling of our infirmities. But he does not limit the emotions of Jesus to his suffering emotions or the defects of soul that are the consequence of Adam's sin. Key roles are assigned to the primary congenial emotions of love and compassion in carrying out Jesus' messianic mission. What is more, Warfield is keen to stress that while Jesus was the "Man of Sorrows," he also knew "exuberant joy" which underlies all his sufferings in doing the Father's good work.[47] With regard to anger, it is noteworthy that Warfield does not treat this passion in negative terms, but conceives of Jesus' anger as the righteous reaction of his moral sense as he encounters evil in carrying forward his mission of mercy.[48] As in the writings of Edwards, the suffering emotions are not the sole focus of Warfield's treatment of Jesus' emotional life, but are always considered in conjunction with the congenial emotions that underlie them, and which together form a unity in Jesus' life and mission. What still remains insufficiently developed in his thought, though, as in the case of Edwards, is the process of development of Jesus' divine-humanity as the two natures mutually interact and advance through each other in the historical life and mission of the Redeemer.

Karl Barth deserves to be singled out as a contemporary Reformed theologian who has sought to systematically develop Calvin's understanding of the Son of God having clothed himself with our flesh. Barth is at pains to stress the importance of recognizing that the Son of God, in his existing as the Son of Man, must have an essence which is the same as our Adamic flesh in order for him to be called our "Brother."[49] Before the event of Jesus Christ can be a real participation of the Son of Man in divine essence, we must admit a real participation of the Son of God in human essence.[50] The conception of a God whose Godhead is unaffected

---

46. Warfield, "Emotional Life," 143.

47. Warfield, "Emotional Life," 126.

48. Warfield, "Emotional Life," 122.

49. Barth, *Church Dogmatics*, vol. IV/II, 86–95.

50. Barth, *Church Dogmatics*, vol. IV/II, 73–75. Barth prefers to avoid talk of "partaking of the divine nature" (2 Pet 1:4), because he wants to emphasize first and foremost the participation of the divine in the human nature—humiliation of the Son of God—for the sake of the exaltation of Adamic flesh to fellowship with God. Barth interprets 2 Pet 1:4 as meaning that human nature has been exalted to "fellowship"

by its union with humanity in the person of Christ is, says Barth, simply "unchristian." The Christian faith affirms that Christ was without personal sin, but *his sinlessness must not be understood in a manner that separates him from our Adamic fleshliness.*[51] Christ shares in the limitations and weakness of the flesh, but given his divine origin and the communication of grace addressed to his human essence, the man Jesus was able to live his humanity in genuine human freedom amidst the repeated assaults from Satan, the unbelief of his own people, and persecution by his enemies. The communication of grace addressed to the human essence of Christ involves, Barth stresses, not the alteration of his humanity, but the perfection of his humanity through the process of his learned obedience to the Father, which reaches its climax on the hill of Golgotha.[52]

Barth insists on historical thinking and does not allow abstract, metaphysical concepts of God to be superimposed upon the gospel story. He conceives of the divine essence in terms of concrete, life-affirming, and relational attributes such as love, freedom, and mercy—God is "the One who loves in freedom"—so that *the temporal realm is thought of as encompassed by God, as the sphere in which the fullness of divinity is revealed* (see Col 2:9).[53] No dualistic modes of thought are permitted to drive a wedge between the divine and the human. The distinctiveness

---

with the divine nature.

51. Barth repudiates the idea of an altered human nature due to Adam's sin. He asserts, "There never was a golden age . . . The first man was immediately the first sinner." Barth, *Church Dogmatics*, vol. IV/I, 508. On this view, no problems arise with the assertion that Christ assumed our Adamic flesh. Orthodox teaching, while holding to a doctrine of original sin, is able to make the same assertion, because what is inherited from the sin of Adam is not the taint of guilt—as Catholic teaching claims—but mortality. Both Christ and Mary are without personal sin, yet both are seen as living under the conditions of fallen humanity. See Ware, *Orthodox Way*, 73–76.

52. Barth says that Christ's humanity does not "possess" all divine power and authority, but rather "mediates" and "attests" the divine power and authority. If his human essence possessed the properties of the divine essence, the result would be that Christ's humanity is "divinized" (i.e., transference of properties from the divine to the human), and thus would no longer be human nature. This is why Barth is opposed to the notion of *apotheosis*. Barth wants to stress the sense of the human "participating" in the divine essence (exaltation of the Son of Man), but before that can happen we must first acknowledge the participation of the divine in the human (humiliation of the Son of God), in accordance with the covenant of grace established from all eternity in the Son of God. See Barth, *Church Dogmatics*, vol. IV/II, 98, 116.

53. Barth regards the self-emptying (kenosis) of God in the event of Jesus Christ as an expression, rather than retraction, of the fullness of the deity. He refutes the theory of surrendered attributes which was popular in his day.

of each essence is upheld, but given the "common actualization" of both essences in the person of Jesus Christ we must repudiate any suggestion of separation between them. Instead, we are required to think in terms of a movement of genuine "action" (*operatio*) where the divine expresses itself in the sphere of the human and the human attests the presence and activity of the divine in history.[54] The twofold movement of action from above to below (humiliation of the Son of God) and from below to above (exaltation of the Son of Man) is not a matter of two different and successive actions, but of a single action because the "going out of God" aims at the "coming in of man."[55] For Barth, *the divinity is mediated by the humanity of Jesus*, and to recognize the divine in the human is to acknowledge that there can be no evading the child in the crib at Bethlehem, the growing in wisdom and stature, the being tempted in the wilderness, the constant need for Jesus to pray to the Father, the episode in the garden of Gethsemane, and the genuine suffering in helplessness on the cross of Golgotha.[56] The following text can be taken as a summary-statement of Barth's thought on the mutual participation of divine and human essence in the one person of Jesus Christ:

> The event of the impartation is the history of Bethlehem, the history of His way from Jordan to Gethsemane, the history of His cross and passion, the history of . . . His resurrection. It is as the Subject of this history that He is the heavenly Head of His earthly body . . . As He is, it takes place that the divine essence in all its distinctiveness is gifted to the human, and the human in all its distinctiveness receives the divine. As He is, there takes place the humiliation of the divine for the exaltation of the human essence, and the exaltation of the human by the humiliation of the

---

54. Barth, *Church Dogmatics*, vol. IV/II, 116.

55. Barth, *Church Dogmatics*, vol. IV/II, 21. By talking of the event of Jesus Christ in terms of a twofold movement, Barth is critical of the older Christology's doctrine of two "states," according to which Christ was first humiliated and not yet exalted, and then subsequently exalted in his resurrection from the dead and no longer humiliated. Barth asserts that the humbling and exalting are present "at the same time," that we must think in terms of two related "moments" that mutually interpret one another. What is more, humiliation applies not to human nature but to the divinity, and exaltation is attributed not to divinity but to the human nature of Christ.

56. Barth changed his model of revelation. The earlier Barth, like Emil Brunner, saw revelation as occurring through the medium of God himself—God reveals himself through himself—whereas the later Barth adopted the view that the human nature per se is the medium of revelation and it mediates the divine nature. See McIntyre, *Shape of Christology*, 157–61.

divine. As He is, nothing is held back. In the height of God and in the depths of man, nothing is excluded from this movement from the height of God to our depths, and back again from our depths to the height of God. As He is, God attains His full glory in the exercise of His mercy, and man attains his in the coming of this mercy. And all this is because and as He, the Son of God, of one essence with the Father and the Holy Ghost, became and is also the Son of Man, of one essence with us and all men.[57]

Barth's insistence that the Son of God assumed our Adamic flesh, when combined with his portrayal of the mutual participation of both essences in the twofold movement of action from above to below and from below to above, certainly does provide a welcome perspective for serious reflection on the emotional life of Christ, although Barth himself does not explicitly embrace this topic of conversation. By portraying the event of Jesus Christ as a movement of action from the height of God to our depths and back again from our depths to the height of God, Barth provides a conceptual framework that is conducive to acknowledging the reality, richness, and depth of Christ's emotional life. For the divine essence is affirmed in terms of relational attributes such as love, freedom, and mercy, which constantly address the human essence of Christ, who grows in wisdom and stature and ultimately suffers in helplessness on the cross of Golgotha. The primary congenial emotions of Christ cannot be thought apart from his suffering emotions, which reveal what it cost the Son to redeem our Adamic flesh. On this view, the process of the common actualization of both essences in Christ's person can be illuminated by an informed study of his emotions, as recorded in the gospels.

The writings of the contemporary Russian Orthodox theologian Sergius Bulgakov bear a strong family resemblance to Barth's thought on the mutual participation of both essences in the life of Christ. Like Barth, Bulgakov does not explicitly engage with the topic of Jesus' emotions. Nonetheless, the full reality and significance of Jesus' emotional life is implicitly implied within the framework of Bulgakov's understanding of a progressive or gradual incarnation that begins with the history of Bethlehem and culminates at Golgotha. The following citation shows the

57. Barth, *Church Dogmatics*, vol. IV/II, 75. It should be noted that for Barth the participation of the divine essence in Christ's human essence is not the same as the participation of his human in his divine essence. There is reciprocity between the two, but they have a different character: the divine essence is that which *gives*—the determination of his divine essence is *to* his human essence—while the human essence is that which *receives*—the determination of his human essence is *from* his divine essence.

similarities with Barth's position on how the union of the two natures in Christ should be conceived in progressive and dynamic, not static, terms:

> In the God-Man, the fallen and infirm human essence, subjecting itself to the divine essence, becomes harmonious with and obedient to it. But this occurs not through the coercion of the human nature by the divine nature but by the spiritual overcoming of the 'flesh' through its free subordination to the commands of the hypostatic spirit. In other words, this harmony and interpenetration of the two natures in the God-Man is *the feat and way of the cross*, which begins in the Bethlehem manger and ends at Golgotha. For the Son this is the path of obedience to the Father's will . . . In this submission to the Father's will the human nature, infirm in its creatureliness and weakened in its sinfulness, is overcome. The union of the two natures in Christ therefore cannot at any instant be understood statically as their mere juxtaposition; instead, it must be understood dynamically, as an actual interaction of energies.[58]

Bulgakov is quite clear about the need to think in terms of the feat of Christ's victorious struggle of spirit against the infirmities of the flesh. We must not think that the power of Christ's divinity was no match for the assumed flesh, or that his human essence was merely passive because coerced and overridden by his divine essence. Rather, the idea of kenosis means that Christ was really tempted by evil—i.e., he experienced interior temptation, not merely external temptation—and had to overcome the disobedient and infirm flesh that resists the spirit. What kenosis implies in respect of the incarnation is that the *Son of God surrendered the power of his divinity, although not its presence*.[59] In order to restore fallen humanity to the fullness of communion with God, Christ was involved in a genuine struggle of spirit against flesh, which he accomplished not by divine power but by free human effort, illuminated and inspired by his divinity. His divinity, though, it should be stressed, is consistently portrayed in the gospels in terms of his modus of being-related to the Father who sent him into the world, and to the Holy Spirit in whose power he was conceived and who comes to rest upon him in his baptism by John.[60]

58. Bulgakov, *Lamb of God*, 243.

59. This assertion by Bulgakov is very similar to Barth's understanding of kenosis. Barth is keen to stress, we saw above, that Christ's humanity does not possess all divine power, but rather mediates and attests the divine power and authority. This is to recognize the real participation of the Son of God in human essence.

60. The principal problem with classical Logos-Christology is that Christ is not

When the divinity of Christ is thought of in relational trinitarian terms, it becomes easier to fathom the idea of kenosis as the Son surrendering the power of his divinity, although not its presence. Bulgakov states this kenotic perspective poignantly when he writes, "the Lord came not into the Garden of Eden, into which the first Adam was placed, but into this world, the earth of anguish, where the creature is groaning and awaiting its liberation."[61] By taking his flesh from his blessed mother Mary, who was not free from original sin, Christ was subject to mortality and subordinates himself to the limits and infirmity of the human essence.

It is time to sum up the findings of this section. The tendency in patristic and scholastic theology to negate the historical dimension of Jesus' life and mission—the incarnation is regarded as complete at the moment of the Son's conception in the womb of the Virgin Mary—is not to be found in the examples of Reformed theology discussed or in the Russian Orthodox theology of Sergius Bulgakov. The examples given highlight a shift in primary focus away from the participation of the human in the divine, towards a concentrated focus on the participation of the divine in the human. The latter is regarded as logically prior to the former, for redemption requires that the Son shares in the limitations and infirmities of Adamic flesh and personally engages in an historical struggle to bring his humanity into full communion with the Father—i.e., the perfection of his humanity—which is finally accomplished on Calvary. Since Calvin, Edwards, and Warfield all give explicit recognition to the strong emotions of Jesus as evidence of his being subjected to the infirmity of this life, they give a wide berth to the use theologians such as Augustine and Aquinas made of the Stoic notion of "propassions," and insist instead that Jesus' emotions ran their full course as we experience them. The reflections of Edwards and Warfield on Jesus' emotional life have the added dimension of establishing strong relations between the suffering emotions of Jesus and the congenial emotions that underlie them, thereby presenting us

---

portrayed as a *human* person—his humanity subsists in the person of the Logos. The hypostatic union is between Jesus' humanity and the Logos, so that his divinity is thought of as an inner core of his person. Such thinking lends itself to the pitfall of Docetism, which has been a persistent temptation throughout Christian history. For a critique of classical Logos-Christology, see Novello, *Death as Transformation*, 46–53.

61. Bulgakov, *Lamb of God*, 290. While Bulgakov maintains that Christ's humanity cannot be identified with the original Adam, at the same time he holds that it cannot be directly identified with our fallen humanity insofar as Christ was without personal sin, although he took upon himself the consequences of sin, for the sake of our salvation.

with a whole spectrum of interrelated emotions of Jesus that are integral to his life and mission.

While the writings of Calvin, Edwards, and Warfield are especially valuable in affirming the strong emotions of Jesus as proof of his real humanity, a shortcoming in their writings is that they do not think of Jesus' divine-humanity in terms of a dynamic process of development—from Bethlehem to Golgotha—wherein the humanity and the divinity mutually interact with one another and advance through each other. The result is that insufficient consideration is given to the role played by Jesus' divinity in the development of his emotional life over the period of his historical life. Are the strong emotions of Jesus merely proof of his real humanity, or should they also be considered as pointers to his divinity that constantly interacts with his humanity, given that his divinity is mediated by his humanity? The validity of this question becomes immediately apparent once we acknowledge the divine emotions recorded in Jewish Scripture—i.e., God's love, compassion, joy, zeal, wrath, mercy, and lament—as belonging to the personal attributes of God in relation to the covenant. On the understanding that these personal attributes of divinity are communicated to the incarnate Word's developing humanity in the concrete circumstances of his life, it is difficult to deny the full reality of Jesus' emotions, both his congenial and suffering emotions. Yet the merit of such a perspective goes beyond its ability to affirm Jesus' emotions as running their full course as we experience them, for it suggests that *Jesus' emotions are deeper and more intense than ours given his involved holiness as Immanuel.* When Jesus weeps bitterly as he approaches Jerusalem (Luke 19:41), for instance, he stands in the prophetic tradition of weeping over the doom that will overtake the city, yet his loud wailing stems from the fact that the covenant people have failed to recognize in his person the visitation of God. Weeping is a human emotion, yet the depth of Jesus' wailing is accounted for by the covenant people's rejection of his messianic mission as the Son, who desires to see the final establishment of God's reign of glory in the New Jerusalem.

Barth and Bulgakov fare better than Calvin, Edwards, and Warfield when it comes to appreciating the breadth, depth, and intensity of Jesus' emotional life, inasmuch as they both elaborate in their respective ways on how the two natures actualize themselves as the one and the other as they confront and address one another in the person of Jesus. The key idea in both these thinkers, which provides a constructive way forward for reflection on the christological mystery and Jesus' emotional life, is that Jesus' humanity mediates and attests the presence of divinity in his person. While both Barth and Bulgakov do not explicitly discuss Jesus' emotions as recorded in the gospels, their thought does nevertheless provide a promising framework for renewed reflection on Jesus' emotional life, understood in terms of the mutual interaction and interpenetration of the two natures in his person. This is the subject matter not only of the following section, but the remainder of this study.

A Progressive Incarnation: The Becoming of the Divine-Humanity

From the perspective of the discussion conducted thus far in this chapter, theological reflection on the event of the incarnation is best approached not by the "taking up" of humanity by the word of God, but by the idea of the descent of divinity to the temporal realm of the human, which has to do with the humiliation or kenosis of divinity. In addition to Karl Barth discussed earlier, Sergius Bulgakov should be singled out as another contemporary theologian whose writings have much to contribute in the area of a kenotic theology that takes seriously the notion of the divine condescension to the human sphere. Bulgakov underscores the true kenosis of the divinity by thinking of the incarnate Word as genuinely subject to human becoming and development, which gives rise to the notion of a progressive or gradual incarnation. The following citation can be taken as a key statement of Bulgakov's thinking on this matter:

> Nowhere in the Gospel can one find the notion that there is such a separation and sundering of the divinity and the humanity in the one life of the God-Man that God, abiding in His divine absoluteness, would only *pretend* to be subject to human becoming and development . . . while in reality having nothing to do with it . . . The mystery, glorious and astonishing, consists precisely in the fact that God Himself lives an authentic life in the God-Man, humbling himself to the level of this life and maturing through it to the consciousness of the God-Man. The Divine-Humanity is a particular form of the Divinity's consciousness of itself *through* the humanity and of the humanity's consciousness of itself *through* the Divinity. It is the fusion of the Creator and creation, a fusion that is simultaneously the kenosis

of the Divinity and the theosis of the humanity, and that concludes with the perfect glorification of the God-Man.[62]

To state the matter another way, we are to think of Christ's humanity as mediating his divinity; that is, the divinity reveals itself in the sphere of his humanity and his humanity expresses itself in the presence of his divinity, so that the two natures progressively actualize themselves as the one and the other as they encounter and address each other in his person. Each nature, as Bulgakov asserts clearly in the citation above, is to be understood as *advancing through the other* in the authentic historical life of the God-Man.[63] The union of Jesus' humanity with the Father is not complete from the beginning of his life, because Jesus, as the incarnate Son, undergoes development as a human being and encounters the *temptation* of evil on the way to the attainment of his glory. The union of his humanity with the Father is perfected on Calvary where he "learned perfect obedience as the Son" (Heb 5:8–9), and, moreover, the power of the Spirit is actuated in a new way in the event of his resurrection from the dead (Rom 1:4), in which his humanity is raised to the glory of the "imperishable" (1 Cor 15:42).[64] The participation of the divine in the human (kenosis) reaches its zenith in Christ's death and burial, but the participation of the human in the divine (theosis) reaches its completion in Christ's resurrection from the dead in the power of the Spirit.

A particular understanding of the christological doctrine of the communication of properties (*commercium idiomatum*) arises from this perspective of a progressive incarnation that reaches its zenith in Christ's

62. Bulgakov, *Lamb of God*, 242. As we have already seen, Bukgakov's argument bears a strong family resemblance to the thought of Barth on this issue.

63. Maximus the Confessor also expresses the view that each nature advances through the other. In the fifth *Difficulty*, for instance, Maximus writes: "For who knows how God assumes flesh and yet remains God, how, remaining true God, he is true man, showing himself truly both . . . and each through the other, and yet changing neither?" Louth, *Maximus the Confessor*, 177. On this point, see also Vishnevskaya, "Divinization," 133.

64. The gospel story makes it plain that the mystery of Jesus' person is rooted in his modus of being-related to the Father in unfathomable love. The man Jesus progressively actualizes his personhood in terms of the I-You relationship; that is, on the basis of the strength of his I in which he calls his You "Father." What is more, the strength of this I-You relationship is not possible without Jesus being anointed with the Holy Spirit. Jesus' divine identity, then, must be understood in relational, Trinitarian terms. The principal problem with classical Logos-Christology is that Jesus' divinity is not thought of in terms of his modus of being related to the Father through the Spirit, but is seen as subsisting in the person of the Logos, hence the life of Jesus is not rendered humanly credible. This will be discussed in chapter 4 of this study.

paschal mystery. What is required is a reading that affirms a genuine mutuality and reciprocity between the two natures, so as to foster a true sense of wonder for the process of the humanization of God (kenosis) in the person of Jesus of Nazareth, which aims at the divinization of humanity (theosis) as the final end of the process of creation. Such a reading gives rise to a *complex view of Jesus' emotional life* as indicative of how each nature advances through the other in his historical life. The life of Immanuel must be taken not only as a definitive statement about the true destiny of our humanity, but as a concrete statement about God: the meaning is that *this* is God, and God is like *this*. This is to say that a conception of the unity of the two natures that remains abstract—i.e., the natures are treated as irreconcilable opposites—and does not think in terms of a concrete event between divinity and humanity, simply fails to grasp the history of the man Jesus as the history of God's subjective engagement in the world. On the view that the humanity of Jesus mediates and attests the personal involvement of God in the world, the actions of Jesus must not be divided up into divine and human actions, as if he had a divine miracle button in one hand and an ordinary human behavior button in the other, so he could act in each case as deemed appropriate. *His actions are at once both divine and human*, for Jesus acts as the Son of the Father when he acts as a human, and as a human when he acts as the Son. Barth affirms this very point when he speaks about the common actualization of both essences in the person of Christ. According to this guiding idea, the event of Jesus Christ is a movement of action from above to below, and from below to above, which is not a matter of two different and successive actions but of a single action that aims at our blessed fellowship with God. Bulgakov certainly lends weight to this understanding when he talks about the dynamic interaction of energies in the historical life of Christ; that is, how the two natures progressively actualize themselves as the one and the other as they encounter and address each other in the person of the God-Man.

In the patristic period, Cyril of Alexandria was effectively able to convey this understanding of the actions of Christ as at once both human and divine with his single-subject Christology, which features the notion of the "one incarnate nature of the Word."[65] In virtue of the interpenetration of humanity and divinity in his person, the actions of

---

65. See Cyril's Second Letter to Succensus, in Wickham, *Cyril of Alexandria*, 87–89. Nestorius, in contrast, put forward the idea of prosopic union; that is, two different "prosopa" or roles, the human and the divine, forming a union by conjunction.

Christ cannot be assigned separately to his humanity (those acts which arise from ignorance or fear) or to his divinity (those acts which manifest divine power). Despite the merits of Cyril's single-subject Christology, questions do arise about whether it borders on monophysitism. Cyril does acknowledge that Christ's soul informs his humanity which is in constant interaction with the Word, but problems arise when the Word as the governing principle is regarded as immediately mastering every emotion experienced by Christ. When speaking about the fear of death that attempts to agitate Christ, for example, Cyril writes: "the power of divinity at once masters the emotion that has been aroused and immediately transforms that which has been conquered by fear into an incomparable courage."[66] Gregory of Nyssa offers us a very similar picture of the Irenaean-Athanasian exchange principle when he asserts that the mingling of the two natures in Christ does not imply a symmetrical interpenetration of two equal constituents; instead, the divine swallows up the human like a drop of vinegar absorbed by a boundless ocean.

Cyril's single-subject Christology "from above" also governs Maximus the Confessor's presentation of the two natures. This is especially apparent in his contention that Christ has no "gnomic" will.[67] In the aftermath of Adam's sin, humanity is seen as having lost the sense of God as its true good, hence it needs to consider various intentions and inclinations in order to deliberate on different possibilities—this is what Maximus calls "gnomic" willing, which is not infallible. In Christ there are two natural wills, a human will and a divine will, but there is no gnomic will, because as a divine person he is without sin and knows God instinctively as the true good. The natural human will of the incarnate Word, therefore, is regarded by Maximus as wholly moved and shaped by the divine will.[68] Bulgakov has criticized this idea as tantamount to denying the divine will in the God-Man as one of two wills, and as implying the "*infallibility* of the divine volition."[69]

The upshot of these notable examples in the theological tradition is the failure of patristic thought to conceive of the interpenetration of the

---

66. *In Johannem* 8. 703d. Cited in Russell, *Doctrine of Deification*, 198. On such a view, Christ simply "passes" from death to life; he does not truly "suffer" the weight of death in order to offer it to the Father, who alone is capable of transforming it.

67. John of Damascus follows Maximus the Confessor in denying a gnomic will in Christ.

68. Louth, *Maximus the Confessor*, 61.

69. Bulgakov, *Lamb of God*, 245n.19.

two natures in terms of a genuine reciprocity of communication of properties in the historical life of the God-Man. What is essentially lacking is an adequately developed idea of kenosis that acknowledges the becoming of Christ's divine-humanity through a process of interaction and mutual reception of the two natures. Even John Damascene with his classical formulation of the notion of "perichoresis" falls short in this regard. While he does affirm as a postulate that each nature accomplishes what is proper to it with the participation of the other, he nevertheless is not able to acknowledge the communication of properties from the human to the divine nature. This is apparent, for instance, when Damascene writes:

> But observe that although we hold that the two natures of the Lord permeate one another, yet we know that the permeation springs from the divine nature. For it is that that penetrates and permeates all things, as it wills, while nothing penetrates it: and it is it, too, that imparts to the flesh its own peculiar glories, while abiding itself impassible and without participation in the affections of the flesh. For if the sun imparts to us his energies and yet does not participate in ours, how much the rather must this be true of the Creator and Lord of the Sun.[70]

Damascene acknowledges that the Word appropriated the sufferings of the body, but he is not prepared to say that the nature of the Word suffered, for the divinity of the Word is impassible and cannot suffer.[71] We can say that God suffered in the flesh, but in no wise can we say that divinity suffered in the flesh. The sufferings of the incarnate Word are regarded as having no relation to the divine nature, which is impassible. But how can one separate the hypostasis from the nature in this clear-cut manner? If the natures are united without separation in the person of the incarnate Word, how can that which occurs with one of the natures have no effect on and no relation to the other nature?[72] The problem with Damascene's thought is that human flesh is received into the hypostatic union for the sake of its redemption, but in itself it remains outside the life of the God-Man: *the human nature does not exist for the divinity itself but is presented as a passive instrument of redemption.*[73]

---

70. Damascene, *Exposition*, 7.

71. Cyril holds the same paradoxical view when he speaks of Christ "suffering impassibly." See Russell, *Cyril of Alexandria*, 41.

72. This question is rightly raised by Bulgakov, *Lamb of God*, 259.

73. Bulgakov, *Lamb of God*, 256. Not only John Damascene, but also "Cyril with his unintentional docetism, the school of Antioch with its radical separation of the

The Lutheran formula also reflects this tendency to deny a genuine reciprocity of communication of properties in the hypostatic union. On a positive note, the Formula of Concord refutes the contention that there can be no communion whatsoever between the two natures themselves, on the grounds that this would effectively result in the separation of the two natures and the emergence of two persons—Christ is one person and the word of God who dwells in him is another. To avoid this unorthodox scenario the Lutheran formula regards the natures as united in such a way that they have *true communion* with each other, which entails a "real exchange" of properties as opposed to a mere "verbal exchange" or mere figure of speech.[74] All this is well and good, but what is less convincing is that the exchange of properties is limited to the *genus majestaticum*: only the divine properties of majesty—i.e., omnipresence, omnipotence, and omniscience—are communicated to Christ's humanity.[75] But how intelligible is it to separate off some properties from others belonging to the divine nature in the event of humanity being addressed by divinity in the person of Christ? Rather than highlighting certain metaphysical properties of the divinity, would it not make more sense to focus on the personal or relational properties of God that are communicated to Christ's humanity? A further problem with the Formula of Concord is that the communication of properties is envisaged as unidirectional: the divine communicates its properties to the human (participation of the human in the divine), but the human does not communicate its properties to the divine (no participation of the divine in the human).

Martin Luther himself, in contrast to the Formula of Concord, did claim a genuine reciprocity and mutuality in the sharing of properties, and he did so on soteriological grounds; that is, to redeem humanity from the powers of death, God has suffered and died in the person of the Word made flesh.[76] When divinity is regarded *in abstracto*, God does not suffer and cannot die, but since the Word has *in concreto* assumed human flesh in the person of Christ, then divinity does suffer and we can talk about God's death, so that the ontological chasm between Creator and

---

two natures, and monophysitism with its de facto abolition of the human nature, considered to be absorbed by the divine nature," all deny that the flesh participates in the proper life of the God-Man.

74. Tappert, *Book of Concord*, 603.

75. This is closely tied to the Lutheran doctrine of "consubstantiation" in sacramental theology.

76. See Lienhard, *Luther*, 342–43; and Nagel, "Martinus," 47.

creature has been overcome. For Luther, the unity of Word and flesh signifies a "communion of being"[77] of God and humanity, which is integral to the fundamental union that obtains between creation and redemption. From the standpoint of the Son's death there is simply nothing "outside" God, including suffering and death, which are now to be seen as loci of relationship to God, the very means by which divine salvation comes to us and makes all things new.

The contemporary Lutheran theologian Eberhard Jüngel has developed Martin Luther's position in respect of a genuine interpenetration of the two natures in the person of Immanuel. In an arresting fashion he maintains that the "death of God" is the story to be told by Christians. Following Heidegger, Jüngel views human existence as characterized by an inescapable rupture between being and time. The present situation of ontological anxiety simply cannot be alleviated by ourselves: only God who comes to us in Christ can overcome the struggle between being and non-being. In light of the gospel story, we must reject the notion of the immutable and impassible metaphysical deity who is defined as the opposite of human existence, and affirm instead that *God is more like us than unlike us*, while still remaining God.[78] Because God must be thought of as being in union with all that is perishable and mutable, temporal existence is freed from an exclusively negative qualification and the process of change and decay is invested with the positive element of *possibility*.[79] The essence of God is to exist through the giving of God's own life, a life that takes death upon itself for the sake of life. "Talk about the death of God implies then, in its true theological meaning, that God is the one who involves himself in nothingness."[80] Death is therefore no longer alien

---

77. See Mannermaa, "Why Is Luther," 11.

78. Jüngel, *God As the Mystery*, 285, 288. He proposes an "analogy of advent" in contradistinction from an "analogy of being," which is designed to convey the sense of a greater similarity between God and humanity, while at the same time revealing the "concrete difference" between us and God. Jüngel's thought, I would note, is not dissimilar to what Kierkegaard says about Christ. He says that in Christ, God himself enters the realm of existential being: Christ is *the* historical, *the* existential individual. In the incarnation, the immutable becomes a changing being, the eternal takes on the temporal process, the suprahistorical enters into history. The object of faith is the "fact that God has existed." See the introduction to this study.

79. Jüngel, *God As the Mystery*, 184–225. Balthasar lends his support to this view when he says that the temporal sphere lies not outside eternity but unfolds within it. See Balthasar, *Theo-Drama*, 5:126.

80. Jüngel, *God as the Mystery*, 218.

to God's own being, and this assertion regarding the death of God ensures that the humanity of God is taken with full seriousness and is not compromised in any way. When God identifies with the crucified Christ, he defines not only himself—as love—but also the nature of death: death is now to be regarded as a locus of relationship to God. The concrete event of Jesus Christ reveals the humanity of God—which is ontologically definitive for all humans—and it directs us toward thinking of God as "the union of death and life for the sake of life."[81] At the place where all relations end, God has interposed the divine being in order to create new relations in the midst of death. Jüngel boldly affirms the genuine penetration of the divine by the human nature of Christ, without which there can be no proclamation of salvation in Christ. There is not so much as a hint of monophysitism in Jüngel's reflections on the christological mystery, for the need to overcome the human struggle between being and non-being ensures that the Son's kenosis is accorded its full ontological realism.

It is time to bring the various elements of this discussion together in some concluding statements. If the concrete event of Jesus Christ reveals the humanity of God, if Christ's humanity mediates and attests the saving presence of the divinity, if there is a genuine process of becoming of the divine-humanity in his person, if his actions are at once both the actions of a human and of the Son of the Father, then this implies that his emotional life cannot be reduced to the mere defects of soul—fear, grief, sadness, and anger—that the theological tradition has long associated with the sickness of sin. The recognition of the reciprocal communication of properties in the God-Man points to his emotional life as the outworking of the mutual interaction of humanity and divinity in his person. It is necessary here to reiterate and underscore the point that when we speak of Jesus' divinity we are dealing with a certain group of divine qualities that are communicated to his humanity. The focus is primarily on the communicable or personal attributes of divinity, which are relational properties of God—such as love, joy, freedom, faithfulness, compassion, mercy, righteousness, wisdom, and holiness. On the view that "God is love" (1 John 4:8, 16), the personal attributes of God should be regarded as prior to the metaphysical attributes of omnipotence, omnipresence, omniscience, impassibility, immutability, and eternity.[82] Yet this is not

---

81. Jüngel, *God as the Mystery*, 299.
82. See Schwöbel, *God*, 46–62.

the whole story. The picture is rendered more complex by the fact that many of the personal qualities of divinity communicated to Jesus' humanity also belong to the sphere of his developing humanity.[83] Love, for instance, is the first and chief of the relational qualities of God, but it is also a common quality and basic emotion of humanity. Therefore, as the two natures progressively address each other and advance through each other in Jesus' historical life, his emotions—love, compassion, joy, righteous anger, indignation, dread, grief, sorrow, and lament—assume an intensity and breadth that is peculiar to the progressive development of his divine-humanity, which culminates in his cry of dereliction on the cross of Golgotha.

When Jesus expresses strong compassion towards his long-suffering people, for example, this congenial emotion is a human emotion informed by his Jewish upbringing, yet at the same time the divine quality of compassion is communicated to his humanity via his unique person as the Son, which intensifies and heightens Jesus' felt experience of this benevolent emotion that underlies all his miraculous and wondrous works. To offer another example, when Jesus expresses indignation or anger towards the Pharisees and scribes, this disturbing emotion is a human emotion that gives voice to Jesus' acute moral sense in the presence of obstacles to his preaching of the kingdom, yet at the same time the divine attribute of anger is communicated to his humanity via his person as the Son, which intensifies and deepens this felt emotion, with the result that it brings him into increasing conflict with the Jewish leaders of his day. Far from thinking of anger as a defect of soul due to Adam's sin, Jesus' righteous anger must be affirmed as an integral element of his proclamation of the kingdom of God to his long-suffering people. As a third and final example, when Jesus is deeply troubled in Gethsemane and experiences overwhelming fear or dread at the prospect of his imminent death, this is a very human emotion in the distressing situation of being handed over to the Jewish and Roman authorities, yet this felt dread is intensified and given a special character by Jesus' peculiar understanding that he as the Son will have to endure "the cup" as a true test of his filial love for the Father. The one who has proclaimed the Father's benevolent love to Israel will now show what it means to be the Son: he who is without sin willingly and completely assumes in his person the human condition of estrangement from God of which the cross is the consummate sign. What

83. This will become clearer in the next chapter of this study, where the formation of Jesus' emotions in the context of the covenant framework is discussed.

Jesus dreads most of all in Gethsemane is that he as the Son will suffer God-forsakenness on the cross, thereby making him the sin-bearer, the one who mercifully and vicariously bears our sorrows in his ineffable sorrow. The suffering emotions of Jesus, then, are actually intensified—not lessened—by his consciousness of being the divine Son, and at the same time they bring into focus the strength and vigor of Jesus' love for the Father, which is able to endure and overcome the agonies of his passion. In these few examples, we are observing the mutual interaction of the two natures in his person in operation.

In light of these examples it becomes apparent that the emotions of Jesus should not and must not be reduced to the mere defects of soul that the theological tradition has long regarded as the consequences of Adam's sin. When we appreciate the richness, intensity, and purity of Jesus' emotional life, we begin to recognize what it means for the divinity to dwell bodily in him (Col 2:9). The general failure of both patristic and medieval theology to accord the idea of kenosis its full ontological realism gave rise to an inability to admit that the man Jesus was subject to becoming and to the interior temptation of evil—"Jesus increased in wisdom and in stature, and in favor with God" (Luke 2:52)—or to acknowledge the common actualization of one nature in the other as integral to the unity of Jesus' person. The human nature is not absorbed into the divine nature like a drop of vinegar absorbed into a boundless ocean. Instead, the divine Word humbles himself to the level of this historical life and matures through his assumed Adamic flesh to the consciousness of his divine-humanity. In this process of becoming implied by a progressive incarnation, the divine nature is firmly established as having a *real* relation to the human nature, which is to say that the human nature is not passive in relation to the divine nature: it plays an active role as it matures and advances through its interaction with the divine nature, an interaction that is ongoing and progressive because subject to the changing historical circumstances of Jesus' life and messianic mission to Israel. The actions of Jesus should not be attributed solely to his divine nature, but should be acknowledged as at once both the actions of God and of a real human.[84] While we must hold fast to the position that the historical

---

84. Barth is not the only modern theologian to contend that the relationship between the divine and the human in the person of Christ is one of genuine action. Colin Gunton holds the same view when he argues that the term "nature" should not be interpreted as a noun but as a verbal adjective—the natures are not things, but refer to ways in which Jesus is fully divine and fully human. When Christ acts, his actions are

figure of Jesus cannot be reduced to the purely human, by the same token there should be no flight into the purely divine realm.

Jesus' Emotions as the Springboard of His Messianic Mission

When the relationship between the divine and the human in the person of Jesus Christ is acknowledged as a movement of genuine action in accomplishing our salvation, this allows us to illustrate the integral role played by the emotions in his life and messianic mission by applying the cognitive theory of emotion elaborated in chapter 1 of this study. One of the fundamental roles of the emotions, it will be recalled, is that they are action potentials or *springs of action* in the world. If basic emotions such as love, hatred, joy, sadness, zeal, anger, hope, fear, and sorrow, were eliminated from our daily lives, the world would be motionless and lacking in any earnest pursuits. Once the emotions are recognized as motivational forces in our personal engagement with the world, then the emotional life of Jesus cannot be downplayed but assumes heightened importance as the springboard of his messianic mission to Israel. The picture is rendered more complex, of course, by the fact that Jesus' emotions are not purely human, since they are in constant interaction with the divinity and communicate the personal attributes of God in relation to the covenant. Since the relational properties of God are synonymous with the divine emotions—e.g., love, compassion, joy, zeal, jealousy, wrath, sorrow, and lament—they can be conceived as springs of God's action in relation to the covenant. The emotions of Jesus are complex because they tend in both a human and a divine direction: his actions as a human are the actions of the divine Son, and his actions as the Son are always the actions of a human. To affirm Jesus as increasing in wisdom and in stature and in favor before God (Luke 2:52) means that he becomes increasingly conscious over time of the presence of the divinity dwelling bodily in him as the Son of the Father (Col 2:9). The growing in wisdom and favor before God implies a process of mutual interaction of the natures united in Jesus' person, where one nature advances through the other. In this process of a progressive incarnation, the consciousness of his divinity is mediated by his humanity, and the development of his humanity takes place through the consciousness of his divinity as the Son of the Father.

---

at once divine actions and those of a man. See Gunton, *Christian Faith*, 91, 95.

Precisely why the emotions are to be acknowledged as springs of action in the world becomes clearer when we turn our attention to the major components of our cognitive theory of emotion. It was shown in chapter 1 how emotions involve a number of interrelated components that account for their motivating force or action potential: they have to do with judgments about important things; they are concerned with value; they embody beliefs about their object; they have a personal biography; and they reveal our vulnerability before parts of the world that we do not fully control. The emotions are not irrational and involuntary, but rather give expression to our engagement in the world from a personal and interested perspective, which always has an ineffable surplus of meaning. The interrelated components that account for the action potential of emotions can quite readily be recognized in the process of the development of Jesus' divine-humanity. The following observations bring this dynamic process to light:[85]

1. Jesus makes *judgments* about the state of the covenant people in the land, the demands of the Torah as the basis of life in the land, and the teachings of the religious authorities of his day. These judgments are human in that he is raised in a devout Jewish family, is steeped in Jewish Scripture and expectations, and experiences first-hand the impoverished state of Jewish life in the land. But his judgments about important matters in relation to the covenant also display a divine dimension insofar as people are amazed by the authority with which Jesus interprets the Torah, forgives sins, drives out demons, is Lord of the Sabbath, and restores people to a state of well-being, all of which leads him into increasing conflict with the religious authorities of his day. The judgments of Jesus reveal that he is both the interpreter of humanity, as well as the interpreter of God. As Jesus' divine-humanity progresses, his judgments become more critical of the Jewish leaders who plot to destroy him, and more focused on his identity as the suffering Son who will be put to death by his enemies.

2. Jesus is concerned with the enduring *value* of God's covenant promises to Israel, which is inseparable from the ineffable value of God's holy name. This value is first acknowledged as a devout Jewish man raised and living in the land under Roman occupation, then later

---

85. What is stated here will become clearer in the following chapter of this study where the history of Jesus' emotions in terms of the covenant and his family upbringing is discussed.

takes on a uniquely personal expression as the divine Son who is intimately related to the Father and makes manifest to Israel God's benevolent love for his long-suffering people. The beautiful prayer in John 17 eminently conveys the ineffable value that Jesus attaches to God's holy name. Jesus prays: "I made known to them your name, and I will make it known, that the love with which you have loved me may be in them, and I in them" (John 17:26).

3. Jesus has concrete *beliefs* about God's fidelity towards the covenant people, and Israel's need for conversion of heart as a concrete response to the demands of the covenant (Matt 4:17; Mark 1:1-8). These beliefs are human in that they are central to Jewish faith and the Jewish experience of history, but in the person of Jesus they are also divine inasmuch as he becomes conscious of himself as God's visitation of Israel (Luke 4:21; 19:44), which calls for a response to his person. To reject Jesus' preaching is to reject the kingdom of God being made manifest in his person. Jesus' Sermon on the Mount can be taken as a good example of the interaction of the two natures in his person. The series of teachings in the Sermon all take the form, "You have heard it said . . . but I say to you." The introductory part—"you have heard it said"—indicates Jesus' humanity as steeped in Jewish traditions, which leads into the subsequent section—"but I say to you"—where Jesus reinterprets the tradition with divine authority. For instance, Jesus says that in the past it was said that you shall love your neighbor and hate your enemy, "but I say to you, love your enemies and pray for those who persecute you" (Matt 5:44). Jesus himself lives out this radical belief when he willingly endures persecution by his enemies, so as to make known the Father's forgiving love towards sinners. The perfection of Jesus' humanity on Calvary, where we see the final triumph of his spirit over his flesh, takes the form of love of enemies.

4. The emotions of the adult Jesus have a history, which is to say that they are formed by a *personal biography*. He is born in the land and takes his flesh from the Virgin Mary, he is raised in a devout Jewish family, he is confronted by misery and sin, fidelity and infidelity, and he undergoes development of his individuality in the concrete historical circumstances of his time. This reveals the human side of his personal biography. But this proves to be insufficient to fathom the mystery of his person, since ultimately his personal biography

is rooted in the bosom of God (John 1:1–18) as the divine Son, who becomes flesh in order to bring the fullness of grace and truth (i.e., salvation) to Israel and the world. It is only from the perspective of the paschal mystery, though, that Jesus' divinity is ultimately manifested to his own.

5. Jesus' emotions reveal a *vulnerability* before parts of the world that he does not fully control. This aspect of Jesus' emotional life is integral to the acknowledgment of the man Jesus as subject to the infirmities and temptations of the flesh, which his spirit seeks to gain mastery over. More specifically, once Jesus begins his messianic ministry, his lack of control over significant parts of his Jewish world is apparent in that he experiences increasing conflict in relation to his preaching of the kingdom. At the same time, this personal experience of mounting rejection of his redemptive message is integral to Jesus' growing consciousness of what it means to be the Son of the Father in a world that refuses to allow goodness to triumph. Jesus' vulnerability is most profoundly evident in Gethsemane where he asks the Father that "the cup" be removed from him, as well as in his cry of dereliction on the cross. Jesus' obedience as the Son is a "learned obedience" (Heb 5:8) through what he suffers. By his perfect obedience Jesus perfects his humanity, and, at the same time, he manifests his divine identity as the Son by his self-sacrificing love to the Father. There is a divine dimension to Jesus' vulnerability, and this is consistent with the view of the pathos of God in Jewish Scripture: God suffers "because" of the people's sinfulness, and, moreover, God suffers "for" the people in that he bears their sins. Jesus the Son suffers in both these senses: he is put to death because of people's sinfulness and hardness of heart, and he suffers for sinners in that he is the sin-bearer, who is the way to the Father.

On this understanding of the emotions of Jesus as the springboard of his messianic mission to Israel and as the manifestation of his divine-humanity, it is not possible to limit and restrict his emotions to those passions that the theological tradition has regarded as the defects of soul—fear, grief, anger, and sadness—due to Adam's sin. The suffering emotions such as anger, sorrow, and lament are not exclusive to the fallen human race, but also belong to the divine pathos, according to Jewish Scripture. God is angry, for example, when his people turn away from him towards the pagan gods; and God laments because of the sin of his people and suffers for the sin of the people. But apart from these suffering emotions, it is the congenial emotions of Jesus—love, compassion, joy, and zeal—that must be recognized above all as the motivating force of his messianic mission as the Son. It is clear from the gospels that one of the chief motivating forces in Jesus' life is his compassion towards his long-suffering people, who had become like sheep without a shepherd. This chief emotion should not be regarded as springing solely from Jesus' divine nature, but from both essences that address each other in his person. Compassion is one of the basic emotions attributed to God in Jewish Scripture, and the Jewish people in the land are required to display compassion as God had shown compassion towards them (Deut 10:12–21; Mic 6:8). When we gaze upon Jesus' astonishing compassion for his people, we are witnessing the most perfect example of human compassion afforded by history, as well as the definitive manifestation of God's compassion towards his people. To offer another example, the strong emotions of dread and sorrow that Jesus experiences in his passion are certainly human emotions. But we should not think that these disturbing emotions are immediately overcome by the power of Jesus' divine essence. Rather, his palpable dread and sorrow are addressed by holy love—his divinity as the Son is made manifest in his love for the Father—in a veritable struggle to carry out his perfect enactment of obedience to the Father's will, for our sake. The chief congenial emotion of love is what enables Jesus to endure the immense suffering of his passion. His astonishing love is not purely divine, but both human and divine, inasmuch as both essences address each other in the person of the Word made flesh. The great commandment to Israel is to "love the Lord your God with all your heart, and with all your soul, and with all your might" (Deut 6:5), and we see the man Jesus fulfilling this commandment perfectly when he sacrificially offers to the Father his tortured, crucified, and broken body as an act of supreme love of God. Each of the natures is never separate or detached from the other, but is involved in a genuine movement of mutual interaction whereby the humanization of God (kenosis) aims at the divinization of humanity (theosis).

An adequately developed idea of kenosis is one that leads to an appreciation of how the incarnate Word knows the totality of the human condition *from within*, so that having lived a genuine human life like ours he remains forever able to be touched by our infirmities, and we are forever able to be touched by his holy affections towards us. In the person of Jesus, God condescends to the historical-existential realm and takes the whole of our Adamic flesh to himself so as to graciously impart what is his to us mortal sinners: God takes the pathos of the flesh, the reality of sin, the limitations and miseries of the temporal realm, the aspirations and desires of the human heart, and the weight of death to himself, in order to impart merciful love, righteousness, holiness, exalted joy, true freedom, and the glory of resurrection life to humanity. As we examine the emotional life of Jesus we must not permit it to slip out of sight, "that we are not only observing the proofs of the truth of his humanity, and not merely regarding the most perfect example of a human life which is afforded by history, but are contemplating the atoning work of the Savior in its fundamental elements."[86] As Jesus carries forth his mission of mercy that makes all things new, his compassion for his long-suffering people reveals the Father's benevolent love for them; his palpable anger and indignation is the righteous reaction of his moral sense in the presence of evil obstacles to proclaiming the kingdom of grace; his exuberant joy stems from his filial consciousness of doing his Father's benevolent work, so as to glorify the Father; in his profound sorrow and lament he bears our sorrow and lament; and in suffering an agonizing death on a cross he bears our death.

In all of these things we are observing Christ's fitness to serve our needs, but at the same time we are witnessing what God is really like and the truth of God's emotional nature—i.e., the personal or relational properties of the divine—as well as what humanity is called to become by the ongoing conversion of our emotions, so that we bear the image of Christ in the world. To put on Christ and bear his image means that his holy affections must become our gracious affections through the Spirit dwelling in our hearts as a new principle of nature. The salvation that Christ proffers us sinners is experienced by way of rightly ordered emotions that flow from a "new heart" (Jer 31:31–34; Ezek 36:26–28; 2 Cor 4:6; Heb 10:22). The emotions have a vital and indispensable role to play in the process of our deification in the person of the incarnate Word, who clothed himself with our flesh in order that we might be "more fully clothed" (2 Cor 5:2–3) with the glory of eternal life. The discussion in this chapter can fittingly be concluded with the formulation of the following proposition that is the main thesis of this book: *As the outworking of the process of mutual interaction of the two natures in his person and the springboard of his messianic mission to Israel, Jesus' emotional life provides*

---

86. Warfield, "Emotional Life," 144.

us with a privileged window to gaze upon the process of deification (i.e., salvation) in his person. The next chapter will endeavor to substantiate this proposition at greater length by first considering the historical development of Jesus' own individuality in relation to the theme of the covenant, his taking flesh from the Virgin Mary, and the consciousness of his filial relationship to the Father, before turning to finally examine Jesus' emotions as recorded in the gospels.

4

Jesus' Personal Biography in the Land

The Full Course of His Emotional Life

THE DISCUSSION IN THE previous chapter has maintained that the key problem with past theological thinking on Christ's emotions is an inadequately developed notion of kenosis. Christ's divinity is commonly regarded as overriding his humanity, which is taken up into his divinity like a drop of vinegar is absorbed into a boundless ocean. In such a perspective, Christ's emotions are (i) regarded as mere signs of his humanity; (ii) restricted to those defects of soul that are considered to be the consequences of sin and mortality; and (iii) conceived as passive in relation to his divinity, which is the active element in his life and messianic mission to Israel. The divine figure of Christ in effect appears as a Stoic sage who displays the ideal state of *apatheia*. In this chapter we shall return to the cognitive theory of emotion formulated in chapter 1, which will be applied to Jesus' temporal life in order to show that Jesus is no Stoic sage who seeks to eliminate the common emotions. It will be recalled how it was said that emotions are subjective in the sense that they have a strong connection to one's personal biography. On this view we cannot ignore the role of cultural-social norms—Jewish life and covenant expectations in first-century Palestine—and the history of childhood development in the shaping of Jesus' attitudes, expectations, and emotions. By acknowledging the complexity of Jesus' emotional dispositions that evolve over time and have a specific history, the result will be a heightened appreciation of his genuine and real humanity—i.e., an adequately developed notion of kenosis—which is not overshadowed by the claim regarding the divinity of his person.

The first major part of this chapter will seek to paint a picture of the cultural-historical background of Jesus in terms of the covenant framework, and it will attempt to say something about the family background of Jesus by focusing on the figure of his mother Mary understood as Daughter Zion. While there is an obvious sparseness of material in the gospels concerning the family upbringing of Jesus, it will be contended that significant light can be shed on the question by reflecting on Mary as Daughter Zion, which captures in an evocative manner the covenant expectations of Israel at the time. Ultimately, though, the mystery of Jesus' person cannot be fathomed without acknowledging that his identity is divine, that he is intimately one with the God whom he calls "Father." The third section of part 1 will discuss Jesus' relational identity to the Father, and will argue that Jesus' divinity should not be thought of statically as an inner core of his person as the Logos, but dynamically in terms of his *modus essendi* of being related to the Father in unfathomable love, through the power of the Spirit who comes to rest upon him in eschatological fullness. The aim of the discussion in part 1 is to provide a credible basis for a more adequate conception of kenosis, where the human and the divine progressively actualize themselves as the one and the other as they address each other in Jesus' person. In such a developmental and biographical framework, Jesus' emotions become most significant as the manifestation of the process of mutual interaction of the two natures in his person, which culminates in his passion.

The second major part of the chapter will then turn to consider Jesus' emotions as recorded in the gospels. Each particular emotion will not be strictly examined within its own narrative context, since the discussion is not intended to be an exegetical examination that aims to highlight the contribution of a particular emotion to that gospel's portrait of Jesus. The primary purpose will be to show the way in which a cognitive theory of emotion is able to illuminate the emotions of Jesus as intelligible in their context, and as providing the springboard of his messianic ministry. Towards the end of the discussion the cognitive character of Jesus' emotions will be reinforced by illustrating how his ineffable love of the Father, as the first and chief of his emotions, serves as the cornerstone of all his other emotions recorded in the gospels. The upshot of all this will be to come to an appreciation of the emotional life of Jesus as the concrete manifestation of the process of mutual interaction of the two natures in his person. At the same time, however, a concomitant purpose throughout the discussion will be to illustrate that there is no warrant for imposing the Stoic notions of *apatheia* and *propatheia* upon the figure of Immanuel. To acknowledge the breadth, depth, and full reality of Jesus' emotional life is to illuminate what it means for the divinity to dwell bodily in the man Jesus (Col 2:9), and to marvel with renewed vigor as we gaze upon the process of salvation (deification) in his person.

The Formation of Jesus' Emotional Life

The Covenant Framework of Jesus' Life

Central to the cultural-religious context of Jesus is the covenantal framework within which the biblical account of Jewish history unfolds. The life, ministry, and emotions of Jesus cannot be properly fathomed without reference to the chosen land, the Roman occupation of the land, and the city of Jerusalem which Jesus acknowledges in the gospel story as the place associated with the destiny of Israel (Luke 13:33-34; 19:41). Jesus, as a devout Jew, was fully immersed in Jewish Scripture, which has the character of "storied place;"[1] that is, a place which has special meaning because of *God's* history of covenant lodged there, which is captured by the name "Zion." Once this fact about Jesus is fully appreciated, Jewish Scripture becomes the concrete ground in which Jesus' life and mission to Israel takes root and is continually nourished.[2] Jewish Scripture, of course, is founded on the rubric of God's covenant relationship with Abraham and his descendants, which is inextricably tied to the promise of the land of Canaan. The discussion that follows seeks to illuminate an understanding of the covenant as a complex phenomenon involving the coming together of right place, right time, and right people.[3] The

---

1. Brueggemann, *Land*, 3-4. Brueggemann distinguishes between "place" and "space."

2. The works of Jewish scholars on the gospel story are particularly informative in respect of reading the story of Jesus from a thoroughly Jewish perspective. Martin Buber, for instance, wrote about Jesus, "I am more than ever certain that a great place belongs to Jesus in Israel's history of faith." Buber, *Two Types of Faith*, 13; Joseph Klausner in the conclusion to his book on Jesus wrote, "In his ethical code there is a sublimity, distinctiveness, and originality in form unparalled in any other Hebrew ethical code." Klausner, *Jesus of Nazareth*, 414; and Geza Vermes acknowledges the special character of Jesus' Jewishness when he claims that Jesus should be placed in "the venerable company of the Devout, the ancient Hasidim." Vermes, *Jesus the Jew*, 223.

3. For a more comprehensive discussion of why Christians should not neglect the land of promise in the covenant between Yahweh and his people, see Novello, "Looking Unto the Hidden Zion," 77-91.

confluence of these three factors allows us to appreciate both the special focus of the covenant on a particular people inhabiting a particular land, as well as the universal horizon of the blessings of salvation connected with the covenant.

The distinction that Walter Brueggemann makes between storied "place" and mere "space" is supported by Gerhard Lohfink's reflections on why the salvation of the world requires the "concrete place" that is Israel.[4] Lohfink asks the basic question, Why begin God's "silent revolution" (see Gen 12:1–3) that will turn everything toward salvation in Palestine, of all places? Why not begin the revolution among more obvious candidates, such as the Egyptians, the Persians, the Greeks, the Etruscans, or the Inca? In his response, Lohfink discusses the coming together into a single constellation of "the right place, the right time, and the right people,"[5] which includes the concept of election. The fact that God starts in a small and inconspicuous way is true not only of Abraham but also of the land. The land of Canaan has little or no significance in respect of size, but when we turn to consider its geographical location its place in the world no longer appears insignificant, for it is uniquely situated. In the book of Ezekiel, the Lord God says that he has set Jerusalem "in the center of the nations, with countries round about her" (Ezek 5:5). The land is truly in the center of the nations inasmuch as it lies at the axis of three continents—Europe, Asia, and Africa—with a plethora of different cultures and it lies between two seas—the Mediterranean and the Red Sea—that opened it to the major trade routes of the world. Precisely because of its unique geographic location, all the great powers of the ancient East sought control of this strategic piece of land.

As a nation, then, Israel was constantly forced to interact with other nations, with their cultures and religions. This inevitable contact with other nations "must have sharpened their understanding and their powers of discernment"[6] in respect of what it means to be the people of God. At the same time, however, this contact posed the constant threat of apostasy and the temptation to manage the land "like all the other nations" (1 Sam 8:5, 19–20). But the miracle of Israel's faith is that it was able not to surrender to the impressive religions of the nations that surrounded it— even in the midst of crises and catastrophes, such as the Babylonian exile

---

4. Lohfink, *Does God Need the Church*, 26–39.
5. Lohfink, *Does God Need the Church*, 32.
6. Lohfink, *Does God Need the Church*, 33.

of 587 BCE, Israel managed to cling to its peculiar faith rooted in the God of Abraham, Isaac, Jacob, and Moses. There is ample evidence in Jewish Scripture of contact with other cultures—e.g., Canaanite myth, Egyptian wisdom, Persian Zoroastrianism, and Hellenistic philosophy—but these imported materials are always placed within the framework of Jewish faith which persistently asserts the sovereignty of Yahweh, the one God, ruler over nature and history, who has entered into covenant relationship with Israel, for the sake of the world's salvation.

The reason why the land of Israel is the right place is intelligible enough, but a more difficult question is, Why was God so late in beginning salvation history with Abraham? The high cultures of the ancient East that preceded the emergence of Israel were centuries older and much more impressive than the culture of Israel, so why did not God begin this new work of salvation with them? Lohfink responds that this is part of God's design inasmuch as the late origins of Israel form "the condition for the possibility of the new."[7] This is to say that only when the cultures of the ancient East had reached their zenith with respect to intellectual thought and the development of social systems, could these be taken up and critiqued by Israel's own peculiar character as the chosen people destined to carry out their divinely-appointed mission in the chosen land. This is apparent in that the founding event of Jewish faith is the exodus—Israel's unique character is forged in the exodus from Egyptian society that "used religion to fortify existing relationships of domination."[8] In light of the exodus, Yahweh reveals himself as the one who does not legitimate existing social conditions, but acts to redeem and liberate his people and pave the way for the creation of a new society centered on the Torah.

The right place and the right time amounts to nothing, of course, without the right people who would willingly accept and commit themselves to living out the truth of the Torah. A Jewish legend tells of how the Torah was offered to all the nations, but only Israel was prepared to place its trust in God and carry out the divine mission of the Torah.[9] The conclusion to the legend corresponds to the way Abraham responds in faith to God's command to leave his country and go to the land that God will show him.[10] Israel's election as the people of God is not to be regarded as

---

7. Lohfink, *Does God Need the Church*, 34.
8. Lohfink, *Does God Need the Church*, 34.
9. See Lohfink, *Does God Need the Church*, 35.
10. Traces of this legend are to be found amongst Christian theologians as well.

something for its own sake, as is made abundantly clear in Moses' address to the people at the boundary crossing of the Jordan. The tradition of Deuteronomy is placed at this momentous juncture when Israel listens to Moses speak about the new existence of Israel in the land promised to Abraham. Central to Moses' speech is not only the theme of *promise*, but also the motif of *demand* that arises out of being party to a covenant relationship with God who gives the land to Israel for a divine purpose. At the heart of Israel's experience as the people of God lies this dialectic of promise and demand. What is asked at the boundary is not courage to overcome enemies in the land, but courage to keep Torah. The crossing of the Jordan is not entry into a safe "space" after the experience of the wilderness wanderings, but entry into a special context of covenant, of historical "place" charged with hidden meaning and the promise of ineffable blessings to come. As gift of God, the land was at no time simply the property of the people, yet the constant temptation of Israel was to forget its gifted existence and to be seduced by the gods—i.e., manipulation of things for human ends. Israel in the land is under a specific mandate to live as the people of God, to make the land what God intends to make of it, which can only come about by a faithful cooperation between the people and the land. The land, in other words, signifies a *mission*, and, as Martin Buber highlights, the cooperation in view is truly reciprocal:

> Just as, to achieve fullness of life, the people needed the land, so the land needed the people, and the end which both were called upon to realize could only be reached by a living partnership. Since the living land shared the great work with the living people it was to be both the work of history and the work of nature. Just as nature and history were united in the creation of man, so these two spheres which have become separated in the human mind were to unite in the task in which the chosen land and the chosen people were called upon to co-operate. The holy matrimony of land and people was intended to bring about the matrimony of the two separated spheres of Being.[11]

Few Christians would be aware of this Jewish understanding of the people in the land as a concrete manifestation of the unity of the God of history and the God of nature, and how God is working to overcome

---

A case in point is Maximus the Confessor who wrote that, "It is not as if God chose Israel alone, but Israel alone chose to follow God." Cited in Lohfink, *Does God Need the Church*, 36.

11. Buber, *Israel and Palestine*, xii.

the separation introduced between the spheres of nature and history by the sin and violence of humankind.[12] There is a fundamental difference, though, Buber explains, between the election of the people and the election of the land; namely, the former arises in the course of history while the latter "must have taken place in the very act of the Creation itself," so that the land is a "microcosm" of the whole world, and the union of people and land concerns the perfecting of the world by the establishment of the kingdom of God on earth.[13] Israel was simply never meant to be like the other nations; rather, it has a God-given destiny and mission to be "a light to the nations" by practicing justice and righteousness in the land so that the *Shekhina* will bring about the regeneration of the land and the eschatological renewal of the face of the earth.[14]

The Jewish understanding of the election of the land as part of the original act of creation serves to bring together the land (creation) and the Torah (redemption) in such a way that redemption is portrayed as the completion of God's work of creation. This is especially the case when the notion of the pre-existent Torah as the foundation of the world, which belongs to Jewish wisdom traditions, is factored into the equation. After the exile, Jewish thinkers began to explore wisdom's relationship with God, and these explorations yielded such writings as the book of Proverbs, Job, Sirach, Qoheleth, and the Wisdom of Solomon. Wisdom came to be acknowledged as pre-existing the creation and as the heavenly original of the Torah, and as having established herself in Zion (Sir 24:8–12).[15] The portraying of Wisdom as God's special agent in the creation of the world (Prov 3:19–20; 8:22–31; Sir 24:3–4) makes it clear that her having pitched camp in Zion is intended for the good of all the lands and all the peoples of the earth.

When we move to the Christian thought-world, the Jewish notion of the pre-existent Torah is further developed into the notion of the *pre-existent Torah incarnate*; that is, Jesus of Nazareth, the Messiah of Israel,

---

12. The earth bears the curses of human sin, as both the story of creation and the story of the flood in the book of Genesis testify (see Rom 8:19–23).

13. Buber, *Israel and Palestine*, 47.

14. Buber, *Israel and Palestine*, 51–52. Buber explains that there are three types of wickedness spoken of by the Haggada: bloodshed, idolatry, and pride. Pride is wicked because it pollutes the land and causes the withdrawing of the *Shekhina*, which the humble cause to dwell in the land.

15. Wisdom was acknowledged as present everywhere in the world (Sir 24:7), but it was believed to have come to dwell pre-eminently in Israel (Sir 24:23).

is the eternal Word of divine Wisdom made flesh.[16] The eschatological revelation of Jesus as risen from the dead is the basis for this Christian profession of faith. The Jewish belief in the resurrection of the dead summed up the firm hope, held on to in the midst of suffering in fidelity to God—this is the wisdom tradition of the *passio justi*—that final justice for Israel, as well as for the world, was to be expected from God, and God alone. By raising Jesus from the dead, God has vindicated and revealed him as "the Holy and Just One" (Acts 3:14) who will be the agent of God's final judgment (Acts 17:31). Jesus, who had an extraordinary sense of the destiny and mission of Israel, came to be regarded as the pre-existent word of God made flesh (John 1:14), which means that he "embodies and personifies to perfection Israel's Torah, the Wisdom of God, faithfully and obediently lived out in a disordered world, that is to say, in a world where goodness does not succeed in being victorious."[17] The mission of Jesus was not to abolish the Torah but to see it lived out to perfection (see Matt 5:17) for the final salvation of Israel and the world. As the Torah incarnate, the mission of Jesus cannot be properly considered apart from the election of the people of God and the election of land promised to Abraham.[18]

The fullness of God's salvation promised to Israel remains elusive though, which is precisely what Buber intends to convey when he talks about "the looking unto the hidden Zion."[19] In Judaism the hidden character of God's reign in the world is expressed above all by the Jewish understanding that the *Shekhina* will not move from the west wall of the temple—the faithful one stands behind the west wall of the shattered sanctuary and "will send down the dew of revival and will give new life

16. For a good discussion of Torah and incarnation, see Beeck, *Loving the Torah*, 59–66.

17. Beeck, *Loving the Torah*, 66.

18. The very fact that the incarnation of the eternal Word of divine wisdom took place in the land of Palestine amongst the Jewish people testifies to the legitimacy of the doctrine of God's election of both the land and the people. As long as creation and history remain an unfinished and fragmented process that is groaning for its final salvation, both the land and the people must be seen as retaining their special, divinely-appointed character. What is more, Christians should be careful not to speak of the fulfilment of the covenant promises with the coming of Christ: the promised fullness of salvation appears *in his person* but is clearly not a finished reality in our world which still groans for its final salvation. The dynamics of human history are basically the same now as they were in the time of Christ. Sin, violence, disease, famine, hatred, war, and death remain disturbing features of our world.

19. Buber, *Israel and Palestine*, 142.

to the dead."[20] To the religious Jew the name Zion conveys the inviolable significance of the land as "holy" land; that is, what the land is to become according to its election by the living God. The name implies a "suprahistorical mystery"[21] that engenders hope and meaning because, being beyond history, it confers to history an open-ended texture, especially when a better and new future seems impossible. Zion symbolizes, then, the steadfast commitment of Yahweh to his land and his people, and Israel's trust in the faithful one who calls into existence the things that do not exist. The prophet Isaiah spoke not only of God creating "new heavens and a new earth" but also of creating a "new Jerusalem" of joy and rejoicing (Isa 65:17-25; see Rev 21:9-27).

Isaiah also spoke, though, of his weeping bitter tears at the prospect of "the destruction of the daughter of my people" (Isa 22:4). The prophetic vision of weeping at the prospect of the destruction of Jerusalem is most pronounced in Jeremiah. He is overcome by grief and dismay for "the wound of the daughter of my people" (Jer 8:21) and he wishes that he "might weep day and night for the slain of the daughter of my people" (Jer 9:1). Jesus clearly stands in this prophetic tradition of weeping over the doom that will overtake the covenant people when Luke records Jesus breaking out in loud wailing as he approaches Jerusalem (Luke 19:41). "The coming of the city into sight draws from Jesus, as a weeping Jeremiah, an announcement of its pending doom as a city that has failed to recognize in the ministry of Jesus the visitation of God."[22] The link with Jeremiah and Isaiah is bolstered by Luke's account of the cleansing of the temple (Luke 19:45-46), which immediately follows the account of Jesus' bitter weeping over Jerusalem. Jesus appeals to Scripture, quoting Isaiah 56:7 ("My house shall be a house of prayer") and Jeremiah 7:11 ("a den of robbers"), thereby making it clear that Jerusalem's judgment has already begun in his action of driving out those who use the temple as a market place and not for worship of the Lord of the covenant. It is not merely Jesus' foreseeing of his own fate in Jerusalem that causes him deep sorrow and distress; it is also the destruction of Jerusalem that causes him profound sorrow and lament. Jerusalem is cherished by Jesus as the place associated with the destiny of Israel and the center of the fully redeemed

---

20. Buber, *Israel and Palestine*, 52.

21. Buber, *Israel and Palestine*, 133, 141, 147. Buber asserts that what the political Zionists fail to acknowledge is the suprahistorical mystery that the name Zion implies.

22. Nolland, *Luke 19-24*, 930. Cited in Voorwinde, *Jesus' Emotions*, 140.

world to come, yet the glory of Zion remains hidden and is anticipated by tested faith in the Lord of the covenant.

In Jewish Scripture the story of the covenant relationship is marked by God's unwavering faithfulness on the one hand, and Israel's persistent failure to keep Torah and to make the land what God intends to make of it. The land, as historical place, is charged with the divine mission of Torah. Israel in the land is under a specific mandate to live as the people of God, hence at the heart of Israel's experience in the land lies the dialectic of promise and demand. This dialectic gives rise to a basic tension within the covenant relationship that provides the setting for the operation of God's emotions. The following are the basic emotions of God recognized in Jewish Scripture, and they all have a distinctly cognitive character in light of the inherently high value placed on their object:

(a) God's abiding *love* for Israel, the setting of his heart on Israel, is the basis of his covenant relationship with his people.[23]

(b) God's *jealousy or zeal* arises out of the exclusiveness and intensity of the covenant bond, which forbids the covenant people to worship other gods, for they are called to be a holy people.[24]

(c) When Israel is seduced by pagan gods and fails to keep Torah, God reacts with *wrath and anger*, which is a legitimate reaction given that God is holy and has given his people the task of upholding justice and righteousness in the land for a divine purpose.[25]

(d) God *laments* Israel's apostasy and *suffers* because of the people's failure to keep Torah. At times the divine pathos takes the form of God choosing to suffer "for" his people, which means that God bears the sins of his people. If God were exacting as to matters of judgment, Israel would simply have no future life.[26]

(e) It is with *mercy* and *compassion* that God restores the covenant relationship. At times Israel is subjected to suffering and hardship, but

---

23. See Deut 7:6-13; Jer 31:1-3; Hos 11:1-4.

24. See Exod 20:4-6, 34:12-16; Num 25:11-13; Deut 4:23-24.

25. See Exod 32:10-13; Lev 26:14-33; Num 25:1-5; Deut 31:16, 17; Josh 7:1-26; Judg 2:20; 1 Kgs 11:9-11; 2 Kgs 17:7-18; Ezek 16:8-63; Hos 8:1, 5.

26. See Jer 1:16, 2:1-13, 4:12; Isa 1:2-3, chs. 40-66; Mic 6:1-8. For a thorough study of God's suffering in Jewish Scripture, see Fretheim, *Suffering of God*.

God does not desert or forget the covenant he has made with his people, and makes a new future possible by taking pity on them.²⁷

(f) When restoration of the covenant relationship has taken place and the people's hearts are once again turned towards their God, God again *rejoices and delights* in his covenant partner.²⁸

A key text in Jewish Scripture that can be taken as a summary statement of God's character by appealing to his major emotional traits, is Exodus 34:6–7: "The Lord, the Lord, a God merciful and gracious, slow to anger, and abounding in steadfast love and faithfulness . . . forgiving iniquity and transgression and sin."²⁹ Since these emotional elements of the divine pathos are based upon God's appraisal of a valued object—God's covenant relationship with Israel—it becomes apparent that they have a cognitive structure. We saw in chapter 1 of this study that emotions address a practical concern from a personal and interested perspective, and this certainly applies to the God of the covenant as recounted in Jewish Scripture. When the history of the Jewish people is recognized as God's special history of engagement in the world for the sake of its salvation, it becomes quite appropriate to speak of the "biographical subjectivity" of God's emotions.³⁰ The divine emotions should not be dismissed as mere metaphorical references, for they assume ontological significance when they are thought of as both personal (i.e., biographically subjective) and sources of knowledge (i.e., epistemically objective). As both personal and sources of knowledge, the divine emotions convey truth about God and his historical involvement with the people of the covenant. The divine emotions are appropriate emotions inasmuch as they are epistemically objective; that is to say, there is a clear sense in which they fit the facts of the changing historical circumstances of the people of God. The covenant operates as a paradigm scenario embedded in Jewish faith, worship, and life, and the divine emotions fit the facts of this overarching paradigmatic narrative. Abraham Heschel's writings on pathos as the central category of the prophetic understanding of God

---

27. See Exod 33:19, 34:6; Deut 4:29–31, 30:3; Neh 9:5–38; Isa 54:1–10; Hos 2:14–23; Zech 10:6.

28. See Deut 30:9, 10; Isa 42:1–6; Jer 32:40, 41.

29. Other key biblical texts that highlight God as merciful, slow to anger, and full of steadfast love include: Ps 145:8; Lam 3:22–24; Isa 54:9–10; Joel 2:13.

30. This term, it will be recalled, is used by Cheshire Calhoun, whose thought on emotions was discussed in chapter 1 of this study.

serve to reinforce this understanding. Integral to the biblical view is the notion that God is affected by what happens in the world. Heschel writes, "This notion that God can be intimately affected, that he possesses not merely intelligence and will, but also feeling and pathos, basically defines the prophetic consciousness of God."[31] Prophetic thought is not focused upon God's absoluteness, as indeterminate being, but upon his subjective being; that is, upon God's expression, pathos, and relationship to the people of the covenant, who are charged with the holy mission of keeping Torah in the land.

The cognitive structure of the divine emotions is further illuminated by the fact that they have a dynamic relationship to one another. In light of God's deep attachment to a valued object outside his own control—Israel's response cannot be forced but must be a free response of keeping Torah in the land—we can appreciate why God will experience various emotions: joy and delight when his beloved object freely obeys the Torah, thereby upholding the holiness of the divine name; jealousy and zeal when the valued object turns to worship rival gods; wrath and anger when Israel fails to honor the holy matrimony of land and people, which the covenant signifies; lament and suffering when Israel commits apostasy; and compassion when catastrophe befalls Israel, which leads to restoration of the covenant relationship and God performing the seemingly impossible in respect of creating a real future for Israel. In this scheme of thinking we begin to understand the divine emotions as value-laden ways of viewing the covenant relationship initiated by God, and of communicating the divine self to the covenant people. Once we begin to appreciate the cognitive structure of the divine pathos spoken about in Jewish Scripture, we can no longer entertain the idea of divine impassibility.[32] God is not indifferent to the plight of Israel but is affected by what happens to his covenant partner. In the exodus tradition, for instance, the people groaning under their bondage cry out to God, who says: "I

---

31. Heschel, "Divine Pathos," 33.

32. The notion of God's impassibility (corresponding to Greek *apatheia*), which is closely tied to the doctrine of divine immutability, originated with Plato and Aristotle as a reaction against the petulance of the gods of Greek mythology. Via Philo of Alexandria it was imported into the thinking of patristic figures such as Clement of Alexandria, Origen, and Augustine. Through them it influenced the thought of Anselm, Aquinas, and Calvin. See Voorwinde, *Jesus' Emotions in the Fourth Gospel*, 32. In twentieth-century Christian theology, the doctrine of divine impassibility has come in for particular criticism in the writings, for instance, of Benjamin Warfield, Jürgen Moltmann, Eberhard Jüngel, and process theologians such as Charles Hartshorne.

have seen the affliction of my people who are in Egypt, and have heard their cry . . . I know their sufferings, and I have come down to deliver them" (Exod 3:7–8). In Christian Scripture the notion of a God who feels the afflictions of his people and comes down to redeem them takes on heightened meaning in the person of Jesus of Nazareth, the Messiah and eternal Word of divine Wisdom made flesh.

Just as the divine pathos in Jewish Scripture is intelligible within the covenant framework, so too Jesus' emotions are intelligible and display their cognitive structure within the rubric of the covenant. As Immanuel, Jesus' entire mission to Israel is portrayed in the gospels as the dawning of the messianic age in the land, as God's promised visitation of his people. In the divine covenants of Jewish Scripture, God is typically the inaugurator of the covenant while humanity is the covenant partner, yet in the synoptic gospels the covenant framework of Jesus' ministry is highlighted by the fact that he is cast in both roles: Jesus is presented as both the ideal covenant partner who brings the blessings of the messianic age, and as the inaugurator of the new covenant by the shedding of his blood on Calvary: "Drink of it, all of you; for this is my blood of the covenant, which is poured out for many for the forgiveness of sins" (Matt 26:27–28). At the Last Supper it is abundantly clear that Jesus understands his whole life and mission to Israel in terms of the covenant, for central to his impending death by crucifixion is his extraordinary declaration that his blood will be sacrificed as the blood of the new covenant. The great prophets had envisaged a new covenant that God would make with his people, whereby their sins would be forgiven and they would receive a "new heart" (Jer 31:31–34; Ezek 36:24–28) to fulfill their holy mission in the land. Jesus clearly interprets his own sacrificial death in this prophetic light. What is extraordinary at this climactic point, though, is that Jesus is portrayed not just as the ideal covenant partner who cooperates fully with God for the fulfillment of the holy mission in the land; he is also depicted as the inaugurator of the covenant, which is a role assigned to God. It is actually the tension between these two poles of covenant partner and covenant inaugurator that "creates the dynamics in which his ministry takes place and also the electrical field within which his emotions operate."[33]

---

33. Voorwinde, *Jesus' Emotions in the Fourth Gospel*, 62. In John's Gospel a covenant structure also operates. In contrast to the Synoptic Gospels, though, Jesus is portrayed as covenant Lord and as covenant sacrifice—the "Lamb of God" imagery conveys the notion of covenant sacrifice, while the divine "I am" sayings reveal Jesus as covenant Lord. It is the disciples of Jesus who function as the covenant partners. See

Once we appreciate Jesus' dual role as both ideal covenant partner and covenant inaugurator, the relationship between his emotions and the covenant becomes more complex by virtue of *his emotions tending in both a human and a divine direction*. This understanding is supported by the arguments of the previous chapter concerning an adequately developed notion of kenosis, which goes hand in glove with the idea of a progressive or gradual incarnation that culminates in the paschal mystery of Christ. In his person we have to do with a complex interweaving and interacting of humanity and divinity, which defies any dualistic conception of the natures as juxtaposed to or separate from one another. It is on the level of person as the incarnate Son of the Father, and not in the sphere of the natures, that the unity of Jesus is established, which means that the mystery of his person is irreducible to either his divine or human nature. We should think of the two natures as progressively encountering and addressing one another in Jesus' person, and hence as advancing through each other in the development of Jesus' own individuality in the historical context of first-century Jewish life in the land. His suffering in connection with the inauguration of the new covenant, for instance, should not be solely attributed to his humanity, while maintaining that his divinity remained immune from suffering and death.[34] Rather, two points must be made here. (i) First, we must appreciate that Jesus' suffering in body and soul is actually intensified, not lessened, by his consciousness of being the divine Son who must drink the cup of God-forsakenness. (ii) Second, if his suffering is not addressed to his divinity—because the divinity is regarded as immune from suffering—then how is it possible for holy love to be communicated to his humanity so that he is able to endure the agony of his passion? If the suffering of Jesus is addressed by holy love in a veritable wrestle to bring his redemptive work to final completion, then the two natures united in his person must perforce be in communication with each other, and advance through each other.

Voorwinde, *Jesus' Emotions in the Fourth Gospel*, 96–115.

34. We saw earlier that Jewish thought acknowledges the divine pathos: God suffers *because* of his people's failure to keep Torah, and at times God suffers *for* the sake of Israel's future by bearing the sins of the people. Jewish thought, unlike patristic and medieval Christian theology, does not shy away from affirming a suffering God. Yet the divine suffering in view when reflecting on Jesus' passion introduces a novel dimension in that God now knows suffering from within the human condition: in the person of Christ, God himself has been subject to human becoming in the historical-existential realm with all its limitations, finitude, sin, and death.

It is helpful when reflecting on this topic to keep in mind that when we speak of the divinity of Jesus we are dealing with a certain group of divine qualities that are communicated to his humanity. The focus is on the *communicable* or personal attributes of divinity, which are relational properties of God as essentially life, love, mercy, righteousness, wisdom, holiness, and freedom.[35] In the divine act of creation, the theological meaning of which is that God enters into relationship with humanity (see Gen 1:26), it is these communicable properties of divinity that humanity is essentially called to share in. The same applies to God's covenant relationship with Israel, which is summed up in the holiness code: "You shall be holy; for I the Lord your God am holy" (Lev 19:2). The purpose of the divine self-communication is the participation of humanity in the very life of God. This means that the measure of our humanity is the degree to which we share in the communicable attributes of God. When our actions are holy and good, they are genuinely human actions, yet they simultaneously attest the personal properties of divinity. There are a couple of significant differences, though, between Jesus and the rest of humanity in respect of sharing in the communicable properties of God. There is a *qualitative* difference in that the man Jesus is the incarnate Son of the Father, and there is a *quantitative* difference in that Jesus shows himself to be perfectly obedient to the Father unto death in the testing circumstances of his saving mission to the covenant people.

Since Jesus is without personal sin, there is a difference between the emotions of Jesus and our emotions, and the difference lies in the purity, intensity, and appropriateness of Jesus' emotions associated with his proclamation of the kingdom of grace, which is met with increasing hostility towards his person and ultimate rejection of his messianic mission. The sinlessness of Jesus must not be understood in a way that separates him from us sinners, inasmuch as he does not appear to share in our Adamic weakness and to be burdened with our daily temptations. On the contrary, Jesus' life, as a life of perfect obedience to the Father

---

35. On the understanding that God is essentially love, the personal attributes of God—love, freedom, mercy, faithfulness, wisdom, righteousness, and holiness—should be regarded as prior to the metaphysical attributes of omnipotence, omnipresence, omniscience, impassibility, immutability, and eternity. The latter do serve, though, as qualifiers of the personal attributes in that they indicate ways in which God's action in the world is distinguished from human action. Human action is always restricted and conditioned action, whereas in the case of divine action in the world God is restricted by nothing apart from himself; that is, by respecting the natural laws of the world and the freedom of human agents. See Schwöbel, *God*, 46–62.

lived in a sinful and cruel world that refuses to uphold justice and allow goodness to triumph, necessarily implies an emotional life that is deeper, purer, and more intense than ours: "He suffered from the repeated assaults of Satan, from the hatred and unbelief of His own people, and from the persecution of His enemies. Since He trod the wine-press alone, His holiness must have been oppressive, and His sense of responsibility, crushing."[36] These heightened qualities of his emotions stem from his intimate oneness with the Father, whose benevolent will Jesus is fully committed to proclaiming despite the increasing hostilities, assaults, unbelief, and rejection that he suffers, which ultimately ends in his crucifixion. *The emotional life of Jesus reveals what it means for the divinity to dwell bodily in the man Jesus* (Col 2:9), in order to bring to fruition the covenant promises of old concerning life in the land as a participation in the very life and holiness of God.

The emotional life of Jesus communicates the intentional action of the divine Father in relation to the valued object of his covenant people, and, at the same time, it offers the most perfect example of a human life that is afforded by history. Jesus is the "interpreter of humanity" in that he shows us through his words, emotions, and deeds what it means to be a truly human being; at the same time, Jesus is the "interpreter of God" in that he shows through his words, emotions, and deeds who and how God himself is.[37] Benjamin Warfield, commenting on Philippians 2:5–8 where Paul talks of Jesus as being in the "form of God" but humbling himself to take on the "form of a servant," makes this very point concerning the need to appreciate the divine pathos, for only a God who is truly affected by human suffering and sorrow is worthy of our trust and love:

> It was our God who so loved us that He gave Himself for us. Now, herein is a wonderful thing. Men tell us that God is, by the very necessity of His nature, incapable of passion, incapable of being moved by inducements from without; that He dwells in holy calm and unchangeable blessedness, untouched by human sufferings or human sorrows . . . Let us bless our God that it is not true. God can feel; God does love . . . our hearts . . . cry out for a God whom we may love and trust . . . Let us rejoice that

---

36. Berkhof, *Systematic Theology*, 337.

37. Schillebeeckx, *Interim Report*, 132. Schillebeeckx talks of only word and deed; he does not mention Jesus' emotions. I have added emotions to this statement, for it should be clear by now that this study argues for the complex unity of intelligence, emotion, and will (action).

> He has plainly revealed Himself to us in His Word as a God who loves us, and who, because He loves us, has sacrificed Himself for us. Let us remember that it is a fundamental dogma of the Christian religion that God so loved us that He gave Himself for us.[38]

Warfield does not believe that talking about God's affections amounts to a gross anthropomorphism or metaphorical language.[39] It is simply the truth of God—i.e., ontological language—and he resists any attempt, as has been commonplace in the past, to yield up the God of the biblical story and the God of our hearts to any philosophical abstraction regarding the Absolute.[40] In the presence of the Absolute we may feel awe and acknowledge our dependence upon it, but we can neither trust it nor love it because our hearts cry out for a God whom we can love and in whom we can trust; that is, a God who is truly affected by the afflictions of his people and is truly concerned for the good of humanity in this vale of tears. The covenant framework of Jewish Scripture, which reaches its zenith in the affirmation of Jesus Christ as the inaugurator of the new covenant by the shedding of his blood on Calvary, presents us with a God who is vulnerable and affected by the cries of his afflicted people. God is understood to be not only transcendent and above the fray, but also immanent and very much in the fray. The God of love and compassion makes the suffering of his people his own (immanence), yet as suprahistorical mystery God is not powerless to do something about human suffering and work some ultimate good out of it (transcendence).

---

38. Warfield, "Emotional Life," 570–71.

39. If God has no emotions, then it logically follows that Jesus' emotions can only be indications of his humanity.

40. Philosophical abstractions regarding the absolute give rise to unsatisfactory notions of divine impassibility and immutability. It is worth noting here that Karl Barth, commenting on the doctrine of divine immutability, maintains that in light of the covenant of grace established from all eternity in the person of Jesus Christ, we must rethink the notion of divine immutability—that God is immutable means that God continues to be what God always is from eternity, namely, "the one who loves in freedom." See Barth, *Church Dogmatics*, vol. II/II, 410. The thought of Jüngel is also worth noting, for he is very critical of Greek philosophical thought for attributing only negative characteristics to the temporal world in which everything changes and is destined to pass away. Jüngel asserts that God in Christ has identified the divine self with the struggle between being and non-being, for the sake of life. Thus the story of the death of God, which expresses the humanity of God, is *the* story to be told by Christians, for it defines the essence of God as love. See Jüngel, *God As the Mystery*, 218, 299.

Jesus' Mother as "Daughter Zion"

Now that Jesus' historical-cultural background in terms of the covenant framework has been discussed, attention can be given to the influence of his parents on the development of his individuality and emotional life. Jesus' world-view was undoubtedly that of Jewish Scripture and it is clear from the gospels that he had an intimate knowledge of Scripture. But what part, if any, did his parents play in developing his individuality and forming his attitudes and emotions? Of course there is a paucity of material in respect of Jesus' parents; what little we know is gleaned from Matthew's Gospel and Luke's Gospel, where Mary is the focus, not Joseph. The figure of Mary is not insignificant, to my mind, when it comes to Jesus' personal biography and the development of his individuality. Christian tradition has long acknowledged the special role that Mary plays in the birth of Immanuel. Her holiness cannot be discounted when reflecting on Jesus' childhood and early development. What is more, Mary's holiness should be thought of dynamically, not statically, as a deep and real involvement with the historical vicissitudes of the Jewish people and their long-suffering expectations in respect of the coming of the Messiah.[41] It will certainly be helpful in this regard to reflect on Mary as "daughter of Zion" (Isa 62:11; Zeph 3:14; Zech 9:9) inasmuch as "she incorporates the whole of the preparation of Israel for him who was to come."[42] This dynamic understanding of Mary's vocation, in which her Jewish faith plays an integral part in her giving birth to the Savior, is expressed concisely in the patristic axiom that Mary conceived Christ spiritually in her heart before she conceived him bodily in her womb (*prius mente quam ventre*).[43] The story of the annunciation reveals that Mary is addressed in a singular way by God's election and covenant promise, but while her office is certainly unique in that she will give birth to the Son of the Most High, it is nonetheless not without analogy to other roles and offices in the biblical narrative of the history of salvation.

In his meditations on Mary, Joseph Ratzinger reminds us that the image of Mary in the New Testament is "woven entirely of Old Testament

---

41. For a discussion of ways in which Mary's holiness can be conceived dynamically rather than statically—the dogma of the immaculate conception conveys a static view of Mary's holiness—see Novello, "Daughter Zion," 238–58.

42. Flanagan, *Theology of Mary*, 20.

43. Flanagan, *Theology of Mary*, 28. The same point was fully acknowledged by no less than Martin Luther. See Yeago, "Presence of Mary," 66–67.

threads" and that the unity of the two Testaments "guarantees the integrity of the doctrines of creation and grace."[44] We must not lose sight of the fact that the spirit that comes upon Mary is the same spirit that hovers over the abyss in the creation story (see Gen 1:2) and that brings forth being out of nothingness. The reversal of values expressed in Hannah's song (1 Sam 2:1–10) is clearly echoed in Mary's *Magnificat* (Luke 1:46–55), where the humble and lowly are exalted while the mighty and haughty are put down from their thrones. In the discussion below it will become apparent that Mary represents the culmination of the history of the great women of Israel, and into that history is woven the theology of Daughter Zion in which the prophets announced the mystery of the covenant and God's steadfast love for Israel.[45] The discussion will also consider the question of whether Mary's holiness entails her complete sanctification from the moment of her conception, or whether it is more plausible to hold that Mary grew in holiness so that by the time of the annunciation she was hailed as "full of grace."

When we reflect upon the history of promises recorded in Jewish Scripture, the Patriarchs of Israel stand out as the bearers of that history. Yet the mothers also play a significant role in that history: Sarah-Hagar (Gen 16:1–16; 21:1–7), Rachel-Leah (Gen 29–35), and Hannah-Penina (1 Sam 1–2) are those pairs of women in whom the extraordinary aspect of the promises becomes apparent.[46] In each of these cases where fertility (Hagar, Leah, Penina) and infertility (Sarah, Rachel, Hannah) stand in opposition, the normal mode of thinking is reversed: the fertile ones are relegated to the realm of the ordinary and are no longer considered the truly blessed; while the infertile ones, who are now elevated to the sphere of the extraordinary, are seen as truly blessed because they are subject to the creative power of God's word of promise. This reversal of values is captured beautifully in the song of Hannah, which is echoed in Mary's *Magnificat*, and it also features prominently in Jesus' Sermon on the Mount. In this history of women who experience earthly infertility as

---

44. Ratzinger, *Daughter Zion*, 12, 33. Jaroslav Pelikan makes the same point as Ratzinger when he laments the tragically forgotten bond between Mary and the Jewish tradition. See Pelican, *Mary Through the Centuries*, 23–36.

45. The brief discussion will be based largely upon strands of Jewish tradition that are identified in the meditations of Ratzinger in his *Daughter Zion*.

46. Ratzinger, *Daughter Zion*, 18. Rebekah, Isaac's wife, is also barren (see Gen 25:21), but she bears a son Jacob.

true fertility is to be found the basis of a theology of virginity.[47] The angel Gabriel's statement to Mary, "For with God nothing will be impossible" (Luke 1:37), reflects this understanding of the creative power of God's word that is made manifest in situations where fertility is not a possibility open to humanity.

Towards the end of the Old Testament canon we come across the woman-savior figures of Esther and Judith as representatives of suffering Jewry. Judith is a widow who represents the apparently forlorn cause of God. When, however, the chosen people triumph over their enemies—the Assyrians—they sing the praises of Judith and go to Jerusalem for a solemn thanksgiving. The book of Esther also tells of the deliverance of Jewry, in Persia this time, by the actions of Esther who is a harem-wife at the Persian court, where she has become queen and uses her position to save the Jews from extermination. Both these women are representative of a defeated Israel that has been dishonored amongst the nations, yet, at the same time, both are depicted as savior figures. This is because they embody the spiritual hope that their powerless state will prove to be the very locus for the revelation of God's redemptive power. As in the case of the infertile woman, the powerless women of Israel represent the people of God; the history of these women "becomes the theology of God's people and, at the same time, the theology of the covenant."[48]

In light of the foregoing discussion, the underlying motif in Luke's portrait of the interaction between the angel Gabriel and the young Mary surfaces: "she is in person the true Zion, toward whom hopes have yearned throughout all the devastations of history."[49] The promise expressed in Isaiah 54:1, where Israel is likened to the childless and barren woman to whom is promised a vast multitude of children, is now fulfilled for Luke in the concrete reality of the Virgin Mary who will conceive the Son of the Most High by the power of the spirit. As daughter of Zion, *Mary represents Israel in eschatological perspective,* for she embodies the realization of Israel's deepest hope in respect of the advent of the Lord who brings final salvation for Israel and the world.[50] The annunciation passage is continuous with prior occasions in which God accomplished the impossible, yet the thrust of the announcement is about the future as

---

47. Ratzinger, *Daughter Zion*, 19.
48. Ratzinger, *Daughter Zion*, 21.
49. Ratzinger, *Daughter Zion*, 43.
50. See Yeago, "Presence of Mary," 69; and Boss, *Empress and Handmaid*, 218.

well as the past, so that Mary becomes the "link" figure between the Old and New Covenants.[51] The uniqueness of Mary amongst the holy ones of Israel is apparent, says Robert Jenson, in that her womb now becomes the container of the Ark of the Covenant:

> It is of course the heart of Christian faith that God's presence in Israel is gathered up and concentrated in Immanuel, God with us, in this one Israelite's presence in Israel: he is in person the Temple's *shekhina*, and the Word spoken by all the prophets, and the Torah. And if that is so, then the space delineated by Israel to accommodate the presence of God is finally reduced to and expanded to Mary's womb, the container of Immanuel. We must note the singularity of Mary's dogmatic tile [*theotokos*]: she is not one in a series of God's mothers, she simply is the Mother.[52]

Mary is continuous with the history of the great women of Israel in whom God accomplished the impossible, yet her unique or singular place is secured by the fact that of no other can it be said that she, or he, contains the uncontainable God. But Mary was not randomly chosen to be the Mother of God, for her response to Gabriel reveals a woman of exceptional Jewish faith and humility, a woman who collaborates with God unreservedly for the much anticipated salvation of Israel. In Luke's portrait of Mary we see a woman who enjoys a loving immediacy to God, which suggests that she was specially elected and consecrated for her mission from the first instant of her conception.

The dogma of the Immaculate Conception holds that Mary was already chosen for her office and consecrated by God from the first instant of her conception. This motif of God choosing and consecrating specific persons even before they are born—i.e., predestining persons—is, of course, not foreign to the prophetic literature of Israel (see Jer 1:5) or Christian Scripture (see Gal 1:15; Eph 1:4–5). But the dogma goes beyond these other cases in claiming that only Mary in her vocation was preserved from inheriting the negative consequences of Adam's sin, which enabled her to live a life of utmost integrity in loving relationship with God in preparation for the incarnation of the Word. An inherent problem with the language of the dogma, however, as stated earlier, is that it suggests a view of holiness which is not congruent with the evidence of

---

51. Gaventa, "Nothing," 29.

52. Jenson, "Space for God," 55. Jenson goes on to say that when we ask Mary, as Mother of God, to pray for us, this is to invoke all God's history with Israel at once, which is contained in her person—"be it done unto me according to your will."

Scripture, where holiness cannot be thought of apart from the concrete situation of human existence and God as historical force who ensures that history remains essentially open to the new, to qualitatively better things to come. As Donald Flanagan has rightly pointed out, the meaning of the dogma can no longer be thought of as Mary having been spared the trials, tribulations, and challenges of daily life. "People today find a Mary so immaculately conceived a totally incredible figure. Such grace is neither inspiring nor in any way supportive for their Christian faith and living."[53] Grace is always grace given in the fray of human existence in this world, and Mary's life should not be treated as an exception to this understanding.

When Mary is reflected upon as Daughter Zion and woven into the history of the great woman of Israel of which she was the flowering, her holiness must be viewed in dynamic terms as an "involved holiness" or a "holiness of preparation" that was not closed-off from her everyday life in Galilee.[54] This means that she was born into Israel's history of fidelity and infidelity, that she had to undergo personal development in a world marked by sin, that she was confronted by human failure and misery, that she was not exempt from the human condition and grew in understanding of her son, and was subjected to suffering and death.[55] It was precisely in this concrete historical situation that Mary was called to radically open herself to God's love and allow her person to be progressively taken over by collaborating with grace. "Mary was by her grace called to open herself more and more to God's love so as to grow towards his coming."[56]

---

53. Flanagan, *Theology of Mary*, 27.

54. Flanagan, *Theology of Mary*, 28; Schillebeeckx, *Mary*, 72.

55. I am of the view that Mary was not spared physical death. Christ himself was not spared death and it is through his redemptive death that death in the full sense is conquered. It is simply untenable, to my mind, to interpret the assumption of Mary in terms of her being taken up straight into heaven without having undergone physical death. Mary shares necessarily with humanity some of the consequences of Adam's sin—i.e., suffering and mortality—so that she is able to impart to her son the humanity of the old Adam with its need of redemption, understood as the supernatural end of union with God.

56. Flanagan, *Theology of Mary*, 28. Mary's growing in grace means that while her fundamental attitude is one of radical receptivity to God, this does not mean that she has full understanding of God's purposes in her son. In Mark 3:31–34, for instance, Mary appears "outside" the company of Jesus; in Luke 2:41–51, Mary lacks understanding of her son and ponders things in her heart right up to the time of Pentecost (see Luke 2:19; Acts 1:14). Just as Jesus "increased in wisdom and in stature and in favor with God" (Luke 2:52), so too Mary increased in wisdom and in stature and in

By interpreting the privilege of the immaculate conception in terms of a growing in grace, we can appreciate the patristic saying that Mary conceived Christ in her heart before she conceived him in her womb.[57] When sin is understood in relational terms as abuse of freedom and distortion of the person's relationship to God, Mary's freedom to grow in holiness points to her capacity to remain resolutely God-centered in a world that groans under the burden of sin, anxiety, and death.[58] Mary's response to Gabriel in Luke 1:38—"Behold, I am the handmaid of the Lord; let it be to me according to your word"—reveals a woman of exceptional Jewish faith, piety, and humility. Such an exceptional faith and humility did not come without any effort on Mary's part; rather, in the harsh and brutal context of the Roman occupation of the land, she lived Jewish life very much in the fray and always looked faithfully to the Lord to perform the impossible and bring salvation to his people. As Daughter Zion she embodies the realization of Israel's deepest hope in respect of the advent of final salvation for the covenant people. In Mary's *Magnificat* it is clear that the ministry of her son will be continuous with hopes that are centuries old (Luke 1:55).

The first two chapters of the Gospel of Luke are not, however, dedicated wholly to Mary. The chapters are replete with material and other persons pertaining to the Jewish expectation of the final coming of God's reign. All the characters without exception are simple, poor, and pious Jews who faithfully await the fulfillment of the covenant promises given to the fathers of Israel. Elizabeth, Mary's kinswoman, is barren but conceives a child (John the Baptist) by the power of the spirit, and she is described as "righteous before God, walking in all the commandments and ordinances of the Lord blameless" (1:6). Elizabeth's husband Zechariah is a priest who is also described as righteous and blameless before God, and

---

favor with God.

57. Mary's growing in grace points to the progressive nature of her "subjective" redemption; that is, the love that God bestows upon Mary is freely reciprocated in her love of God. This process of subjective redemption culminates in Mary's death as total dispossession of herself in love of God, and her sharing in Christ's resurrection as the perfect reality of "objective" redemption.

58. The grace of the immaculate conception is the privilege of radical openness or total dispossession of self in freedom before God. On the basis of Irenaeus of Lyon's anthropology, where a distinction is made between the "image" of God and "likeness" to God, it can be argued that the privilege of the immaculate conception confers upon Mary the perfect image of God, but Mary still has to grow in her likeness to God. See Novello, "Daughter Zion," 245–51.

when the child John is born Zechariah in his *Benedictus* (1:68–79) foretells the greatness of the child as the "prophet of the Most High" who will "go before the Lord to prepare his ways, to give knowledge of salvation to his people." There is an old devout man named Simeon who was looking for the consolation of Israel (2:22–35), and Simeon's Oracle (*Nunc Dimittis*) adds the dimension of salvation for the gentiles—the oracle therefore anticipates the Acts of the Apostles. There is an aged widow and prophetess named Anna who spent all her time in the temple and who recognizes the baby Jesus as the one who would bring "the redemption of Jerusalem" (2:36–38). Finally, Luke includes shepherds in his birth narrative (2:8–20). Shepherds were a lowly class in Jewish society, yet it is to them that an angel of the Lord brings the "good news of a great joy which will come to all the people."

When we try to picture Jesus' family upbringing, the one thing that certainly can be established is the strong Jewish piety and deep humility of his parents. The special character of Mary as Daughter Zion stands out in Luke's account of Jesus' virgin birth. Joseph is barely mentioned, but the little that is said about him is sufficient to indicate that he was "a just man" (Matt 1:19) of the "house and lineage of David" (Luke 2:4; also Matt 1:20). Joseph, like Mary, was a righteous and upright man who awaited God's visitation of his people. With regard to extended family, we know that Mary's cousin Elizabeth is certainly a pious and humble Jewish woman, and Elizabeth's priestly husband Zechariah is just as assuredly pious, humble, and faith-filled. The picture that emerges concerning Jesus' family background is that he grew up in an atmosphere of exceptional Jewish faith, piety, and humility. We should not discount the influence of Jesus' family with regard to his acquiring a deep knowledge of Jewish Scripture, the formation of his Jewish faith and beliefs, his appreciation of foundational core values based on God's abiding covenant with Israel, and hence the development of his emotional life. The emotions of adult life have a history, it was argued in chapter 1 of this work, and we can well imagine that Jesus' history was one in which he received a steady dose of Jewish instruction, based on a family life of keeping Torah in the land and maintaining trust in God who is true to his covenant promises.

His childhood could not have been a normal one typical of other Jewish youth, for he was conceived in the womb of Daughter Zion by the power of the spirit. His mother and father, as well as Elizabeth and her husband Zechariah, were all recipients of the angel Gabriel's communication to them, so they knew the special identity of Jesus as Son of God, who had come into the world to bring final salvation to God's people. Jesus was simply no ordinary child, and his parents would have made known to him the extraordinary manner in which he was born into Jewish life in the land. At the same time, in light of the understanding that the history of Jesus' mother as Daughter Zion is the flowering of the history of the powerless women of Israel who represent the people of God, we can well imagine that Jesus would have received from his parents a special education in respect of the theology of the covenant. The study of Jewish Scripture would have been integral to Jesus' understanding of the theology of covenant, yet we should not ignore the role played by his parents in faithfully and steadfastly keeping Torah and instructing the young Jesus with regard to trusting in God's abiding covenant with Israel. There can be little doubt, either, that Jesus' parents would have cherished him dearly, given his holy status as Immanuel, and their love for him would have been the young Jesus' first experience of the benevolence of God. While we have a paucity of knowledge regarding the family upbringing of Jesus, it would not be stretching matters too far to suggest that Mary and Joseph, together with Elizabeth and Zechariah, must have had a significant influence on the formation of Jesus' faith, core values, and personal attitudes, and hence his emotional life.

The fact that Jesus was a precocious child raised in a pious Jewish family is evident in Luke's Gospel when we read of his parents journeying to Jerusalem for the feast of the Passover when he was twelve years old (2:41-51). This scriptural passage recounts the story of Jesus remaining in the temple, unbeknownst to his parents, and when they return to Jerusalem after three days to seek out the young Jesus they find him in the temple, "sitting among the teachers, listening to them and asking them questions; and all who heard him were amazed at his understanding and answers" (vv. 46-47). When Mary begins to reprove the young Jesus for causing his parents anxiety, Jesus perplexes his parents with the response, "Did you not know that I must be in my Father's house?" (v. 49). Here we see the divine consciousness being awakened in the young adolescent Jesus. The fact that Jesus' parents did not understand his response, and his mother pondered all these things in her heart (v. 51), shows that despite being the recipients of the angel Gabriel's communication to them regarding the special birth of Jesus by the power of the spirit, they could not fathom the extraordinary sense of Jesus' identification with the Father or his precocious understanding of Jewish Scripture. Jesus, though, did not possess the fullness of knowledge or self-consciousness as the divine Son of the Father by the age of twelve, for we are told that Jesus was *obedient to his parents* and returned with them to Nazareth where he "increased in wisdom and in stature, and in favor with God and man" (Luke 2:52).[59] He underwent, in other words, temporal development of his individuality in the historical situation of his time: he was born into Israel's history of fidelity and infidelity; he lived under Roman occupation of the land; he had to grow up in a world marked by sin; he was confronted by human failure, misery, and suffering; he attended the local synagogue and the religious festivals in Jerusalem and was a keen learner of wisdom; and he worked as a carpenter (Mark 6:3) to make a humble living in Nazareth. The divine-humanity of Immanuel, in accordance with the testimony of the gospels, is manifested not from the very beginning but only gradually; he is subject to a process of temporal development that is proper to "the kenotic idea of the Incarnation."[60] Being in the "form of God" but humbling himself to take on the "form of a servant" (Phil 2:5-8), Jesus' consciousness of self as the divine Son who is obedient to his Father is subject to a process of gradual awakening in time.

At a particular point in his life history, around the age of thirty (Luke 3:23), Jesus reaches a level of maturity that sees him leave his home in Nazareth to seek the baptism of John. Once he is baptized by John and receives his anointing with the spirit, he begins his special proclamation of the kingdom of God's mercy to Israel.[61] As Jesus carries out

59. It is interesting to note that before the gospels depict the adult Jesus as being obedient to the Father who sent him to preach the kingdom, he is portrayed in Luke 2:41-51 as being obedient to his parents. Obedience to parents could be seen as a precursor to obedience to the Father, in which case we have another indication of the influence of Jesus' family life on the formation of his basic attitudes and beliefs, and thus emotional life.

60. Bulgakov, *Lamb of God*, 254. While the person of Jesus was divine, his divinity was concealed in kenosis, thus his personal consciousness of self undergoes a process of awakening in the temporal sphere.

61. According to Schillebeeckx, Jesus is presented as the "eschatological prophet" who ushers in God's time of mercy. Jesus is not to be thought of as a prophet in the line of the prophets, but as the latter-day prophet who redeems Israel and ushers in God's reign of mercy. When Jesus is called the Christ, he is being interpreted as the latter-day prophet who, being anointed with the Spirit, possesses the true doctrine; he speaks in a definitive way of God, he is the true interpreter of the Torah. The eschatological prophet was to be one who was like Moses but greater than Moses. With Moses, God spoke face to face, mouth to mouth (see Num 12:6-8; Exod 33:11), whereas with other prophets God makes himself known to them through a dream or vision. Moses was also a suffering servant of God (see Num 16:47; Isa 53:4), and this theme is fused in Deutero-Isaiah. See Schillebeeckx, *Jesus*, 475-99; and his *Interim Report*, 65.

his mission of mercy to Israel according to his interpretation of what it means to keep Torah in the land, he is always presented as the one who possesses the fullness of the spirit and who enjoys a unique and intimate relationship of oneness with the Father. What is clear from the gospels is the relational character of Jesus' identity, although his divine identity as the Son cannot be fathomed apart from his increasingly difficult and testing relationship with the covenant people to whom he brings the glad tidings of the Father's merciful love and benevolence. When Jesus begins his messianic activity in the land, it soon becomes apparent that the history of his virginal birth and pious Jewish upbringing are not sufficient to illuminate the mystery of his person, which causes such astonishment and amazement among the people: "Is not this the carpenter, the son of Mary?" (Mark 6:3). His personal biography, which leads to the formation of specific orientations and attitudes and therefore the emergence of his emotional life, simply cannot be restricted to his being conceived in the womb of Daughter Zion by the power of the spirit, and to the process of his pious Jewish upbringing. The personal biography of Jesus must be extended all the way back into the suprahistorical life of God himself—he is the eternal Word of divine Wisdom (Torah) made flesh, who brings the glad tidings of salvation for Israel and the world. The following section will seek to illuminate the manner in which the gospels establish this ontological aspect of Jesus' identity.

Jesus' *Modus Essendi*: Obedience to His Father

On the basis of the foregoing discussion, we should now be able to appreciate the assertion that in light of the play of his emotions, Jesus appears before us as "a distinct human being, with *his own individuality*."[62] It is often suggested in writings on Christology that the Son of God assumed not "a" human nature manifesting itself in a concrete individual, but "generic" or "universal" human nature. This thinking is of a philosophical kind, based on a static concept of a generic nature. This idea receives no support from the discussion hitherto concerning the distinctly historical framework of the covenant and the land—the convergence of right place, right time, and right people—and the particular social-religious milieu of Jesus' family upbringing in Galilee in the first century of the

---

62. Warfield, "Emotional Life," 139.

Common Era. The person of Immanuel is simply "not man in general."[63] He was conceived in the womb of Daughter Zion by the workings of the spirit, was born into a specific historical milieu in the land under Roman occupation, shared the long-suffering aspirations of his Jewish people, spoke the language of Aramaic, brought the glad tidings of God's benevolent visitation to Israel, underwent development of his individuality in his messianic mission to a people burdened by sin and misery, was ultimately rejected by his own people and religious authorities and put to death, but was raised from the dead by the Father and exalted to God's right hand. It is certainly correct to maintain that our Adamic humanity has been assumed by the person of Jesus, but the term "humanity" should not be thought of philosophically as a static or closed system— i.e., a definitively known quantity—but theologically as a dynamic system that is fundamentally open to the transcendent reality of God. Humanity should be regarded as an emerging reality beyond every definition and every boundary. We can say that Jesus as a distinct human being with his own individuality is the *interpreter of humanity*, in that he shows us in word and deed and through the play of his emotions what it can mean to be a truly human being; and at the same time Jesus as a distinct human being with his own individuality can be said to be the *interpreter of God* in that he shows us in word and deed and through his emotional life who and how God himself is.

We are to understand that what is commonly referred to as "human nature" is not a fixed and closed system, and, moreover, neither should "divine nature" be thought of as a fixed and closed system. As both open and dynamic systems, the human and divine essences in the person of Jesus mutually interpenetrate, interact, communicate, and address each other in a movement of genuine action where the humanization of God (kenosis) aims at the deification of humanity (theosis). An appreciation of the development of Jesus' individuality certainly serves to bolster the assertion that in the man Jesus we have before us a human being like ourselves, who knows our temporal human condition intimately from within. Yet the import of this notion of the development of Jesus' own individuality should not be limited to merely establishing Jesus' real humanity. This line of thinking is also valuable when it comes to reflecting on the uniqueness of Jesus' person as the Son of the Father, and demonstrating the need to adopt a dynamic or progressive view of the incarnation

---

63. Bulgakov, *Lamb of God*, 274.

rather than a static perspective characteristic of patristic and medieval thought. The following discussion concerning a literary approach to the gospel story has more to say on the development of Jesus' individuality in relation to the Father, on the one hand, and to the increasing isolation and rejection of his messianic preaching to Israel on the other.

In recent decades we have witnessed not only the introduction of an historical approach to the Bible, but also a literary approach that draws attention to what a text means on its own terms: content and form are inseparable. Reflection on the person and work of Jesus is strengthened when it includes literary interpretation analogous to the ways Christians at worship listen to the gospels as aesthetic wholes and respond to them in their proclamation of who Jesus is. Thinkers such as Frans Jozef van Beeck, for instance, stress that the gospel story is not a history but a "witnessing story" that attests to the actions of Jesus and of God through his person, and the response of those committed to following him.[64] The thought of van Beeck draws on the work of David Kelsey who has argued that what we know about the gospel story's central protagonist is not known by inference from the story; rather, "he is known quite directly in and with the story, and recedes from cognitive grasp the more he is abstracted from the story," hence the gospels are to be treated as "identity descriptions" of the man Jesus.[65] In the gospel narratives, persons are viewed as agents, they enact their intentions, so that their identity arises out of their interaction with one another within the changing circumstances of their lives. In light of this realism that draws us into the world of the gospels, Hans Frei sums up the literary approach by saying that what the gospels tell us "is the fruit of the stories themselves."[66] While the gospel narratives are not to be seen as historical accounts of the life of

---

64. Beeck, *Christ Proclaimed*, 327, 360–75. The kerygma is viewed by Beeck as first and foremost the Christian *homologia*, that is, testimony in the form of narrative recital of the great things God has done in our midst through Jesus. There are three characteristics of kerygma: it attests to a present and future person, not just to a past figure; it speaks about God as well as Jesus Christ; and it tells not only about Jesus' actions but also about the responses of the witnesses who proclaim the great things God has done for us.

65. Kelsey, *Uses of Scripture*, 39. Terrence Tilley explains that a narrative theology is more fundamental than a propositional theology since "propositional theology is derivative from narratives as literary criticism is derivative from literature." Tilley, *Story Theology*, 14. Propositional theology cannot carry the gospel message, but it is nevertheless an indispensable guide in exploring ways of telling the stories of Christianity anew.

66. Frei, *Identity*, xiv.

Jesus, nevertheless we must appreciate that they do have a "history-like" quality that conveys the identity of the man Jesus.[67]

When we examine the gospel story we find that one of its fundamental characteristics is that it takes the shape of "realistic narrative." That is to say, the man Jesus is portrayed as leading a personal life which is conveyed by a story in which his intentions and actions, on the one hand, and the circumstances of his surroundings, on the other, are involved in a dynamic interplay which lead to the climactic point of his sacrificial death on Calvary. The identity of the man Jesus emerges by means of the constant interplay of intention and circumstance, which shows that he was fundamentally obedient to the Father who "sent" him. It is the great merit of Hans Frei to have restored the role that realistic narrative plays in biblical hermeneutics. Let us listen to what Frei has to say about the gospel story's depiction of Jesus' obedience to the Father's will:

> His obedience exists solely as a counterpart to his being sent and has God for its indispensable point of reference. Jesus' very identity involves the will and purpose of the Father who sent him. He becomes who he is in the story by consenting to God's intention and by enacting that intention in the midst of the circumstances that devolve around him as the fulfillment of God's purpose. The characterizing intention of Jesus that becomes enacted – his obedience – is not seen 'deep down' in him, furnishing a kind of central clue to the quality of his personality. Rather, it is shown in the story with just enough strength to indicate that it characterized him by making the purpose of God who sent him the very aim of his being.[68]

The central point which Frei is making here is that the enacted intention of Jesus to obey the Father's will meshes with external circumstances devolving around him, so that Jesus becomes who he is through the specific actions and circumstances surrounding his public life, especially his last

---

67. Frei, *Eclipse*, 10. Frei argues that, since the rise of the historical-critical methods, we have become aware of the fact that the gospels are not biographies of the life of Jesus; we cannot read them as we would a history. This has resulted, though, in the tendency to go behind the gospels in order to extract their meaning; we no longer consider them on their own terms. We must return to treating the gospels according to their verbal sense, that is, we must recover the narrative character of the gospels.

68. Frei, *Identity*, 107. Many works have appeared since the 1970s on narrative theology, including: Stroup, *Promise*; Goldberg, *Theology and Narrative*; Tilley, *Story Theology*; Thiemann, *Revelation and Theology*; Krieg, *Story-Shaped Christology*; and Frei, *Theology and Narrative*.

days. The identity of Jesus in the gospel story is therefore not given simply in his inner intention, but in the enactment of his intentions that coincide with circumstances partly initiated by him, partly imposed upon him.[69] The gospel narrative as story should therefore be taken in its own right as testimony to Jesus' perfect obedience to the Father, which is of a piece with his intention to do what had to be done for the sake of the redemption of his own people. Once the gospels are considered as realistic narrative, then we can appreciate the view that the identity of Jesus is not given from the very beginning but develops as the drama of the gospel story unfolds. This is why we read in Luke 2:41–51, for instance, that Jesus' parents were mystified by the young Jesus' response to them—"Did you not know that I must be in my Father's house?"—when they were able to seek him out in the Jerusalem temple. After the incident in the temple we are told that Mary "pondered all these things in her heart" (v. 51). Even as Daughter Zion, Mary was not able to fathom the person of her son, and it is not until she kneels at the foot of the cross and the risen Jesus appears to her after three days, that she gains true knowledge of his divine identity and the accomplishment of God's good work in his person.

When we examine the synoptic gospels we quickly realize that the identity of the man Jesus is never presented unequivocally. From the outset, of course, Jesus identifies with the kingdom of God (Mark 1:15), yet this pointing away from himself to God's reign almost immediately starts up an interplay. In the very act of pointing to the kingdom of God being made manifest in his mission of authoritative teaching, exorcising and healing, and associating with tax collectors and other undesirables, Jesus places himself at the heart of the people's concerns: they are simply amazed, astonished, and stupefied by the manner in which Jesus addresses them, hence they find themselves compelled to respond to his person. As we engage with the synoptic story we find that the question about Jesus' identity is not established from the beginning but is kept alive throughout, for there is "a developing relationship between the individuality of Jesus and the response of his surroundings."[70] It is clear that Jesus adopts a profoundly compassionate stance towards his own people: he is acutely aware of the impoverished condition of his people who are like sheep without a shepherd, and identifies their legitimate concerns

---

69. Note how the line of thought here fits in well with the discussion in chapter 1 of this study concerning emotions as subjective engagements with the world.

70. Beeck, *Christ Proclaimed*, 362.

with precision and sets about healing their lives by the power of the spirit resting upon him in eschatological fullness (see Acts 10:38).[71]

The whole of Jesus' ministry, and the wonder it evokes, inevitably gives rise to questions about his authority: "Why does this man speak thus? It is blasphemy! Who can forgive sins but God alone?" (Mark 2:7; see Matt 9:2–8). Closely related to this theme of Jesus' authority is the inability or unwillingness of the characters in the synoptic story to understand who Jesus is. His family comes to the conclusion, "He is beside himself" (Mark 3:21); the scribes and Pharisees claim, "He is possessed by Beelzebul" (Mark 3:22; Matt 12:24; Luke 11:15); and even Jesus' disciples are lacking in perception—"Are your hearts hardened?" (Mark 8:17).[72] The extent of the disciples's lack of understanding is clearly revealed in the question that Jesus puts to them: "But who do you say that I am?" (Mark 8:29; Matt 16:15). Peter answers correctly by saying that Jesus is the "Christ," but whatever he understood by this title had little to do with what was about to happen to Jesus. By Peter rebuking Jesus' prediction of his suffering and death at the hands of the elders and the chief priests and the scribes, he shows himself to be on Satan's side, not God's. "It is not that Jesus merely "corrects" Peter's confession. He turns it upside down. The Messiah doesn't win the world by a display of divine power. He wins it in death."[73] The exchange between Jesus and Peter at Caesarea Philippi serves as the fulcrum for the synoptic story and sets the stage for the telling of Jesus' entry into Jerusalem, which culminates in his crucifixion and the confession of the Roman centurion that he is the "Son of God."

As the reader is drawn into the synoptic story by its realistic narrative, it soon becomes apparent that the very beneficiaries of Jesus' compassionate ministry of healing become obstacles to the establishment of

---

71. Biblical texts which speak of Jesus' awareness of people's thoughts include: Mark 2:8; Matt 9:4, 12:25; Luke 6:8, 9:47; and John 2:25. In Heb 4:15, we are told that Jesus is able to "sympathize with our weaknesses" on the basis of his common humanity with us—he is one who "in every respect has been tempted as we are, yet without sinning."

72. The motif of the disciples's lack of understanding is particularly pronounced in Mark's Gospel where it is linked to the motif of the messianic secret. The intention of Mark is to show that the cross is the decisive event for understanding who Jesus is and what it means to call him the Christ. The cross, then, determines what it means to be a follower of Christ, as is made clear when after Jesus' rebuke of Peter, Mark has Jesus say, "If any man would come after me, let him deny himself and take up his cross and follow me" (8:34). See Stroup, *Promise*, 154–64.

73. Tilley, *Story Theology*, 139.

the kingdom of God. Those who are the recipients of God's benevolent love seek to possess the gifts of God's kingdom on their own terms (see Mark 10:35-45); that is to say, "they want to own what can be theirs only gratuitously."[74] In losing sight of the utter gratuitousness of that which they have received in Jesus' address to them, the beneficiaries of Jesus' ministry in effect join forces with those who have failed to recognize his person from the very beginning. As the gospel story unfolds, therefore, resistance to the teachings and blessings of Jesus—not only from the religious leaders and the people in general but also from his disciples—grows to the point of overshadowing any sense of deep gratitude and true conversion of heart. The upshot of this realistic narrative of the synoptic story is that the *identity of Jesus becomes increasingly established with reference to the profound loneliness and isolation that he experiences in relation to his hostile surroundings.* It would be unsatisfactory to think that the identity of Jesus emerges only with reference to his identification with the human concerns of his covenant people, on the one hand, and his identification with the kingdom of his Father, on the other. The way of obedience to the Father is for the man Jesus a way of righteous suffering that carries him forward all the way to the cross of Golgotha.

This increasing isolation of Jesus becomes the wellspring of a new dynamic interplay in which Jesus and those whom he addresses are individualized in a new way. In failing to recognize Jesus, those around him make it plain that they prefer to live by the norms of self-established assurances rather than by the unmerited gifts of a selfless God who calls them to genuine freedom. But when those around Jesus reject him, he does not, it is important to underscore, seek to defend himself or walk away from them in a disconsolate state. Instead, Jesus freely decides to continue to stand in front of a people with hardened hearts; he chooses to remain in steadfast relationship to sinners, and by doing so his individuality is increasingly established as he becomes the one in whom "humanity's inhumanity" is revealed in all its ugliness.[75] There simply is no basis in the synoptic story for the proposition that Jesus' individuality remains unchanged from beginning to end, and that it is only his surroundings that change. While the gospels furnish us with no direct evidence of a psychological development on the part of Jesus—with the notable exception of Luke 2:52—nonetheless the process of Jesus' individualization is

---

74. Beeck, *Christ Proclaimed*, 364.
75. Beeck, *Christ Proclaimed*, 367.

indirectly conveyed by the narrative shape of the gospel account of the present significance of Jesus as the risen one: he who is rejected and put to death is vindicated by his being raised from the dead and exalted by the Father in whom he had kept faith to his very last breath.[76]

The development of Jesus' individuality as discussed hitherto, since it highlights Jesus' subjective engagement with his increasingly hostile surroundings as he proclaims the Father's kingdom of grace, also helps to bring into sharper relief Jesus' emotional life. This is especially the case concerning those emotions associated with the Jerusalem section of the synoptic story. These include: (i) his bitter weeping over the impending destruction of Jerusalem due to the people's rejection of his person and their failure to recognize in him God's visitation of his people (Luke 19:41–44); (ii) his overwhelming sorrow and grief in the garden of Gethsemane as he contemplates the dreadful prospect of drinking "the cup" (Matt 26:36–39; Mark 14:32–36); and (iii) his deep anguish and suffering of God-forsakenness on the cross (Matt 27:46; Mark 15:34), which he endures in order to secure the blessings of the new covenant by the sacrificial shedding of his very own blood—he is the "lamb of God." Ultimately it is not so much the increasing isolation and rejection of Jesus' person by his own people that causes Jesus to experience overwhelming grief and sorrow: it is the prospect that he as the Son will have to endure the suffering of the cup; that is, his bearing of the sins of others will ultimately require him to suffer the God-forsakenness that is the destiny of sinners.[77] Jesus' true identity as the Son is put in sharpest relief when he endures the cup of God-forsakenness on the cross. *It is not until Jesus is presented as the one forsaken by God that his individuality becomes complete.* The one forsaken by God is the very Son of God! The increasing isolation of Jesus in a sinful, cruel, and hostile world does not mean, it is important

---

76. Frei argues convincingly that Jesus is identified in his resurrection. It is in the passion-resurrection narrative, rather than in the account of his sayings and teachings, that the person of Jesus is most clearly accessible. Frei explains that in the resurrection of Jesus, the "intention-action" description of personal identity becomes intermingled with the "self-manifestation" description, for "Jesus is set forth in his resurrection as the manifestation of the action of God." Frei, *Identity*, 117–25, 139–52.

77. In Jewish Scripture, "the cup" stands for God's wrath and judgment. See Ps 75:8; Isa 51:17, 22; Jer 25:15–17, 49:12; Ezek 23:31–34. By bearing the judgment of God in the place of sinners, Jesus the Son reveals the primacy of God's love for us. In the new covenant sealed by the shedding of Jesus' blood, the blessings of the new covenant spoken of by Jeremiah (Jer 31:31–34), namely, forgiveness of sins and a new heart to keep Torah, have now become a reality.

to emphasize, that he is depersonalized in any way; on the contrary, Jesus stands out as an individual in ever sharper relief as he endures repeated assaults by his own people and by satanic forces opposed to the kingdom of God, all of which reaches its zenith in his ineffable sorrow and suffering on the hill of Golgotha.[78]

Once we understand the process of the development of Jesus' individuality according to the realistic narrative of the gospel story, we can better appreciate that what we are dealing with in the person of Jesus is the redefinition of humanity. On the cross the utterly rejected Jesus concretely identifies with the fallen human condition, yet at the same time he is totally individualized as he surrenders himself unreservedly to the Father in a final prayer of forgiveness for humanity's inhumanity (see Luke 23:34), which is the other side of the God-forsakenness that he suffers on Calvary. What the people reject is not some abstract idea of humanity taught by Jesus, but Jesus himself who embodies the ideal of a humanity that gratefully accepts its true identity as something given gratuitously by the living God. In respect of the assumption of humanity by Jesus the Son, van Beeck therefore has the following to say:

> Jesus does not confront his opponents with an idea of humanity that they have rejected. He presents them with himself as he willingly accepts their rejection. Thus the incorporation of humanity into the crucified Jesus is *a matter of sustained relationships*. The rejected one does not reject. The rejectors, in rejecting Jesus, reject the one who does not reject them; they also reject themselves, for Jesus has received the imprint of their inhumanity into his own person. Yet precisely because Jesus does not cease to relate to them, they cannot help but respond: their very rejection of Jesus becomes an implicit testimony to the defectiveness of their own humanity and to the fullness of his.[79]

The fullness of Jesus' humanity must not be thought of as being of a philosophical kind, based on a static concept of a generic nature. Rather,

---

78. See Frei, *Identity*, 26–34. Frei explains that nowhere in the gospel story does the figure of Jesus appear as purely symbolic. Jesus is not the "archetypal man" who represents all humanity in its homelessness—he is not the "universal stranger." Rather, the gospels make it clear that Jesus "owns his own presence" and yet he "turns and shares it with us." To the modern imagination, however, this is problematic since it would mean that Jesus is at a different level from our own true being, that he is precluded from sharing his own presence with us.

79. Beeck, *Christ Proclaimed*, 367.

given the manner in which the gospel story depicts Jesus as continuing to stand in relationship to those who reject him, the fullness of his humanity takes the form of "love of enemies" (Matt 5:44).[80] In respect of the redefinition of humanity in the person of Jesus, what the term humanity refers to is a dynamic system that is fundamentally open to the transcendent reality that we name "God" or "Holy Mystery"—*mysterium tremendum et fascinans*. Humanity is an emerging reality conformed to the person of Jesus, which is a new being and transformed life beyond every definition and every boundary.

To conclude, the complex picture of Jesus' personal biography presented in the first major section of this chapter serves not only to uphold the true humanity of Jesus—against the traditional tendency in Christology to pay only lip service to his humanity—but also makes plain the need to appreciate the assumption of humanity in his person as taking place in a gradual and progressive fashion. The incarnation of the eternal Word should not be regarded as fully consummated at the moment of Jesus' conception in the womb of the Virgin Mary. Instead, the assumption of humanity progresses with the development of his individuality, which occurs through a process of mutual interaction of the divine and the human over the course of Jesus' historical life and messianic mission that culminates in his passion. This way of viewing the christological mystery is not only able to guarantee the true and genuine humanity of the God-Man, but also ensures that Jesus' divinity is depicted as having a real relation to his humanity, since each nature is to be thought of as advancing through the other. Once we embrace this truly kenotic line of thinking, the extraordinary character of the Word become flesh can be acknowledged with renewed vigor that does justice to Kierkegaard's statement: "that the eternal truth has come into being in time, that God has come into being, has been born, has grown up, and so forth, precisely like any other individual human being."[81]

The above discussion of Jesus' personal biography has also afforded us the opportunity to appreciate the ability of our cognitive theory of

---

80. Bonhoeffer, in his reflections on this radical commandment of Jesus, speaks of the "extraordinary" quality of the Christian life as a life committed to the person of Christ whose compassionate love requites evil with good. To love one's enemies is to live the way of the cross. The right way to requite evil is not to resist it violently; rather, evil is disarmed by the unfathomable depths of a compassionate love that sustains relationships to enemies so as to requite evil with good.

81. Kierkegaard, *Concluding Unscientific Postscript*, 188. Cited in the introduction to this study.

emotion to shed light on the formation and function of Jesus' emotions, which are the springboard of his messianic mission to Israel. The import of our cognitive theory of emotion for examining Jesus' personal engagement with his covenant people can be enumerated according to the major components of the proposed theory, as follows:

(a) Jesus' emotions involve *judgments* about important matters in relation to the supreme value and enduring promises of the covenant, and what a renewed life of keeping Torah in the land entails.

(b) Jesus' emotions embody *beliefs* about the God of the covenant, the divine purpose of the people in the land, the nature of the kingdom of God, and the destiny of Israel. The conversion of heart taught by Jesus is succinctly summed up in his radical commandment regarding love of enemies.

(c) Jesus' emotions are directed toward *intentional* objects, including his friends—e.g., Lazarus, Mary, and Martha—his disciples, his long-suffering people, the holy city of Jerusalem, the religious leaders, his enemies who persecute him, and, of course, God the Father, whose benevolent will Jesus obediently seeks to make manifest to his people.

(d) In light of the increasing rejection, hostility, isolation, and suffering that Jesus experiences as he seeks to carry forward his messianic mission, his emotions register his *vulnerability* and *passivity* before parts of his world that he does not fully control. This is especially evident in his passion, where his helplessness and powerlessness are in full display.

(e) Finally, while Jesus' emotions are cognitive and hence not reducible to mere bodily feelings, nonetheless there is an *involvement of the body* in his emotional life, which is apparent in two main ways. First, there are physiological changes appropriate to the emotion, as, for instance, when Jesus sheds tears at the tomb of Lazarus (John 11:35); weeps bitterly on his approach to Jerusalem (Luke 19:41); sweats drops of blood in Gethsemane (Luke 22:44); and offers up to God an agonizing cry of dereliction on the cross. Second, the involvement of the body is implied by his resurrection from the dead by the Father. The risen body of the crucified Jesus underscores the involvement of the body in the glorious life of beatific communion with God in the age to come.

These integral components of our cognitive theory of emotion account for the motivating force or action potential of Jesus' emotions in carrying him forward in his messianic ministry as the Son. When we examine Jesus' emotional life, we must not regard his emotions as mere proofs of his humanity or limit the scope of inquiry to the defects of soul that have long been regarded as the consequences of Adam's sin. Instead, we are required to recognize the emotional life of the Savior as a privileged window through which to gaze upon the wondrous process whereby the divine expresses itself in the sphere of the human, and the human attests the presence and activity of the divine in history. In such a framework, Jesus' emotions—both his congenial and suffering emotions, which form an integral unity—emerge as the outworking of the mutual interaction of the two natures in his person. In the event of the incarnate Word, what takes place is the participation of the divine in the human (kenosis), which aims at the participation of the human in the divine (theosis), and Jesus' emotional life—which tends in both a human *and* divine direction—is at the heart of this process of deification. In this process, God takes finitude, the pathos of the flesh, the reality of sin, and the weight of death to himself, in order to bestow upon us mortal sinners merciful love, righteousness, wisdom, holiness, joy, freedom, and the glory of the risen life. The man Jesus does not complete this process of deification in a facile manner, but has to win this victory of salvation in the veritable struggle of his passion, where we see his overwhelming emotions of dread, grief, and sorrow overcome by the exercise of his holy love of the Father. Ineffable love of the Father ultimately manifests itself as perfect obedience to the Father unto death on a cross, from which springs the salvific blessings of the new covenant.[82]

The Emotions of Jesus in the Gospels

In light of the discussion hitherto, we can now turn our attention to the emotions of Jesus recorded in the gospels. When we turn to examine the references to Jesus' emotions, we find that they number sixty. By far the

---

82. It is not correct, in my view, to maintain, as does Matthew Elliott, that Jesus experiences sorrow and grief, but he does not fear anything because he is the Son of God who has an understanding of the future and knowledge of God's provision and power. See Elliott, *Faithful Feelings*, 202. The one thing that the incarnate Son does dread, which causes him to sweat drops of blood in Gethsemane, is the judgment of God that he must bear for us sinners on the hill of Golgotha.

most are in John where there are twenty-eight references; next is Mark with sixteen; Matthew has ten; and Luke just six. Mark's portrayal of Jesus' emotional life is richer and fuller than the other two synoptic gospels. In light of the fact that the synoptic accounts overlap in significant ways in their presentation of Jesus' emotions, this would suggest that we could treat each emotion generally without reference to the specific context in which it arises. The best approach, though, would be to consider each occurrence of an emotion within its own narrative context. In this fashion the contribution to that gospel's portrait of Jesus can be better appreciated. This is especially true when we draw attention to the fact that there is very little overlap between the emotions of the Synoptic Jesus and those of John's Jesus, hence "John's portrayal of Jesus' emotions may confidently be regarded as unique among the Gospel accounts."[83]

Be that as it may, we shall not strictly examine each occurrence of an emotion of Jesus within its own narrative context, since the discussion is not intended to be an exegetical examination that seeks to highlight the contribution to that gospel's portrait of Jesus. The primary purpose here is to show how our cognitive theory of emotion functions to illuminate the emotions of Jesus as intelligible within the context of his life and messianic mission, and how it provides us with a lens through which to observe the process of salvation in his person. At the same time, however, a concomitant purpose will be to illustrate that the Stoic ideal of *apatheia* is simply not something that can be imposed upon the figure of Immanuel. For the man Jesus experiences real isolation and rejection, he becomes truly angry and indignant, he genuinely suffers and grieves, he bitterly weeps over the fate of Jerusalem, he is overwhelmed with sorrow to the point of death, he shudders at the dreadful prospect of "the cup," and he profoundly laments his sense of God-forsakenness on the cross. To acknowledge the breadth, depth, and full course of Jesus' emotional life is to illuminate what it means for the divinity to dwell bodily in the man Jesus, so as to bring to fruition the fullness of the covenant of grace.

Jesus' Love, Compassion, and Joy—The Congenial Emotions

The emotions of love and compassion are the two emotions that the gospels most frequently attribute to Jesus. Love is highlighted in John's Gospel, while compassion is frequently attributed to Jesus in the Synoptic

---

83. Voorwinde, *Jesus' Emotions in the Gospels*, 5.

Gospels where a pattern is evident; namely, the emotion of compassion is associated with his miracles, while other less congenial emotions, such as grief, anguish, anger, distress, and lament, are associated with his journey to Jerusalem and his passion. In the Synoptic Gospels the emotion of love is attributed to Jesus only once (Mark 10:21), but compassion often, while in John's Gospel compassion is attributed to Jesus not even once, but love often. This love, however, is the love of compassion, or perhaps it would be better to broaden this and say that it is the "love of benevolence."[84]

The cognitive character of love is apparent in that love is an attraction towards an intentional object that is judged as good, valuable, and desirable for the flourishing of life. In Jewish Scripture the most fundamental emotion is a vigorous love of God (Deut 6:4–5), from which springs a fervent love of neighbor (Lev 19:18). The chief affection of love is clearly in operation in the person of the God-Man. Jesus exhibits a profound love towards his long-suffering people as he goes about his messianic ministry, and his love for his own springs from his ineffable love of God, whose kingdom Jesus wholeheartedly preaches in word and deed: "I do as the Father has commanded me, so that the world may know that I love the Father" (John 14:31). The Father, as the ineffable fount of life and delight, has unsurpassable value and surplus of meaning, and Jesus as the Son is conscious of being in "the bosom of the Father" (John 1:18). His mission to Israel is purely and simply to make known the Father's benevolent love for the covenant people. Yet it is important to appreciate that Jesus is not conscious of being in the bosom of the Father from the very beginning of his life, but arrives at this consciousness of self through a historical process of development of his individuality. His parents, as well as extended family, are all portrayed in the gospel story as devout Jews who practice humility and profess steadfast faith in the God of the covenant—summed up most powerfully in the figure of Mary as Daughter Zion. In the context of Jesus' family life, love of God would have been extolled above all else, thus Jesus comes to affirm the chief emotion of love of God through his humanity that develops according to the religious beliefs and practices of his devout family.

The humanity of Jesus, however, cannot be thought of apart from the presence of the divinity, which means that as Jesus' individuality develops he becomes conscious of his divinity as the Son through his humanity. The emotions that are first formed in the context of Jesus' family

---

84. Warfield, "Emotional Life," 102.

upbringing develop and intensify as he becomes conscious of his special relationship to the Father. The incidence in the Jerusalem temple when Jesus is twelve years old (Luke 2:41–52) is a good indicator of this movement of a gradual incarnation where the two natures advance through each other. The young Jesus refers to the Jerusalem temple as his "Father's house" (Luke 2:49), which causes his parents to be baffled by what he is saying. What is on display in this narrative is Jesus' emerging consciousness of his filial relationship to the Father, or, to express it another way, *his humanity is becoming conscious of itself through his divinity*. Jesus is not yet, though, at the level of maturity required to begin his mission to Israel, for we are told in respect of his parents that he remained "obedient to them" (Luke 2:51). Obedience to his parents is a precursor to obedience to his Father, which is the springboard of his messianic proclamation of the kingdom to Israel. While there is no explicit mention of Jesus' love for his parents in the gospels, it is nevertheless implicitly conveyed by the understanding that his love for them—as his first teachers of the God of the covenant—is the basis of his obedience to them. Jesus humanly loves his parents, who teach him love of God as the first and chief of the emotions in Jewish life. But as Jesus grows in consciousness of his special relationship to God, his humanity develops less in relation to his Jewish family life and more directly through his personal relation to the Father. This does not mean, however, that Jesus no longer enters into human relationships as his individuality develops. In the moving story of raising Lazarus from the dead (John 11:1–44), it is clear that Jesus' love for Lazarus, Martha, and Mary is in every way natural, since it is the affection for friends who have given him devotion and hospitality. Jesus therefore risks going to Bethany and being caught by the Jewish authorities in order to reach his friend Lazarus and resuscitate him. This story is then transposed to a higher key when Jesus lays down his life for his friends on the cross. He is the "Lamb of God" (John 1:29) who offers himself as covenant sacrifice, and in so doing his sacrificial death "on behalf of" his friends reveals a love that is sublime and divine.

There is only one explicit mention of Jesus' love in the Synoptic Gospels, which occurs in the story of the rich young man (Mark 10:17–22), who asks Jesus what he must do to inherit eternal life. Jesus replies by reciting part of the Decalogue, to which the rich young man responds by saying that he has observed all these commandments since his youth. We then read: "And Jesus looking upon him loved him" (v. 21). Jesus senses a sincerity and goodness in the young man who has observed the commandments since his youth, which he finds instantly appealing and admirable. However, Jesus also identifies a basic problem in that the young man is more devoted to his "great possessions" (v. 22) than to the God of the covenant. By being too attached to his riches and hence not willing to sell what he has in order to give to the poor, the young man fails to keep the greatest and first commandment of love of God and to value "treasure in heaven" (v. 22) above all else. Jesus humanly loves the rich young man, yet is critical of him for failing to respond adequately to what God's love for his people demands. Jesus has an acute sense of the demands of divine love, of what holiness in the land requires, which is underlined in the narrative by his injunction to the rich young man to "come, follow me" (v. 21). Jesus displays a love towards the young man that is human, yet at the same time his injunction reveals that his person is intimately in touch with divine love and its demands.

It is clear from the gospels that the primary object of Jesus' love is the Father—the *mysterium tremendum et fascinans*. This is explicitly the case in John's Gospel, and although the Synoptic Gospels do not explicitly mention Jesus' love for the Father, it is implicitly conveyed by Jesus' obedience to the Father, since the latter springs from the former. It is the ineffable love of the Father that motivates and carries Jesus forward in his salvific mission to his own, all the way to his passion. In John's Gospel, Jesus' crucifixion is depicted not as a victory for the ruler of this world but as "the most profound expression of Jesus' love for the Father."[85] At the same time, though, the crucifixion is portrayed as the ultimate manifestation of Jesus' love for his disciples, which forms the basis of the new commandment that Jesus gives them: "This is my commandment, that you love one another as I have loved you. Greater love has no man than this, that a man lay down his life for his friends" (John 15:12–13). The mutual love between the disciples is to have its source in Jesus' sacrificial love for them, and such love sets a new standard in respect of the commandment in the Torah concerning love of neighbor. It is precisely when Jesus offers himself as covenant sacrifice that "he proves himself to be covenant Lord;" his sacrificial death on behalf of his friends is the flowering of the covenant of grace and "reveals a love that is sublime and divine."[86] The trajectory of Jesus' love of God starts with the teaching of his pi-

---

85. Voorwinde, *Jesus' Emotions in the Fourth Gospel*, 243. In the Synoptic Gospels, also, Jesus' crucifixion is depicted as his ultimate act of love for the Father (see Mark 14:36; Matt 26:39; Luke 4:13, 22:3, 23:46).

86. Voorwinde, *Jesus' Emotions in the Fourth Gospel*, 253.

ous parents and reaches its climax in his passion as the Son, where "he learned obedience through what he suffered" (Heb 5:8). In this trajectory we observe a continuous process of reciprocal interaction of humanity and divinity in his person, and therefore his "being made perfect" (Heb 5:9) for the sake of our salvation.

Jesus' love of God, which in John's Gospel is presented as the love of sheer delight in its object (14:21, 31), accounts for the exuberant joy of Jesus as his messianic mission is being fulfilled. Ineffable love of the Father is the source of Jesus' obedience to the Father's commands, and exuberant joy is portrayed as the result of obedience. Obedience is the link between love and joy, and this applies to the disciples also. The disciples's joy is dependent on their keeping the commandments of Jesus: "If you keep my commandments, you will abide in my love, just as I have kept my Father's commandments and abide in his love. These things I have spoken to you, that my joy may be in you, and that your joy may be full" (John 15:10–11). In Luke's Gospel the theme of joy is also in evidence in the passage where the seventy disciples commissioned by Jesus return to him with joy (Luke 10:17–24). The disciples rejoice at their success in driving out demons, but Jesus reminds them that there is a greater reason for joy: "do not rejoice in this, that the spirits are subject to you; but rejoice that your names are written in heaven" (v. 20). The greater joy, in other words, must be the joy of their salvation. Jesus also rejoices, but his joy is not solely due to the successful mission of the disciples; rather, he rejoices "in the Holy Spirit" (v. 21) and in his unique filial relationship with the Father (vv. 21–22). "Nowhere else in Luke's Gospel is the Father-Son relationship as developed as it is here."[87] Due to the intimate reciprocity of this relationship, which no human being will ever be able to fathom, Jesus' joy is more exuberant than that of the disciples: they return with "joy" but Jesus is "filled with joy" (v. 21) as the task close to his heart as the Son is being successfully carried out by the seventy disciples. While both Jesus and the seventy share the experience of joy, Jesus' joy is of a distinctly different class. The pinnacle of Jesus' joy is to do the good work of his heavenly Father, to bring his Father's benevolent love to those who are like sheep without a shepherd, and thus exposed to many forms of evil. This is why Jesus rejoices with such religious exuberance: "This is divine joy at its most sublime."[88]

---

87. Voorwinde, *Jesus' Emotions in the Gospels*, 131.
88. Voorwinde, *Jesus' Emotions in the Gospels*, 132.

When we observe the movement of Jesus' love and joy in the gospel story, what we are really gazing upon is the extraordinary nature of his compassion for his long-suffering people. Compassion is frequently attributed to Jesus in the Synoptic Gospels, where it is associated with his healing miracles, exorcisms, and his feeding of the hungry crowds. Jesus is deeply affected by the dismal state of the covenant people's spiritual condition and his heart goes out to his suffering people. In Matthew's Gospel we read that Jesus has compassion for the crowds because "they were harassed and helpless, like sheep without a shepherd" (Matt 9:36). In the preceding chapters Jesus has been proclaiming the kingdom of God in word (Matt 5–7) and deed (Matt 8–9), and here in the description of the crowds as being like sheep without a shepherd we are "given insight into the motivation that drove the activity of the previous chapters."[89] It is the deep compassion of Jesus that is presented as the *motivating force* behind his healing ministry to Israel. Jesus is certainly not portrayed as a Stoic wise man who is completely unaffected by the dismal condition of his own people. The external realities of Jewish life in the land are of the utmost importance to Jesus, because the state of his people is invested with intrinsic and inviolable value in virtue of God's covenant relationship with Israel.

At the same time, though, Matthew 9:36 is a stinging indictment on the Jewish religious leaders, which recalls the reproof of the shepherds of the people in Jewish Scripture (see Num 27:17; Ezek 34; Zech 10:2). Jesus is not like the Jewish leaders, for he is the "good shepherd" (John 10:14) who has deep compassion on his flock (see Isa 40:11; 54:7–10). He has compassion on the crowd of 5,000 and miraculously feeds them with five loaves and two fishes (Matt 14:13–21; Mark 6:32–44; Luke 9:10–17; John 6:1–13); on another occasion he has compassion on a crowd of 4,000 and miraculously feeds them with seven loaves and a few small fish (Matt 15:32–39; Mark 8:1–10); he has mercy on two blind men in Jericho and gives them sight (Matt 20:29–34; Mark 10:46–52; Luke 18:35–43); Jesus is moved with pity by a leper and makes him clean (Mark 1:40–42); he has pity on the epileptic boy and heals him instantly (Mark 9:14–29; Matt 17:14–18); and Jesus' heart goes out in compassion to the widow of Nain and he brings her dead son back to life (Luke 7:11–17). The new exodus prophesied by Isaiah is replete with references to God's compassion on his afflicted (Isa 49:8–13; 54:7–10; 60:10). In displaying the extraordinary

---

89. Voorwinde, *Jesus' Emotions in the Gospels*, 26.

degree of compassion on his suffering people as he does, Jesus is presented in the gospels as performing God's good work of restoration and ushering in the much-anticipated messianic age.[90] The divine nature of Jesus' compassionate healing is epitomized in Psalm 146 where God "gives food to the hungry" (v. 7) and "opens the eyes of the blind" (v. 8). God's love for his covenant people is expressed most eminently through the richness of his compassion on them, which restores the "covenant of peace" (Isa 54:10). The divine compassion has a distinct object, which is highly valued, and its workings in history bring about a renewed life of peace and justice in the land. Once restoration has taken place through the workings of divine compassion, God rejoices and delights in his covenant people whose hearts are renewed and again turned towards him in praise and worship.

From the standpoint of the foregoing discussion of the congenial emotions of Jesus, we can recognize the subtle interplay of humanity and divinity in the person of Jesus. This interplay is not static in the sense that the human nature is passive while the divine nature is the active element in the life of Jesus. Rather, the interplay in view is dynamic and developmental, for Jesus becomes conscious of his divinity through the process of maturation of his humanity, and his humanity is conscious of itself through his divinity, so that each nature advances through the other in his historical life and messianic mission to Israel. This developmental process reaches its zenith in Jesus' passion, when Jesus perfects his humanity by virtue of his perfect obedience to the Father unto death, which springs from his ineffable love of the Father. The congenial emotions of Jesus, which form the springboard of his proclamation of the kingdom of grace, are truly human emotions, yet they are not merely human emotions, for they also communicate God's congenial emotions which are mediated by his humanity. What the congenial emotions of Jesus the Son make manifest is the ineffable character of the Father's saving will toward his people, which makes all things new and knows no bounds.

Jesus' Amazement and Stern Warning

In both Matthew (8:5–13) and Luke (7:1–10), the first recorded emotion of Jesus is amazement or astonishment at the centurion's humility and faith in him: "Truly I say to you, not even in Israel have I found such

---

90. Voorwinde, *Jesus' Emotions in the Gospels*, 42.

faith" (Matt 8:10; also Luke 7:9). Amazement is a very human emotion and it serves as a reminder that "for all the divinity that has been ascribed to him Jesus is still the son of Mary, a human being who can be genuinely surprised."[91] What is it about the centurion that so impresses Jesus? It is not only the centurion's humility—"Lord, I am not worthy to have you come under my roof"—but his belief that all Jesus need do is "say the word" and his servant will be healed. Up to this point in the gospel story Jesus has performed no miracle by the power of his word, yet the centurion believes that Jesus need only say the word and all will be well with his servant. The centurion is able to see in Jesus something of the Immanuel (Matt 1:23), and he anticipates the gentile mission (Matt 28:18–19) that will go beyond the people of the old covenant to include all peoples of the earth as recipients of the divine compassion.[92]

A very different emotion of Jesus is recorded in Matthew 9:27–31. Two blind men, who respectfully address Jesus and have faith in his authority, plead with him to have mercy on them. Jesus responds to their supplication by touching their eyes and their eyes are opened. But immediately Jesus sternly warns them not to say anything to anyone. The Greek word used, *embrimaomai*, which occurs only four times in other parts of the New Testament, conveys harshness in Jesus' warning and overtones of anger and indignation.[93] Jesus knows that the two recipients of his merciful healing will not be obedient to his request; they will spread the news like wildfire, thereby making Jesus' mission more difficult and more dangerous because he will come into conflict with the Jewish religious leaders. The emotion expressed by Jesus is perfectly intelligible since it addresses a practical concern from a personal and interested perspective. In the very next passage (Matt 9:32–34), though, the conflict with the religious leaders is already a concrete reality, for the Pharisees in response to Jesus' exorcisms say: "He casts out demons by the prince of demons" (v. 34). This groundswell of opposition to Jesus is also a feature of Mark's Gospel, where conflict with the religious leaders grows steadily from the early stages of Jesus' ministry. The scribes and Pharisees watch Jesus' every move and his emotions are deeply stirred by their legalistic and antagonistic attitudes towards him. The conflict reaches a climax with

---

91. Voorwinde, *Jesus' Emotions in the Gospels*, 124.
92. Voorwinde, *Jesus' Emotions in the Gospels*, 20.
93. Voorwinde, *Jesus' Emotions in the Gospels*, 23.

the statement in Mark 3:6: "The Pharisees went out and immediately held counsel with the Herodians against him, how to destroy him."

In his emotion of amazement in response to the centurion's faith Jesus foresees the gentile mission, whereas in Jesus' stern warning to the two blind supplicants he foresees the inevitable conflict and increasing trouble with the Jewish leadership of his day. In both instances the supplicants address Jesus with much respect and by the correct titles that acknowledge his divine authority, yet Jesus' emotional response is very different in each case. This makes eminent sense within the framework of a cognitive theory of emotion. What Jesus values above all else is strong faith in God and he expects such faith to form the foundation of the life of the covenant people in the land. Therefore, when the Roman centurion expresses such strong faith in Jesus as a person with divine authority, this comes as a positive surprise to Jesus and becomes a pointer in the gospel story to the prospective good of divine salvation extended to the gentiles. The surprise of Jesus in respect of the centurion's supplication, moreover, shows that he is not fully in control of his ministry in the sense that he foresees all that lies before him according to a predetermined divine plan. Surprise is a very human emotion that highlights the dimension of unpredictability in the affairs of the present age. Jesus does, however, foresee the inevitability of increasing conflict with the religious leaders, which explains the strong emotion that he expresses in his stern warning to the two Jewish supplicants, whose eyes have been opened by Jesus' healing touch. The cognitive nature of Jesus' emotional response is evident in that Jesus clearly foresees a prospective evil; namely, mounting conflict with the Jewish religious leaders, which will make his proclamation of the kingdom of grace increasingly difficult, and ultimately will lead to overwhelming grief and the agony of his death on the cross.

How can we think of the human and divine natures in the person of Jesus as addressing each other in these emotions? Jesus' emotion of astonishment at the centurion's faith is a very human emotion, yet in the context of the gospel narrative this emotion bears a close relationship to the divine compassion being made manifest in his person. Compassion is the motivating force that carries Jesus forward in his redemptive mission to Israel, and the emotion of amazement serves as a pointer to the eventual extension of Jesus' mission of compassion to the gentile world. The emotion of amazement also serves to clearly show that his human nature is very real and not passive in relation to his divinity. The amazement at the centurion's faith in him indicates that the humanity of Jesus is involved in a process of ongoing interaction with his divinity. This process of mutual interaction of the two natures is further evidenced by the strong emotion expressed in Jesus' stern warning to the two blind men who have received the gift of sight. The stern warning, which has overtones of anger and indignation, is clearly a human emotion in the context of the gospel narrative. Yet there is also a definite overlap here with the testimony of Jewish Scripture concerning the manifestation of divine anger and displeasure when the divine purpose in the land is thwarted and corrupted. Conflict with the Jewish religious leaders will restrict and hamper Jesus' mission of proclaiming God's visitation of his people, hence Jesus sternly warns the two healed blind men not to say anything to anyone. As the gospel story unfolds, however, Jesus does inevitably encounter mounting isolation and rejection, and begins to focus more and more on his disciples as he comes to realize that his preaching will require him to undergo a unique baptism that no other can undergo: "I have a baptism to be baptized with; and how I am constrained until it is accomplished!" (Luke 12:50). This means that the stern warning of Jesus is to be interpreted as a pointer to his passion as the climactic point of his messianic mission to Israel. Jesus' emotion of zeal for the temple, which is recorded very early in John's Gospel (see below), bolsters considerably this perspective of Jesus' conflict with the Jewish leaders as a pointer to his passion. It is in the passion of Jesus where we see the mutual interaction of the two natures in his person come to a climactic point, for his humanity is finally perfected as he reveals what it means to be the divine Son who obediently does the Father's will, so as to inaugurate the blessings of the new covenant of grace.

Jesus' Anger and Indignation

Jesus' stern warning to the two healed blind men, it was said above, has overtones of anger and indignation. There are further and more explicit examples of these emotions expressed by Jesus. In Mark 10:13-16, for example, Jesus gets angry with his disciples because they prevent the children from coming to him. Both Matthew and Luke also record this incident, but neither mention Jesus' indignation at his disciples. In order to understand why children are candidates for the kingdom of God, it is necessary to contrast them with the story of the rich young man (Mark 10:17-22) that immediately follows. The latter thinks he can merit the kingdom by adhering to the commandments, but Jesus points to the young man's failure to uphold the first and greatest of the commandments by refusing to give up his great possessions to the poor. Children, by contrast, are models for entry into God's kingdom, for their entry is by grace alone, not merit.[94] The point Jesus makes by becoming indignant with his disciples is that they should not stand in the way of God's grace, which Jesus demonstrates by taking the children in his arms and blessing them (Mark 10:16). The object of Jesus' entire mission to Israel is the inauguration of the covenant of grace, and the children epitomize the reality of this kingdom of gifted benevolence, which turns everything on its head.

Another instance of Jesus' anger is recorded in Mark 3:1–6. Here Jesus enters the synagogue at Capernaum on the Sabbath and heals the withered hand of a man. When Jesus asks whether it is "lawful on the sabbath to do good or to do harm, to save life or to kill?" (Mark 3:4), and his question is met with silence, he then "looked around at them with anger, grieved by their hardness of heart" (v. 5). Jesus' claim to authority has been steadily rising in the opening chapters of Mark—he teaches with authority (1:22), with authority he commands the unclean spirits (1:23–27), he has authority to forgive sins (2:10), and he is Lord of the Sabbath (2:28)—and in this particular text his claim to authority reaches a level that causes the Pharisees to "hold counsel with the Herodians against him, how to destroy him" (Mark 3:6). The reason Jesus is angered by the silence of those gathered in the synagogue is that they are "unwilling to allow Jesus to do good and to save life, while at the same time they themselves are prepared to do evil by plotting to kill him."[95] On account of their hardness of heart, they fail to acknowledge the mercy and grace of God being made manifest in Jesus' person. It is this indifference to dire human needs in favor of legalistic stipulations that angers Jesus. His reaction of anger is very real and eminently reasonable in that it signifies Jesus' *strong moral sense* informed by the covenant of grace. The cognitive character of Jesus' anger is readily apparent in that his emotion is directed toward the object of the Pharisees, who are proving to be a veritable obstacle to what Jesus truly cherishes as supremely valuable; namely, the benevolence of God who desires the flourishing of life for his people in the land. The anger of Jesus is therefore a righteous anger as he confronts

---

94. Voorwinde, *Jesus' Emotions in the Gospels*, 107.
95. Voorwinde, *Jesus' Emotions in the Gospels*, 78.

the evils of his time, which are obstacles to the realization of the divine purpose in the land.

In addition to the emotion of anger we read that Jesus is also "grieved" by the hardness of heart of the Pharisees and their plot to kill him. This causes him deep distress. Later in the gospel story Jesus' disciples also display a hardness of heart (Mark 6:52; 8:17), but what is in view there is a certain spiritual obtuseness and lack of understanding—nothing like the Pharisees who have murderous intent against Jesus. The deep-seated grief expressed in Mark 3:1–6 sets Jesus on an inevitable pathway of suffering, which will culminate at Gethsemane and Golgotha, when Jesus as Lord of the Sabbath offers himself as the sacrificial lamb for the forging of the new covenant of grace. While emotions of anger, indignation, and grief on Jesus' part do not feature regularly in the gospels, nevertheless we could and should imagine these emotions as occurring with a degree of frequency in the course of Jesus' ministry, given that they pertain to Jesus' acute moral sense that brings him into mounting conflict with the religious leaders in particular, as well as increasing rejection of his messianic mission on the part of his own people in general.

Jesus' anger and indignation is a human emotion which is directed at an object that is judged as a slight upon or threat to what Jesus values and cherishes most highly, but at the same time it is also an expression or communication of divine anger. For in Jewish Scripture, as was discussed earlier in this chapter, when Israel fails to live up to the demands of the Torah, God reacts with wrath and anger because divine justice and righteousness are not being upheld in the land. The prophets before Jesus had offered stinging indictments on Israel's moral failures, and Jesus is well versed in the prophetic traditions and stands in the line of the prophets when he criticizes the Jewish leadership. But Jesus as the Son is greater than the prophets. The strong moral sense of the Son springs from his profound sense of the Father's justice and compassion, which Jesus desires to make known in concrete terms to his suffering people. In light of this ineffable oneness of the Son with the Father, which accounts for the acuteness of Jesus' moral sense, his anger should not be ignored or played down or regarded as inconsequential. Instead, his anger is a very real and significant emotion that registers the sizeable gap that exists between the Jewish leadership's narrow legalistic understanding of the kingdom and Jesus' proclamation of God's reign of benevolent love, which leaves people spellbound.

The anger of Jesus in the gospel story should be affirmed as both human and divine. It is neither a merely human emotion that serves as a sign of Jesus' humanity—i.e., a defect of the soul which is the result of Adam's sin—nor is it an undesirable human emotion that is quickly brought under the control of Jesus' illuminated reason as the divine Son. There is no warrant for applying either the Stoic notion of *apatheia* to the man Jesus, or the Stoic idea of Jesus' emotions as first movements or "prepassions" (*propatheia*) that are quickly brought under the control of his superior reason. The anger of Jesus is expressive of his acute moral sense as the Son and is justified by the judgment of its object—hardness of heart of the religious leaders, the people in general, and his disciples—as an obstacle or hindrance to God's benevolent visitation of his people. Jesus is not a Stoic sage, but the Word become flesh, who proclaims the fullness of the covenant of grace to his long-suffering people, who are like sheep without a shepherd. Jesus' emotions of anger and grief are indispensable to fathoming the way in which the gospel story establishes the development of Jesus' individuality as the Son who is obedient to the Father's will. Once we acknowledge the Son as mediating his divinity through his humanity, then this ensures that we think of divine anger as conscious of itself through Jesus' humanity, and human anger as conscious of itself through his divinity. In this perspective, again, Jesus' human nature cannot be regarded as passive in relation to his divinity, which is tantamount to saying that his divinity has a real relationship to his humanity, as the two natures progress and advance through each other in accomplishing salvation in his person.

Jesus' Zeal for His Father's House

In John's Gospel the first reference to an emotion of Jesus is the "zeal" for his Father's house (John 2:13–17), which impels him to drive out from the temple "those who were selling oxen and sheep and pigeons, and the money-changers at their business" (v. 14).[96] This narrative can be seen as supporting the synoptic narratives in Matthew 9:27–31 and Mark 3:1–6, insofar as the expressed emotion serves as a pointer to Jesus' passion.

---

96. All three Synoptic Gospels record the incidence of Jesus' cleansing of the temple (Mark 11:15–17; Matt 21:12–13; Luke 19:45–46), but the emotion of zeal is absent from their accounts. While no emotion is recorded in the Synoptic accounts, it is difficult to see how Jesus would have performed such an act without feeling revulsion at the dismal state of worship in the temple.

Zeal or jealousy is a divine emotion that is especially aroused by Israel's lack of fidelity to the God of the covenant.⁹⁷ What is recorded in Jewish Scripture about the affect on God of Israel's idolatry, Jesus now experiences upon entering the Jerusalem temple: "Take these things away; you shall not make my Father's house a house of trade" (v. 16). The cleansing of the temple occurs immediately after Jesus' first sign at Cana, where he turns the water into wine. The wine symbolizes the new wine of the messianic era, the time of receiving "grace upon grace" (John 1:16) from the fullness of "the only Son who is in the bosom of the Father" (John 1:18). Jesus thus enters the temple and expresses zeal in his capacity as the divine Son. His zeal is "driven by his revulsion at the blighted worship that is now being offered at the place where God had chosen to establish his name."⁹⁸

The portrayal of Jesus as expressing zeal for his Father's house is intelligible given that he as the Son looks to the Father as the object of his ineffable love (John 14:31), and is dedicated to upholding the holiness of the divine name. Yet the narrative in John's Gospel goes on to replace the temple with Jesus since the divine glory resides in his person as the incarnate Word: "And the Word became flesh and dwelt amongst us, full of grace and truth; we have beheld his glory, glory as of the only Son from the Father" (John 1:14). Jesus says in response to those who ask for a sign from him: "Destroy this temple and in three days I will raise it up" (John 2:19). Jesus here speaks of the temple of his body; his resurrected body is presented as the building of the new temple, the new locus of encounter between divinity and humanity. Jesus, like the psalmist (Ps 69:9), is consumed by zeal for God's cause, but he "will be consumed not just by calamity but by death itself."⁹⁹ An intimate connection exists, therefore, between Jesus' zeal and his sacrificial death as the "Lamb of God who takes away the sin of the world" (John 1:29). By situating Jesus' zeal for his Father's house at the beginning of the book of Signs, the intention is to portray this strong emotion as the motivating force of the Son's ministry to Israel and as a pointer to his passion, when his zeal as covenant Lord "creates the circumstances that will eventually make him the covenant sacrifice."¹⁰⁰

97. See Exod 20:5, 34:14; Num 25:11; Deut 4:23–24, 6:14–15, 29:20, 32:16; Ps 78:58.
98. Voorwinde, *Jesus' Emotions in the Fourth Gospel*, 138.
99. Voorwinde, *Jesus' Emotions in the Fourth Gospel*, 132.
100. Voorwinde, *Jesus' Emotions in the Fourth Gospel*, 138.

While the zeal that Jesus displays in his cleansing of the temple has a fundamentally divine tone in John's Gospel, we should not lose sight of the fact that Jesus as the Word become flesh reveals his divine glory through his humanity (John 1:14). The operation of the divine emotions in the incarnate Word simply cannot be thought of apart from his humanity that mediates his divinity. This implies that the divine zeal of the Son is also at the same time the human zeal of the man Jesus in upholding the exclusivity of the covenant relationship. His zeal, though, is greater than the zeal of the prophets who preached the divine pathos, for Jesus' origin as the Son is in the bosom of the Father, thus he is the personal revelation of the unfathomable pathos of God. It is also important to note the manner in which Jesus' zeal for his Father's house bears an intimate relationship to other fundamental emotions in John's Gospel, which were discussed above, namely: Jesus' ineffable love for the Father, and his sublime joy that results from obediently keeping the Father's commands. Zeal for the Father implies that Jesus loves the Father and desires to please the Father, which gives him as the Son the deepest and most sublime joy. Jesus' zeal and love for the Father is revealed most powerfully on the cross, yet at the same time his sacrificial death is the ultimate manifestation of Jesus' love for his disciples, which forms the basis of the new commandment that Jesus gives them: "This is my commandment, that you love one another as I have loved you" (John 15:12–13). There exists, then, in accordance with our cognitive theory of emotion presented in chapter 1, a logical and dynamic relationship between these basic emotions of Jesus recorded in John's Gospel, which provide the action potential for his saving mission to the people of God.

Jesus' Sighing and Weeping

There are two recordings in Mark's Gospel of Jesus sighing. In the first narrative Jesus sighs at the plight of a death-mute (7:31–37), while in the second recording he sighs at the testing of the Pharisees (8:11–13). These are quite different situations. In the story of healing the deaf-mute, Jesus looks up to heaven and sighs before he performs his miracle. To interpret Jesus' emotion in the context of this healing act, it is helpful to have recourse to Paul's writings where he talks about the whole of creation "groaning to be set free from its bondage to decay," and we ourselves as groaning for the "redemption of our bodies" (Rom 8:18–25). The appropriate response to being caught in the tension between the present age of toil and suffering and the future age of glory and delight is to sigh. "Jesus therefore sighs for the Day when sighing will be no more. He longs for the New Jerusalem, the destination to which he will lead his people along a New Exodus way."[101] The sigh of Jesus as he looks up to heaven is a very human emotion that acknowledges the limitations and sufferings of this age, while expressing the heart's longing for God's establishment of the New Jerusalem when sighing will be no more: "He will wipe away every tear from their eyes, and death shall be no more, neither shall there be mourning nor crying nor pain any more, for the former things have passed away" (Rev 21:4). Jesus' longing for the New Jerusalem is expressed in an especially powerful way in Luke's account of Jesus' bitter wailing on his approach to Jerusalem, which is discussed below.

In the second incidence of sighing recorded in Mark's Gospel, Jesus sighs at the testing of the Pharisees who demand from him "a sign from heaven" (Mark 8:11). In the healing of the deaf-mute Jesus merely "sighs" as he looks up to heaven, but in the context of the request from the Pharisees for a heavenly sign we read that Jesus "sighs deeply" (Mark 8:12). His emotional response expresses utter dismay at the unbelief of the Pharisees and their request for a spectacular sign, such as the mighty deeds of liberation that God worked in the event of the exodus. What the Pharisees are expecting is a political Messiah who will liberate them from the Roman occupation of the land, but Jesus' emotional response leaves us in no doubt that he is not that kind of Messiah. For up to this point in the gospel story Jesus has announced the advent of the kingdom of God by his authoritative exorcisms, his authoritative teaching, his deeply compassionate acts of healing, and the miraculous feeding of the 5,000 and the 4,000. Notwithstanding these wondrous happenings that herald the advent of the messianic age, the Pharisees harbor exceptionally strong feelings against Jesus (see Mark 3:6) and demand from him a sign from heaven, which causes Jesus to sigh deeply.

It is worth drawing attention to the fact that in the very same chapter of Mark we read that it is not only the Pharisees who are without understanding, but also Jesus' own disciples (Mark 8:17). This theme of the disciples' hardness of heart is strongly reinforced at the end of the chapter (Mark 8:27–33), which marks a turning point in the gospel narrative as Jesus shifts his focus to the prediction of his passion. Jesus

---

101. Voorwinde, *Jesus' Emotions in the Gospels*, 100.

teaches his disciples that he will be rejected by the Jewish leaders, suffer many things, and be put to death, but after three days he will rise again (Mark 8:31). Peter and the other disciples cannot accept Jesus' passion prediction—Peter actually rebukes Jesus—for they do not understand what Jesus is saying to them. This is forcefully conveyed by Jesus' strong rebuke directed at Peter: "Get behind me, Satan! For you are not on the side of God, but of men" (Mark 8:33; also Mark 9:32). Despite the fact that the disciples of Jesus are on the "inside" (see Mark 4:11), they truly struggle to accept his status as Messiah in terms of his passion prediction, which shows that even they share the kind of messianic expectations held by the Pharisees (cf. Luke 24:21). We can well imagine, then, that Jesus would have sighed at the spiritual obtuseness and hardness of heart of his disciples as well, and not just on one or two occasions but on many occasions in the course of his messianic ministry, especially in the final phase when his focus is very much on his journey towards Jerusalem for the Jewish festival of *Pesah*.

The sighing of Jesus makes perfect sense as Jesus' emotional response to various objects with which he is subjectively engaged. These objects include: the hardness of heart and unbelief of the Jewish leaders; the spiritual obtuseness of his disciples whose hearts are transformed only in light of his resurrection from the dead; and his earnest desire to see the establishment of the New Jerusalem, when God will reign supreme from Mt. Zion and all will worship and glorify the Lord with new hearts. The emotion of sighing is a common human emotion that expresses not only the tribulations and toil of this life, but also the aspirations and desires of the human heart for a better age to come (i.e., a prospective good). Jesus' sighing is an indicator of his true humanity that is lived very much in the fray of the present age with its infirmities, unbelief, and hardness of heart, yet Jesus always looks to his heavenly Father for the coming of the New Jerusalem when sighing will be no more. The sighing of Jesus should not be attributed merely to his human nature, though, for there is also a distinctly divine dimension to his sighing. In Jewish Scripture, God sighs because of the sinfulness of his people who fail to keep Torah and promote the divine purpose in the land, and Jesus the Son in his proclamation of his Father's kingdom of grace expresses this divine sighing as he confronts the hardness of heart and infirmity of his own people. The sighing of Jesus is deeper and more intense than any merely human sigh, though, in virtue of the fact that his humanity mediates his divinity as the Son, who desires to make known the Father's benevolent goodness towards his covenant people. It is not difficult to imagine that Jesus would have sighed on a regular basis, given the increasing opposition and rejection of his person and mission, as conveyed by the gospel story as realistic narrative.

In addition to the two recordings of Jesus' sighing, there are two recorded instances of Jesus' weeping. The first is recorded in Luke's Gospel (Luke 19:28–44), where Jesus weeps bitterly on his approach to Jerusalem. The second recording is in John's Gospel, where Jesus weeps at the tomb of Lazarus (John 11:35). The latter is quite different from the former, though, for the verb *klaiō* in Luke conveys a strong emotion of loud wailing, whereas the verb *dakruō* in John is rendered "broke out in tears."[102] What causes Jesus to weep so bitterly in Luke's narrative is not merely his own impending fate in Jerusalem, but the impending destruction of the holy city of Jerusalem. Isaiah spoke of his weeping bitter tears at the prospect of "the destruction of the daughter of my people" (Isa 22:4), and Jeremiah is overcome by grief and dismay for "the wound of the daughter of my people" (Jer 8:21). Jesus stands in this prophetic tradition of weeping over the doom that will overtake Israel as the people of God. Jesus' own fate is intimately linked with the fate of Jerusalem, so the coming of the city into sight draws from Jesus a prophetic announcement of its impending doom. Jesus' rejection by Israel and the failure to recognize in his ministry God's visitation of his people will bring the destruction of Jerusalem.[103] Jesus yearns for the New Jerusalem, but as he approaches the holy city he is overcome by the strong emotion of loud wailing as he contemplates the destruction of the Jerusalem. The cognitive character of the bitter weeping of Jesus is apparent in that the holy city of Jerusalem is deeply cherished by him as the place associated with the destiny of Israel and the center of the fully redeemed world to come. Jesus believes that Israel has a God-given mission to keep Torah in the land, so as to bring about the regeneration of the land and the eschatological renewal of the face of the earth. Israel's rejection of Jesus as the Torah incarnate signifies the doom of Jerusalem, which causes Jesus to weep bitterly.

Jesus also weeps at the tomb of Lazarus (John 11:35), but his weeping in this instance is very different to his bitter wailing on his approach to Jerusalem.[104] The text says explicitly that Jesus loves Mary,

102. Voorwinde, *Jesus' Emotions in the Gospels*, 138.

103. Voorwinde, *Jesus' Emotions in the Gospels*, 140. See 2 Kgs 8:11, 12; Isa 22:4; Jer 8:21, 9:1, 13:7.

104. The raising of Lazarus from the dead is the climactic sign in the book of Signs.

Martha, and Lazarus (John 11: 3, 5, 36), and it is because of this love that Jesus leaves the security of his place of retreat (John 11:8) and ventures to a place of danger—Bethany near Jerusalem—so he can visit the sisters Mary and Martha and the tomb of their brother Lazarus.[105] Jesus' love for these three persons is very natural, since it is the affection for friends who have given him devotion and hospitality. It also seems very natural that Jesus is "deeply moved" (John 11:33, 38) by the grief he encounters in Bethany, so that he enters the grief of those around him and weeps at the tomb of Lazarus. Jesus' human love for his friends is then transposed to a higher key when Jesus sacrificially lays down his own life for his friends on the cross. As the "Lamb of God who takes away the sin of the world" (John 1:29), Jesus' sacrificial death on behalf of his friends reveals a love that is sublime and divine. The cross is the ultimate manifestation of Jesus' love for his own, which forms the basis of the new commandment that Jesus gives them: "This is my commandment, that you love one another as I have loved you. Greater love has no man than this, that a man lay down his life for his friends" (John 15:12–13).

The cognitive nature of Jesus' weeping in the gospels of Luke and John is indicated by the value he attaches to, and the importance he places upon, the object of weeping. Lazarus is a much loved friend, and Jesus' love for Lazarus, together with his sisters Mary and Martha, shows that Jesus has a personal history and is truly engaged with his world. His earthly life is a truly human life in which he develops affectionate and valued friendships with persons who offer him devotion, support, and hospitality. His love for Lazarus appears as a genuinely human love, which accounts for Jesus' expression of grief at the tomb of Lazarus. While it is true to say that John paints a picture of Jesus as being in control of his life and mission as the Son, nonetheless the evangelist does not want us to think of Jesus as unmoved by the events in which he is subjectively involved.[106] Jesus is genuinely affected by happenings that involve him per-

---

There is a clustering of emotions in this narrative—Jesus "loves," is "glad," is "troubled," "weeps," and is "deeply moved"—which indicate a complex interweaving of the human and the divine into the fabric of the narrative. Voorwinde, *Jesus Emotions in the Fourth Gospel*, 185.

105. This theme of leaving a safe place to venture to a place of danger could be seen as a parallel to the prologue to John's Gospel: the eternal Word, out of unfathomable love for us, leaves the safe haven of life with the Father in heaven and becomes flesh so as to offer us the fullness of salvation, understood as the conquest of the powers of death and the glory of eternal life.

106. In John's Gospel, Jesus is not only "troubled" by the grieving atmosphere that

sonally; he is not a Stoic sage who is detached from things in the external world and who seeks to distance himself from disturbing emotions such as grief. Jesus is deeply distressed and moved at the sight of the tomb of Lazarus, and he is even more deeply distressed and moved at the coming into sight of the holy city of Jerusalem, which draws from Jesus a prophetic announcement of its impending doom. Jerusalem is deeply loved, cherished, and valued by Jesus as storied place, as having special meaning because of God's history of covenant lodged there. Its impending doom due to Israel's rejection of Jesus stirs up in him the strong emotional response of loud wailing. Here again Jesus is not portrayed as a Stoic sage, for he is not detached from his external world but is personally attached to Jerusalem as storied place. Jesus deeply desires the establishment of the New Jerusalem and feels overcome with grief at the prospect of the holy city's impending doom due to Israel's rejection of his person. The grief in view here is very human and is in line with the prophets who experienced similar grief, yet there is also a divine dimension to Jesus' grieving. Jesus is greater than the prophets, for he is the Son who is commissioned by the Father to proclaim the kingdom of grace to Israel. This means that *his rejection by Israel is felt more deeply than the prophets*. To reject Jesus the Son is to reject God's visitation of his people. Jesus grieves as a human, yet the process of each nature advancing through the other in his person means that his grief is intensified and deepened by virtue of the consciousness of his divinity as the Son who proclaims the Father's kingdom of benevolent love, yet ends up being rejected by his own and put to death.

Jesus' Grief, Distress, and Lament—The Suffering Emotions

The emotions of grief, distress, and lament feature prominently in Jesus' journey to Jerusalem and his passion. We have just seen that in Luke the pathos of Jesus is introduced at an earlier stage than in the other Synoptic

---

he finds in Bethany (11:33): his soul is "troubled" as his hour strikes (12:27), although he knows that the "ruler of this world" will be cast out (12:31); and he is "troubled" in spirit due to his impending betrayal (13:21), although he has chosen Judas in order that "the scripture may be fulfilled" (13:18). For all Jesus' divine foreknowledge, John does not want us to neglect the mystery of the eternal Word who became flesh and dwelt amongst us. Since the divinity cannot be thought of apart from the humanity, Jesus is moved and troubled by historical events that involve him personally. In John there is "a subtle and mysterious interplay between the divine and the human." Voorwinde, *Jesus' Emotions in the Fourth Gospel*, 218.

Gospels, with the account of Jesus' loud wailing on his approach to Jerusalem. What's more, Luke highlights in an arresting fashion the great suffering and agony of Jesus in Gethsemane when he writes: "his sweat became like great drops of blood" (Luke 22:44).[107] What Jesus finds so deeply distressing is the dreadful prospect of having to endure the suffering of "the cup" (Luke 22:42; Mark 14:36; Matt 26:39; John 18:11). In Gethsemane, Jesus is acutely aware of the terrifying ordeal of the cross that awaits him, hence he is deeply "troubled" and "overwhelmed with sorrow to the point of death" (Mark 14:34; Matt 26:38; John 12:27). We see Jesus in Gethsemane as we have never seen him before. He pleads with the Father that the cup be removed from him and he is overcome by such powerful passions that he is rendered vulnerable and emotionally out of control. His heart is about to break with overwhelming grief, yet he steels himself for the mammoth struggle that lies ahead in his ultimate enactment of perfect obedience to the Father. This episode marks a point of transition in the gospel story for the enactment of Jesus' obedience to the Father. The emphasis in the narrative falls on Jesus as truly tested in his fidelity to the Father as he gives himself over to the Jewish and Roman authorities. By doing so, Jesus renounces a certain liberty of action that he had enjoyed as a figure of power and authority in his proclamation of the kingdom, and now enters a distressing situation of powerlessness and helplessness.[108] The words that the chief priests and scribes utter as Jesus hangs on the cross poignantly express this transition: "He saved others; he cannot save himself" (Mark 15:31; Matt 27:42; Luke 23:35).

In the cry of lament on the cross—"My God, my God, why have you forsaken me? (Mark 15:34; Matt 27:46)—it becomes apparent that what Jesus dreads in Gethsemane is the prospect of being abandoned by God. There are a few salient observations that need to be made in respect of Jesus' lament, which lead to the formulation of a complex view of Jesus' suffering for our sake.[109] First, in light of the process of development of Jesus' identity as the Son in the gospel story, his cry of lament appears as the culminating point of the mounting isolation and opposition he experiences in carrying out his messianic mission. Jesus is abandoned by the covenant people in general, the Jewish religious leaders, his very own

---

107. This condition is known medically as "hematidrosis." In cases of severe anguish, stress, and strain, it is possible for blood to mingle with sweat.

108. See Frei, *Identity*, 102–15.

109. For a more comprehensive discussion of these points in relation to Jesus' cry of lament, see Novello, "Jesus' Cry," 38–60.

disciples, and now he feels abandoned even by God to terrible adversity as he is delivered into the hands of his enemies. Jesus clearly suffers "because" of the hardness of heart of the people, which is to say that he takes upon himself the *consequences of sin*. Since the rejected one, however, does not reject those who condemn him to death—"Father, forgive them, for they know not what they do" (Luke 23:34)—this means that Jesus becomes their "representative" before the Father. A second and related point here is that Jesus' solidarity with Adamic flesh implies that he too was judged by God, but not in the sense of appeasing the wrath of God against the sinner.[110] Rather, his being *made sin* (2 Cor 5:21) for our sake recognizes the dimension of his suffering as the sin-bearer.[111] The suffering of Jesus "for" sinful humanity is captured by the concept of "substitution," according to which the Son takes the place of the sinner and suffers the hell of God-forsakenness so as to conquer the "second death" (Rev 20:6). Jesus suffers not merely at the hands of sinners, but also at the hands of God, although it is important here to stress love of the Father as the exegesis of the event, not Stoic submissiveness to the Father.

A third aspect of Jesus' suffering emerges when his participation in Adamic flesh is not reduced to his solidarity with sinners, but is broadened to include his *solidarity* with all the suffering just and with suffering humanity in general in this vale of tears. From the vantage pint of this particular aspect of Jesus' suffering, salvation in his person assumes a broader dimension beyond the forgiveness of sin to include his compassionate solidarity with all those who cry to God out of the depths of their afflicted hearts.[112] Jesus suffers not only "because" of sin and "for" sinners, but "with" the afflicted, with all those who mourn, who suffer loneliness, who suffer rejection and persecution, who suffer grief and sorrow,

---

110. Jesus' drinking of the cup should not be interpreted in the manner that the Reformers in the past proposed; namely, in juridical terms as Jesus appeasing the wrath of God against the sinner (i.e., penal substitution theory). Karl Barth and Hans Urs von Balthasar, it is worth noting, both reject penal substitution theory: they stress that God's love, not wrath, is the cause of Jesus' passion, yet they retain the notion of substitution to convey the Son's suffering endured as the "second death" (Rev 20:6). The notion of substitution serves to convey the exclusive aspect of the Son's conquest of the second death. See Lauber, *Barth on the Descent*.

111. The church fathers tended to affirm that Christ took upon himself the "consequences" of sin, not that he was "made sin" for our sake. Hans Urs von Balthasar has been critical of the church fathers for not following through on the exchange principle expressed in 2 Cor 5:21. See Balthasar, *Theo-Drama*, 4:244–54.

112. See Miller, *Interpreting the Psalms*, 109–10.

who sigh and lament, and who suffer death. While the suffering emotions come into sharp relief in Jesus' passion, we should not lose sight of the fact—as the discussion above has sought to demonstrate—that Jesus expresses an array of disturbing and suffering emotions during the course of his messianic mission: he is angered by obstacles to his proclamation of the kingdom of grace; he is angered by corrupt worship and legalistic attitudes to Jewish faith; he sighs at the physical infirmities that afflict his people; he sighs at the spiritual obtuseness of his disciples; he suffers increasing loneliness, isolation, and rejection as his messianic mission unfolds; he sighs deeply for the New Jerusalem; and he is deeply grieved and troubled by the death of Lazarus. Many of these disturbing and suffering emotions of Jesus are the focus of Jesus' teaching in the Beatitudes recorded in Matthew's Gospel. Jesus teaches: "Blessed are those who mourn, for they shall be comforted" (5:4); "Blessed are those who hunger and thirst for righteousness, for they shall be satisfied" (5:6); "Blessed are the pure in heart, for they shall see God" (5:8); "Blessed are those who are persecuted for righteousness' sake, for theirs is the kingdom of heaven" (5:10). The blessed are those who follow Jesus, whose emotional life exemplifies the teachings of the Beatitudes.

A properly formed interpretation of Jesus' cry of lament is one that holds together both the reality of Jesus' torment of God-forsakenness,[113] as well as the enactment of his perfect obedience to the Father as the definitive manifestation of personal unity with the Father in unfathomable love. Jesus' cry, as belonging to the Wisdom motif of the suffering just one (*passio justi*), presents as a radical test of his love for the Father. He as the Son "learned obedience through what he suffered" (Heb 5:7–8). Love is the basis of obedience, and Jesus' love for the Father is truly put to the test in his passion, as his very strong human emotions of dread, grief, and anguish make plain. These suffering emotions are involved in a mighty struggle with the vigor and strength of the Son's love—for both God and humanity—which is able to endure and overcome the agonies of his passion. Here we see the mutual interaction of the two natures in his person in stark operation. It is the exercise of Jesus' holy love that

---

113. The view of the scholastic period, where the problem was how to reconcile the beatific vision of Christ with his suffering on the cross, tended to undermine his genuine cry of lament. Aquinas, for instance, offered a solution on the basis of the two natures of Christ: the incarnate Word suffers in his body and in the "inferior" part of his soul, but the "superior" part of his soul, which has to do with the redemption of humanity, cannot suffer from God's non-intervention. See Aquinas, *Summa theologiae* I 47.3, 50.2.

wins the victory in his torturous sufferings, when he drinks the cup to its bitter dregs because he is set upon our salvation. Love is not merely one of the affections, but the first and fount of all the affections in Jesus' life and mission to Israel. "I do as the Father has commanded me, so that the world may know that I love the Father" (John 14:31). The primary object of Jesus' love is the Father, and the consummate expression of this ineffable love is that the Son willingly sheds his blood as "the blood of the covenant" (Matt 26:28). The cry of lament on Calvary indicates that the one forsaken by God is the righteous Son of God, in whom our salvation is accomplished.

We have seen in this chapter that Jesus' love of the Father is presented in the gospels as the love of sheer delight in its object (John 14:21, 31; Luke 10:17-24), which accounts for the exuberant joy of Jesus as his messianic mission is being fulfilled. In his authoritative proclamation of the kingdom of grace, Jesus experiences the Father as the *mysterium fascinans*. In respect of his passion, though, the situation is markedly different, for Jesus is deeply troubled as his hour strikes. Exuberant joy gives way to overwhelming distress and anguish as Jesus is truly tested in his love for the Father, who is now experienced as the *mysterium tremendum*. The followers of Jesus should not think that the life of discipleship is all about the congenial emotions of love, joy, and delight, without any regard for the manner in which love of the Father is the cornerstone of all Jesus' emotions, including his suffering emotions that culminate in his passion and cry of lament.[114] The suffering emotions of Jesus spring from his love of the Father, which translates into his ineffable love for us, which carries him forward in his redemptive mission all the way to shedding his blood on the cross to inaugurate the new covenant of grace. The grace of redemption does not come cheaply, but is a costly grace that leaves us spellbound. The recipients of this grace experience joy, peace, and gratitude for the forgiveness of sins and the new life that is on offer, but the mature Christian knows that imitating Christ is inevitably costly since crucifixion is what makes a Christian. The Christian cannot expect to be exempt from suffering, because to live the way of the cross is to imitate the self-sacrificing love of Christ for others. The driving force for this

---

114. Jesus' love of God accounts for the compassion he has for his own, his exuberant joy as he carries out his mission, his zeal for his Father's house, his anger at whatever gets in the way of the kingdom of grace, his sighing at the testing of the Pharisees and at the plight of the deaf-mute, his bitter wailing as the holy city of Jerusalem comes into sight, and his willingness to endure the agony of his passion.

process of imitating Christ and becoming sons and daughters of God in the Son, is the transformation of our emotional life as we allow the crucified Christ to become the new object of both our congenial and suffering emotions, which form an integral unity.

The emotions of Christ must become the emotions of his followers, and in light of Jesus' emotional life as reaching its zenith in his cry of lament on Calvary, the suffering of Christian discipleship assumes a distinctive character as testimony to the saving power of Jesus' crucifixion, which brings new life to Israel and the world. The complex nature of Jesus' suffering expounded above is to be reflected in the life of his disciples. (i) Christians must expect to suffer "because" of people's sinfulness and hardness of heart, yet they are required to adopt the attitude of not rejecting those who reject them, so that they may represent sinners before Christ. (ii) Christ's disciples must be prepared to suffer "for" sinners, which entails bearing the sins of others and suffering in the place of sinners, rather than being exacting as to matters of justice. (iii) The followers of Christ must be prepared to suffer in solidarity "with" the afflicted and display compassion for all those who cry to God out of the depths of their afflicted hearts. Once this complex view of Christian suffering is embraced as a living witness to the first and chief emotion of love of God, then the event of the incarnation should not be treated purely as a past event, but should be regarded as a process that continues in the baptized, who are the embodiment of Christ in the world.

Jesus' Involved Holiness and the Process of Passionate Deification in His Person

With regard to Jesus' love as the fount of his emotions, we have seen that its cognitive nature is plainly evident in that it has an intentional object that is supremely valued; namely, God the Father. The cognitive character of Jesus' love is further in evidence when we consider the covenant framework into which Jesus is born, which this chapter has sought to highlight by focusing on Jesus' Jewish upbringing and his mother as Daughter Zion. God's love for Israel is the basis of the covenant relationship (Deut 7:6–13), just as God's love is the motivating force behind the new covenant associated with the sending of the Son into the temporal realm: "For God so loved the world that he gave his only Son, that whoever believes in him should not perish but have eternal life" (John 3:16).

The required response of the covenant people to God's love for them is obedience to Torah as the pathway to a transformed life of holiness in the land. Jewish history, though, tells the story of the people of God as a less than ideal covenant partner, and Jesus is born into this history of fidelity and infidelity.

This chapter has argued that we must not overlook the role played by Jesus' Jewish family upbringing in shaping the formation of basic attitudes—love of God, trust in God, humility before God, joy in God, and hope in God—in respect of the God of the covenant and Jewish life in the land. To recognize the import of Jesus' family upbringing in the matter of the development of his individuality is to avoid the past tendency to downplay or undermine the eternal Word's condescension into the human temporal realm. The Word truly enters into the sphere of Adamic flesh, for the child Jesus takes his flesh from the Virgin Mary and he undergoes a familial process of faith formation and childhood development in the context of his cultural-religious situation. Love of God is the most fundamental orientation to Jewish life and Jesus first acquires this basic attitude in the context of his Jewish family. The love that the young Jesus has for God is to be thought of as a human love, yet by the time the more mature Jesus begins his messianic ministry he is conscious of his uniquely filial relationship to the Father, and thus surfaces a distinctly divine dimension to his love of God. Human love of God is transposed to the higher key of the divine Son's love of the Father, which is always, however, mediated by his humanity. What is in view here is the process by which one nature advances through the other in the maturing consciousness of the Word become flesh. If Jesus' love of God were a merely human love, then this would mean that he could not in person be the historical revelation of the Father's benevolent love for his people, or the inaugurator of the new covenant by the shedding of his blood, which brings the blessings of forgiveness of sins and a new heart that imitates the sacred heart of Jesus. If, on the other hand, we were to ignore the genuine humanity of Jesus and insist that his love of God is purely divine because he is the Son of God, then this would in effect amount to a disregard for the genuine process of development of Jesus' individuality. The latter is integral to affirming that Jesus is the Redeemer and Savior who knows the human condition intimately from within—though he is without sin—and has exalted our lowly and infirm status to the glory of beatific communion with God.

Before Jesus begins his authoritative proclamation of the kingdom of God, he undergoes a preparatory process of maturation in the harsh and testing conditions of Jewish life in first-century Galilee. The basic Jewish attitudes to life that the young Jesus acquires from his family upbringing are not forged in a vacuum of detachment from his concrete surroundings. Instead, the formation of basic attitudes or orientations to life—i.e., emotions—involves an involved process whereby the young Jesus subjectively engages with the grim realities of Jewish life in the land. For he grows up in a world marked by sin and infidelity; he is confronted by human failure and misery; he devoutly attends the local synagogue and keeps the Jewish festivals; he maintains fidelity and trust in the God of the covenant in the harsh realities of the Roman occupation of the land; he works as a humble carpenter in his home town of Nazareth; and he grows in wisdom and understanding, which brings him to the point of baptism by John. The array of emotions that Jesus displays in his messianic mission to Israel has a personal biography or history of formation, yet we must not think that this process of formation ceases once Jesus begins his proclamation of the kingdom of grace. The gospel story shows that Jesus the Son must learn what obedience to the Father involves. His identity as the Son is put into progressively sharper relief as he is subjected to mounting opposition from the Jewish leaders, as well as increasing rejection and hardness of heart on the part of his own people in general, including his disciples. Ultimately, Jesus accomplishes his mission as the Son by enacting perfect obedience to the Father unto death, which is expressed in a poignant and arresting fashion in his cry of dereliction on the hill of Golgotha.

From the perspective of this process of a gradual incarnation—starting with his birth from the Virgin Mary and culminating in his self-sacrificing death on the cross—the holiness of Jesus cannot be thought of as an ahistorical holiness cut-off from the toil and grim realities of Jewish life in first-century Galilee. His holiness is very much an *involved holiness* lived in the fray of first-century Galilee, which does complete justice to the notion of the kenosis of the Son. That is to say, the real participation of the divine in the human existential realm, for the sake of effecting the fullness of the covenant of grace—i.e., participation of the human in the divine, by means of the participation of the divine in the human. The human essence and the divine essence should not be thought of as juxtaposed to one another, or the human essence as purely passive in relation to the divine essence. The two natures must be affirmed as mutually interpenetrating each other in Jesus' person, so that each nature advances through the other in the process of a progressive incarnation. The present chapter has sought to illustrate that the richness of Jesus' emotional life is the concrete manifestation of the process of mutual interaction of divinity and humanity in his person, and the springboard of his messianic mission to Israel. The emotional life of Jesus should not be downplayed, therefore, for it provides a special window through which to observe the extraordinary manner in which the process of deification (i.e., salvation) in his person is achieved.

The notion of Stoic *apatheia* is simply incongruous with the gospel picture of Jesus and should not be superimposed on the Savior so as to enforce a particular metaphysical conception of his divinity, which bears no real relationship to his humanity. Nor should the emotions of Jesus be regarded as mere signs of his humanity and restricted to those defects of soul that are considered to be the consequences of sin and mortality. Jesus' emotions must be affirmed as running their full course as we experience them, with the exception of sin. Moreover, Jesus' emotions should be acknowledged as purer and more intense than ours in virtue of his emotions being both qualitatively and quantitatively different to our emotions. Jesus is no ordinary human being, for his identity is divine as the only Son who is in the bosom of the Father, thus a qualitative difference emerges in that Jesus personally makes known the Father's kingdom of grace. There is also a related quantitative difference in that the emotions of Jesus flow out of his purity of heart as the only Son who makes known the Father's merciful love for his people, which means that the man Jesus feels far more intensely the disjunction that exists between the present age of sin and suffering and the kingdom of grace he proclaims to Israel. In the end, the kingdom of grace comes by way of Jesus' very real and profound suffering in his sacrificial death on Golgotha, which is the definitive manifestation of Jesus' ineffable love for the Father, as well as his perfect love for his friends and his perfect love for his enemies who condemn him to death. The full course of Jesus' intense emotional life illustrates the reality of the divine Son having clothed himself with our Adamic flesh, so that we might be "more fully clothed" (2 Cor 5:2) with the unfathomable gift of salvation in his person, which makes all things new. As the divine Son clothed in Adamic flesh, the crucified Jesus is forever able to be touched with a profound feeling of our vulnerabilities and infirmities, and, conversely, we are forever able to be deeply moved and affected by his self-sacrificing love for us, which knows no bounds.

The purity, breadth, and depth of Jesus' emotional life, which our cognitive theory of emotion has been able to illuminate in conjunction with an adequately developed notion of kenosis, provides a privileged window through which to gaze upon the mystery of the incarnation and the manner in which the fullness of the covenant of grace is accomplished in his person. The deification of humanity in Jesus Christ, when observed through the window of his emotional life, is a truly passionate deification. This has implications for how we understand the life of Christian discipleship, for the process of ongoing conversion and imitation of Christ fundamentally involves an ongoing conversion of the emotions, as the crucified Christ becomes the new object of both the congenial and suffering emotions. The process of our salvation cannot be thought of apart from our emotional life, for salvation in Christ involves the ongoing conversion of our emotional life through the indwelling Spirit of the risen Lord—we receive a *new heart* by means of which we are transformed into the Son's likeness with ever increasing glory (see 2 Cor 3:18). The role of the emotions in the Christian ascent to God was discussed in chapter 2, but the topic will now be revisited in the following concluding chapter, which takes into account the findings of chapters 3 and 4 of this study.

5

Christian Life as the Transformation of the Emotions

THIS STUDY BEGAN BY stating that human beings experience a wide range of emotions and it would be difficult to imagine life without the motivating force of the emotions that account for the drama of our lives in the world. It was said that the language of emotion so pervades the lives of ordinary people that it is the primary or first-order language. This was based on the understanding that emotions are closely intertwined with people's goals or desires, values, beliefs, morality, and ethics. As evaluative judgments directed upon actual or prospective states of affairs, the emotions disclose that we humans are personally bound up with our world and appraise given situations as beneficial or harmful to human flourishing. At times the emotions might appear as compulsive forces in opposition to the powers of reason, but closer examination reveals that the emotions of adult life have a biography: they are historically formed in the context of social-cultural norms, although our childhood upbringing, as well as individual proclivities, are also contributing factors to the emotions of adult life. Far from being irrational forces opposed to reason, the intellectual, emotional, and volitional elements of the human person are to be thought of as closely intertwined distinctions that belong within a living whole.

The Stoic theory of the emotions as judgments concerning present and prospective state of affairs still has significance today, although this study has repudiated the Stoic claim that all common emotions must be extirpated in the pursuit of virtue, because all are based on false judgments. Anger, for instance, is a legitimate emotion when one suffers a personal insult or injury, or encounters moral evil as an obstacle to human flourishing; and grief is a valid emotion that registers the loss of something deemed important for our human flourishing, such as the breakdown of a close relationship or the death of a loved one. Grief is an ineluctable emotion that registers our passivity before the world; that is, our attachment to external things, our being bound up with the world that is not fully within our control. Negative emotions that disturb the soul are invariably experienced within the historical setting of this life and palpably reveal the limited human capacity to secure the kind of future we would like for ourselves. Human desires (goals) are invariably frustrated and remain unfulfilled, and negative emotions give voice to this dimension of passivity before the world. When we experience our vulnerability in the world and find ourselves wondering about the meaning and purpose of human existence, this experience of wonder is often associated with emotions such as grief, sorrow, and lament.

Not merely negative emotions, though, but also positive emotions such as love and joy are referred to a transcendent object of wonder, which is invested with unsurpassable value and a surplus of meaning. We saw that for Jesus—who is the interpreter of humanity as well as the interpreter of God—the object of wonder is his heavenly Father and his fundamental desire is to make manifest the Father's benevolent love to the covenant people. This study has argued that Jesus the Son experiences the Father as both the *mysterium fascinans* (congenial emotions of love, joy, and delight) and the *mysterium tremendum* (suffering emotions of dread, grief, sorrow, and lament). Jesus knows exuberant joy which stems from his consciousness of carrying out his Father's work of benevolent love, and at the same time the gospels depict Jesus as the man of sorrows: he suffers "because" of the hardness of heart of the covenant people, who reject his person; he suffers "for" sinners in that he vicariously bears the sins of Israel and of the whole world; and he suffers "with" those who endure innocent suffering in seeking to uphold justice and righteousness in a world where truth and goodness struggle to triumph. The full course of Jesus' emotions are directed upon actual states of affairs in the land of promise, and reveal the extent to which Jesus as the Son is subjectively bound up with Jewish covenant expectations on the one hand, and his ineffable love of the Father on the other, which is put to a severe test as his increasing rejection and isolation culminates in the suffering of his passion.

To acknowledge the full course of Jesus' emotional life is to acknowledge the truth of his Adamic flesh, of his being subjected to the infirmity, limitations, and tribulations of this life. At the same time, though, we have seen that Jesus' emotions also reveal the truth of his divinity. The latter proposition should not strike us as entirely novel, for it builds upon the Jewish understanding of the God of the covenant as exhibiting pathos in relation to his people. Basic emotions such as love, joy, delight, jealousy, anger, compassion, and lament, are not confined to the human sphere but are also ascribed to God as personal or communicable properties in relation to the people of the covenant. When we shift our focus to the Christian claim that Jesus of Nazareth is the word of God become flesh, his emotional life assumes primary significance as the special lens through which to observe what it means for the divine Word to dwell bodily in the man Jesus. In the past the notion of kenosis was not accorded its full ontological realism, for the Word's humanity was thought of merely as a passive instrument of our redemption. In itself, the Word's humanity was regarded as remaining outside the life of the God-Man; it was not truly affirmed as the divine-humanity, as the culmination of God's personal history of engagement with Israel and the world. To accord the idea of kenosis its full ontological realism is tantamount to acknowledging the incarnate Word as subject to becoming, to the interior temptation of evil, and to a process of development of his own individuality in the socio-historical context of first-century Palestine. This study has sought to demonstrate that a close examination of Jesus' emotional life, informed by a contemporary cognitive theory of emotion, is able to effectively illuminate the kenotic process whereby the divine and the human mutually interact with each other, and progressively actualize themselves as the one and the other as they encounter and address each other in Jesus' life and mission to the people of the covenant.

Once we observe the process of salvation through the window of Jesus' rich and intense emotional life, we can better appreciate why it is not possible to separate out human from divine actions in the man Jesus. Instead, we must think in terms of a single divine-human subject where the two natures mutually interact and reciprocally penetrate each other, not in terms of two juxtaposed natures where the divine (active element) penetrates the human but the human (passive element) does not penetrate the divine. On the view that the emotions are the springs of action in the world, both the humanity and the divinity assume active roles as they mutually interact in the process of a progressive incarnation in Jesus' person. To study Jesus' emotional life is to behold the wondrous process of deification in his person and to appreciate what it cost the Son to win the decisive victory over the powers of death in the world, so that we humans might be "further clothed" (2 Cor 5:4) with the grace and glory of divine salvation; that is, the fullness of human flourishing in relation to God, to one another, and to the cosmos.

The recognition of the full course of Jesus' emotions allows us to appreciate the Son's holiness as an involved holiness: he is truly immersed in the temporal-historical realm, he is truly vulnerable before the world, and is thus involved in a mammoth and veritable struggle to carry forward the proclamation of his Father's kingdom of grace. The Word made flesh has to learn what perfect filial obedience involves. Since he is truly tested in his fidelity to the Father, the Crucified One is forever able to be touched by our infirmities, by the limitations of our flesh, and we are forever able to be moved and affected by his self-emptying, compassionate love for us, which elevates us to the glory of union with his Father. The emotions of Jesus recorded in the Gospels should not be treated as "pre-passions" (*propatheia*), nor should they be limited to the defects of soul that have traditionally been regarded as the consequences of Adam's sin. We are required to acknowledge the full course of Jesus' emotions as the manifestation of what it means for the divinity to dwell bodily in the man Jesus. We should be "spellbound by the intensity of Jesus' emotions."[1] His unfathomable love, heartbroken compassion, his exuberant joy, his palpable anger and strong indignation, his deep sighing, his bitter weeping, his groans of anguish, and his loud cry of dereliction on Calvary, are all integral to and the manifestation of the salvific process of the mutual interpenetration of divinity and humanity in his person.

In light of the process of passionate deification elaborated in this study, we are required to think of salvation in Jesus Christ as involving the ongoing conversion of our emotions. It is not sufficient to be merely spellbound by the intensity and richness of Jesus' emotional life: "we are to be unbound by his Spirit so that his life becomes our life, his emotions our emotions, to be 'transformed into his likeness with ever increasing glory' (2 Cor 3:18)."[2] The participation in the divine life—to be sons and daughters of God in the Son—has to do with the transforming of human desire away from earthly objects towards God as the new object

---

1. Hansen, "Emotions of Jesus," 46.
2. Hansen, "Emotions of Jesus," 46.

of love, delight, and joy. To put on Christ and imitate his life is *to see as God sees, and feel as God feels*. This is aptly conveyed by the reception of a "new heart" that inclines the soul towards the infinite God, who is the fulfillment of the fundamental desire that accounts for the movement of the human being's subjective engagement in the world. This putting on of Christ does not involve new faculties of the soul, but the same faculties of the soul: God's grace in Christ brings about a new inward perception that inclines the soul toward God as its ultimate end. Normal human affections and Christian affections are not two different stories, but integral parts of one and the same story. If we take first the congenial emotions of love, joy, and compassion, a Christian understanding of these emotions should proceed along the following lines of thought.

1. The object of love is no longer limited or confined to other humans or earthly pursuits deemed desirable for achieving certain goals in life, but now opens out to the transforming and transcendent horizon of God as the new object of delight. The directing of human love to God has the effect of redirecting human goals to supremely good objects that have eternal value and which alone can satisfy the deep yearning of the human heart. The redirecting of love to the ineffable object of God, who addresses humanity personally in Jesus Christ, has the effect of loving sinful and fallible humans more profoundly, patiently, and faithfully, as Christ loves them. This includes not merely those who are closest and most familiar to us—such as family members, fellow Christians, and friends—but also love of enemies. The love in view here is no ordinary love; it is not romantic ecstasy or sentimental love, but a self-sacrificing love that is refined through the process of suffering as the embodiment of Christ in the world. To actively engage in love towards enemies highlights the "extraordinary" character of Christian life, which is not "a matter of course."[3] Love of enemies is the love of Jesus Christ himself, which is the way of the cross. To put on Christ means that our lives are caught up in Christ's love of the Father and of sinners; we are required to patiently endure evil and forego revenge in giving witness to the ineffable love of God towards sinners, which brings about personal conversion and a transformed worldview. Love of

---

3. Dietrich Bonhoeffer keenly emphasized the Christian life as characterized by the quality of the "extraordinary," the "peculiar," that which is not "a matter of course." See Bonhoeffer, *Cost of Discipleship*, 136.

God is the first and chief of the Christian emotions, for "God is love" (1 John 4:8, 16). The truth and meaning of human life in this world is thus known through love of God, which empowers and motivates us to continue the work of Christ's proclamation of the kingdom of grace, by loving our fellow humans as Christ loves them.

2. Christian joy should not be thought of as limited to experiencing the goodness of other persons or delighting in certain earthly activities, but assumes a much more profound dimension as the joy of the Father's benevolent love for us in sending his only Son into the world to offer us the gift of salvation. Jesus experiences exuberant joy in obediently carrying out his Father's good work, and the source of his obedience to the Father's will is his ineffable love of the Father. Jesus' disciples too must exhibit the unsurpassable joy of proclaiming the Gospel of Christ to the world. Jesus gives his disciples a "new commandment" (John 13:34; 15:12) that they must love one another as he has loved them. The joy of his disciples is dependent upon their keeping his commandments: "If you keep my commandments, you will abide in my love, just as I have kept my Father's commandments and abide in his love. These things I have spoken to you, that my joy may be in you, and that your joy may be full" (John 15:10–11). The joy of the Christian springs from obeying Jesus' commandments and abiding in his love. The hearts of his disciples should be on fire with the joy of the Gospel, even when the world seems to be collapsing around them.[4] This kind of joy is not a fickle or superficial joy based on self-indulgence and self-interest, but a robust joy that springs from the ineffable gift of salvation in the risen Lord.[5] As a robust joy, Christian joy is not extinguished when things in our world are not going well, but comes into its own as a joy based upon the love of Jesus Christ himself, in whom is to be found the fullness of salvation.

3. Compassion also assumes a broader horizon that challenges Christians to go beyond feeling mere sympathy for those who suffer some form of evil or mishap. Worldly expressions of sympathy tend to be

---

4. Pope Francis, in his apostolic exhortation *Evangelii Gaudium* (Joy of the Gospel), asserts that joy is the distinguishing atmosphere of the Christian life, and is necessary to effectively proclaim to the world the good news of God's extraordinary address to humanity in the person of Jesus Christ.

5. See Novello, "Robust Joy," 323–33.

of the type that does not involve any personal attachment to the suffering situation of others. Christians, in contrast, must display the type of compassion that is the hallmark of the God-Man; they must bear in their bodies the dying of Jesus in order that the life of Jesus may be manifested to the world (see 2 Cor 4:10–11). To be the embodiment of the crucified Jesus in the world means that his disciples cannot keep the suffering of others at arm's length; they must bear in their bodies the divine pathos incarnated in the person of Jesus the Christ. The God of the covenant is a compassionate God who is affected by the cries of his afflicted people, and Jesus' followers are called to imitate the divine pathos in bringing the glad tidings of salvation to a suffering humanity. Jesus suffers not only "because" of the hardness of heart of his people and "for" sinners in that he bears their sin, but "with" the afflicted. The compassion of Jesus is manifested in his solidarity with all those who cry to God out of the depths of their afflicted hearts, who mourn, who suffer grief and sorrow, who suffer loneliness, who suffer rejection and persecution, who sigh and lament, and who suffer death. The followers of Christ must be prepared to suffer in solidarity with the afflicted, as living witness to the first and chief emotion of love of God.

The congenial emotions of love, joy, and compassion should not be treated as separate emotions but as intimately intertwined emotions that provide the springboard of Christian life, just as they formed the basis of Jesus' life and messianic mission to Israel. The congenial emotions are summed up in Jesus' commandment that we love one another as he has loved us. Just as love for the Father is the basis of Jesus' obedience to the Father and the source of the exuberant joy that is in him, so our abiding in Christ's love is the basis of our keeping his commandments and the source of our robust joy that transcends the normal boundaries of human existence. Love of God is the fount of the emotions of joy and compassion that form the distinguishing atmosphere of Christian life, and they give poignant expression to the *already* present dimension of the kingdom of God in our midst. The presence of the kingdom in our midst comes through our witnessing to God's salvation in Christ, not as a socio-political program for the transformation of the world. The socio-political task of Christians is not so much to transform the world, as "*how* to be in the world, in what form, for what purpose."[6] The task of Christians in the

---

6. Hauerwas and Willimon, *Resident Aliens*, 43.

present age is to endeavor to "influence the world by being the church, that is, by being something the world is not and can never be, lacking the gift of faith and vision, which is ours in Christ."[7] The congenial emotions of Christian life flow out of a *new heart* born of the Spirit dwelling in the soul as a new principle of nature—i.e., the participation of human nature in the divine nature. The Christian vision is the vision of the New Jerusalem, which transcends anything the unstable and self-serving socio-political order of this world could ever envision, let alone achieve. Yet precisely because Christian love of God is expressed in this sinful and groaning world as living witness to the Gospel of Christ, this chief emotion is not only the fount of Christian joy and compassion, but also of rightly directed emotions such as anger, indignation, and sighing, as well as the suffering emotions of grief, sorrow, and lament. An inextricable relationship obtains between the three congenial emotions of Christian life and the disturbing and suffering emotions. In respect of the Christian emotions of anger and indignation, sighing and weeping, they should be understood in the following manner.

1. The problem with normal human anger is that it too often leads to violence, murder, and broken relationships. The type of anger shown by Jesus is distinctly different. We saw in the previous chapter 4 of this study that Jesus gets angry and indignant with his disciples when they prevent children from coming to him, and with the scribes and Pharisees when they challenge his proclamation of God's visitation of his people. Jesus generally gets indignant with whomever and whatever stands in the way of God's kingdom of grace, which addresses human needs in a radical fashion. Jesus' anger expresses his strong moral sense of the covenant of grace, and the supremely high value he attaches to the divine goodness that brings about human flourishing in its totality—i.e., in relation to God, to one another, and to the cosmos. As the embodiment of Christ in the world, Christians are required to take up Jesus' moral stance and sense of indignation and not aspire to the cool detachment of the Stoic sage, who attributes no significance in the life of virtue to happenings in the external world. Anger is a perfectly legitimate and appropriate emotion when justified by the correct judgment of its object. Christian emotions of anger and indignation are indicative of concrete attachment to and personal engagement

---

7. Hauerwas and Willimon, *Resident Aliens*, 46.

with this world, in the name of Christ, and serve as action potentials for confronting moral evil and promoting more just relationships that will bring greater peace to our world.

2. It is common for people to sigh when they are sad, tired, relieved, or long for friends and home. The sighing of Jesus in the Gospels, though, has distinctly different objects, namely: the hardness of heart of the Jewish religious leaders, the spiritual obtuseness of his own disciples, and his strong desire to see the establishment of the New Jerusalem. What Jesus' sighing serves to express is the gap that exists between Jesus' proclamation of the kingdom and the worldly realities of the present age. This age is burdened with unbelief, hardness of heart, falsehoods, infirmities, and much toil. Christians, like Christ, can be expected to sigh as they subjectively engage in this world and seek to proclaim the kingdom of grace in the harsh realities of the here and now. The "not yet" dimension of the kingdom of God means that sighing is an inevitable emotion of Christian life in the present age. This sighing occurs not only in relation to the church's engagement in the world, but is also a dimension of the internal life of the church community, inasmuch as believers encounter hardness of heart and spiritual obtuseness amongst their own community of faith. The church constantly fails to fully live up to the demands of the Gospel of Christ, and sighing serves to express the constant need for reform and ongoing conversion as the embodiment of Christ in the world. A church that is not familiar with sighing is a church that has become complacent and comfortable with its settled arrangements. A church that does not sigh is a church that feels no need to challenge its leaders, fails to recognize the spiritual obtuseness of its own members, and expresses little desire to nurture the vision of the New Jerusalem or its establishment.

3. Weeping is common to human beings, for it is a physical manifestation of anguish, sorrow, grief, or joy. Jesus' sighing at times gives way to weeping, as when Jesus weeps bitterly as he approaches Jerusalem, or when he sheds tears over the death of his beloved friend Lazarus. Far from being a Stoic sage, Jesus at times is deeply moved by disturbing events unfolding around him; he is so overcome by happenings that he personally responds by weeping. His weeping shows in a powerful way his vulnerability before the world. Christians, like Christ, can expect that their passivity before the world will manifest

itself at times in bitter weeping. To be incorporated into the body of Christ is no recipe for Christians to feel that they are in full control of their own lives, or the lives of their loved ones, or the desired outcomes of their various church ministries. The tragic dimension of human existence remains very much with us. At times it is perfectly acceptable to feel so overwhelmed by disturbing happenings or bitterly disappointing outcomes that Christians respond by weeping profusely. Sighing and weeping rightly belong to Christian life. Not only do they testify to the fact that faith in the God of the covenant is always a tested faith lived in the fray of the present age, at the same time they are expressive of the deep yearning and longing for the coming glory of God's kingdom of goodness and beauty. This longing is succinctly expressed in the New Testament by the Greek word *maranatha*: "Our Lord, Come!" (1 Cor 16:22)

The common emotions of anger and indignation, sighing and weeping, should not be regarded as inappropriate to Christian life. Far from being obstacles to growth in virtue and wisdom, these emotions give expression to the *not yet* dimension of the kingdom of God, inasmuch as they highlight the disjunction that exists between the anticipated advent of the kingdom of God and the present age of sin, toil, and hardship. The congenial emotions are inevitably accompanied by anger and indignation, sighing and weeping, as Christians struggle with the infirmities of this life, come to terms with their passivity before the world, battle against the many forms of evil in this age, and yearn deeply for the full manifestation of God's covenant of grace in the crucified and risen Christ. The suffering emotions of dread, grief, and lament, which dominate the emotional landscape of Jesus' journey to Jerusalem and his passion, add further weight to this view of Christian life as a veritable struggle and "straining forward to what lies ahead" (Phil 3:13). The suffering emotions of Christian life should be conceived as follows.

1. In ordinary life, people dread their own mortality and grieve the loss of loved ones. Jesus knows what it is to grieve over a loved one, for he weeps at the death of his beloved friend Lazarus. But the dread Jesus experiences in his final days and hours is not the normal dread over one's own mortality. Rather, in Gethsemane Jesus is deeply troubled by the dreadful prospect of suffering "the cup," which is no ordinary death. As he considers this dreadful prospect, he does not display the cool demeanor and stiff upper lip of the Stoic sage,

but is so overwhelmed by powerful passions that his vulnerability is in full view. Jesus' love for the Father is truly put to the test. The strong emotions of dread and grief are involved in a mighty struggle with Jesus' holy love for the Father; this love is perfected when Jesus drinks the cup to its bitter dregs because he is set upon our salvation and the glory of the divine name. Christians too must be prepared to be overwhelmed with dread and grief at times, both in relation to God and our fellow human beings. It is a fearful thing to fall into the hands of God, and it is a fearful thing to be subjected to possible persecution by enemies for promoting gospel truth and goodness in a world that refuses to allow truth and goodness to flourish.

Christian fear, though, is distinct from normal human fear in that it does not lead to either despair or violence. The disciples of Christ, despite acknowledging their own sinfulness before God, remain hopeful of God's infinite mercy manifested in the crucified Christ; and their preparedness to suffer vicariously "because" of moral evil and "for" the wicked shows that evil is ultimately overcome by a holy love that transforms all things from within, not violently from without. The followers of Christ grieve over their own sins and the hardness of people's hearts, and must be willing to bear in their bodies the sins of their enemies and persecutors, so that the life of the crucified Christ may be manifested to the world. Love of enemies, that most challenging of Jesus' commandments, implies that Christians will inevitably be overwhelmed by emotions of grief and sorrow at times, as they strain forward towards the promises of the new covenant forged in the blood of Christ.

2. Complaints in ordinary life are many and reflect the insecurity, vulnerability, and imperfections that human persons feel so profoundly. Complaints arise out of natural disasters, disease and sickness, the ravages of war, fear of death, persecution by enemies, the injustices of this age, and the awareness of guilt. Complaints or laments in the biblical narratives arise out of the same temporal dynamics, although they are set within a covenant framework that creates the atmosphere for the divine pathos. The pathos of God recorded in Jewish Scripture is portrayed as a complex phenomenon that is not limited to God's suffering with his afflicted people, but includes his suffering because of the sinfulness of his own people, and his suffering for the people in that God bears their sin so as to make a future

life possible for Israel.[8] By addressing God in the lament speech-form, which is the winter voice of prayer,[9] the biblical complainant places their trust in God to work some good out of a situation of distress and suffering. The human lament addressed to God is therefore not an opportunity to wallow in sorrow, self-pity, and misery, but an appeal to God out of the depths of the heart, which functions as "the mode by which hope is reborn."[10] The hope of transformation expressed in lament is not something automatic though; rather, "it tracks a fierce struggle for faith in God that has its ups and downs and that may last a lifetime."[11] The praise and worship of God that accompanies lament does not come automatically or cheaply. While biblical lament resists notions of God as unaffected by either the sufferings of his people or their persistent sinfulness, at the same time it affirms the paradoxical notion of the nearness of God in his radical hiddenness: "My God, my God, why have you abandoned me?" (Mark 15:34; Ps 22:1). The whole history of biblical lament reaches its zenith in Jesus' cry of dereliction on the cross, where divinity and humanity "are united together in the ultimate agony."[12]

The cry of lament on the cross brings to a definitive conclusion the process of kenosis—i.e., the participation of the divine in the human—in the person of Jesus the Son. The Son is the one who enters into the realm of Adamic flesh, all the way to the extreme point of abandonment by the Father on the cross, for the sake of our salvation and the glory of the divine name. The suffering of Jesus takes on the complex nature of divine suffering recounted in Jewish Scripture: the Son is in complete solidarity with the infirmities of the flesh and the human cries of affliction lifted up to God (concept of solidarity); the Son suffers at the hands of sinners who reject his person and put him to death (concept of representation); and the

---

8. Fretheim, *Suffering of God*, 107-26, 140, 148. God is not exacting as to matters of judgment, for if God were to apply strict justice, Israel and the world would not exist.

9. Prayers in the Christian churches tend to be limited to penitential prayers and prayers of praise and thanksgiving. But prayer has many voices and many seasons: there is the summer voice of praise (Ps 150:6: "Let everything that breathes praise God!") and the winter voice of lament (Ps 129:1: "Out of the depths I cry to you, O God). See Billman and Migliore, *Rachel's Cry*, 4.

10. Hicks, "Preaching Community Laments." 79.

11. Billman and Migliore, *Rachel's Cry*, 124.

12. Terrien, *Psalms*, 236.

Son suffers in the place of sinners so that by bearing our sins he makes a future life possible for us (concept of substitution). The Son suffers not merely out of solidarity with suffering flesh and at the hands of sinners (human judgment upon his person), but also at the hands of God (divine judgment on the Son as the sin-bearer).

As sons and daughters of the Father in Jesus the Son, Christians can expect to be deeply grieved and anguished at times by the hiddenness of God, when God seems to have forsaken his people to forces of darkness, both within and without. Lament testifies to the fact that faith in Jesus Christ is never a stagnant or superficial affair, but is always a faith tested by the trials and tribulations of this age, in which Christians pledge to live the way of the cross as the embodiment of Christ in the world. Love of God is the first and chief of the emotions of Christian life, yet lament voices the veritable struggle involved in living faithfully the demands of the gospel in a troubled world "groaning" (Rom 8:22) for its final salvation. Christian life as a "straining forward to what lies ahead" (Phil 3:13) requires the constant nurturing of hope, and the lament speech-form is an effective mode by which hope is reborn. For the cries of the faithful out of the depths are lifted up to God, trusting that God hears them and is affected by their affliction, so that from the divine pathos will spring a new divine action to alleviate the distressing situation. The suffering, though, might not be alleviated, in which case *suffering is to be accepted as the vocation of the faithful*. This particular perspective of the suffering just is notably conveyed by Isaiah's notion of the suffering servant of God (Isa 52:13–53:12). To suffer precisely *because* one is faithful and just—not despite the fact that one is just—is not a formula for the cessation of hope in God, but it does mean that hope takes on the character of a hope against hope. In order to fathom this perspective on suffering as the vocation of the faithful, it must be borne in mind that God's response to Jesus' cry of lament comes with his raising Jesus from the dead, yet in the wonderful joy of Easter Sunday we should pause to remember that God did not wipe away the lacerations and scars of the Son's saving death (see Luke 24:39; John 20:27). "The wounds of the Messiah's crucifixion are the inexpungible identification by which God has embodied himself for us, for our healing, for the salvation of all."[13] The faithful

---

13. Black, "Persistence of the Wounds," 56.

followers of the crucified Messiah are required to accept suffering as their distinct and specific vocation, for they represent the ongoing embodiment of God in a world groaning for its salvation.

The suffering emotions of dread, grief, and lament are very real emotions of Jesus associated with the great drama of his passion, where we see the process of deification in his person reach its climactic point. Jesus is subjected to great suffering, both at the hands of sinners and at the hands of God. He endures this suffering out of unfathomable love for the Father, which is one with his merciful and compassionate love for us sinners. The tortured, crucified, and broken body of the man Jesus is the extraordinary revelation of what it means for the fullness of divinity to dwell bodily in him. As the embodiment of Christ in the world, Christians cannot focus exclusively on the congenial emotions and ignore the suffering emotions, for "crucifixion is what makes a Christian."[14] To put on Christ is to fix our gaze on *the crucified Christ as the new object of not only the congenial emotions, but also the suffering emotions*. The suffering emotions give poignant expression to what is involved in carrying out Jesus' commandment that we love one another as he has loved us.

Love of neighbor refers not merely to those who belong to our family group or church community or are in need of our help, but includes "love of enemies" (Matt 5:44). Love of God is not a sentimental type of love, but the love of Jesus Christ himself, which is the way of the cross. The radical commandment of love of enemies epitomizes the radical interior conversion of heart that Jesus' disciples are to display, from which flows the exterior or visible element of the kingdom of God at work in our midst. Many might object that love, when understood as an emotion, cannot be commanded, but what is in view here is a "change of heart" from which springs the action commanded by Jesus.[15] Just as the divine quality of Jesus' joy as the Son is *a communicable quality* that is shared with human characters in the gospel story (see Luke 10:17–22), so too the command to love our enemies is a quality which is communicated via the acquisition of a new heart that imitates the sacred heart of Jesus. Equipped with this new sense of the heart, the command to love our neighbor is no sentimental teaching about being nice to others, but involves the

---

14. Murphy-O'Connor, "Even Death," 43.

15. Piper, *'Love Your Enemies,'* 144–45, 161. Jonathan Edwards's writings on the religious affections, which were discussed in chapter 2 of this study, offer much support to this line of thinking.

acceptance of suffering as the vocation of the faithful. The suffering in view here is a comprehensive suffering that consists in our readiness to suffer in solidarity with all suffering flesh, as well as our preparedness to suffer at the hands of sinners, and our willingness to suffer for sinners by bearing their sins. It is true to say that the suffering emotions voice the "not yet" dimension of the covenant of grace, yet we should not lose sight of the fact that they also witness to the "already" present dimension of the new covenant forged by the shedding of Christ's blood on the cross, where divinity and humanity are united together in the ultimate agony. On the view of Christian life as a bearing in our bodies of the dying of Jesus so that the life of Jesus is manifested to the world, suffering is integral to the process of our becoming sons and daughters of the Father in the crucified Son. The congenial emotions of love of God and joy in God are therefore to be thought of as forming an integral unity with the suffering emotions of grief, sorrow, and lament, since they all have the crucified Christ as their intentional object.

The above discussion has sought to show how normal human emotions become Christian emotions by directing our emotional life to Jesus Christ as the new object of the emotional life. Since the full course of Jesus' emotional life is integral to the process of deification in his person, we are required to think of our salvation as involving the transformation of our emotions. In order for Christ's life to become the primary motivating force in Christian life, his emotions must become our emotions. It must be borne in mind here, however, as was pointed out earlier, that a qualitative and quantitative difference exists between Jesus' emotions and Christian emotions—by virtue of being the Son who is the personal revelation of the Father to Israel and the world, Jesus' emotions are purer, deeper, and more intense than Christian emotions could ever be.[16] The ongoing conversion of the emotions in Christ's followers—who are not without sin—is a process of ongoing embodiment of God for the sake of proclaiming the kingdom of God in our midst. Christian life must never lose touch with its setting in this life—the Word became flesh and dwelt amongst us—by focusing too much on heavenly things beyond

16. The qualitative and quantitative differences are also apparent from the standpoint of the covenant structure that operates in the four gospels, as discussed in chapter 4 of this study. In the Synoptic Gospels, Jesus is portrayed as the ideal covenant partner as well as the inaugurator of the new covenant, and in John's Gospel, Jesus is depicted as covenant Lord as well as covenant sacrifice. It is the tension between these two poles that creates the atmosphere in which his emotions operate, and that accounts for his emotions tending in both a human and divine direction.

this life. One of the distinct advantages of conceiving of Christian life in terms of the ongoing transformation of both the congenial and suffering emotions, is that discipleship remains firmly rooted in this earthly life. Yet another distinct advantage of such a perspective is that it ensures that Christian life is not reduced to nothing more than a "veneer" over a secular way of thinking about the world.[17] Many Christians today have been too compromised by the secular culture and give witness to a watered-down version of historical Christianity, which has little to do with putting on Christ and much do with subjective happiness, improving self-esteem, and getting along well with others.[18] To bear the image of Christ, though, according to historical Christianity, has to do with our gracious participation in the ineffable life of God, which is the true vocation of the human creature. This high calling involves the ongoing conversion of our passions—which are captive to capitalism's ensemble of technologies of desire that shapes and corrupts desire—by putting on the passionate life of Christ, so that more and more in this life we are able to see things as God sees them, and feel things as God feels them. In this way, the followers of Christ become the ongoing embodiment of God in the world, as they are "transformed into his likeness with ever increasing glory" (2 Cor 3:18).

This implies that Christian life ineluctably involves asceticism—the ongoing conversion of the emotions—in imitating the virtuous life of the Word become flesh. Asceticism is the practice of educating ourselves to direct our physical and intellectual appetites to the lofty goods of the kingdom of God; it involves sacrificing the lesser for the greater, so that life may be held high in honor and become fruitful on the level of its deepest significance in relation to God. In other words, asceticism is simply the "refusal to capitulate to the forces of barbarism."[19] Regrettably

---

17. Dreher, *Benedict Option*, 158.

18. A sociological study of the religious and spiritual lives of young Americans, conducted in 2005, found that most adhered to a mushy pseudo-religion, which the researchers named "Moralistic Therapeutic Deism" (MTD). There are five basic tenets to MTD: a God exists who created the world and orders it; God wants people to be good, nice, and fair to each other; the goal of life is to be happy and to feel good about oneself; God is only needed in one's life when a problem arises; and good people go to heaven when they die. The researchers found that this creed is especially prominent among Catholic and mainline Protestant teenagers. See Smith and Denton, *Soul Searching*.

19. Guardini, *End of the Modern World*, 217. For a powerful analysis of the forces of barbarism in the Western world today, see Henry, *Barbarism*. Henry regards our

there is little evidence of asceticism amongst Christians today, whose lives fit too readily into the framework of a secularist, consumerist, and technological society that has lost its historical memory. Since Christians today are no longer nourished by the Great Tradition[20]—Augustine of Hippo, Gregory of Nyssa, and Jonathan Edwards are all exponents of the Great Tradition—they are not capable of reaching for the future upon the scaffolding of the past. As G. K. Chesterton is often quoted as saying, "a dead thing goes with the stream, but only a living thing goes against it."[21] In order for the Christian churches to have future relevance in this technological age, they must reach for the future on the scaffolding of the crucified yet living Christ who is "the way, the truth, and the life" (John 14:6). This will involve a rediscovery of the Great Tradition, essential to which is the practice of asceticism. The ascetic life is one in which we recognize the folly and wrongs within ourselves and set about righting them by directing our emotional life to wiser and loftier goods. The Christian churches of the future must display the courage to become counter-cultural to a significant degree, inasmuch as to acknowledge the crucified Christ as the "wisdom of God" (1 Cor 1:24) means that his followers see things as God sees them, and feel things as God feels them.

Talk of asceticism and the life of virtue (wisdom) should not be interpreted as meaning that Christian life is nothing but the fulfilling of moral obligations and serving penance for our sins. Everything in Christian life should flow out of making God, who has manifested himself in Christ, the new object of our love and delight. Pope Francis in his apostolic exhortation *Evangelii Gaudium* (*The Joy of the Gospel*) makes this very point when he stresses that Christian morality is not a form of Stoicism or a catalogue of sins and faults. Before all else, the gospel "invites us to respond to the God of love who saves us," and "all of the virtues are at the service of this response of love."[22] The pontiff is keen to counteract the deadening effect of an overly moralistic attitude to

---

own epoch as characterized by "an unprecedented development of knowledge going hand in hand with the collapse of culture." Henry, *Barbarism*, preface.

20. When Lewis proceeded to write *Mere Christianity*, he explained that he was trying to articulate the Great Tradition—those bedrock beliefs of the Bible, the early church, the creeds, the Reformers, and orthodox Christians throughout the ages. He was not, in other words, trying to explicate something that he could call "my religion," but to expound "mere" Christianity; that is, what Christianity is and what it was long before he was born.

21. Chesterton, *Everlasting Man*. Cited by Dreher, *Benedict Option*, 173.

22. Francis, *Evangelii Gaudium*, 39.

Christian life and reminds us that what is essential and counts above all else is "faith working through love."[23] In the proclamation of the gospel the church should not appear to be imposing new obligations on people, but rather should convey the sense of eagerly wanting to share the joy of the gospel, which points to a transcendent horizon of truth and goodness that makes all things new. It is not by proselytizing that the church grows, but by *attraction*. "I bring you good news of a great joy which will come to all the people" (Luke 2:10). Above and beyond the faults and failings of people, what people need is to be touched by the attraction of God's saving love in Christ. When God's merciful love dwells in our hearts, we are motivated to lead a virtuous life and the church "goes forth" to offer everyone the saving and transforming life of Christ.[24]

What the pontiff wishes to highlight in his apostolic exhortation are the congenial emotions of love and joy as the distinguishing atmosphere of proclaiming the Gospel to the world. The pontiff does briefly mention the grief and lament of people who have to endure great suffering, yet he writes that "slowly but surely we all have to let the joy of faith slowly revive as a quiet yet firm trust, even amid the great distress."[25] In situations of great distress and suffering, we should call to mind the steadfast love of the Lord, for hope is founded on the Lord's faithfulness towards his suffering people. Thus we cannot expect Christian joy to be expressed the same way at all times; joy changes depending on the real situations that we find ourselves in. What the pontiff wishes to convey is the view that joy endures in the measure that it hopes in the coming salvation of the Lord. This is all well and good. However, I believe the pontiff should have made more than a passing mention of lament in his lengthy exhortation. He offers no reflections on the role of lament in proclaiming the Gospel,

---

23. Francis, *Evangelii Gaudium*, 36, 37.

24. In this going forth into the world, Pope Francis acknowledges many challenges that will have to be faced. Francis, *Evangelii Gaudium*, 50–109. These challenges include: the new idolatry of money; an economy of exclusion; a financial system that rules rather than serves; the inequality that spawns violence; new attacks on religious freedom and new persecutions of Christians; the process of secularization that reduces religious faith to the private sphere; the proliferation of new religious movements; a growth in various forms of a "spirituality of wellbeing" or a "theology of prosperity" divorced from the common good and communal life; a pessimism that diminishes our commitment to fighting many forms of evils in our world; and a spiritual sloth amongst Christians who are more keen to protect their free time than take on any missionary responsibility or some form of ministry.

25. Francis, *Evangelii Gaudium*, 6.

or the *special character of Christian lament as ontologically joined to Jesus' cry of lament on the cross*. The latter would seem to be crucial to his vision of the church, which he describes thus: "I prefer a Church which is bruised, hurting, and dirty because it has been out on the streets, rather than a Church which is unhealthy from being confined and from clinging to its own security."[26] The pontiff desires the kind of Christians who do not deliberately keep Christ's wounds at arm's length, who are willing to touch the suffering flesh of others. Yet he fails to acknowledge that such Christians cannot go forth without appreciating the function of lament in their lives of self-sacrificing love, which is the way of the cross. The weakness in the pontiff's thinking is that he does not sufficiently appreciate the intimate interweaving of the congenial emotions of love of God and joy in God, and the suffering emotions of grief, sorrow, and lament, all of which share the same object; namely, the crucified Christ. Christian life as the way of the cross means that suffering is the vocation of the faithful, yet this peculiar form of suffering as the embodiment of Christ in the world cannot be borne unless our hearts extoll love of God above all else.

Lament pronounces faith in God as a tested faith, which implies that worship does not come cheaply. The gospel is a divine gift of exuberant joy addressed to humanity, yet it comes to us not only as abundant gift but also as a divine command that causes us to tremble—the *mysterium fascinans* can never be divorced from the *mysterium tremendum*. It is no easy thing to put on Christ, to step out of ourselves onto the sea of holy love, to forsake every safety net we know, and to walk the way of the cross. In the gospel narration of Jesus walking on the sea (Matt 14:22–32), Peter says to Jesus: "Bid me to come to you on the water" (v. 28). As Peter starts to walk on the water he quickly begins to sink as fear overcomes him. It is indeed a difficult thing to step out of ourselves onto the sea of divine love. Like Peter we experience an initial astonishing joy, but quickly we are besieged by the winds of fear and waves of doubt that threaten to destroy us. But when we begin to sink, we can always cry out, "Lord, save me" (v. 30), trusting the Lord will stretch out his hand and catch us. Then, with renewed worship of the Lord, we can once again attempt to step out of ourselves onto that sea of holy love, for the Lord bids us, "Come." The Christian emotions of love and joy, which are the focus of the pontiff's exhortation, cannot be highlighted and given prominence without at the same time acknowledging the situations of fear and doubt that will

---

26. Francis, *Evangelii Gaudium*, 49.

inevitably overwhelm Christians when they are besieged by threatening forces in following Christ. The practice of lament is integral to the task of renewing hope and deepening faith in God, who calls us to live the way of the cross for the sake of the world and the glory of the divine name. The Christian goes forth into this world clothed with the wisdom of God manifested in the crucified Christ, which is diametrically opposed to the wisdom of the world. This implies that suffering is to be expected and accepted as the vocation of the followers of Christ, and is integral to the process of our deification in his person as the Word become flesh.

Augustine of Hippo, Gregory of Nyssa, and Jonathan Edwards Revisited

In chapter 2 of this study it was shown how Augustine of Hippo, Gregory of Nyssa, and Jonathan Edwards all repudiate a severe asceticism and affirm the emotions as playing a constructive role in the ascent to God. All three maintain, in their respective ways, that Christian life consists not in the elimination of the emotions, but the conversion of the emotions by redirecting them to God as their proper object. In light of the foregoing discussion on Christian life as the ongoing conversion of both the congenial and suffering emotions, some concluding comments on the views of these three eminent theologians of the Great Tradition can now be offered. It will be recalled how Augustine uses erotic language to convey the soul's deep yearning and longing for union with God, and conceives of the emotions as revealing the true human condition before God; that is, how the Christian is still embroiled in the force of habit and ardently yearns for the anticipated bliss of eternal peace in the age to come. Augustine rejects the Stoic notion of *apatheia* on the grounds that it fails to acknowledge the enduring problem of sin, and he develops his thought on Christian emotions in terms of the rightness of the object of the emotions. We saw that there were, however, aspects of Stoic philosophy that did exert a strong influence on Augustine's thought, especially the Stoic notion of the passions as sicknesses of the soul. Augustine in his *Confessions* talks at length about the impoverished condition of his soul plagued by the sickness of sin, and how the common emotions (passions) of fear, grief, sadness, and anger bring to light the extent of his sickness, which can only be healed by God, the all-merciful physician.

An inherent problem with Augustine's thought is that because the sickness of sin tenaciously persists in the soul despite receiving the blessings of God's grace in Christ, we are presented with a restricted view of the emotional life of the Christian. Augustine's soul is so deeply troubled by the sickness of sin that the congenial emotions of love of God and joy in God are not presented as the atmosphere of Christian life. Images of descent, rather than ascent to God, prevail in Augustine's thinking on Christian life. For instance, he fears the danger of eternal condemnation for sin; he feels sorrow for sins committed and affirms his poverty and lowness; he struggles with virtue and is resigned to a life of toil and obscurity; and he grieves for the redemption of his mortal body, which will bring exaltation and final peace. In respect of more positive and congenial emotions, Augustine experiences only occasional moments of delight in God, he affirms joy as more of a prospective joy in the hope that death will be swallowed up in victory, he does feel gladness when he is able to do good works, and he feels compassion for fellow sinners insofar as they are in fundamental need of God's redemption in Christ. All in all, though, Augustine gives much more weight to the suffering and disturbing emotions in virtue of the sickness of his soul, so that sighing and lament assume more prominence as the atmosphere of Christian life. Without doubt Augustine's *Confessions* is a moving account of the emotional life of the Christian, yet for all its merit it fails to recognize the broader and fuller dimensions of the transformed emotions involved in putting on Christ, which were discussed above. The shortcomings in Augustine's treatment of Christian emotions can be stated thus:

(a) Augustine limits fear to the danger of eternal condemnation for individual sins, but this suffering emotion should be broadened to include the dread associated with the acknowledgment that crucifixion is what makes a Christian. The gospel of Christ is received as a wonderful gift of salvation that forms the basis of Christian joy, but with this joy comes the demand to imitate Christ's self-sacrificing love, which is the way of the cross. Christian life as the way of the cross is especially highlighted by Jesus' commandment concerning love of enemies, which is no ordinary or sentimental love, but the love of Jesus Christ himself. The emotion of dread is integral to Christian life as the way of the cross, although the dread in view here does not lead to despair or violence, because it has a different object: namely, the crucified Christ, who is the embodiment of divine love for the world. The Christian must be prepared to suffer all sorts of afflictions for the sake of the gospel, "but not driven to despair" (2 Cor 4:8). The feeling of dread gives realistic expression to what is being asked of Christ's followers in living the way of the cross.

(b) Augustine feels sorrow for individual sins committed, but this suffering emotion should be expanded to include the sorrow that Jesus' followers can expect to experience when, as the ongoing embodiment of Christ in the world, they suffer at the hands of sinners, and for the sins of others by bearing their sins. To embrace the view that Christians carry in their bodies the death of Jesus so that the life of Jesus is manifested in their bodies (2 Cor 4:10), inevitably means that Christians will experience levels of sorrow that go beyond the realm of their own individual sins as they gladly assume the role of being suffering servants of the living God.

(c) Augustine grieves for the redemption of the body, but this suffering emotion should be broadened to include a considerable number of additional aspects, such as: grieving for the hardness of people's hearts, which is an obstacle to the flourishing of goodness in our world; grieving the loss of friends and loved ones, which recognizes our human vulnerability in the world; grieving in solidarity with all suffering flesh that groans for its final salvation; and grieving for ways in which the church has failed to uphold the holiness of the divine name—the contemporary scandal of clerical child sexual abuse is a case in point.[27]

(d) The emotion of anger does not feature in Augustine's view of Christian life, other than offering proof of the ongoing detrimental consequences of Adam's sin. Anger is simply recognized by Augustine as a manifestation of the sickness of his soul. But this study has shown that there is such a thing as righteous anger and indignation, which Jesus clearly displays in the gospel story. The righteous anger of Christian life is indicative of a strong moral sense that serves as a motivating force to confront evil in the world and commit to benevolent works that manifest the loftier goods of the kingdom of God in our midst.

---

27. See Novello, "Sexual Abuse of Minors," 222–40.

(e) Augustine certainly does feel compassion for others, but this congenial emotion is restricted to fellow sinners who are also the object of redemption in Christ. Christian compassion should be thought of in much broader terms than this, however, which reflects more fully the compassion of Christ displayed in the gospel story. Christian compassion, as the imitating of Christ's compassion—which is the driving force of his healing ministry to his own—must include solidarity in suffering with those who suffer innocently, are outcast or downtrodden, suffer rejection and persecution, are like sheep without a shepherd, or are deprived of the basic goods necessary for a dignified life in this world.

(f) Augustine feels the tragic dimension of this life so profoundly that he can only rejoice in the hope of eternal life to come. This study has argued that since putting on Christ involves the reception of a new heart, love of God and joy in God become the distinguishing atmosphere of the Christian life. The reception of a new heart implies that already in the here and now we participate in God, although we strain forward to the there and then of the age to come. If the Christian churches are to have a future, the way forward is not by announcing a message of pessimism and gloom; rather, the churches will grow by attraction—"I bring you good news of a great joy which will come to all the people" (Luke 2:10). What people need is to be touched by the attraction of God's ineffable love for them revealed in Christ. With God's merciful love dwelling in their hearts, Christians are motivated to lead a virtuous life and the churches can then "go forth" to offer everyone the saving and transforming life of Christ.

(g) Augustine certainly gives much weight to the emotion of lament, which serves to underline his soul's deep yearning for the eternal peace of union with God. But he proffers no notion of Christian lament as ontologically joined to Christ's lament on the cross. This study has argued that once the crucified Christ is acknowledged as the new object of both the congenial *and* the suffering emotions, the practice of lament becomes integral to the acceptance of suffering as the vocation of the faithful, and to renewing radical hope in God, as Christians walk the way of the cross in order to manifest the transforming life of Jesus to the world.

In addition to displaying a restricted view of Christian emotions, Augustine presents us with a narrow view of Christ's emotions. The full course of the emotional life of the Word made flesh is not recognized on account of Augustine's doctrine on Christ as free of original sin, and his acceptance of Stoic teaching on the passions as sicknesses of the soul. On the basis of these teachings, we saw that Augustine formulates the view that Christ experiences only pre-passions (*propatheia*), and since Christ's reasoning faculty is in full control of his soul, his pre-passions—which reveal his humanity, which the divine Son takes up for the sake of our redemption—are never permitted to develop into full-fledged passions. This means that Christ, for all intents and purposes, is depicted as a Stoic sage who is unperturbed by the passions that plague the rest of Adamic flesh. Gregory of Nyssa does not fare any better in this regard, for he conceives of Christ's humanity as absorbed into the divine nature like a drop of vinegar is absorbed into a boundless ocean. The emphasis falls very much on the divinity of Christ who shows fallen humanity what the life of virtue, as the pathway to God, consists in. It follows that when the focus shifts from Christ's life to Christian life, Gregory stresses those emotions which are consistent with his guiding idea of imitating the divine nature: love of God and courage for the ascetic discipline are put forward as the chief emotions in the educating of erotic desire in an ascending order of creation. The strength of this perspective is that Gregory does affirm the chief and congenial emotions of love of God, as well as courage for the ascetic life of pursuing loftier goods, as the atmosphere of Christian life.

The weakness in Gregory's position, though, is that the suffering emotions such as fear, anger, grief, sorrow, and lament are not accorded any constructive role in the ascent to God, for they are seen as belonging to sinful Adamic flesh. By virtue of the redeeming grace of Christ, Gregory emphasizes the rational soul of the Christian as focused on the divine goodness and beauty, and as progressing in the life of virtue as testimony to the educating of erotic desire. In Augustine, the erotic desire for God always remains unfulfilled and frustrated by the darkness of sin, thus Christian life is never free of the suffering emotions. But Gregory is quite different in his thinking. He describes the Christian's erotic desire for God as an "impassible desire;" that is, desire that shifts its focus from the flesh (errant judgment) to the divine goodness and beauty (good judgment), and hence is free from the common passions of lust (leads to adultery), anger (leads to murder), fear (associated with mortality), and grief (due to human vulnerability). The conception of a progressive participation in the divine nature—both in this life and in the age of the eschaton—when combined with the doctrine of the impassibility of the divine nature, does not permit Gregory to assign any significant role to the suffering emotions. There is no cause for lament in this life, for Christians are called servants and friends of God by virtue of their lives lived as an imitation of the divine nature. This study has argued that a constructive role should be attributed to the suffering emotions and to Christian lament insofar as they are ontologically joined to Christ's suffering and lament in his passion, but there is no room in Gregory's thinking for supporting this proposition. The basic problem with Gregory, as in Augustine, is that there is *no recognition of the crucified Christ as the new object of the suffering emotions, including lament.* The cross of Christ only elicits the chief emotions of love of God and courage for the ascetic life of pursuing virtue, as the pathway to union with God.

When we turn to Jonathan Edwards's writings on the religious affections, we find that his thought is markedly distinct from the positions held by both Augustine and Gregory, for he does not hesitate to plainly acknowledge the rich emotional life of Christ. Edwards asserts that he whom God sent into the world to be the perfect example of true religion was not a Stoic sage but a person of affectionate heart. The virtues of Christ—such as humility, meekness, love, forgiveness, and mercy—are expressed very much in the exercise of his holy affections, which give insight into the whole orientation of Christ's life and provide the springboard of his mission of redemption. This is especially the case in his passion, where the depth and vigor of Christ's holy love is revealed in the veritable struggle with the natural affections of fear and grief. The virtues of Christ are most dramatically on display in the unutterable sufferings of his passion, which he endured as the dreadful effects of our sins. But Christ was full of affection not only in his passion, but also in the entire course of his life. Edwards gives examples of Christ's great zeal, his being grieved for the hardness of people's hearts, his bitter weeping over Jerusalem, the tenderness of his heart full of pity and compassion, his being moved by the mourning of Mary and Martha over the death of Lazarus, and his earnest desire to eat the Passover with his disciples. Far more than Augustine and Gregory, who are most reluctant to acknowledge the emotions of the God-Man as running their full course, Edwards presents us with a moving and dramatic picture of the emotional life of Christ in carrying forth his redemptive mission.

In respect of the emotions of Christian life, Edwards is quite optimistic about the transforming power of the gracious affections that involve a change of nature. The saints are those who bear the image of Christ, who put on Christ, which is to say that the holy affections of Christ are reflected in the gracious affections of the saints. Edwards repudiates the notion of *apatheia* as the ideal of Christian life and maintains instead that from the chief emotion of love of God arise other emotions, such as: hatred of sin, fear of sin, dread of God's displeasure, gratitude to God for his goodness, joy when God is present and grief when God is absent, hope when enjoyment of God is expected, and zeal for the glory of God. The merit of Edwards's position is that he clearly extolls the chief emotions of love of God and joy in God as the atmosphere of Christian life. Yet notwithstanding his positive appraisal of the gracious affections of the saints, Edwards still displays, in a manner similar to Augustine, the tendency to restrict and confine Christian emotions to the problem of sin. Thus most of the criticisms raised earlier in respect of Augustine's limited treatment of Christian emotions apply also to Edwards. (a) Fear should not be limited to the prospect of eternal condemnation for individual sins, but should be broadened to include the real dread of living the way of the cross as the ongoing embodiment of Christ in the world. (b) Grief should not be restricted to moments when God is felt to be absent, but should be broadened to include grief for the hardness of people's hearts, grief at the loss of friends and loved ones, grief that arises from being in solidarity with all suffering flesh, and grief at ways in which the church has failed to exhibit zeal for the holiness of the divine name. (c) Edwards has no place for anger in the life of the saints, yet anger, when referred to a legitimate object, should be regarded as an essential emotion that motivates Christians to confront evil and injustice in the world in the name of Christ. (d) Edwards regards compassion as springing from a spirit of forgiveness and mercy, but Christian compassion should not be limited to seeing others as the object of redemption in Christ and should include solidarity with those who are outcast and downtrodden, suffer innocently, suffer rejection and persecution, or are denied the basic goods necessary for a dignified human life. (e) While Edwards does recognize that Christians at times voice lament when God is felt to be absent, this emotion is not developed in any meaningful or constructive way by joining the lament of the Christian to Jesus' cry of lament on the cross.

Despite the notable optimism regarding the transforming power of the gracious affections of the saints, Edwards's reflections are confined to the problem of sin and the individual's need for redemption. No reflections are offered on the distinctive character of Christian life as the way of the cross, or on suffering as the vocation of the faithful who bear in their bodies the dying of Jesus so that the life of Jesus is manifested to the world (2 Cor 4:10), or the indispensable role of Christian lament as ontologically joined to Christ's cry of lament. The same can be said of Augustine and Gregory whose writings also portray a limited understanding of the integral role played by the suffering emotions in the life of Christian ascent to God. It is true that Augustine's soul endures much suffering, but his suffering is due to the enduring problem of sin in his life and his deep yearning for the peace of eternal life. It is not a suffering that springs from having before us the crucified Christ as the object of the suffering emotions, as well as the congenial emotions. Gregory too acknowledges that there is suffering in the Christian life, but this suffering stems from the difficulty of pursuing the life of virtue, which is why courage is required to continue along the path of the soul's ascent to God. As in the case of Augustine, suffering is limited to the individual's ongoing struggle with the reality of sin, although Gregory is considerably more optimistic about the educating of erotic desire in this life than Augustine is.

To conclude, suffering is simply not something that the Christian faithful should seek to avoid, as people in general do. To put on Christ and bear his image in the world means that the suffering emotions assume a normative role in witnessing to the transformative power of the way of the cross. This holy suffering of the faithful is integral to Christ's commandment that we love one another as he has loved us, which is most powerfully conveyed by his radical teaching concerning love of enemies. The practice of lament is integral to the holy suffering of the faithful, not as an opportunity to wallow in self-pity and misery, but as a statement of tested faith and renewed hope in living Christian life as the way of the cross, and keeping our gaze firmly fixed on the vision of the New Jerusalem. The process of deification in Christian life inevitably involves the willingness of Christians to suffer as the ongoing embodiment of Christ in the world, which is borne by the chief emotions of love of God and joy in God, as well as courage for the ascetic life. When the process of deification in Christ's life and in Christian life is conceived along the lines of the ongoing mutual interaction of human emotions and divine emotions—through the operation of the indwelling Spirit—then the event of the incarnation of the eternal Word "should be understood not as a past event, but as the ongoing embodiment of God in those who follow Christ."[28] The followers of Christ, since they receive a new heart with which to see as God sees and feel as God feels, are called to an involved holiness in imitating Christ, "the Holy and Righteous One" (Acts 3:14). The springboard of Christian life lived as an involved holiness is the ongoing transformation of the emotions, as the crucified Christ becomes the new object of both the congenial and suffering emotions, which form an indissoluble unity. The following passage from St Paul's writings serves as an appropriate conclusion to this chapter on the emotional life of Christ's followers, who seek to embody or incarnate the treasure that is Christ—in whom the fullness of divinity dwells bodily—in their vulnerable and mortal flesh:

> But we have this treasure in earthen vessels, to show that the transcendent power belongs to God and not to us. We are afflicted in every way, but not crushed; perplexed, but not driven to despair; persecuted, but not forsaken; struck down, but not destroyed; always carrying in the body the death of Jesus, so that the life of Jesus may also be manifested in our bodies. For while we live we are always being given up to death for Jesus' sake, so that the life of Jesus may be manifested in our mortal flesh (2 Cor 4:7–11).

We saw that Mary as Daughter Zion is unique amongst the great figures in Israel's history in that of no other can it be said that she, or he, contains the uncontainable God. In the process of preparation leading up to the event of the annunciation, Mary freely collaborates with God for the much-anticipated salvation of Israel, so that she conceives Christ spiritually in her heart before she conceives him bodily in her womb. In a similar way, Christians too, equipped with the sense of the new heart as gift of the Spirit, first know Christ spiritually in their hearts, and then subsequently give bodily form to Christ by being his embodiment in the world. By making manifest the ineffable life and unsurpassable treasure of Jesus Christ in their mortal bodies, Christians, like Mary, can be said to contain the uncontainable God, insofar as their lives are a beholding of the glory of the Lord "with unveiled face" (2 Cor 3:18).

This bearing and beholding of Christ is always imperfect in the here and now, though, as Christ's followers strain forward towards the there

---

28. Behr, *John the Theologian*, preface. The writings of Edward Schillebeeckx on Christ as the primordial sacrament of God, and the church as the basic sacrament of Christ, can be used to support and bolster this conclusion. See Schillebeeckx, *Christ the Sacrament*.

and then of the fullness of deification (salvation) to come. The process of deification in Christ is never completed in this life, for while we live in the earthly tent of our mortal flesh we sigh and long to be "further clothed" (2 Cor 5:4) by sharing in the glory of Christ's resurrection, where death is swallowed up by life. In this pilgrim life, the followers of Christ "are being changed into his likeness from one degree of glory to another" (2 Cor 3:18), and at the heart of this ongoing transformation into Christ's likeness is the process whereby Christ's emotions increasingly become the emotions of his disciples. The emotional life does not cease, however, once we have entered our eternal dwelling place through the suffering gateway of death—in which the full saving power of Christ's conquest of death is made known to the deceased[29]—but assumes even greater significance as we are transformed and transported to a higher degree of glory in Christ, and therefore eternally praise God through the chief emotions of love of God and joy in God, who is "life, love, and freedom" (Barth).

---

29. See Novello, *Death as Transformation*.

Bibliography

Aquinas, Thomas. *Summa Theologica*. Translated by Fathers of the English Dominican Province. First Complete American Edition in Three Volumes. New York: Benzinger Brothers, 1948.

Arnold, Magda B., ed. *The Nature of Emotion*. Penguin Modern Psychology Readings. Harmondsworth, England: Penguin, 1968.

Augustine, Saint. *The City of God, XI–XXII*. In *The Works of Saint Augustine: A Translation for the 21st Century*. Translated by William Babcock. New York: New City, 2013.

———. *The City of God, I–X*. In *The Works of Saint Augustine: A Translation for the 21st Century*. Translated by William Babcock. New York: New City, 2012.

———. *The Confessions*. In *The Works of Saint Augustine: A Translation for the 21st Century*. Translated by Maria Boulding. 2nd ed. New York: New City, 2012.

———. *Enchiridion*. In *The Library of Christian Classics*, vol. 7, translated and edited by Albert C. Outler, 337–412. London: SCM, 1955.

———. *On the Trinity*. In *Nicene and Post-Nicene Fathers of the Christian Church*, edited by Philip Schaff, vol. III. Grand Rapids: Eerdmans, 1978.

Balthasar, Hans Urs von. *Theo-Drama: Theological Dramatic Theory / Vol. 5, The Last Act*. Translated by Graham Harrison. San Francisco: Ignatius, 1998.

———. *Theo-Drama: Theological Dramatic Theory / Vol. 4, The Action*. Translated by Graham Harrison. San Francisco: Ignatius, 1994.

Barth, Karl. *Church Dogmatics*. Vol. II/II. *The Doctrine of God*. Translated by G. W. Bromiley et al. Edinburgh: T. & T. Clark, 1957.

———. *Church Dogmatics*. Vol. IV/I. *The Doctrine of Reconciliation*. Translated by G. W. Bromiley. Edinburgh: T. & T. Clark, 1956.

———. *Church Dogmatics*. Vol. IV/II. *The Doctrine of Reconciliation*. Translated by G. W. Bromiley. Edinburgh: T. & T. Clark, 1958.

Barton, Stephen C. "Eschatology and the Emotions in Early Christianity." *Journal of Biblical Literature* 130 (2011) 571–91.

Bate, W. Jackson. *Samuel Johnson*. New York: Harcourt Brace Jovanovich, 1975.

Beeck, Frans Jozef van. *Christ Proclaimed: Christology As Rhetoric*. New York: Paulist, 1979.

———. *God Encountered: A Contemporary Catholic Systematic Theology*. Vol. 2/3. *The Revelation of the Glory: Finitude and Fall*. Collegeville, MN: Liturgical, 1995.

———. *Loving the Torah More Than God? Toward a Catholic Appreciation of Judaism*. Chicago: Loyola University Press, 1989.

Behr, John. *John the Theologian and his Paschal Gospel: A Prologue to Theology*. Oxford: Oxford University Press, 2019.

———. "The Rational Animal: A Reading of Gregory of Nyssa's *De hominis opificio*." *Journal of Early Christian Studies* 7 (1999) 219–47.

Bell, Daniel M. *Liberation Theology After the End of History: The Refusal to Cease Suffering*. London: Routledge, 2001.

Ben-Ze'ev, Aaron. "The Logic of Emotions." In *Philosophy and the Emotions*, edited by Anthony Hatzimoysis, 147–62. Royal Institute of Philosophy Supplement 52. Cambridge: Cambridge University Press, 2003.

———. "The Nature of Emotions." *Philosophical Studies* 52 (1987) 393–409.

Berkhof, Louis. *Systematic Theology*. Edinburgh: The Banner of Truth Trust, 1958.

Billman, Kathleen D., and Daniel L. Migliore. *Rachel's Cry: Prayer of Lament and Rebirth of Hope*. Eugene, OR: Wipf and Stock, 1999.

Black, C. Clifton. "The Persistence of the Wounds." In *Lament: Reclaiming Practices in Pulpit, Pew, and Public Square*, edited by Sally A. Brown and Patrick D. Miller, 47–58. Louisville: Westminster John Knox, 2005.

Bonhoeffer, Dietrich. *The Cost of Discipleship*. Translated by R. H. Fuller. New York: Touchstone, 1995.

Bonner, Gerald. "Augustine's Conception of Deification." *Journal of Theological Studies* 37 (1986) 369–86.

Boss, Sarah Jane. *Empress and Handmaid: On Nature and Gender in the Cult of the Virgin Mary*. London: Cassell, 2000.

Brown, Peter. *Augustine of Hippo*. London: Faber and Faber, 1967.

Brueggemann, Walter. *The Land*. Philadelphia: Fortress, 1977.

Buber, Martin. *I and Thou*. Translated by Walter Kaufman. New York: T. & T. Clark, 1970.

———. *Israel and Palestine: The History of An Idea*. Translated by Stanley Godman. London: Horovitz, 1952.

———. *Two Types of Faith*. Translated by Norman P. Goldhawk. New York: Macmillan, 1951.

Bulgakov, Sergius. *The Lamb of God*. Translated by Boris Jakim. Grand Rapids: Eerdmans, 2008.

Calhoun, Cheshire. "Subjectivity and Emotion." In *Thinking About Feeling: Contemporary Philosophers on Emotions*, edited by Robert C. Solomon, 107–21. Oxford: Oxford University Press, 2004.

Calvin, John. *Institutes of the Christian Religion*. The Library of Christian Classics, vol. 20. Edited by John T. McNeill. Translated by Ford Lewis Battles. Philadelphia: Westminster, 1960.

Cates, Diana Fritz. *Aquinas on the Emotions: A Religious-Ethical Inquiry*. Washington, DC: Georgetown University Press, 2009. http://ebookcentral.proquest.com/lib/flinders/detail.action?docID=537038.

Chadwick, Henry. *Augustine*. Oxford: Oxford University Press, 1986.

———. *Boethius: The Consolations of Music, Logic, Theology, and Philosophy*. Oxford: Clarendon, 1990.

Chesterton, G. K. *The Everlasting Man*. New York: Dodd & Mead, 1925.

Clapper, Gregory Scott. *John Wesley on Religious Affections: His Views on Experience and Emotion and Their Role in the Christian Life and Theology*. PhD diss., Emory University, ProQuest Dissertations, 1985.

Coolman, Boyd Taylor. "Hugh of St. Victor on 'Jesus Wept': Compassion as Ideal Humanitas." *Theological Studies* 69 (2008) 528–56.
Corrigan, John. *Religion and Emotion: Approaches and Interpretations*. New York: Oxford University Press, 2004.
Daly, Gabriel. *Creation and Redemption*. Dublin: Gill & Macmillan, 1988.
Damascene, John. *Exposition of the Orthodox Faith*. In *The Nicene and Post-Nicene Fathers of the Christian Church*. Second Series, vol. IX. Translated by Rev. S. D. F. Salmond. Grand Rapids: Eerdmans, 1979.
Damasio, Anthony R. *Descartes' Error: Emotion, Reason and the Human Brain*. New York: Avon, 1994.
De Sousa, Robert. *The Rationality of Emotion*. Cambridge: MIT Press, 1987.
Descartes, René. *The Passions of the Soul and Other Late Philosophical Writings*. Oxford World's Classics. Translated by Michael Moriarty. Oxford: Oxford University Press, 2016.
Dreher, Rod. *The Benedict Option: A Strategy for Christians in a Post-Christian Nation*. New York: Sentinel, 2017.
Edwards, Jonathan. *The Works of Jonathan Edwards, Vol. 2: Religious Affections*. Edited by John E. Smith. New Haven, CT: Yale University Press, 1959.
Elliott, Matthew A. *Faithful Feelings: Rethinking Emotion in the New Testament*. Grand Rapids: Kregel, 2006.
Flanagan, Donal. *The Theology of Mary*. Theology Today Series 30. Dublin: Mercier, 1976.
Francis. *Evangelii Gaudium: The Joy of the Gospel*. London: Catholic Truth Society, 2013.
Frei, Hans W. *The Eclipse of Biblical Narrative*. New Haven, CT: Yale University Press, 1974.
———. *The Identity of Jesus Christ*. Philadelphia: Fortress, 1975.
———. *Theology and Narrative: Selected Essays*. Edited by George Hunsinger and William C. Placher. Oxford: Oxford University Press, 1993.
Fretheim, Terence E. *The Suffering of God: An Old Testament Perspective*. Philadelphia: Fortress, 1984.
Gaventa, Beverly Roberts. "Nothing Will be Impossible with God." In *Mary, Mother of God*, edited by Carl E. Braaten and Robert W. Jenson, 19–35. Grand Rapids: Eerdmans, 2004.
Gibson, Margaret, ed. *Boethius: His Life, Thought and Influence*. Oxford: Blackwell, 1981.
Goldberg, Michael. *Theology and Narrative*. Nashville: Abingdon, 1982.
Gondreau, Paul. *The Passions of Christ's Soul in the Theology of St. Thomas Aquinas*. Münster: Aschendorff, 2002.
Graver, Margaret. *Stoicism and Emotion*. Chicago: University of Chicago Press, 2009.
Greer, Rowan A. *Christian Hope and Christian Life: Raids on the Inarticulate*. New York: Crossroad, 2001.
Gregersen, Niels Henrik. "The Emotional Christ: Bonaventure and Deep Incarnation." *Dialog* 55 (2016) 247–61.
Gregory of Nyssa. *The Life of Moses*. The Classics of Western Spirituality. New York: Paulist, 1978.
———. "On What it Means to Call Oneself a Christian." In *Ascetical Works*, translated by Virginia Woods Callahan, 79–89. The Fathers of the Church, vol. 38. Washington, DC: The Catholic University of America Press, 1967.

Griffiths, Paul E. *What Emotions Really Are: The Problem of Psychological Categories.* Chicago: University of Chicago Press, 1997.

Grillmeier, Aloys. *Christ in Christian Tradition. Vol. 1, From the Apostolic Age to Chalcedon (451).* Second Revised Edition. London: Mowbrays, 1975.

Guardini, Romano. *The End of the Modern World.* Wilmington, DE: ISI, 1998.

Gunton, Colin E. *The Christian Faith: An Introduction to Christian Doctrine.* Oxford: Blackwell, 2002.

Hansen, G. Walter. "The Emotions of Jesus." *Christianity Today* 41 (1997) 42–46.

Hart, Mark D. "Reconciliation of Body and Soul: Gregory of Nyssa's Deeper Theology of Marriage." *Theological Studies* 51 (1990) 450–78.

Hauerwas, Stanley, and William H. Willimon. *Resident Aliens: Life in the Christian Colony.* Expanded 25th anniversary edition. Nashville: Abingdon, 2014.

Heidegger, Martin. *Being and Time.* Translated by John Macquarrie and Edward Robinson. New York: Harper, 1962.

Henry, Michel. *Barbarism.* Translated by Scott Davidson. New York: Continuum, 2012.

Heschel, Abraham J. "The Divine Pathos: The Basic Category of Prophetic Theology." In *Faith and Reason: Essays in Judaism,* edited by Robert Gordis and Ruth B. Waxman, 33–58. New York: Ktav, 1973.

———. *The Prophets.* New York: Harper and Row, 1962.

Hicks, John Mark. "Preaching Community Laments: Responding to Disillusionment with God and Injustice in the World." In *Performing the Psalms,* edited by David Bland and David Fleer, 67–82. Danvers, MA: Chalice, 2005.

Hilary of Poitiers. *On the Trinity.* In *Nicene and Post-Nicene Fathers of the Christian Church.* Second Series, vol. 9. Translated by Rev. E. W. Watson and Rev. L. Pullan. Edited by Rev. W. Sanday. Grand Rapids: Eerdmans, 1979.

Horner, Robyn. *Jean-Luc Marion: A Theo-logical Introduction.* Aldershot: Ashgate, 2005.

James, William. "What is an Emotion?" In *The Nature of Emotion: Selected Readings,* edited by Magda B. Arnold, 17–36. Penguin Modern Psychology UPS 12. Harmondsworth: Penguin, 1968.

Jenson, Robert. "A Space for God." In *Mary, Mother of God,* edited by Carl E. Braaten and Robert W. Jenson, 49–57. Grand Rapids: Eerdmans, 2004.

Jüngel, Eberhard. *God As the Mystery of the World: On the Foundation of the Theology of the Crucified One in the Dispute between Theism and Atheism.* Translated by Darrell L. Guder. Grand Rapids: Eerdmans, 1983.

Kelly, J. N. D. *Early Christian Doctrines.* Fifth Revised Edition. London: A & C Black, 1977.

Kelsey, David H. *The Uses of Scripture in Recent Theology.* Philadelphia: Fortress, 1975.

Kenny, Anthony. *Action, Emotion and Will.* London: Routledge, 1963.

Kierkegaard, Søren. *Concluding Unscientific Postscript.* Translated by David F. Swenson. Princeton: Princeton University Press, 1941.

Klausner, Joseph. *Jesus of Nazareth.* Translated by Herbert Danby. London: Allen and Unwin, 1925.

Krieg, Robert A. *Story-Shaped Christology: The Role of Narratives in Identifying Jesus Christ.* New York: Paulist, 1988.

Laird, Martin. "Under Solomon's Tutelage: The Education of Desire in the *Homilies on the Song of Songs.*" *Modern Theology* 18 (2002) 507–25.

Lauber, David. *Barth on the Descent into Hell: God, Atonement and the Christian Life.* Aldershot: Ashgate, 2004.
Lazarus, Richard S., and Bernice N. Lazarus. *Passion and Reason: Making Sense of Our Emotions.* Oxford: Oxford University Press, 1994.
Lewis, C. S. *Mere Christianity.* New York: HarperCollins, 1952.
Lienhard, Marc. *Luther: Witness to Jesus Christ.* Minneapolis: Augsburg, 1982.
Lohfink, Gerhard. *Does God Need the Church? Toward a Theology of the People of God.* Translated by Linda M. Maloney. Collegeville, MN: Liturgical, 1999.
Lombardo, Nicholas E. *The Logic of Desire: Aquinas on Emotion.* Washington, DC: Catholic University of America Press, 2011. http://ebookcentral.proquest.com/lib/flinders/detail.action?docID=3135109.
Louth, Andrew. *Maximus the Confessor.* London: Routledge, 1996.
Ludlow, Morwenna. *Universal Salvation: Eschatology in the Thought of Gregory of Nyssa and Karl Rahner.* Oxford: Oxford University Press, 2000.
Lutz, Catherine A. *Unnatural Emotions: Everyday Sentiments on a Micronesian Atoll and Their Challenges to Western Theory.* Chicago: University of Chicago Press, 1988.
Lyons, William. *Emotion.* Cambridge Studies in Philosophy. Cambridge: Cambridge University Press, 1980.
Macquarrie, John. *Existentialism.* London: Penguin, 1972.
Mannermaa, Tuomo. "Why Is Luther So Fascinating? Modern Finnish Luther Research." In *Union with Christ: The New Finnish Interpretation of Luther,* edited by Carl E. Braaten & Robert W. Jensen, 1–21. Grand Rapids: Eerdmans, 1998.
Markus, Robert. *The End of Ancient Christianity.* Cambridge: Cambridge University Press, 1990.
McIntyre, John. *The Shape of Christology.* London: SCM, 1966.
Merton, Thomas. *Contemplation in a World of Action.* Garden City, NY: Image, 1973.
———. *Seeds of Contemplation.* Wheathampstead, UK: Anthony Clarke, 1972.
Miller, Patrick D. "Heaven's Prisoners: The Lament as Christian Prayer." In *Lament: Reclaiming Practices in Pulpit, Pew, and Public Square,* edited by Sally A. Brown and Patrick D. Miller, 15–26. Louisville: Westminster John Knox, 2005.
———. *Interpreting the Psalms.* Philadelphia: Fortress, 1986.
Murphy-O'Connor, Jerome. "Even Death on a Cross: Crucifixion in the Pauline Letters." In *The Cross in Christian Tradition: From Paul to Bonaventure,* edited by Elizabeth A. Dreyer, 21–50. Mahwah, NJ: Paulist, 2000.
Nagel, Norman. "Martinus: Heresy, Doctor Luther, Heresy! The Person and Work of Christ." In *Seven-Headed Luther. Essays in Commemoration of a Quincentenary 1483–1983,* edited by Peter Newman Brooks, 25–49. Oxford: Clarendon, 1983.
Nolland, John. *Word Biblical Commentary, Volume 35C: Luke 19–24.* Nashville: Thomas Nelson, 1993.
Nouwen, Henri J. M. *In Memoriam.* Notre Dame, IN: Ave Maria, 1980.
Novello, Henry. "Daughter Zion and the Advent of Salvation: Mary in Eschatological Perspective." *Irish Theological Quarterly* 76 (2011) 238–58.
———. *Death as Transformation: A Contemporary Theology of Death.* Farnham, UK: Ashgate, 2011.
———. "Jesus' Cry of Lament: Towards a True Apophaticism." *Irish Theological Quarterly* 78 (2013) 38–60.

———. "Looking Unto the Hidden Zion: A Christian Appreciation of the Holy Land." *Australasian Catholic Record* 87 (2010) 77–91.

———. "New Life as Life out of Death: Sharing in the 'Exchange of Natures' in the Person of Christ." In *The Role of Death in Life: A Multidisciplinary Examination of the Relationship between Life and Death*, edited by John Behr and Conor Cunningham, 96–119. Eugene, OR: Cascade, 2015.

———. "The Robust Joy of the Christian Life." *Australasian Catholic Record* 91 (2014) 323–33.

———. "The Sexual Abuse of Minors in the Church: Reform through the Practice of Lament." *Worship* 92 (2018) 222–40.

Nussbaum, Martha C. *The Therapy of Desire: Theory and Practice in Hellenistic Ethics*. Princeton: Princeton University Press, 1994.

———. *Upheavals of Thought: The Intelligence of the Emotions*. Cambridge: Cambridge University Press, 2001.

O'Daly, Gerard. *Augustine's City of God: A Reader's Guide*. Oxford: Clarendon, 1999.

———. *Augustine's Philosophy of Mind*. Los Angeles: University of California Press, 1987.

O'Murchu, Diarmuid. *The Transformation of Desire: How Desire Became Corrupted—And How We Can Reclaim It*. Maryknoll, NY: Orbis, 2007.

Ortony, Andrew, et al. *The Cognitive Structure of Emotions*. Cambridge: Cambridge University Press, 1988.

Otto, Rudolf. *The Idea of the Holy: An Enquiry into the Non-Rational Factor in the Idea of the Divine and its Relation to the Rational*. London: Oxford University Press, 1958.

Pelican, Jaroslav. *Mary Through the Centuries: Her Place in the History of Culture*. London: Yale University Press, 1996.

Piper, Joseph. *'Love Your Enemies': Jesus' Love Command in the Synoptic Gospels and in the Early Christian Paraenesis*. Cambridge: Cambridge University Press, 1979.

Power, Mick, and Tim Dalgleish. *Cognition and Emotion: From Order to Disorder*. Hove, East Sussex, England: Psychology Press, 1997.

Rahner, Karl. *Foundations of Christian Faith: An Introduction to the Idea of Christianity*. Translated by William Dych. New York: Crossroad, 1978.

Ratzinger, Joseph. *Daughter Zion: Meditations on the Church's Marian Belief*. Translated by John M. McDermott. San Francisco: Ignatius, 1983.

Ricoeur, Paul. *Fallible Man*. New York: Henry Regnery, 1965.

Roberts, Robert C. "What an Emotion Is: A Sketch." *The Philosophical Review* 97 (1988) 183–209.

Russell, Norman. *Cyril of Alexandria*. London: Routledge, 2000.

———. *The Doctrine of Deification in the Greek Patristic Tradition*. Oxford: Oxford University Press, 2004.

Sartre, Jean-Paul. *Being and Nothingness: A Phenomenological Essay on Ontology*. Translated by Hazel E. Barnes. New York: Pocket, 1956.

Schillebeeckx, Edward. *Christ the Sacrament of Encounter with God*. London: Sheed and Ward, 1963.

———. *Interim Report*. Translated by John Bowden. New York: Crossroad, 1981.

———. *Jesus: An Experiment in Christology*. Translated by Hubert Hoskins. London: Collins, 1979.

———. *Mary, Mother of the Redemption*. Translated by N. D. Smith. London: Sheed and Ward, 1964.
Schleiermacher, Friedrich. *The Christian Faith*. Edited by H. R. Mackintosh and J. S. Stewart. 2nd ed. Edinburgh: T. & T. Clark, 1928.
Schwöbel, Christoph. *God: Action and Revelation*. Kampen, Netherlands: Kok Pharos, 1992.
Seneca, Lucius A. *De Consolatione ad Helviam*. In *Seneca Moral Essays*, vol. II, translated by John W. Basore, 416–89. Cambridge: Harvard University Press, 1958.
———. *De Consolatione ad Marciam*. In *Seneca Moral Essays*. Vol. II. Translated by John W. Basore, 2–97. Cambridge: Harvard University Press, 1958.
———. *De Consolatione ad Polybium*. In *Seneca Moral Essays*. Vol. II. Translated by John W. Basore, 356–415. Cambridge: Harvard University Press, 1958.
Smith, Christian, and Melinda Lundquist Denton. *Soul Searching: The Religious and Spiritual lives of American Teenagers*. New York: Oxford University Press, 2005.
Smith, J. Warren. *Passion and Paradise: Human and Divine Emotion in the Thought of Gregory of Nyssa*. New York: Crossroad, 2004.
Solomon, Robert C. "Emotions, Thoughts, and Feelings: Emotions as Engagements with the World." In *Thinking About Feeling: Contemporary Philosophers on Emotions*, edited by Robert C. Solomon, 76–88. Oxford: Oxford University Press, 2004.
———. "Emotions, Thoughts and Feelings: What is a 'Cognitive Theory' of the Emotions and Does it Neglect Affectivity?" In *Philosophy and the Emotions*, edited by Anthony Hatzimoysis, 1–18. Royal Institute of Philosophy Supplement 52. Cambridge: Cambridge University Press, 2003.
Sorabji, Richard. *Emotion and Peace of Mind: From Stoic Agitation to Christian Temptation*. Oxford: Oxford University Press, 2000.
Stead, George C. "The Concept of Mind and the Concept of God in the Christian Fathers." In *The Philosophical Frontiers of Christian Theology. Essays Presented to Donald MacKinnon*, edited by Brian Hebblethwaite and Stewart Sutherland, 39–54. Cambridge: Cambridge University Press, 1982.
Stroup, George. *The Promise of Narrative Theology*. Atlanta: John Knox, 1981.
Studer, Basil. *The Grace of Christ and the Grace of God in Augustine of Hippo*. Collegeville, MN: Liturgical, 1997.
Tappert, Theodore G., ed. *The Book of Concord*. Philadelphia: Fortress, 1959.
Terrien, Samuel. *The Psalms: Strophic Structure and Theological Commentary*. Grand Rapids: Eerdmans, 2003.
Thiemann, Ronald F. *Revelation and Theology*. Notre Dame, IN: University of Notre Dame Press, 1986.
Tilley, Terrence W. *Story Theology*. Wilmington, DE: Michael Glazier, 1985.
Tillich, Paul. *Perspectives on 19th and 20th Century Protestant Theology*. Edited by Carl E. Braaten. London: SCM, 1967.
Vermes, Geza. *Jesus the Jew: A Historian's Reading of the Gospels*. London: Collins, 1973.
Vishnevskaya, Elena. "Divinization as Perichoretic Embrace in Maximus the Confessor." In *Partakers of the Divine Nature*, edited by Michael J. Christensen and Jeffrey A. Wittung, 132–45. Grand Rapids: Baker Academic, 2008.
Voorwinde, Stephen. *Jesus' Emotions in the Fourth Gospel: Human or Divine?* London: T. & T. Clark, 2005.
———. *Jesus' Emotions in the Gospels*. London: T. & T. Clark, 2011.

Ware, Bishop Kallistos. *The Orthodox Way*. Crestwood, NY: St Vladimir's Seminary, 1995.

Warfield, Benjamin B. "The Emotional Life of Our Lord." In *The Person and Work of Christ*, 93–145. Philadelphia: Presbyterian and Reformed, 1970.

Wickham, Lionel R., ed. *Cyril of Alexandria: Select Letters*. Oxford Early Christian Texts. Oxford: Clarendon, 1983.

Williams, Rowan. "Macrina's Deathbed Revisited: Gregory of Nyssa on Mind and Passion." In *Christian Faith and Greek Philosophy in Late Antiquity*, edited by L. Wickam and C. Bammel, 227–46. Leiden: Brill, 1993.

Wollheim, Richard. "The Emotions and their Philosophy of Mind." In *Philosophy and the Emotions*, edited by Anthony Hatzimoysis, 19–38. Royal Institute of Philosophy Supplement 52. Cambridge: Cambridge University Press, 2003.

Yeago, David S. "The Presence of Mary in the Mystery of the Church." In *Mary, Mother of God*, edited by Carl E. Braaten and Robert W. Jenson, 58–77. Grand Rapids: Eerdmans, 2004.

Index

abandonment, of Jesus, 190
Abraham, 170
the absolute, 182, 182n40
acquired empirical knowledge, 135
action(s)
    of Christ, 158n84-59n84
    as the creative work of dedicated love, 66
    predisposed to, 50
Action, Emotion and Will (Kenny), 4
action potentials
    of contemplation, 67
    of emotions, 61, 62, 88, 160
    necessary to emotional experience, 28
"action readiness," associated with anger, 49
active intelligence, 96
"activities and powers," of the soul, 99
Adam, 117, 123
Adam and Eve, 78-79
Adamic flesh
    Christ's real solidarity with, 21
    difference between Christ's humanity and, 127
    divine Son clothed himself with our, 231
    God taking to himself, 164
    Jesus' participation in, 225
    Jesus sharing, 142
    not the same as the essence of the Word becoming flesh, 137
    truth of Jesus's, 235
    the Word truly entering into, 229
Adam's sin, 81-82, 82n28, 127
adversity, 81
affection language. *See also* emotion language
    for Wesley, 14
affectional life of our Lord, 137
affections
    of Christ, 140, 257
    connection with the understanding and the will, 106
    as the fruits of the Spirit, 105
    kinds of, 107
    as more extensive than passion, 106n100
    as motivational forces, 112-13
    role in human life, 13
    true religion consisting in gracious, 104-14
    as truly human, 83-84
affective elements, to human existence, 9
affective language, 8
affective responses, as rational and good, 33
affectus or *affectio* (affection), as parallel to emotion in Latin, 10n29
the afflicted, 225-26, 228
agape (holy love), 101
"alliance" (*oikeiōsis*), rational and non-rational, 99

"already" present dimension, of the new covenant, 247
amazement or astonishment, of Jesus, 210–13
"analogy of advent," Jüngel proposing, 155n78
"analytic" rules, of formal logic, 54n109
anger
  associated with personal insult or injury, 3
  challenging a present evil, 12n38
  Edwards having no place for, 258
  as an emotion, 1, 234, 240
  of God, 162
  of Jesus, 213–16, 240
  leading to violence, murder, and broken relationships, 103, 240
  not featured by Augustine, 254
  as righteous reaction, 164
"Angst" (anxiety), for Heidegger, 5
anguish and suffering, of God-forsakenness, 199
Anna, recognizing the baby Jesus, 189
annunciation, 183, 185–86
anxiety, as an emotion, 1, 5
apatheia
  Augustine rejecting the Stoic notion of, 79, 84, 252
  Augustine's understanding of, 127
  Calvin condemned, 137
  Christians working toward, 18n57
  as denial of our human condition, 114
  described, 86
  as dispassion, 94
  displaying the ideal state of, 166
  Edwards on, 114, 258
  as extirpation of emotions, 4, 27, 74
  as freedom from any materialistic impulse or passion, 97
  as incongruous with the gospel, 231
  Jonathan Edwards rejecting, 117, 119
  Nussbaum rejecting, 29, 56
  repudiating, 22
  state of, 117
  Stoic ideal of, 9, 27, 31, 204, 216
Aphthartodocetae, 133
Apollinarian "one physis" doctrine, 131
apotheosis, Barth opposed to, 143n52
appetite(s)
  Aquinas' concept of, 10–12
  as the defining characteristic of goodness, 11
  directing to the kingdom of God, 248
  Gregory elaborating on, 97
  as judgment that there is a prospective good, 32
  kinds of for Aquinas, 12
  subordinating to the peace of the rational soul, 83
appetitive faculty, desire for goods, 99
appraisal, 3, 28, 29
apprehension, appetites involving, 11
"appropriate emotions," 52
Aquinas, Thomas
  on basic passions, 63
  on Christ born free of original sin, 134–35
  on Christ sharing in the condition of Adam, 123–24
  on Christ's passions, 123, 123n5, 134
  on the emotions, 19n58
  on kinds of knowledge in relation to Christ, 135
  never used the term "emotion," 10n29
  not permitting any inclinations toward sin in Christ, 136
  on the passions (*passiones*), 10–12

on the two natures of Christ, 226n113
Arians, 132
Aristotelian tradition, of non-dualistic mind, 26
Aristotle
   on emotions, 26n8, 35n38
   "functionalist" model of mind, 3
Arnold, Magda, 15
ascending order of creation, Gregory on, 94–95
ascent to God
   Augustine on, 79
   involving the body, 92
   as a matter of receptivity and love, 87
   redirecting love and desire away from earthly objects toward God, 20, 24, 86
   of the soul, 19
   through reason, spirit, and desire, 100
asceticism, 19n59, 92, 248–49
assaults of fortune, accepting, 39
assents. *See* judgments
Athanasius, 130n20
attachment, danger of, 93
attraction, church growing by, 250, 255
Augustine of Hippo
   on affective movements in Christ's soul, 126
   on anger, 254
   on *apatheia*, 114
   on the body as good, 95n59
   casting all his cares upon the Lord, 116
   on Christ as free of original sin, 256
   on Christ as not being too perturbed by the affections, 138
   on Christian ascent, 19, 74, 92, 109
   on Christ's human nature, 127
   on Christ's humanity, 130
   on compulsive force of habit (*consuetudo*), 41
   on constant danger of falling away from God, 89
   on a descending order of creation, 74–75
   on desire, 68, 69
   on emotions, 104n92, 252
   on the gap between the here and now and the there and then, 115
   on the Gospel of Christ, 100nn82
   on grieving, 254
   on human emotions compared with the cognitive theory of emotion, 86–92
   on human emotions shown by Christ, 126
   on a mediatory role of the God-Man, 129
   on the passions as modes of willing, 97n69
   on perturbations of the soul, 117
   on redirecting affections, 71
   rejoicing in the hope of eternal life to come, 255
   relating emotions of the Christian to emotions of Christ, 125
   representative of Western Latin Christianity, 19
   restless longing of the heart and, 75–92, 110, 119
   shortcomings regarding emotions, 253–55
   on the sinful soul, 94n52
   on Stoic teaching on the passions, 256
   on suffering, 259
   talking of Christ in more sanguine terms, 138
   on the training or educating of desire, 115
   on transformation of the basic emotions, 71
   understanding of Stoic first movements, 128
   upholding Christ's genuine humanity, 126

authority, of Jesus, 197, 214
awe, 59n129

Balinese, on sad feelings associated with death, 59
Balthasar, 155n79
baptism, 76–77
barbarism, in the Western world today, 248n19–49n19
Barth, Karl
   on Adam's sin, 143n51
   avoiding "partaking of the divine nature," 142n50
   as a contemporary Reformed theologian, 142
   contributing in the area of a kenotic theology, 149
   critical of Christology's doctrine of two "states," 144n55
   on divine and human essence in Jesus Christ, 144
   on the doctrine of divine immutability, 182n40
   on the emotional life of Jesus, 148
   on the essences in the person of Christ, 151
   not allowing abstract concepts of God, 143
   on the self-emptying (kenosis) of God, 143n53
   on the Son of God assuming Adamic flesh, 145
Barton, Stephen, 16
basic emotions. *See also* emotion(s)
   as anger, fear, disgust, sadness, and happiness, 63
   ascribed to God, 235
   Augustine's treatment of, 89
   listed by Descartes, 25n2
   scholars on, 63n140
   Stoics taught the notion of, 62–63
   undergoing transformation, 71
basic orientation to life, 113
basic passions, 32n24, 63, 63n138
Bate, Jackson, 41, 85–86

bearing the image of Christ, 248
beatific joy, 135
Beatitudes, 120, 226
behaviorist theory of emotion, 26, 26n4
Behr, John, 94–95
being and non-being, struggle between, 155
Being and Time (Heidegger), 5n11
"being-there" (*Dasein*), 6
"belief-desire" analysis, of emotions and intentions, 47
beliefs
   compared to emotions, 2
   connection to personal biographies, 50
   as dispositions and/or propositional attitudes, 48
   emotions based on false, 4
   emotions embodying, 57, 62
   function of, 52
   of Jesus, 161, 202
   shaped by social norms, 59
Bell, Daniel, 69
beneficiaries, of Jesus' ministry, 198
Ben-Ze'ev, Aaron, 54–55
Bernard of Clairvaux, 69
bestial passions, 100, 103
bifurcated anthropology, former view of, 98
biographical subjectivity, 50, 51, 176
blind men, warned by Jesus, 211
bodiliness, mutuality mediated by, 49–50
bodily life, of the rational human being, 95
body
   in emotional life, 104
   in emotions, 62, 91
   as good, 82, 91
   in Jesus' emotional life, 202
   as not altogether discrete, 50
   role in emotion, 47, 49
body and soul, 92, 96
body sensation, as emotion for James, 14
Boethius, 39

Bonhoeffer, Dietrich, 120–21,
    201n80, 237n3
boredom, 5n13
Brueggemann, Walter, 168n1, 169
Buber, Martin
    on the chosen land, 171
    on election of people versus
        land, 172
    on the inner "I," 65n152
    on Jesus, 168n2
    on "looking unto the hidden
        Zion," 173
    on the mystery of the name
        Zion, 174n21
    on types of wickedness, 172n14
Bulgakov, Sergius
    on both essences in the life of
        Christ, 145
    on Christ's humanity, 147n61
    on Christ's victorious struggle of
        spirit, 146
    on the "infallibility of the divine
        volition," 152
    on the interaction of energies in
        the life of Christ, 151
    on Jesus' emotional life, 148
    on kenosis, 146n59, 149–50
Bultmann, Rudolf, 7n19
"but I say to you," Jesus
        reinterpreting tradition, 161

Calhoun, Cheshire, 46, 50–52,
    60n133
Calvin, John
    elevating the heart above the
        mind, 42–43
    on the emotional life of Jesus,
        137, 138, 147
    on Jesus' divine-humanity, 148
    on one thought dominating the
        minds of Christians, 139
    Warfield compared to, 141
Calvinists, 105n94
Canaan, 169
carpenter, Jesus worked as, 191
caution (*eulabeia*), 33, 34
celibate life, 93

centurion, 197, 211, 212
character or virtuous behavior,
    control of, 34
Chesterton, G. K., 249
childhood, developmental phase
    of, 29
children, 213–14
Christ. *See* Jesus Christ
Christian ascent. *See* ascent to God
Christian faith. *See* faith
Christian life
    bearing of the image of Christ,
        117
    consisting in right ordering of
        the emotions, 19
    as the "extraordinary" and the
        "unusual," 121, 237
    as an imitation of Christ's
        emotional life, 120
    sighing and weeping rightly
        belonging to, 242
    as transformation of the
        emotions, 23, 233–61
Christian mediocrity, Augustine
    defending, 76n6
Christian norm, Augustine created
    a new, 87
Christian religion, Edwards on
    extreme poles of, 13
Christian scholarly neglect, of the
    emotions, 15
Christian thinkers, 73–75, 120
Christianity, 116
Christians
    accepting sorrow and suffering,
        43
    anguished by the hiddenness of
        God, 245
    appropriate emotions for, 79
    carrying in their bodies the
        death of Jesus, 254
    directing passions toward their
        right objects, 73
    infected with sin, 76
    knowing Christ spiritually in
        their hearts, 260
    metamorphosed into the image
        of Christ, 141

Christians (*continued*)
   seeing sinfulness and neediness in neighbors, 89
   taking up Jesus' moral stance, 240
christology, avoiding a dualizing, 15, 15n52–16n52
Chrysippus, 4n5, 27n9, 32
church, as the basic sacrament of Christ, 260n28
church fathers, 9, 225n111
Cicero, 35n39–36n39
City of God (Augustine), 81, 126, 128
classic Hellenistic period, writings on emotions, 3
classical Logos-Christology, 146n60–47n60, 150n64
clichés, on emotion, 2, 3, 14
Clore, G., 46
Cogito ergo sum, 65
cognition, 12n36, 46, 47–48, 61
cognitive approach to emotions, 26, 46
cognitive character, of Jesus, 167, 214
cognitive framework, on the emotions, 17
cognitive nature
   of Jesus' emotional responses, 212
   of Jesus' love as the fount of his emotions, 228
   of Jesus' weeping, 222
"cognitive structures," of emotion, 46
cognitive theory of emotion, 25–72
   acknowledged by all three Christian thinkers, 74
   on the action potential of Jesus' emotions, 203
   applying, 159
   components of, 61–62, 160
   comprehensive nature of, 28n12
   illuminating the emotions of Jesus, 167, 204
   implications for the Christian life, 15
   on Jesus' emotions, 201–2
   rejecting the notion of *apatheia*, 4
cognitive therapy, compared with Stoic therapy, 31
cognitive-evaluative thesis, of Nussbaum, 56
Collins, A., 46
Commentary on the Song of Songs (Gregory), 101
"common actualization," of both essences in the person of Jesus Christ, 144
common emotions, Augustine on, 252
common passions, tied to sickness of the soul, 119
communicable attributes of God, sharing in, 180
communicable quality, of Jesus' joy, 246
communication of properties (*commercium idiomatum*), christological doctrine of, 150–51
communion, true, 154
"communion of being," of God and humanity, 155
communion with God, longing or yearning for, 71
compassion
   attributed to God in Jewish Scripture, 163
   attributed to Jesus in the Synoptic Gospels, 204–5
   Augustine on, 255
   broadening Edwards' concept of, 258
   carrying Jesus forward, 209, 212
   of Christians, 239
   displaying for all those who cry to God, 228
   distinct object of divine, 210
   examples of results of Jesus,' 209–10
   of God, restoring the covenant relationship, 175–76
   Jesus expressing strong, 157

INDEX 277

of Jesus for his long-suffering
people, 163, 196–97, 209
restoration of, 89
complaints (laments), in the biblical
narratives, 243
compulsive force of habit
(*consuetudo*), 76, 87–88
concupiscible passions, of Aquinas,
63
"concupiscible" power, of appetite,
12
Confessions (Augustine)
baring his restless soul, 90
on Christ as the fulfillment of
true desire, 69
as a classic treatment of the
emotions, 9
coming to terms with true
human condition, 75
on compulsive force of habit
(*consuetudo*), 41
failing to recognize transformed
emotions, 253
on glimpses of supreme good, 42
as the image of a traveler on a
long journey, 77
as a moving portrayal of the
lament genre, 116
patterned after the book of
Psalms, 91
congenial emotions
accompanied by anger and
indignation, sighing and
weeping, 242
described, 24
as holy affections in Christ, 141
informed by Jewish upbringing,
157
of Jesus, 145, 163, 204–10
providing the springboard of
Christian life, 239
understanding of, 237–40
unity with the suffering
emotions, 247
consciousness, "levels" of, 48
consequences of sin, Jesus taking
upon himself, 225

"consolation," philosophical genre
of, 36
Consolation of Philosophy
(Boethius), 39
"consubstantiation," Lutheran
doctrine of, 154n75
contemplation, 65, 66, 67
continuity, Gregory focused on,
85n36
contracting soul, Stoic idea of, 32,
107n101
conversion to Christ, 117
corruptible body, 83
cosmos, 49
courage, 103
covenant, 169, 175, 176
covenant framework, of Jesus' life,
168–82
covenant people, God's love for, 210,
229
covenant relationship
of God with Israel, 180
human zeal of Jesus in
upholding, 218
with Israel as a valued object for
God, 176
marked by God's unwavering
faithfulness, 175
restoration of, 177
creation, 95, 180, 218
creative power, of God's word, 185
Creator and creation, fusion of,
149–50
cries of the faithful, lifted up to God,
245
"crimes of passion," 3
cross, 197n72, 222
crucifixion, 207, 227
cry of lament, on Calvary, 227
cultural rankings, of paradigms, 52
cultural-social norms, shaping Jesus,
166
cultures, in Jewish Scripture, 170
"the cup"
enduring the suffering of, 199,
224
Jesus deeply troubled by, 242–43
Jesus' drinking of, 225n110

278 INDEX

"the cup" (*continued*)
  standing for God's wrath
    and judgment in Jewish
    Scripture, 199n77
Cyril of Alexandria, 151–52,
  153n71, 153n73

Dalgleish, Tim, 27–28
Damascene, John, 133, 134, 153
danger, causing the emotion of fear,
  27
Daughter Zion
  embodying Israel's deepest hope,
    188
  Mary as, 183, 185, 187, 196
  theology of, 184
De anima et resurrectione (Gregory),
  96
De Consolatione ad Helviam
  (Seneca), 37
De Consolatione ad Marciam (To
  Marcia on Consolation), by
  Seneca, 36
De Consolatione ad Polybium
  (Seneca), 38
De diversis Quaestionibus
  (Augustine), 127n11
De fide orthodoxa (Damascene), 133
De hominis opificio, 94
de Sousa, Ronald, 52
deaf-mute, Jesus sighing at the
  plight of, 218
death, 36, 155–56
death of God, told by Christians,
  155, 182n40
decisiveness, in subjectivity, 7
"deep transcendent self," awakening
  of, 65
"defects of soul," Christ's passions
  restricted to, 123
deification
  of Adamic humanity, 22
  Augustine not often using the
    term, 130n20
  beginning in the virgin's womb,
    131
  of Christ as a truly "passionate
    deification," 125
  at the heart of, 203
  of humanity in Jesus Christ, 232
  of Jesus, 236, 246
  as mutual interaction of human
    and divine emotions, 259–60
  process of, 24, 164, 231, 259, 261
delight
  as beyond human control, 78
  emotions of the genus, 63
  of God, 176
  in God, 253
  moments of an inward sense
    of, 87
  motivating the human will, 42,
    84
  psychology of, 9, 77
"delight" or "pleasure" (*hēdonē*),
  emotions of the genus, 32
Descartes, René
  on emotions, 4, 25
  individual as purely a thinking
    subject (*Cogito ergo sum*), 5
  non-cognitive conception of the
    emotions, 14
  six primary emotions or
    passions, 63, 64
descent, Augustine more focused
  on, 80, 118
"descriptive" sense, of rational,
  54n108
Desdemona, 2
desire(s)
  as "appetite" (*epithumia*), 32
  in basic emotions, 68
  bodily and carnal persisting, 76
  considering as basic emotion, 18
  defying all human categories, 70
  different types of, 97
  directed into the paths willed by
    God, 83
  directed toward God as its right
    object, 114
  educating, 10, 94, 95, 98, 102,
    103
  emotions of the genus, 63
  in the eschaton, 97, 101

as essential to participation in God, 102
as the final end or inalienable goal, 70, 99
giving emotion motivational force, 53
as goals, 234
of the heart, 85
integral to human knowing and willing, 70
longing (*epithymia*) and, 104n92
as love of God for Gregory, 98
malleable quality of, 83n31, 97, 102–3, 114
as part of how mind realizes itself, 98
providing targets or goals in life, 68
rightly or wrongly directed, 97
as rightly or wrongly ordered, 19
role of, 53
transforming away from earthly objects, 236–37
wonder making reference to, 67
desolation, as unwanted emotion, 35
despair, 12n38
developmental process, of Jesus, 210
disciples
bearing the divine pathos, 239
hardness of heart of, 215
Jesus' love for, 207
joy of, 208, 238
messianic expectations of, 220
without understanding, 219
discipleship, keeping rooted in this earthly life, 248
discontinuity, Augustine stressing, 85n36
disobedience, 82
dispassion (*apatheia*), 94
"dispassionate passion," 99, 103, 114
"distress" (*lupē*), 1, 32, 63
disturbing and suffering emotions, 240–42
divine
participation of in the human, 142n50, 143n52, 144, 203, 230
swallowing up the human like a drop of vinegar absorbed by a boundless ocean, 131, 152
divine affections, interacting with "natural," 140
divine emotions. *See also* emotion(s)
as both personal and sources of knowledge, 176
cognitive structure of, 177
listed, 159
recorded in Jewish Scripture, 148
divine essence, 143, 144, 145n57
divine glory, residing in Jesus' person, 217
divine illumination, 78n12
divine immutability, 177n32, 182n40
divine impassibility, 177, 177n32
divine nature
impassibility of, 132
not a fixed and closed system, 193
progressive participation in, 256–57
real relation to the human nature, 158
divine pathos. *See also* pathos of God
emotional elements of, 176
intelligible within the covenant framework, 178
Jesus followers called to imitate, 239
suffering emotions belonging to, 162–63
divine person, Christ's knowledge as, 135
divine qualities, 156, 157, 180
divine Son. *See* Son of God
divine Word, 158, 235
divine-human encounter, 78
divine-humanity, 142, 149, 160–62
divinity
attributes of, 156
in Christ's mission of redemption, 130

280 INDEX

divinity (*continued*)
  communicating to the covenant people, 177
  descent to the temporal realm of the human, 149
  dwelling bodily in the man Jesus, 236
  of Jesus Christ, 21, 124, 146, 201, 216
  mediated by the humanity of Jesus for Barth, 144
  revealing itself, 150
  of the Word, 153
divinization of humanity (theosis)
  completion in Christ's resurrection from the dead, 150
  as the final end of the process of creation, 151
  kenosis (self-emptying) aiming at, 163, 193
"divinized" humanity, of Christ, 143n52
docetism, 147n60, 153n73
dread
  integral to Christian life, 253–54
  Jesus experienced in his final days and hours, 157, 242
  as a natural affection, 112
  as a strong emotion, 243
  as a suffering emotion, 227, 234
dread and sorrow, addressed by holy love, 163
dual creation, "synthetic" presentation of, 94
dual role, of Jesus, 179
dualistic modes, of thought, 143–44
dualistic theory of mind, in the Platonic tradition, 25
dynamic relationship, of emotions, 58–59, 62

earth, bearing the curses of human sin, 172n12
earthly life, 37, 81
Ecclesiastes, exercising "the passionate faculty," 98

Edwards, Jonathan
  on the affections of Christ, 139
  concluding comments on, 257–59
  on the congenial emotions of Christ, 140–41
  distinction between the "affections" and the "passions," 106n100
  on gracious affections, 20
  on Jesus' divine-humanity, 148
  on the problem of sin, 119
  representative of Protestant Christianity, 19
  repudiating *apatheia*, 117, 119
  on the rich emotional life of Christ, 257
  on the significance of the emotions, 13
  on the strong emotions of Jesus, 147
  on true religion consisting in gracious affections, 74, 104–14
  on true saints having a fear of sin and a dread of God's displeasure, 114
  on the virtuous life of Christians, 117
Egyptian society, exodus from, 170
election of the land, as part of the original act of creation, 172
Elizabeth, Mary's kinswoman, 188, 189
Elliott, Matthew, 15, 16, 203n82
emerging consciousness, of Jesus, 206
emotion(s). *See also* divine emotions; passions
  as about something, 57
  acknowledging as subjective engagements, 87
  as acknowledgments of profound neediness, 78
  as action potentials or springs of action, 159
  addressing a practical concern, 55, 176

as always about something, 71
Aquinas on, 10n28
as bad guides to good human
    behavior, 27
basic ascribed to God, 235
behavioral sequence of, 83n32
as bodily, 56–57
as both personal and sources of
    knowledge, 51
as both positive and negative, 1
as a broader concept than the
    ancient term "passion," 4n5
broken down into species within
    each genus, 32n25
capacity to experience, 31
central to perpetual progress in
    God, 20
Christian life as the
    transformation of, 233–61
clichés about, 2
complexity of, 45, 48–49
components of, 17, 28
connection with personal
    biography, 88
constituent parts of an, 28
contemporary cognitive theories
    of, 45–61
in contemporary thought, 25–72
correcting ordinary, 40
defined by propositional
    content, 71–72
directing
    to Jesus Christ, 247
    towards God, 9
    towards the right objects, 80
dismissed as mere subjectivity,
    25, 45
distinguished on the basis of
    "stimulus" or appraisal,
    26–27
dynamic relationship of, 58–59
enabling the soul's ascent to
    God, 74, 100
experienced by God, 177
extirpating rejected by
    Augustine, 84
as far from being irrational, 30

fifteen discussed by Lazarus and
    Lazarus, 30n19
formation of involving an
    involved process, 230
giving expression to our
    engagement in the world,
    160
good, 86
    as a foretaste of the blessed
        life, 83
    if accompanied by a morally
        right will, 79
as good or bad judgments, 103
grouping together as a class, 58
grown out of human
    ambivalence and neediness,
    60
having
    a biography, 233
    a cognitive structure, 71
    heat and urgency, 54, 58
    a logic of their own, 30
    a role to play in the process
        of deification, 164
    us under their control,
        34n30
as highly complex phenomena,
    30–31
history of, 53, 60
human, 59n129, 60, 157
implying false judgments, 31
as an impulse turned away from
    reason, 40
introduced by Adam's sin, 127
involving
    appraisal or evaluation, 56
    judgments about important
        things, 29, 32, 43, 55
    physiological movements, 32
as irrational, 2–3
of Jesus Christ
    according to Calvin, 43
    addressing a practical
        concern, 211
    associated with the
        Jerusalem section of the
        synoptic story, 199

emotions (*continued*)
  of Jesus Christ (*continued*)
    Augustine presenting a narrow view of, 256
    becoming the emotions of his disciples, 247, 261
    in both a human and a divine direction, 179
    in constant interaction with the divine, 159
    directed toward the object of the Pharisees, 214
    as evidence of being subjected to this life, 138
    flowing out of his purity of heart, 231
    forming an integral unity, 203
    in the gospels, 203–28
    heightened qualities of, 181
    as intelligible and displaying cognitive structure, 178
    in John's Gospel, 16, 218
    not limiting to suffering emotions, 142
    not mere defects of soul, 158
    not mere signs of his humanity, 231
    as passive in relation to his divinity, 166
    purity, intensity, and appropriateness of, 180, 247
    reflected in his followers, 120
    revealing his human soul, 127n11
    revealing the truth of his divinity, 235
    shedding light on the dynamics of the gospel story, 23
    showing, 125–26
    as the springboard of his mission, 159–65
    in the theological tradition, 122–65
    "latching onto false beliefs," 27
  as "localized," 44
  moderating (*metriopatheia*) or eradicating (*apatheia*), 35n38
  as modes of willing, 83, 88
  as non-reasoning, unthinking energies, 56
  not inherently evil, 100, 103
  as not rational, 54
  occurrences within narrative context, 204
  ongoing transformation of, 260
  placed amongst the mental dispositions, 52
  power to heal or to wound, 2
  range of, 1
  recording vulnerability and imperfect control, 58
  redirecting, 74, 115
  registering
    the human subject's deep vulnerability, 87
    neediness and vulnerability, 43
  related to value, morality, and ethics, 3
  relationship with bodily sensations, 91–92
  role in the Christian ascent to God, 9–10, 93, 102
  role of, 53–54, 118
  shaped by individual history and social norms, 59
  some more basic than others, 62
  as the springs of action in the world, 235
  as subjective, 47, 50, 196n69
  as uncontrollable and involuntary, 3
  unique logic of, 54–55
  viewing as irrational forfeiting humanity, 84
  as voluntary, 47
Emotion and Personality (Arnold), 4
emotion language, as the primary language, 1–24
emotional life

assuming greater significance, 261
development of Jesus' individuality and, 199
formation of for Jesus, 168–203
of the human subject, 69
of Jesus Christ, 15, 22, 23, 124, 125, 141, 151, 156, 164–65, 167, 181, 204, 231, 232
emotional mode, 54, 55
emotional nature, witnessing the truth of God's, 164
emotional paradigm scenarios, 52
emotional person, as not in control, 3
emotional reality, differing from intellectual, 55n109
emotional reasoning, 55
emotional subjectivity, conceptions of, 50
emotional traits, development of, 60
Enchiridion (Augustine), 127n12
enemies, love of, 201, 201n80, 237, 243, 246, 253
engagement with the world, emotions as, 47, 57n119
Enlightenment, 8
epectasy, 101, 102, 111
epistemic objectivity, 51
epistemic subjectivity, 50
equanimity, achieved, 39
erōs
  dispassionate form of, 101
  of Gregory compared to Plato, 102n89
  in the life to come, 102
  persisting even in the eschaton, 97
  in Plato's *Symposium*, 102n89
  role for in the age to come, 19–20
  as a "soaring *stasis*," 19
  stressing intensity of the soul's desire for God, 97
  of this life as not tragic, 102
  transformed nature of in the eschaton, 93

erotic desire (*epithymia*), for God, 101, 118, 256
erotic longing, Augustine using language of, 9, 78
eschatological *erōs*, as a "soaring *stasis*," 102
eschatological love, as "impassible desire," 101
"eschatological prophet," Jesus presented as, 191n61
eschaton
  desire in, 97, 101
  erōs persisting in, 97
  erōs transformed in, 93
  Gregory's view of desire in, 101
essences, actualization of in Christ's person, 145
Esther, 185
eternal life, as the supreme good, 81
eternal rest in God, bliss of, 9
eudaimonia, 29, 29n17, 43, 87
eudaimonistic, emotions appearing to be, 57
eupatheia (good judgments), Stoic category of, 4n5
eupatheiai
  as the affective responses of the sage, 33
  class of affective responses known as, 39
  experiencing stable states after extirpating the passions, 79n18
  wise person remaining subject to, 34
evaluations, associated with emotions, 55–56
evaluative judgments, emotions as, 61
Evangelii Gaudium (Joy of the Gospel), by Pope Francis, 238n4, 249–50, 250n24
events, transforming hope into grief, 56
evil, 11n30, 94, 201n80, 243
evil passions, ensuing from bad judgment, 103
evocative language, 7

evolutionary view, of the world, 49
exile, as nothing more than a "change of place," 37
existence, ending in death, 6n14
existentialists, 4–5, 5n11, 6, 7
existing, 5, 6
exitus-reditus structure, of *Summa theologiae* (Aquinas), 11
exodus, as the founding event of Jewish faith, 170
expanding soul, Stoic idea of, 107n101
experience, emotion as, 48
"exterior" senses, 11n35
"exterior" temptation, experienced by Christ, 136
external goods, invested with no intrinsic value, 34
extirpation of the emotions (*apatheia*), 4, 27, 74
exuberant joy, 208, 227

"facticity" of existence, 5–6
faith
　of the centurion, 212
　Christian, 7, 7n19, 143
　of Israel, 169–70
　Jewish, 170, 176
　lament and, 245, 251
　requiring risk, 7
the faithful, holy suffering of, 259
fallen humanity, experiencing emotions, 91
family life, of Jesus, 189, 205, 229
fascinans affective state, 8, 64–65
fascination, as the rational side of wonder, 67
the Father. *See also* God
　Jesus' love for, 205, 207, 217, 218, 227
　Jesus' obedience to, 192–203
　submission to the will of, 146
Father's house, Jesus' "zeal" for, 216–18
fear
　Augustine on, 253

　based upon an appraisal of danger, 3
　broadening to include dread, 258
　Christ not experiencing like a human would, 135n31
　distinct from normal human fear, 243
　as an emotion, 1
　emotions of the genus, 63
　experienced by Jesus Christ, 138, 203n82
　future evil seeming impossible to overcome, 12n38
　as the judgment of prospective evil, 32
　overcoming, 36
　seeing oneself threatened, 57
fear and anger (*thymos*), reacting to painful sense data, 104n92
fear and doubt, overwhelming Christians, 251–52
"feeling," 8, 78
feeling theory, 25, 26n3
feelings
　of Augustine, 78
　intentionality of, 5
　as judgments of the body, 49
　mobilization of, 42
　role of in emotions, 47
　teaching about our world, 6
fertility, 184, 185
filial obedience, Jesus learning perfect, 236
finite, having a capacity for the infinite, 109n105
first movements, Stoic idea of, 17n57
fixed plan, for all things, 36
Flanagan, Donal, 187
flesh, 81, 91, 143, 153
Flesh and Logos, considered as a separate physis, 131
"flesh" and "spirit," unresolved tension between, 41
fomes peccati (the tinder of sin), theme of, 136

"form of a servant," Christ's
    obedience in, 139
formation of attitudes, function
    of, 53
forms of judgment, emotions as,
    4, 27
Formula of Concord, 154
Pope Francis
    challenges acknowledged by,
        250n24
    on joy, 238n4, 249–50
freedom, 35, 68–69
freedom of choice (*liberum
    arbitrium*), 82n28
Frei, Hans, 194, 195, 195n67,
    199n76, 200n78
frustration of desire, 53
function, of emotion, 28
"functionalist" model of mind, 26
fundamental desire, 18, 68
fundamental feelings, 5n13

Gabriel, 185, 188
"garments of skin," postlapsarian
    addition of, 94
Gellius, Aulus, 128
generic emotions, 32
generic nature, static concept of, 192
gentile mission, Jesus foreseeing,
    212
genuinely good, belonging to an
    ethical system, 35
genus majestaticum, exchange of
    properties limited to, 154
"gnomic" will, Christ having no, 152
goals, 45
God. *See also* the Father
    addressing humanity personally,
        237
    affected by what happens in the
        world, 177
    appetite of, 11n33
    Augustine's dialogue with, 90
    basic emotions of, 175–76
    bearing the sins of his people,
        175
    choosing and consecrating
        specific persons before they
        are born, 186
    desire of, 70
    emotions of, 235
    entering the realm of existential
        being, 7
    as essentially love, 180n35
    existing only for subjectivity in
        inwardness, 7
    feeling the afflictions of his
        people, 178
    feelings of, 181
    giving the land to Israel for a
        divine purpose, 171
    identifying with the crucified
        Christ, 156
    involving himself in
        nothingness, 155
    living an authentic life in the
        God-Man, 149
    love of, as motivating force
        behind the new covenant,
        228
    loving us, 182
    as merciful, slow to anger, and
        full of steadfast love, 176n29
    as more like us than unlike us,
        155
    as neither a "what" nor a "thing,"
        but a pure "Who" or "Thou"
        or "I AM," 65
    as not exacting on matters of
        judgment, 244n8
    not wiping away the wounds of
        the Messiah's crucifixion,
        245
    as the object
        of Augustine's delight, 81
        of endless desire, 101
        of *erōs*, 10, 97
        of wonder, 18, 70n160
    as our greatest desire, 70
    overcoming separation between
        nature and history, 171–72
    personal attributes of, 148, 156
    personal or relational properties
        of, 154

God (*continued*)
    prospect of being abandoned by, 224
    reacting with wrath and anger, 215
    redemption of enemies of, 140
    sighing in Jewish Scripture, 220
    Son suffering at the hands of, 245
    suffering of, 162
    as "the union of death and life for the sake of life," 156
    united to man to constitute Christ, 129
God-forsakenness, Jesus suffering on the cross, 158
Godhead, conjunction with the material body, 130
God-Man, 125, 149, 156
"going out of God," 144
Gondreau, Paul, 123
good, purified desire of, 97
good affections, generic kinds of, 33
good and bad, distinction between, 32n24
good life, consisting in activity, 29
"good shepherd," Jesus as, 209
goodness, evoking appetite in all existing things, 11
Gordon, R., 46
gospel, as a divine gift of exuberant joy, 251
gospel narratives, 194–95, 196
gospel story, depicting Jesus, 201
gospels
    emotions of Jesus recorded in, 22
    recovering the narrative character of, 195n67
grace
    addressing to the human essence of Christ, 143
    of the immaculate conception, 188n58
    involving a new inward perception or sensation, 109
    kingdom of, 231
    Mary growing in, 187n56, 188n57
    offer of as existential, 66n153
    participation of nature in, 115, 117
gracious affections
    attended by a change of nature, 110n106
    exercise and fruit in Christian practice, 111n112
    signs of, 105n95, 109–10
The Great Awakening in the 1740s, 104
great commandment to Israel, 163
Great Tradition, 249, 249n20, 252
Greek philosophical tradition, guilty of the sin of pride, 76
Greer, Rowan, 84
Gregory of Nyssa
    on ascending order of creation, 74
    on the ascent to God, 118–19
    challenging Macrina's understanding, 100
    on Christian ascent, 109
    concluding comments, 256–57
    on conjoining nutritive and sentient powers to rational faculties, 104
    on the connection between emotions and judgments, 103
    on desire (*erōs*) as never exhausted, 110
    on desire as a basic emotion, 68
    on the educating of desire and the erotic relation of humanity to God, 74
    on emotions, 9–10
    on the erotic relation of humanity to God, 19
    on the event of the incarnate Word, 131
    idea of perpetual progress (*epectasy*), 115
    on the mingling of the two natures in Christ, 152

on the moral qualities or virtues
of the Christian, 115
on participating in God and
growing in virtue, 115
on participation in the new age
in the earthly life, 84n36
on the passions of lust and
anger, 118
on progressive education of
desire, 69, 92–104
representative of Eastern Greek
Christianity, 19
restricting the passions to the
problem of sin, 118
restricting the role of the
suffering emotions, 119
retaining the language of desire
(*epithymia*), 99
on suffering, 259
on the two natures of Christ, 131
understanding of the passions,
103–4
viewing the animal as included
in the rational, 96
grief
as anger, 56
broadening Edwards' concept
of, 258
containing judgments, 43
divine dimension to Jesus', 223
as an emotion, 1
overcoming, 36
regarded by Stoics as unwanted
emotion, 35
seeing an object or person as
lost, 57
as a valid emotion, 134
groaning, for the "redemption of our
bodies," 218
growing in wisdom and favor before
God, 159
Gunton, Colin, 158n84

habitual sin, Augustine on, 87
Hannah, song of, 184
Hansen, G. Walter, 16–17

happiness, misguided expectations
of, 93
happy life, rejoicing in God, 81
hardness of heart
amongst communities of faith,
241
bringing about sighing by Jesus,
241
of the covenant people, 234
of the disciples, 219
grieving for, 254
Jesus grieved by, 214, 215
as the object of anger, 216
unbelief of the Jewish leaders
and, 220
Hart, Mark, 93
hatred, leading to aversion of an evil
object, 12n38
healing, 210, 214, 218
hearts
crying out, 182
religion affecting, 106
Heidegger, Martin
admitting two other affects or
moods, 5n13
on "being-in-the-world," 6
Jüngel following, 155
as a pupil of Husserl, 5n11
using *Befindlichkeit* meaning
"the-way-one-finds-oneself,"
5
Helvia, 37, 38
"hematidrosis," blood mingling with
sweat, 224n107
hereditary "pattern-reaction,"
emotion as, 26
Heschel, Abraham, 176–77
hiddenness of God, 245
Hilary of Poitiers, 132
historical-critical methods, 195n67
historical-existential realm, God
condescending to, 163
history
of the affections of adult life, 113
of emotions of adult life, 87
"history-like" quality, of the gospel
narratives, 195

holiness
    of Jesus, 230, 236
    of Mary, 187
holy, coming to through awe and
        wonder, 64
holy affections
    of Christ, 111, 117, 140
    religion of heaven consisting of,
        110–11
    true religion consisting in, 13
holy love
    of Christ, 111–12
    power of the exercises of, 140
"holy mystery," 18, 68, 69, 70
Homilies on the Song of Songs
        (Gregory), 98
hope
    as an anticipation of what will
        be, 84–85
    arising when a future good
        seems possible, 12n38
    with a good chance for a good
        outcome, 57
    as hope against hope, 245
human action, as restricted and
        conditioned, 180n35
human agency, Augustine
        questioning, 85
human and divine emotions, overlap
        between, 141
human and divine natures, in the
        person of Jesus, 212
human beings. *See also* humanity
    ascending toward God, 80
    disobedience to self, 82
    liberating from bondage to
        emotion, 27
    never meant to be solely
        intellectual beings, 95
    as not helpless, 40
    treating as living creatures, 29
human desire. *See* desire(s)
human essence
    of Christ, grace addressing, 143
    participation with divine
        essence, 144, 145n57
    Son of God's participation in,
        142, 146n59
    as that which receives, 145n57
human existence, 155
human life, 41, 81, 164
human mortality, emotions due
        to, 36
human nature
    affirming in Christ, 122
    of Christ, 21
    "fellowship" with the divine
        nature, 142n50–43n50
    mediating the divine nature,
        144n56
    as not a fixed and closed system,
        193
    not passive in relation to the
        divine nature, 158
    participation in the divine
        nature, 240
    as passive in relation to the
        divine nature, 130
    as a passive instrument of
        redemption, 153
human needs, indifference to,
        angering Jesus, 214
human predicament, reassessment
        of by Augustine, 76
human relationships, legitimate
        expectations of, 93
human self-transcendence, 49
human sinfulness and mortality,
        condition of, 79
human species, wonder as the
        hallmark of, 64
human task, attaining virtue
        (wisdom), 34
human tragedies, bearing nobly and
        calmly, 42
humanity. *See also* human beings
    complex interweaving with
        divinity, 179
    conscious of itself through his
        divinity, 210
    desire for union with God, 69
    as an emerging reality, 193
    erotic relation with God in this
        life, 93
    of God, taken with full
        seriousness, 156

of Jesus Christ
   as clearly different from the rest of humanity, 124
   experienced suffering or other human experiences, 131
   integral to the proclamation of redemption and salvation, 139
   mediating his divinity, 22, 150
   not "possessing" all divine power and authority, 143n52
   taken up into his divinity like a drop of vinegar is absorbed into a boundless ocean, 166
Jesus perfecting his, 162
not a static or closed system, 193
participation in the very life of God, 180
progressing with the development of Jesus' individuality, 201
raised to the glory of the "imperishable," 150
referring to a dynamic system, 201
testifying of the divine, 144
humanity's inhumanity, prayer of forgiveness for, 200
humanization of God (kenosis). See kenosis (self-emptying)
humbling and exalting, "at the same time," 144n55
humiliation, of the divine for the exaltation of the human essence, 144
Husserl, Edmund, 5n11
hypostatic union, 124, 147n60

I and Thou (Buber), 65n152
Iago, 2
The Idea of the Holy (Otto), 8, 64
identity, of Jesus, 195, 196, 198, 231
"identity descriptions," of the man Jesus, 194
Ifaluk, 59
ills, none suffered after death, 37
Immaculate Conception, 186–87, 188
Immanuel. *See also* Jesus Christ
   Mary's womb as the container of, 186
   as "not man in general," 193
immediate beatific knowledge of God, 135
impassibility, of God, 177n32
"impassible desire"
   ceasing to be a passion in the pejorative sense, 99
   Christian's erotic desire for God as, 256
   conveying desire wholly focused on God, 101
   of Gregory, 114
   shifting its focus from the flesh, 118
In canticum canticorum (Gregory), 97
inanimate objects, inclined toward a good, 12n36
incarnate Son, not exempt from the human condition, 22–23
incarnate Word, 149, 153, 235
incarnation
   of the eternal Word, 201
   gazing upon the mystery of, 232
   notion of a progressive or gradual, 149
   as the "ongoing embodiment to God in those who follow Christ," 120
   as a process continuing in the baptized, 228
   process of, 159, 230
   progressive or gradual, 145
inclination of the soul in action, as "will," 106
increase and nutrition, power of, 95
indifference, Stoic theory of, 35
individual history, of a person affecting emotions, 60

individuality
  diminishment of the richness of, 88
  of Jesus, 192, 193, 198–99, 205, 229
infancy, cognitive views ignoring, 60
infertile women, seen as truly blessed, 184
infused supernatural knowledge, 135
inmost "I," giving rise to "fruitful action," 67
inner "I," awakened by a "Thou" or "I AM," 65n152
inner self, as portrayed by Augustine, 89
instigating event, of an emotion, 28
Institutes of the Christian Religion (Calvin), 42
intellectual activity, contemplation involving much, 66
intellectual appetite or will, 12n36
intellectual awareness, 99
intellectual cognition, 12n36
intellectual deliberations, 55
intellectual enjoyment of God's beauty, 101
intelligence, hand in hand with emotions, 61
intensity, of Jesus' emotions, 236
intention, 12n36, 195
"intention-action" description, of personal identity, 199n76
intentional objects, 57, 62, 202
intentionality, 47
"interior" senses, 11n35
interior temptation, Christ and, 136, 146
interplay, of humanity and divinity in Jesus, 210
interpreter of God and humanity, Jesus as, 181, 193
interrelatedness, of the affections, 113
intuitive awakening, contemplation as, 66–67
involved holiness, 22, 230
Iranaeus, 130n20

irascible passions, 12n38, 63
"irascible" power, of appetite, 12
Irenaeus of Lyon, 188n58
irrational parts of the soul, training to control, 25n1
Isaiah, 174, 221
isolation, of Jesus, 198
Israel
  faith of, 169–70
  forced to interact with other nations, 169
  God-given destiny and mission, 172, 221
  God's love for, 228
  Jesus' mission to, 178
  late origins of, 170
  managed to cling to its peculiar faith, 170
  mandate to live as the people of God, 171
  rejection of Jesus, 221
"It," realm of, 65n152
I-You relationship, 150n64

James, William, 14, 25, 49
jealousy, 1, 175
Jenson, Robert, 186, 186n52
Jeremiah, 174, 221
Jerusalem. *See also* New Jerusalem
  in the center of the nations, 169
  deeply cherished by Jesus, 174–75, 221, 223
  place associated with the destiny of Israel, 168
Jesus Christ. *See also* Immanuel; Son of God
  abandonment of, 224–25
  accepted sorrow and sufferings, 43
  actions both divine and human, 151
  actualizing his personhood, 150n64
  affected by personal happenings, 222–23
  assaults by his own people and by satanic forces, 200

bearing and beholding of, 260–61
bearing his image, 164
becoming conscious of
   himself as God's visitation of Israel, 161
   his divinity, 205, 210
   his special relationship to the Father, 206, 208, 229
being made sin for our sake, 225
born into a history of fidelity and infidelity, 229
bound up with Jewish covenant expectations, 234
commandments taught by, 108
comparing to Adam, 123, 134
compassion of, 164, 209
confronted by human failure, misery, and suffering, 191
conquered sin and death, 73
"deeply moved" by grief in Bethany, 222
on desire, 70
desire to make known the Father's love, 18–19, 70n160–71n160
as a distinct human being, 192
distressed at the sight of the tomb of Lazarus, 223
divine consciousness awakened adolescence, 190
divine qualities of, 180
divine-humanity of, 141
divinity of, 147, 191n60
education received from his parents, 190
embodying the ideal of humanity, 200
emotions of
   in the gospels, 203–28
   intensity and breadth peculiar to divine-humanity, 148, 157
   as the springboard of his mission, 159–65
   in the theological tradition, 122–65
eternal life and final peace coming through, 80
as eternal Word of divine Wisdom made flesh, 172–73
as an existential individual for Kierkegaard, 155n78
experiencing
   exuberant joy, 238
   the Father, 234
   fear or dread at the prospect of death, 157
   real emotions, 204
   supernatural joy, 135
   the whole gamut of emotions, 138–39
expressing
   disturbing and suffering emotions, 226
   indignation or anger, 157
   utter dismay at the unbelief of the Pharisees, 219
   zeal, 217
family life of keeping Torah, 189
"filled with joy," 208
foreseeing conflict with the religious leaders, 212
free of original sin and its associated effects, 124
as a genuinely surprised human being, 211
giving himself over to the Jewish and Roman authorities, 224
as the history of God's engagement in the world, 151
holiness and deification in his person, 228–32
holy affections of, 111
as "the Holy and Just One," 173
human ignorance in, 127
humanity of, 124
   absorbed into the divine nature, 256
   mediating the presence of divinity in, 149
as ideal covenant partner, 178
identified in his resurrection, 199n76

292   INDEX

Jesus Christ (*continued*)
  identifying with the fallen human condition, 200
  as the inaugurator of the covenant, 178
  increasing in wisdom and in stature and in favor before God, 159
  interplay of the human and the divine in, 22
  irreducible to either his divine or human nature, 179
  isolation and rejection of, 213
  justifying us, 139
  knowing the human condition intimately, 229
  laying down his life on the cross, 127n12, 206
  learning what obedience to the Father involves, 230
  leaving home in Nazareth, 191
  like Moses but greater than Moses, 191n61
  living in genuine human freedom, 143
  love
    for Mary, Martha, and Lazarus, 206, 221–22
    for the rich young man, 207
    towards his long-suffering people, 205
  as the man of sorrows, 234
  moved and troubled by historical events, 223n106
  natural and divine emotions, 141
  need to pray to the Father, 144
  not experiencing ordinary human joy, 135n31
  not feeling pain, 132
  not fully in solidarity with the human condition, 135–36
  not liable to death by any sin, 126n10
  not possessing the fullness of knowledge or self-consciousness by the age of twelve, 190–91
  not spared death, 187n55
  obedience
    to the Father, 191n59, 195–96, 224
    to his parents, 206
  object of wonder as his heavenly Father, 234
  "owning his own presence," 200n78
  "passing" from death to life, 152n66
  personal biography, 161–62, 166–232
  pleading with the Father in Gethsemane, 224
  as a precocious child, 190
  as the pre-existent word of God made flesh, 173
  reality of the body of, 132
  rebuke directed at Peter, 220
  rejoicing in his unique filial relationship with the Father, 208
  remaining in the temple, unbeknownst to his parents, 190
  revealing
    his divine glory through his humanity, 218
    the primacy of God's love for us, 199n77
  risking going to Bethany in order to reach his friend Lazarus, 206
  sighing and weeping of, 218–23
  special identity as Son of God, 189–90
  standing in front of people with hardened hearts, 198
  stricken by dread and sorrow, 139
  strong emotions of, 139
  struggle of spirit against flesh, 136, 146
  subject to
    first movements according to Jerome, 136n33

INDEX 293

infirmities and temptations
  of the flesh, 162
mortality, 147
suffering of, 179, 223–28, 239,
  246
teaching his disciples about his
  death, 220
transformation into the likeness
  of, 261
"troubled" by the grieving in
  Bethany, 222n106–23n106
two natural wills, 152
undergoing development as a
  human being, 150, 191, 230
unique characteristics of, 193
as the unity of two spiritual
  substances, 129
venturing into the dangerous
  Bethany near Jerusalem, 222
wailing approaching Jerusalem,
  174, 223
weeping, 148, 241
as well versed in the prophetic
  traditions, 215
winning the victory of salvation,
  203
without personal sin, 126,
  143n51, 180
as the Word become flesh, 216
zeal for his Father's house,
  216–18
Jewish expectation, of the final
  coming of God's reign, 188
Jewish history, covenantal
  framework of, 168
Jewish life, love of God fundamental
  to, 229
Jewish people, required to display
  compassion, 163
Jewish religious leaders, Matthew
  as a stinging indictment on,
  209
Jewish scholars, on the gospel story,
  168n2
Jewish Scripture
  final object of desire as God
    himself, 70
  founded on God's covenant
    relationship with Abraham,
    168
  history of promises recorded
    in, 184
  Jesus fully immersed in, 168,
    189
  on the manifestation of divine
    anger and displeasure, 213
  reproof of the shepherds of the
    people in, 209
Jewish thought, acknowledging
  divine pathos, 179n34
Jewish world, Jesus' lack of control
  over, 162
John Damascene, 123, 153
John the Baptist, 146
John's Gospel, 178n33, 204, 205,
  222, 247n16
Johnson, Samuel, 85–86
Jordan, crossing of, 171
Joseph, as "a just man," 189
joy
  changing depending on real
    situations, 250
  Christian, as robust, 238
  of delight, 1
  in the Father's benevolent love,
    238
  in God, 255, 258
  of Jesus, 164, 208, 234, 238
  judgment involved in the
    affective response of, 33
  no commerce with laughter and
    elation, 34
  ontological significance of, 5n13
  as prospective for Augustine,
    253
  as reasonable, 33–34
  resulting from keeping the
    Father's commands, 218
  of the Stoics as emotion-free, 34
  theme of in Luke's Gospel, 208
judgments
  of appropriate actions, 32
  of the body, 49, 62
  as both human and divine, 160

judgments (*continued*)
  emotions as, 31, 40, 47, 56, 114, 233
  of good or bad at hand, 32
  Jesus' emotions involving, 202
  Jesus making, 160
  maintaining close ties to perception, 48
  as not articulate or deliberate, 48n88
  as not involuntary, 31
Judith, 185
Jüngel, Eberhard, 155, 156, 182n40

Kelsey, David, 194
kenosis (self-emptying)
  according its full ontological realism, 235
  adequately developed, 21, 163, 179
  aiming at deification of humanity (theosis), 163, 193
  development of an adequate understanding, 21
  divine and the human mutually interacting, 235
  of God, 143n53
  inadequately developed notion of, 166
  Karl Barth on, 143n53
  meaning that Christ was really tempted by evil, 146
  more adequate conception of, 167
  not according its full ontological realism, 131
  in the person of Jesus the Son, 244
  sense of wonder for, 151
  Sergius Bulgakov on, 146n59, 149–50
  of the Son, 147, 230
  traditional patristic and scholastic notion of, 139
  unsatisfactory remaining undeveloped, 130
kenotic theology, 149

Kenny, Anthony, 15
kerygma, characteristics of, 194n64
Kierkegaard, 7, 155n78, 201
kingdom of God, 161, 196
Klausner, Joseph, 168n2
knowledge, 51, 68, 135

Laird, Martin, 98–99
"Lamb of God," 178n33, 206
lament
  and anticipation, Augustine on, 116
  Augustine on, 255
  cry of, on the cross, 224
  Edwards on, 258
  Pope Francis offering no reflections on, 250–51
  of God, 162–63, 175
  integral to the acceptance of suffering, 255, 259
  Jesus' cry of, 226
  joined to Christ's lament on the cross, 251, 255
  place of centrality in this pilgrim life, 89
  pronouncing faith in God as a tested faith, 251
  speech form, 116, 244
  testifying to faith, 245
the land, charged with the divine mission of Torah, 172, 175
language of emotion, as primary, 233
Last Supper, 178
latter-day prophet, redeeming Israel, 191n61
Lazarus, 206, 221, 221n104, 222
Lazarus, Richard, 30, 46
"learned obedience," of Jesus as the Son, 162
life
  as but a journey towards death, 38
  characterized by emotions other than love and joy, 79
  on earth, 81
  of grace, 66n153

Life of Moses (Gregory), 101
lifeless morality, religion reduced to, 13, 104
literary approach, to the gospel story, 194
literature, as a microcosm of the real world, 2
living according to self, becoming like the devil, 82
"lofty goods," directing appetitive faculties to, 100
"lofty ideas," conveyed by names of the virtues, 116
logic, Seneca's focus on, 39
Logos, as the active element, 131
Lohfink, Gerhard, 169, 170
longing for union with God, 84
Lord God. *See* God
love
    attributed to Jesus once in the Synoptic Gospels, 205
    as the basis of obedience, 226
    cognitive character of, 205
    as defined by its direction or goal, 83
    directing of human to God, 237–38
    as an emotion, 1
    enabling Jesus to endure immense suffering, 163
    as the first and chief of relational qualities, 157
    as first and chief of the affections, 108, 113, 227
    foundational role of, 115
    highlighted in John's Gospel, 204
    invested with a special sort of radiance, 57
    of Jesus for his friends, 222
    leading to desire and pleasure, 12n38
    of neighbor, 205
    not wrath as the cause of Jesus' passion, 225n110
    to our fellow human beings, 113
    of our neighbor, 246–47
    as the principal cause of the soul's ascent to God, 100
    sublimated love of God, 103
    as the tendency an entity has to be itself for Aquinas, 11
    tending to remain superficial, 66
    victory of divine, 121
love and compassion, congenial emotions of, 142
love and joy in Christ, true religion consisting in the affections of, 107–8
love of enemies. *See* enemies, love of
love of God
    as the basis of Jesus' obedience to the Father, 239
    as chief affection, 23, 107
    as chief emotion, 119, 245, 258
    as the fount of joy and compassion, 239
    giving rise to intense hatred of sin, 113
    giving rise to love of one's fellow human beings, 108
    for Israel, 175
    of Jesus, 207–8, 227, 227n114
    in Jewish Scripture, 205
    motivating and carrying Jesus forward, 207
    transposed to the divine Son's love of the Father, 229
    truth and meaning of human life known through, 238
"lover of the good," 83
Ludlow, Morwenna, 97–98
lust, leading to adultery, 103
Luther, Martin, 154, 155
Lutheran formula, on the hypostatic union, 154

Macquarrie, 6n13
Macrina (Gregory's sister), 100
Magnificat, of Mary, 184, 188
"making a face," feeling of, 49
"Man of Sorrows," 142
maranatha: "Our Lord, Come!" 242
Marcia (sister of Seneca), 36–37
Marion, Jean-Luc, 64n146

Mark (Gospel of)
    cross as the decisive event, 197n72
    opposition to Jesus as a feature of, 211
marriage, 93, 94
Martha, 206
Mary (Jesus' mother)
    chosen for her office and consecrated by God, 186
    conceived Christ spiritually in her heart, 183, 260
    conceiving the Son of the Most High, 185
    contained the uncontainable God, 260
    as "Daughter Zion," 183–92
    holiness of, 184
    lacking understanding of her son, 187n56
    looked faithfully to the Lord, 188
    not exempt from the human condition, 187
    not free from original sin, 147
    sharing with humanity consequences of Adam's sin, 187n55
    as the true Zion, 185
    without personal sin, 143n51
Mary (sister of Martha), Jesus' love for, 206
materialistic impulses, 97
Maximus the Confessor, 150n63, 152, 171n10
mediatory role, of Christ's rational soul, 129–30
medieval theologians, on Christ's emotions, 123
medieval theology, Jesus' emotions in, 20
memory, 76, 77
mental dispositions, 52, 52n102, 53
mental states, 52, 52n102
mercy, restoring the covenant relationship, 175–76
Mere Christianity (Lewis), 249n20
Merton, Thomas, 65

Messiah, winning the world in death, 197
metaphors, for the irrationality of the emotions, 45
metaphysical deity, as the opposite of human existence, 155
Miller, Patrick, 90, 91
mind, 38, 96, 114
ministry, of Jesus, 197
misfortune, bringing a certain blessing, 37
mission
    of Jesus, 173, 205
    the land signifying, 171
mode, by which hope is reborn, 244
modern Western world, attitude to emotion in, 14
modes
    of the mental system, 54
    of willing, 83n32, 115
Modus Essendi, of Jesus, 192–203
monophysitism, 152, 154n73, 156
moral agency, 89
moral sense, 214, 215
"Moralistic Therapeutic Deism" (MTD), 248n18
Moses, 171
mothers
    emotion at the death of, 44, 56
    role in Jewish Scripture, 184
motivational forces, 61, 159
movement of genuine "action" (*operatio*), 144
Murphy, Jeffrey, 46
mysterium, 65
mysterium fascinans (congenial emotions of love, joy, and delight), 227, 234, 251
mysterium tremendum et fascinans, 8, 64, 67, 201, 207
mysterium tremendum (suffering emotions of dread, grief, sorrow, and lament), 227, 234
mystery of Jesus' person, 150n64

natural affections, 112, 140, 141

"natural and innocent passions," of
    Christ, 133
natural appetite, 12n36
natural desire, for the beatific vision
    of God, 69
Nature, 36, 38
natures, in Jesus, 179, 230–31
nearness of God, 244
negative concupiscible passions,
    12n38
negative emotions
    of Aristotle, 26n8
    bringing to light the sickness of
        the soul, 117–18
    fear and grief as, 73
    human subject experiencing, 69
    revealing limited human
        capacity, 234
neo-Stoic theory of emotion, 28–29,
    44, 55–61
Nestorius, 151n65
Neu, Jerome, 46
"new commandment," of Jesus, 238
new heart
    emotions flowing from, 164, 240
    imitating the sacred heart of
        Jesus, 246
    participating in God in the here
        and now, 255
    possessing, 23
    receiving, 178, 232
    reception of, 237
    to see as God sees and feel as
        God feels, 260
new inwards perception, inclining
    the soul towards God, 115
New Jerusalem. *See also* Jerusalem
    Jesus desiring the establishment
        of, 220, 223
    Jesus longing for, 116, 219, 221,
        241
    vision of, 240
"new nature," Edwards' principle
    of, 109
new spiritual sense, Edwards on, 109
New Testament, key texts on desire,
    70

"noetic-erotic" capacity, for God,
    98–99
non-cognitive approach to
    emotions, tracing back to
    Plato, 3
non-cognitive theories, 4, 26
non-emotional beliefs, 50
normal emotions, versus emotional
    disorders, 28n12
"normative" sense, of rational,
    54n108
normative teachings, of different
    societies, 59–60
not yet dimension, of the kingdom
    of God, 241, 242
Nouwen, Henri, 44
numinous experience, transcending
    the ordinary, 8
"numinous" state of mind, as
    irreducible, 64
Nussbaum, Martha
    on Augustine's account of
        Christian ascent, 80
    on Augustine's work for
        restoring compassion, 85
    on emotions as different from
        desires, 54n105, 68
    on emotions as evaluative
        judgments, 46
    on neo-Stoic theory of emotion,
        43, 55–61
    story of her mother's death, 56
    on thoughts about the good, 45
    within a broadly functionalist
        framework, 28–29
nutritive and sentient powers of the
    soul, 99
nutritive soul, 95

obedience
    to the Father, 198, 226
    of Jesus, 191n59, 195–96
    linking love and joy, 208
    to parents, 206
objective accent, falling on "what"
    is said, 7
O'Murchu, Diarmuid, 70

On the Expression of the Emotions in Man and Animals (Darwin), 63
On the Soul and Resurrection (Gregory), 101
"one incarnate nature of the Word," 151
ongoing conversion and imitation of Christ, 232
ontological language, 7
opposition, to Jesus as a feature of Mark's Gospel, 211
ordeal of earthly life, Augustine's view of, 80–81
orexis (drive for pleasure, glory, and wealth), purging of, 101
Origen, 136n33
original justice, 91n46, 127n12
Orthodox teaching, on the sin of Adam, 143n51
Ortony, A., 46
Othello, 2
Othello (Shakespeare), 1–2
Otto, Rudolf, 8, 64

pain, Christ not feeling, 132
paradigm scenarios, embedded in our culture, 52
parents, influence on the development of Jesus, 183
Pascal, Blaire, 55
paschein, meaning to suffer or undergo, 34n30
passio justi, wisdom tradition of, 173
passionate life of Christ, 248
passion-resurrection narrative, 199n76
passions
  Aquinas listing eleven basic, 12
  befalling the Stoic wise man, 129
  caused by "evil husbandry of the mind," 95
  characterizing relationship to God, 7
  of Christ, 123, 133, 136, 257
  human directed to God prior to Adam's sin, 82–83
  as impulse or affect, 96
  as motivating forces, 103
  not attributable to God, 11n33
  referring to effects on the "animal spirits," 106n100
  regarded as defects of soul due to Adam's sin, 162
  right ordering of, 104
  as sicknesses of the soul, 75
  in the soul of the wise person, 79
  Thomas's positive account of human, 123
passivity, 58, 202
pathē (bad judgments), 4n5, 39
pathē (principal emotions), 104n92
pathos of God. *See also* divine pathos
  in Jewish Scripture, 162, 243–44
patristic and medieval theology, 158
patristic and medieval thought, 125–37
patristic and scholastic theology, 147
patristic reserve, toward Christ's emotions, 122–23
patristic theology, 20, 122, 147, 158
patristic thought, 21, 124, 125–37, 152–53
Paul, 65, 70, 76, 260
peace, attaining, 83
Pelikan, Jaroslav, 184n44
penal substitution theory, 225n110
people, in the land, 171
people of God, 229
perceived object, liking or disliking of, 108
perception, as the cognitive element in emotion, 48
perfected saint in heaven, undergoing perpetual progress, 97
perfection
  of Jesus' humanity, 161
  normative goal of, 60
  as taught by the ancient Stoics, 45
"perichoresis," notion of, 153
personal attributes, of God, 180n35

personal biography
  affections having, 113
  complex picture of Jesus's, 201
  connection of emotions with, 50, 51–52, 55
  of Jesus, 161–62, 166–232
  of subjective engagement, 62
personal history, of Jesus, 222
personal knowledge, including the recognition of emotional beliefs, 51
personal meaning, emotions as products of, 30
personal sin, Christ without, 147n61
personal values, emotion as an expression of, 3
perturbatio, used by Cicero, 35n39–36n39
perturbations of the soul, 79, 127, 128
perverse will, persisting, 88
Peter, 197, 220, 251
Pharisees
  feelings against Jesus, 219
  hardness of heart of, 215
  held counsel on how to destroy Jesus, 212, 214
  Jesus sighing at the testing of, 218, 219
  responding to Jesus' exorcisms, 211
phenomenology, 5n11
Philo of Alexandria, 177n32
philosophical abstractions, regarding the absolute, 182n40
philosophical behaviorism, 26n4
philosophical schools, in Aristotle's time, 35n38
philosophy, beginning with wonder, 64
physical death, Mary not spared, 187n55
physical things, desire for, 97
physiological changes, of Jesus, 202
piety, articulating positive "signs" of true, 13
pity, as an emotion, 1

plants, natural disposition of, 12n36
Plato, 3, 25, 25n1
Platonism, 76
pleasure, 32, 93, 135
plot and personal meaning, of an emotion, 30
political Messiah, Pharisees expecting, 219
Polybius, 38
positive concupiscible passions, 12n38
positive emotions, 26n8, 69, 79, 234
possibility, positive element of, 155
Power, Mick, 27–28
"power of animation," 96
power of life and soul, distinctions of, 95
powerless women, of Israel, 185
powerlessness and helplessness, Jesus entering a distressing situation of, 224
praise and worship, of God, 244
prayers, 90, 244n9
precipitating factor, selection of, 53
predestining persons, 186
preexistent Torah incarnate, notion of, 172
preferred indifferents, Stoic attitude of, 35
pre-passions (*propatheia*), 17n57, 22
  Christ experiencing, 128, 256
  emotions of Jesus as not, 216, 236
present and future, distinction between, 32n24
pride, wickedness of, 172n14
primary language, emotion language as, 1–24
"primitivist" conception, of emotions, 46
principal emotions (*pathē*), 104n92
"principle of identity," 8
"principles of nature," 109
progress, Augustine's position on the limits of, 85n37
progressive incarnation, 125, 149–59, 235–36

"progressive integration," of the power of animation with the material world, 96
promise and demand, dialectic of, 175
propassio term, coined by Jerome, 136n33
"propassions," 124, 147
propatheia (pre-passion). *See* pre-passions (*propatheia*)
prophetic thought, focused upon God's subjective being, 177
prophets, offered indictments on Israel's moral failures, 215
propositional content, defining of emotions by, 31
propositional theology, derivative from narratives, 194n65
prosopic union, idea of, 151n65
prosperity, Augustine longing for, 81
Proverbs, exhorting to desire virtue, 98
pseudo-religion, of young Americans, 248n18
psychological development, on the part of Jesus, 198
psychologists, on emotions, 26
public and personal spheres, polarization of, 51
Puritan Protestantism, central question of, 105
putting on Christ, meaning of, 246

Rahner, Karl, 66n153, 68, 69n157
rational persons, 3
rational soul
    animal instincts and appetites included in, 92
    as a blending of rational and non-rational, 99
    of the Christian, 118
    emphasized by Gregory, 256
    goal of attaining union with God, 96
    in the image of God, 95
    transforming the bestial passions, 10, 102

rationality, 45–46, 54
Ratzinger, Joseph, 183–84
realistic narrative, 195, 196
reality, becoming fully alive, 65–66
reason
    distinguished from emotion, 2
    exerting control over the appetitive impulses, 100
    making us rich and wise and virtuous, 39
    passions requiring the guidance of, 12
    prevailing for Christ, 136
reason and passion, disjunction of, 96
reasonableness (*eulogon*), 33–34
Rebekah, 184n46
recipients, of God's benevolent love, 198
redemption, 137, 140, 172
Reformed theology, 141, 147
rejection of Jesus, 200
rejoicing, of God, 176
relational attributes, 145
relational character, of Jesus' identity, 192
relational properties, of God, 159, 180
religious affections, 14, 104, 112–14
representation, of the Son, 244
reproduction, prelapsarian angelic mode of, 94
restless heart, finding no peace in the pilgrim life, 84
resurrected body, of Jesus as the new temple, 217
resurrection, sharing in the glory of Christ's, 261
revelation, Barth changed his model of, 144n56
reverence or awe, related to wonder, 66n155
revivalism, spectacular commotions of, 13, 105
rich young man, 206–7, 213–14
Ricoeur, 5n13–6n13
right will, locked in battle with a perverse will, 88

righteous anger, of Jesus, 157, 254
rightly directed emotions, 240–42
rightness, of the object of the emotions, 79
risen body, of the crucified Jesus, 202
Roberts, Robert, 46
Roman centurion. *See* centurion
Romanticism, principle of the infinite within the finite, 8
Russian Orthodox theology, on participation of the divine in the human, 147

sacraments, as the heart of redemption, 130
sacrificial death, of Jesus on behalf of his friends, 222
sacrificial love, of Jesus, 207
sadness, experienced by Christ, 138
safe place, leaving to venture to a place of danger, 222n105
saints
    bearing the image of Christ, 258
    carrying out Christ's healing mission, 20
    having a heart of flesh, 112
salvation
    having to do with the illumination of the mind, 91
    in the here and now as very incomplete, 85
    humanist notion of, 42
    involving ongoing conversion of emotions, 232, 236
    observing through Jesus' rich and intense emotional life, 235
    regarded as a matter of the mind, 39
Sartre, Jean-Paul, 6
Satan, 143
satisfaction, 53
"saturated phenomenon," 64n146
Schillebeeckx, Edward, 260n28
Schleiermacher, Friedrich, 8
scholastic period, 226n113

scribes and Pharisees, watching Jesus' every move, 211
scriptural scholars, not considering cognitive theory, 15
Scripture
    Jesus having an intimate knowledge of, 183
    laments of, 90
secular culture, Christians today too compromised by, 248
self-deception, 41, 86
self-emptying (kenosis). *See* kenosis (self-emptying)
self-sacrificing love, 227, 237
self-transcendence, 68
self-understanding, 35
Seneca, 4n5, 27n9, 36, 40, 73
sensations, feelings as a physiological set of, 25–26
sense and perception, activity of, 95
sense appetite, directed toward proper objects, 136
sense cognition, 12n36
sense of self, forfeiting, 77
"sense of the heart," 13, 105
sensitive soul, 95
sensory appetite, 12, 12n36
sentient beings, inclined toward good, 12n36
Sermon on the Mount, 161, 184
servant of God, becoming, 115–16
service, of bringing children into the world, 94
seventy disciples, commissioned by Jesus, 208
sexual desire, 83n32
sexual images, imprinted by former habit, 76
Shekhina, 172, 172n14, 173–74
sickness of sin, 118, 253, 256
sighing, of Jesus, 218–23, 241
"a sign from heaven," Pharisees demanding, 219
"signs" of true piety, articulating positive, 105
"silent revolution," turning everything toward salvation in Palestine, 169

Simeon, 189
sin
    Edwards restricting Christian emotions to the problem of, 258
    Jesus bearing of, 199
    leading to death, 73
    as not natural, 133
    of pride, 80
    reducing engagements in the world to the problem of, 88
    referred to as hardness of heart, 112
sin-bearer, Jesus' suffering as, 225
sinful soul, 82, 91
sinfulness and hardness of heart, Christians suffering for, 228
single-subject Christology, of Cyril, 152
sinlessness, of Jesus, 143, 180
sinners, 198, 228, 237
Smith, J. Warren, 99–102
"soaring *stasis*," as ever ascending, 102
social context, vulnerability of the individual before, 41
social justice, not embraced by Augustine, 89
social norms, shaping emotions, 29, 56, 59
societies, emotions shaped differently by, 59, 63–64
socio-political task, of Christians, 239
solidarity, of Jesus, 225, 244
Solomon, Robert, 46, 47–50
Son of God. *See also* Jesus Christ
    humiliation of, 22
    Jesus acting as, 151
    Jesus' consciousness of being, 162
    making manifest to Israel God's benevolent love for his long-suffering people, 161
    mediating his divinity through his humanity, 216
    participation of in human essence, 142, 146n59
    raised human lowliness to the realms of the divine, 130n20
    sharing in the limitations and infirmities of Adamic flesh, 147
    surrendered the power of his divinity, 146
Son of the Father. *See* Son of God
Song of Songs, 98
sons and daughters of God, becoming in the Son, 228
Sorabji, Richard, 31–32, 34
sorrow, 38, 135n31, 254
sorrow and grief, in the garden of Gethsemane, 199
soul
    of Augustine plagued by sin, 118
    being "carried out," 107n101
    contractions or expansions of, 32
    as immaterial united to the body, 129
    inclined or disinclined in every act of the will, 108
    leading into the apophatic space of the inner sanctuary, 98
    love of God of, 101
    as a protective screen between immaterial and material, 130
    requiring memory for progress, 77
    rising above the drives of the spirited and appetitive faculties, 10
    struggling against the weight of the flesh, 37
    unity of the trichotomous structure of, 104
spirit, coming upon Mary, 184
Spirit of Christ, influencing hearts of the saints, 117
spirited faculty (*thymos*), 100
"spirit-flesh" conflict, cannot be applied to Christ, 124
spiritual obtuseness, 220, 241
Mr. Spock, complete lack of emotions, 2

spring of human actions, affections as, 107
"stable states" (*eupatheiai*), 79n18
stasis, of the soul, 102
Stead, Christopher, 96
stern warning, of Jesus to the blind men, 212, 213
Stoic ethical system, 31, 34
Stoic first movements (*propatheia*) or pre-passions, 128, 128n16
Stoic philosophers, 3-4, 4n5, 27
Stoic philosophy, Calvin's repudiation of, 43, 137-38
Stoic sage
    attributing no significance to happenings in the external world, 240
    Augustine on perturbation of soul in, 129
    Christ having the mind of a, 128
    Christ possessing the virtuous qualities of, 137
    depicting Christ as, 256
    divine figure of Christ appearing as, 166
    Jesus as not detached from things like a, 223
Stoic therapy, 4
Stoic view
    of emotion, 17-18, 31-45
    of emotions as judgments, 57
    of the passions as sicknesses of the soul, 117, 233, 252
Stoics, 44, 68, 107n101
"storied place," Jerusalem as, 168
strong emotions, of dread and grief, 243
subjective accent, falling on "how" it is said, 7
subjective engagements with the world, emotions as, 57n119, 62
"subjective" redemption, of Mary, 188n57
substitution, of the Son, 225, 225n110, 245
suffering
    Augustine and Gregory on, 119
    of Christians, 228
    of God, 175
    integral to becoming sons and daughters of the Father, 247
    integral to deification, 252
    of Jesus, 224, 225, 228, 234, 239, 244, 246
    Jesus on an inevitable pathway of, 215
    as the vocation of the faithful, 245, 251, 259
suffering emotions, 240-47
    belonging to the divine pathos, 162-63
    crucified Christ as the new object of, 257
    described, 24
    Gregory not assigning any significant role to, 257
    integral role played by, 259
    of Jesus Christ, 140, 141, 158, 223-28
    no constructive role in the ascent to God, 256
    not the sole focus of Warfield's treatment of Jesus' emotional life, 142
    relations with congenial emotions, 147-48
    role in witnessing the way of the cross, 259
    in a struggle with the vigor and strength of the Son's love, 226
    voicing the "not yet" dimension of the covenant of grace, 247
suffering flesh, grieving in solidarity with all, 254
suffering God, Jewish thought on, 179n34
suffering servant of God, Isaiah's notion of, 245
Summa theologiae (Aquinas), 68n156
superficial external self, as not our real self, 65
"supernatural existential," notion of, 66n153

suppression, of emotion, 31
suprahistorical life of God himself, extending Jesus' personal biography, 192
"supra-historical mystery," name of Zion conveying, 174
supreme good, 77, 81
surprise, as a very human emotion, 212
symbiōsis, desire for in marriage, 93
sympathy, worldly expressions of, 238–39
Synoptic Gospels
    on Jesus' cleansing of the temple, 216n96
    on Jesus' ministry, 178
    Jesus portrayed as covenant Lord, 178n33, 247n16
    one explicit mention of Jesus' love in, 206
Synoptic Jesus, little overlap with the emotions of John's Jesus, 204
"synthetic" rules, of reasoning, 55n109
system of value, no well-structured, 45

tears of blood, on the body of Christ during his passion, 138
telos (perfection and completion), 11, 12n36
temple
    Jesus cleansing, 174, 216n96, 217
    resurrected body of Jesus as the new, 217
    young Jesus referring to, 206
    young Jesus remaining in, 190
temporal existence, 155
temporal realm, as encompassed by God, 143
temptations, discussed by Augustine, 76n4
temptations and sin, coming in when assent is given, 17n57
tension
    in the appetitive faculty, 99
    between Christ's natural will (sensory appetite) and his intellectual appetite (will) and the divine will, 136
    between covenant partner and inaugurator, 178
    between a sinless passible Christ and a Christ sharing in the defects of human affectivity, 126
    unresolved between "flesh" and "spirit," 41
theologians, not considering cognitive theory, 15
theological reflection, on the incarnation, 149
theological thinking, logical relations with emotion, 9
theory of the mind, going with a theory of the emotions, 52
theosis. *See* divinization of humanity (theosis)
"therapy of desire," Christianity as, 69–70
thoughts
    divide between emotion and, 2
    emotions involving, 57
    Jesus' awareness of people's, 197n71
    not applying to all emotions, 48
thymos, 100, 104n92
Tilley, Terrence, 194n65
Tillich, Paul, 7n19, 8
Torah, 170, 172
Torrell, Jean-Paul, 122
touch, nearest sense to inward experiences, 5n10
tragedies, defying logic, 42
tragic dimensions, of existence, 6n14
tranquility, 35–36
transcendental experience, 18
Treatise on the Passions (Aquinas), 10, 10n28, 135
tremendum affective state, 8, 64
trichotomous soul, 99n76
Trinitarian terms, for Jesus' divine identity, 150n64

true communion, 154
true freedom (*libertas*), lost, 82n28
true knowledge, in the public realm, 51
true religion, 105–6, 107, 114
two "states," doctrine of, 144n55

understanding, 106, 197, 197n72
union, 150, 172
union with God, 65, 90
unity
    of body and soul, 129
    of Christ, 131
universal human emotions, 59
universal nature, as most admirable, 38
unwelcome emotions, 31
urgency, of emotions, 58

value
    emotions concerned with, 57
    of God's covenant promises to Israel, 160–61
value-laden ways, of seeing the world, 62
van Beeck, Frans Jozef, 194, 200
The Vanity of Human Wishes (Johnson), 41, 85–86
Vermes, Geza, 168n2
Virgin Mary. *See* Mary (Jesus' mother)
"virginity," as a metaphor for an attitude of non-atachment, 93
virtue
    of Christ, 112, 116n121
    extirpating common emotions in pursuit of, 233–34
    as most admirable, 38
    pursuing the life of, 115
    at the service of response of love, 249
    worth choosing for its own sake, 34
virtuous action, subject matter (*hulē, materia*) of, 35

virtuous life, easier to attain for souls freed early, 37
virtuous person, 29, 34
voice of lament, as the voice of humanity, 117
volitional self-mastery, of Christ, 134
voluntarist thesis, of Solomon on emotions, 46
von Balthasar, Hans Urs, 225n111
Voorwinde, Stephen, 15, 16
vulnerability
    emotions registering, 62
    experiencing, 234
    of Jesus, 162, 236, 241–42, 243
    Jesus' emotions registering, 162, 202

Walton, Kendall, 46
Warfield, Benjamin, 141
    on Calvin's portrayal of Jesus's emotional life, 137
    on examining the emotional life of Christ, 15
    on God's affections, 182
    on Jesus' anger, 142
    on Jesus' divine-humanity, 148
    on Jesus taking on the "form of a servant," 181–82
    on observing the movements of Jesus' emotions, 141
    on the strong emotions of Jesus, 147
Watson, James, 26
weeping
    common to human beings, 241
    a human emotion, 148
    of Jesus, 218–23
    over the impending destruction of Jerusalem, 199
Wesley, John, 13–14, 19n58
Western philosophical thought, on the emotions, 3
Western philosophy, dichotomy between emotion and intellect, 25
wickedness, types of, 172n14

will, 33
   of Christ, 152
   delight motivating human, 77
   described, 106
   divine as appetite in God, 11n33
   of the incarnate Word, 152
   involved in the emotions, 83
   as a reasonable desire, 34
Williams, Rowan, 95–97, 100n78
wine, symbolizing new wine, 217
winter voice of prayer, addressing God in, 244
Wisdom, 172, 172n15
wisdom and understanding, Jesus growing in, 230
Wisdom motif, of the suffering just one (*passio justi*), 226
"wisdom of God," crucified Christ as, 249
wise person, 34, 37
Wollheim, Richard, 52–54, 60n133, 68
women, 184, 185
wonder (*mysterium fascinans et tremendum*)
   associated with emotions, 234
   basic emotion of, 18
   departing from focus on one's own scheme, 59n129
   emotion of, 64–67
the Word, became flesh, 139–40, 154, 201
"a word-bearing animal," human being as, 95
Word's humanity, not truly affirmed as the divine-humanity, 235
worship and prayer, as the way to God, 116
wrath and anger, of God, 175

Yahweh, acting to redeem and liberate his people, 170
yearning, for blissful perfection, 42
"you have heard it said," 161
young Jesus, Jerusalem temple and, 206
young man, devoted to his "great possessions," 207

zeal, 175, 216–18, 257
Zechariah, 188–89
Zeno, 32
Zion, 168, 174, 175, 185

www.ingramcontent.com/pod-product-compliance
Lightning Source LLC
Chambersburg PA
CBHW050621300426
44112CB00012B/1604